Cazaly
THE LEGEND

The Slattery Media Group Pty Ltd

Text © Robert Allen 2017

Design © The Slattery Media Group Pty Ltd 2017
First published by The Slattery Media Group Pty Ltd 2017

All images and artwork reproduced with permission. All images and artworks used with permission. See images for credit information. Every effort has been made to verify the source of each photograph.

Inquiries should be made to the publisher. All rights reserved. No part of this publication may be reproduced, stored in a retrieval system or transmitted in any form or by any means without the prior written permission of the copyright owner. Inquiries should be made to the publisher.

Images on jacket—Roy Cazaly circa 1941 [© News Ltd.] ; Back Cover: A Thorps Chocolate Fudge swap card issued in 1922 and a JJ Schuh tobacco swap card issued in 1921 [author's collection]. Inside Flap: Roy Cazaly in his North Hobart uniform, circa 1932 [Cazaly family] End Papers: Roy Cazaly signature ™ used with permission of Cazaly Sports Pty Ltd as trustee of the Roy Cazaly Family Trust; Spine, contents page, preface and 'quarter' headings: trade mark no. 1373861, used with permission of Cazaly Sports Pty Ltd as trustee of the Roy Cazaly Family Trust.

National Library of Australia Cataloguing-in-Publication entry

Creator: Allen, Robert, author.

Title: Cazaly: the legend / Robert Allen

Edited by Simone Egger

Designed by Kate Slattery.

ISBN: 9780992363161 (hardback)

Subjects: Cazaly, Roy, 1893-1963.
Australian football players--Biography.
Sports--Australia--Biography.
Heroes--Australia.
Australian football.
Australia--History--Biography.

Other Creators/Contributors:
Slattery, Geoff, editor.
Slattery, Kate, book designer.

Group Publisher: Geoff Slattery
Editor: Simone Egger
Creative Director and Design: Kate Slattery
Printed and bound in China by Everbest Printing

books.slatterymedia.com

Robert Allen

visit *slatterymedia.com*

1938
Roy Cazaly portrait
(CAZALY FAMILY)

DEDICATION
For my family

CAZALY
THE LEGEND

CONTENTS

PREFACE 9
1 BEGINNINGS 11
2 MIGRATION ON A MASSIVE SCALE 17
3 BOOM AND BUST 24

First Quarter 31
4 A CHILDHOOD BY THE LAKE 32
5 A RAW COLT FROM THE PADDOCK 42
6 A PREMIERSHIP THROWN IN THE AIR 51
7 FOOTBALL DURING WAR 58
8 RECESS AND RESUMPTION 65
9 PEACE AND INSTABILITY 73

Second Quarter 79
10 'UP THERE CAZALY!' 80
11 AN UNHAPPY COACHING STINT 91
12 TRIALS AND TRIBUNALS 99
13 CARNIVAL CAPERS 106
14 A SPELL IN THE COUNTRY 114
15 BACK TO THE LAKE 124

Third Quarter 133
16 ROAST CHICKEN EVERY SUNDAY 134
17 DEPRESSION FOOTBALL 144

18 FIGHTS AND A FLAG 153
19 FROM UGLY DUCKLINGS TO PREMIERS 160
20 LAKESIDE LAMENT 169
21 THE LEGION OF THE LOST 177
22 AMONG THE WOWSERS 185

Fourth Quarter 191

23 MODEST EXPECTATIONS 192
24 FROM MAYBLOOMS TO HAWKS 201
25 HOME-FRONT 207
26 HEALING HANDS 217
27 RETURN OF THE PRODIGAL SON 223
28 ONE LAST HURRAH 233
29 TIME ON 240
30 SIREN 247

31 POST 1963 251
32 THE LEGEND GROWS 260
33 REAPPRAISING THE LEGEND 267
34 AFTERWORD 275

Appendices

1 LIFE AND CAREER HIGHLIGHTS 282
2 CONTEMPORARY HONOURS 284
3 ROY CAZALY'S ADVICE TO PLAYERS 285
4 'UP THERE CAZALY' OVER TIME 290
5 PLAYING CAREER SUMMARY 293
6 COACHING CAREER SUMMARY 307
7 TRUTH CAZALY AWARD WINNERS 323
8 A NOTE ON OBJECTIVES, METHODS
     AND SOURCES 324
9 ACKNOWLEDGEMENTS 330
10 CHAPTER ENDNOTES 335
11 REFERENCES 383

INDEX 391

A 1914 postcard of Maurice Guillaux' Blériot XI monoplane.
(CROME COLLECTION, MUSEUM OF APPLIED ARTS AND SCIENCES, SYDNEY)

Distance, measures and currency

This book uses the imperial measurement system established under Britain's Weights and Measures Act 1824 and adopted by its Australian colonies.

1 INCH = 2.54 CENTIMETRES (CM)
12 INCHES = 1 FOOT (FT)
1 FT = 30.5 CM
1 MILE = 1.61 KILOMETRES (KM)
1 ACRE = 0.4 HECTARES
16 OUNCES (OZ) = 1 POUND (LB)
1 LB = 454 GRAMS (GM)
2 LB 3 OZ = 1 KILOGRAM (KG)
100 DEGREES FAHRENHEIT = 37.8 DEGREES CELSIUS
12 PENCE (D) = 1 SHILLING (S)
20 SHILLINGS = 1 POUND (£)
1 GUINEA (COMMONLY USED FOR SPORTS PRIZES) = 21 SHILLINGS

PREFACE

It was June 1914, and the St Kilda and Carlton teams were playing a game of Australian Football at the Junction Oval. Just as the third quarter began, the players and crowd paused to look skyward, distracted by the unfamiliar drone of an approaching aeroplane. The monoplane's large wings and long, slender frame led more than one observer to compare it to a huge black dragonfly suspended in mid-air.[1] French aviator Maurice Guillaux was on a promotional tour of Australia, exciting crowds with his aerobatic displays. He had modified his 50 horsepower *Blériot XI* for stunt flying and just months earlier, in April, he had thrilled a 60,000-strong Sydney crowd by performing the first loop-the-loop seen in Australian skies.[2]

To the delight of the players and spectators, Guillaux proceeded to buzz the football ground in his fragile plane, climbing steeply into the clouds before diving so low he could read the numbers on the scoreboard. When the umpire eventually blew his whistle for play to resume, a reporter at the game noted that:

> Even football could not hold its own against such an attraction, and the thousands of spectators sent their cheers aloft to the bird-man. To have one eye on the plane and the other on the ball was a task that tried most of the footballers to the limit in optics.[3]

Within weeks the Great War would begin. A number of players from both sides enlisted and two—Carlton's George Challis and Stan McKenzie—would not return.[4] Maurice Guillaux was another victim of the conflict, killed in 1917 while testing a prototype plane for the French Air Force.[5]

One of the St Kilda players at the Junction Oval that day in 1914 was a young man in his third season with the club. Just 21 years old, Roy Cazaly was already making a name for himself as a high-flyer. In subsequent years his gravity-defying leaps for the ball would see him compared to the pioneering aviators who were setting records and captivating crowds.

But Cazaly's career was still in its infancy in the winter of 1914. No one at that match could have predicted that his playing and coaching career would span four decades or that his feats would inspire a phrase that would make him him a legend in his own lifetime.

Cazaly led a crowded life that didn't begin and end with football. Long after his on-field exploits were over, a new generation who had never seen him play came to know him as a skilled physiotherapist, successful horse trainer, shrewd philosopher and loving grandfather. It was his sporting prowess which first drew me to his story, but learning the extent of his exuberant life made me want to tell it.

It is tempting to begin Cazaly's story with his first VFL game for St Kilda in 1911, when he was plucked from relative obscurity to play against his boyhood idols from Carlton. But that would imply that nothing that came before then mattered. To understand the forces that influenced Cazaly's life—and how he shaped our national game—we must go back even further.

Robert Allen,
MARCH 2017

1

BEGINNINGS

FRANCE AND ENGLAND, 1700-1854

Roy Cazaly's story begins, not in the streets of St Kilda or South Melbourne, but with his ancestors in the rugged mountains and on the fertile plains of southern France. His forebears were Huguenot, the minority of Calvinist Protestants who lived within France's overwhelmingly Catholic population.

The Huguenots suffered state-sanctioned repression because of their beliefs, and a series of bloody religious wars were fought in France during the second half of the 16th century. In the face of continued and systemic persecution, many Huguenots either converted to Catholicism under threat of execution or practised their faith in secret.

The proclamation of the Edict of Nantes by the Protestant-raised Henry IV in 1598 theoretically guaranteed Huguenots greater religious and civil freedoms, but the uneasy truce which followed ended with its official revocation by Henry's grandson Louis XIV in 1685. Protestantism was again declared illegal and fears of renewed persecution caused as many as 200,000 Huguenots to flee France. Many sought the safety of the Netherlands, England, Prussia or Switzerland. Some went even further afield, to the American colonies or the Dutch Cape Colony in South Africa. Much of this exodus occurred during the decade between 1680 and 1690, but the entire emigration period lasted until the late 18th century.[6]

More than 50,000 Huguenot refugees fled to England in the years immediately following the revocation. Many were skilled craft workers who helped revolutionise its silk-weaving industry.[7] The Huguenots developed a reputation for industry and piety; in 1738, pictorial satirist and painter William Hogarth's engraving *Noon* was published, contrasting a family of Huguenots leaving their French church with a group of debauched native Londoners on the other side of the street.[8]

There were many branches within the local silk trade, a rigid hierarchy of skills and a strict division of roles between men, women and children. Designers, master weavers and merchants could earn a handsome income but life was much more precarious for ordinary weavers. An early tradesman's handbook described the various types of work available:

> The plain Silk Weaver requires but little Ingenuity, but the Weavers of flowered Silks, Damasks, Brocades and Velvets are very ingenious Tradesmen ... The Journeyman Weaver in most Branches in the Silk Way requires moderate Strength: A Boy may be bound about Eleven or Twelve Years of Age ... [The] Tradesman buys raw Silk from the Importer, and sometimes imports it himself and sells it to the Manufacturer ... The Silk-Throwster prepares it for the various Uses of the Weaver; he employs mostly Women, to whom he gives but small Wages ... Spinning the hard Silk and winding it employs a great Number of Female Hands, who may make good Bread of it, if they refrain from the common Vice of Drinking and Sotting away their Time and Senses.[9]

The Cazaly family originated from the Languedoc province in southern France. The area was a stronghold of Huguenot resistance whose residents—both Catholic and Protestant—had endured numerous atrocities and reprisals during the religious wars.[10] Languedoc was famous for its silk-weaving. Italian weavers had introduced the industry during the 15th century and rapid improvements in design, dyes and weaving techniques meant the region boasted Europe's most advanced silk industry by the end of the 16th century.[11]

The original Cazalys are known only as Monsieur Cazaly, who was born around 1700, and his wife Marguerette. According to later accounts, the couple owned considerable property, including a chateau near Sommieres named 'Puech Bouquet', but their assets were confiscated by the state after Monsieur Cazaly died.¹²

With few other options and no doubt fearing further reprisals, Marguerette and her 12 children sailed for England around 1745, where they settled in London's East End. Marguerette may have had relatives there, or at least would have known that the district housed a large number of Huguenots who could provide employment and support. The family lived first in Bethnal Green, where they were closely associated with the church of St Matthew, but by the time Marguerette died in 1783 they were living in Spitalfields, the heart of the local silk-weaving industry.

Spitalfields' close-knit Huguenot community was united by a shared religion and a common language. Huguenots worked together, worshipped together and married into each other's families. The poor and infirm were cared for at La Providence, the French Hospital in Bath Street, which had been founded by Huguenot emigrants in 1718. Huguenot ancestry had to be proven to gain admission, and several members of the Cazaly family did so over subsequent generations.¹³

By 1803 the Cazaly family were living at Norton Folgate on the corner of Spital Square.¹⁴ Marguerette's eldest child Guillaume (or William) manufactured silk stockings, one of the more delicate and therefore expensive silk products. Over time he became a textile merchant, a director of the French Hospital and an *ancien* (or elder) of the French Protestant Church in Brick Lane.¹⁵ Eventually he earned enough money to return to Sommieres and buy back the family's former 'Puech Bouquet' estate, where he died in 1824, aged 96.¹⁶ William's story was unusual, however, for the vast majority of Huguenot emigrants remained in England, their children and grandchildren gradually assimilating into the wider community.

Marguerette's second child Jean Pierre (or John Peter) also became a silk weaver. In 1757 he married Jeanne Poulain at St Matthew's in Bethnal Green.¹⁷ John and Jeanne's ninth child, Jaques, was born on 4 October, 1779 and was baptised on All Hallows' Eve at the Artillery French Huguenot Church in Spitalfields. Jaques, also known as James, would become Roy Cazaly's grandfather.¹⁸

Unlike his father and uncle, James did not work directly in silk production but became a bookkeeper and accountant for the merchant firm of Doxat and Company from about the age of 16. The company's Huguenot founder, John Doxat, had emigrated from Switzerland as a young man. He established his business in 1779 and specialised in importing raw and thrown silk from Italy. In 1792 Doxat became a naturalised citizen, probably to prove his loyalty to England during a time of immense social and political upheaval in Europe.[19]

John Doxat was illustrative of the wealthy Huguenot immigrants who prospered in their adopted country.[20] A prominent philanthropist, he chaired a gathering of businessmen at the City of London Tavern in September 1821 to assist a Swiss Huguenot colony in Brazil. James Cazaly attended the meeting and pledged £1/1 towards the fund.[21]

James was clearly a loyal and trusted employee. On one occasion he gave evidence at the trial of a man accused of stealing £500 worth of jewellery, which James had delivered to the West India Dock on behalf of a wealthy client. Cazaly identified the recovered jewellery in court and the thief was sentenced to 10 years transportation to the penal colony of New South Wales.[22]

By the 1830s Britain's silk industry was in serious decline. High duties levied on imported manufactured silk had protected the local industry for decades but falling tariffs, changing consumer tastes and the growing availability of cheaper woven alternatives such as cotton were hastening its demise. Frequent economic downturns meant thousands of Spitalfields weavers were often out of work, resulting in destitution, social unrest and occasional street riots.

Succumbing to growing political pressure, the House of Commons appointed a Select Committee in 1832 to inquire into the state of the industry. The Committee heard that most of the 100,000 people living in Spitalfields depended on silk weaving for their livelihood. John Doxat was one of the inquiry's key witnesses.[23] He gave detailed testimony and tabled documents showing the impact of wages, tariffs and foreign competition on production, costs and profits.[24] James must have assisted Doxat compile his evidence; he would have been acutely aware of the precarious state of an industry on which his livelihood depended.

James had married Elizabeth Eagles in December 1827 at St George's Parish in Hanover Square. The last of four children, Elizabeth was 26 when she married; James was 48. For the next few years they lived at Claremont Cottages in West Hackney, a more genteel district than down-at-heel Spitalfields had become. The couple had nine children. Their first son Charles was born in West Hackney in 1828, followed by Charlotte, Peter and Henry. By the time their fifth child, Owen, was baptised in 1836 the family was living at Barrett Grove in Stoke Newington. Foy (better known as John) was born there in 1837 and Catherine (known as Kate) in 1839. James' occupation during this period was variously described as accountant, merchant's clerk and gent. Despite the fluctuating fortunes of the silk trade the household was able to employ two Irish-born servants.[25]

The exact birth date of James Charles, later to become Roy's father, is unclear. A scribbled note in the margin of his baptism record states he was born on 30 November 1841 but this is at odds with a June 1841 census form, which recorded his age as seven months. It seems more likely that he was born in late 1840.[26] By 1851, the older boys were working as clerks while the four youngest children, including James jnr, were 'scholars'.[27] Studio photographs of the children reveal several distinctive features that Roy would later inherit: a long, straight nose, a prominent chin and large, slightly protruding ears.[28] The siblings appear to have enjoyed the benefits of a middle-class upbringing: Kate became an accomplished pianist under the guidance of royal court composer John Henry Griesbach, and several of the boys rowed competitively.[29]

Rowing was enjoying enormous popularity during the mid-19th century. Sponsored at first by local publicans and later by rowing associations, races between rival crews and champion scullers attracted large crowds. The growth of the railway as a means of transporting large numbers of people helped establish rowing as Britain's first mass spectator sport. The crowds watching the regattas may not have drawn social distinctions between the various competitors but the organisers certainly did. Strict demarcations were drawn between working class watermen who plied boats for their living, professional rowers who competed for prizes and amateurs deemed "gentlemen" by virtue of their birth, education or occupation. As a result, regattas often featured separate races for each category.[30]

The Cazaly brothers rowed as gentlemen with the Albion Rowing Club, a strictly amateur club based at Hackney on the River Lea.[31] In August 1855 Owen, Peter and Charles rowed for Albion in the Gentlemen's Four Oared race at the Royal Thames National Regatta and Charles won a sculler's race. James and John were part of an Albion crew that won the Gentlemen's Junior Four Oared race the next year.[32]

James snr died of chronic bronchitis in June 1854, aged 74.[33] Unusually for someone who had spent his life keeping accounts he appears to have left no will because the following notice appeared in several newspapers three months later:

> MR JAMES CAZALY ... Any person who may possess or who can give any information respecting any WILL, money, or other property of the deceased, are requested to send the same to his widow, Mrs Cazaly, of No. 1, Barrett-grove, Stoke Newington; or to communicate with her, or her solicitors and they will be liberally REWARDED for their trouble.[34]

Elizabeth decided to leave England soon after. Her motives are unknown but they can be guessed. Her parents had both died so there were no remaining family ties to keep her in England. She would have known that the local silk trade no longer promised secure employment for her children and the impecunious state of the family's affairs may have provided the final incentive to make a fresh start.

Having resolved to emigrate, Elizabeth chose Victoria, Australia. London was abuzz with stories of fortunes being made on the goldfields of the distant colony named for the ruling British monarch. News of rich discoveries accompanied each returning vessel and the writer Charles Dickens described crowds of prospective emigrants "struggling and elbowing" at shipping agent offices.[35] Scarcely a century after Marguerette Cazaly and her family had left France for a new life in England, her grandson's widow and children sailed halfway around the world to begin a new chapter in their own lives.

2

MIGRATION ON A MASSIVE SCALE

BALLARAT, 1855-70

The shipping records are sketchy, but they suggest that Elizabeth and seven of her nine children sailed to Victoria over several voyages, beginning with Peter and Henry in 1855. Owen and John arrived in early 1856, followed by Elizabeth and her three youngest children Kate, James and Bessy in 1857.[36] Her two eldest children, Charles and Charlotte, remained behind in London.[37]

The family made their way to the Ballarat district, 65 miles north-west of Melbourne. The area's name is thought to have originated from the local Aboriginal words "Balla arat", meaning "resting place". White pastoralists arrived in 1837 but the discovery of gold at nearby Golden Point in August 1851 was followed by chaotic scenes as thousands converged on the district hoping to strike it rich. By October there were 5000 people on the diggings and a journalist who had spent nine days travelling on boggy roads from Melbourne reported that "an insane rush has taken place to a small spot."[38]

Gold strikes continued throughout the 1850s and Melbourne experienced severe labour shortages as thousands flocked to the fields. Around £4 million worth of gold was discovered at Ballarat in 1856 alone and the total yield between 1851 and 1859 was more than 4 million ounces. By 1860 the colony was producing a third of the world's gold and four in every 10 Victorians were living in gold towns.[39]

The rush drew people from everywhere. Victoria's population mushroomed from 77,000 to more than 540,000 in the decade from 1850, and soon accounted for almost half of everyone living in Australia.[40] It was migration on a massive scale.

More than half of the new arrivals to Ballarat came from the United Kingdom. Unlike earlier waves of immigration, gold attracted a larger proportion from the middle and upper classes. Those with the means to pay their own way far outnumbered assisted migrants, and this influx of education and skills materially shaped Victoria's subsequent development.[41]

Elizabeth and her children arrived in the district at a time when men still outnumbered women by almost two to one.[42] The Eureka Stockade uprising, in which a number of Ballarat diggers were shot dead by state troopers after demanding an end to taxation without representation, had occurred less than three years earlier.

The family initially settled at Weatherboard Hill on the western shore of Lake Learmonth, 10 miles north-west of Ballarat. The area was originally part of a large pastoral estate but portions were sold off during the mid-1850s to grow wheat and vegetables for the nearby goldfields. The district had rich volcanic soils and a common refrain from visitors was that the crops were bountiful but the roads were "frightfully bad".[43] Henry Cazaly purchased an allotment at Weatherboard Hill when the first land parcels were offered for sale in early 1857. Local agent William Smith had described the area's potential in wildly exuberant terms:

> For quality the land is not to be surpassed, for situation it is unequalled. For the rapidity with which this district has and is progressing it stands unparalleled in the history of the known world.[44]

The town lot Henry bought was just over five acres in size—large enough for a house and market garden, but too small for growing crops or grazing livestock. Some of these lots were bought by those who worked on the nearby Ercildoune sheep property and the Cazalys may have had a connection with the Learmonth family who owned the run.[45]

For reasons unknown the family decided to relocate to Ballarat around 1859. Once there, they had the choice of settling in the older, brasher eastern side of town or the newer, more ordered western side.[46] They chose Ballarat West and moved in to a cottage in Drummond Street.

Their arrival coincided with a frenetic burst of consolidation. The canvas tents and wooden shanties of the early 1850s were being replaced by more substantial structures of brick and stone. Frequent fires and floods provided an excuse for municipal leaders to tear down and rebuild the rapidly growing town.[47] The local hospital was built in 1856, the Mechanics' Institute was founded in 1860 and the railway line to Melbourne was opened in 1862.[48] Improving Ballarat's suburban amenities was a lower priority, however, and ratepayers began petitioning the council on numerous issues requiring redress. Popular demands included preventing mine tailing sludge from oozing into nearby houses, installing more street lamps and banning the keeping of pigs within a hundred feet of private dwellings.

Several of the Cazaly siblings seized the opportunity to lobby the civic authorities. In October 1861, Peter initiated a petition seeking local street improvements and both he and James signed a petition supporting the establishment of a new produce market. Owen also instigated several petitions making increasingly strident demands for improved roads and footpaths in Ballarat West. In a muted echo of the Eureka miners' uprising, residents threatened to withhold their rates if the Council didn't provide the services they felt they were entitled to.[49]

Elizabeth Cazaly died in August 1863 from 'phthisis', an archaic medical term commonly used to describe tuberculosis. She was 59.[50] By this time most of her children were busy putting down roots in Ballarat. Owen, Peter and Kate had all married during 1862 and they were followed by Bessy in 1864 and Henry in 1867. By the end of the decade only James and John remained unwed.

Each of the siblings made their own mark on Ballarat through various cultural, business, civic and sporting pursuits.[51] The family had brought a piano with them from England, and Kate became a prominent soloist, piano teacher and organist at the Wesleyan Church.[52] She married William Little, an auctioneer and Freemason who later became mayor of Ballarat. They bred a musical family and Kate continued to play the church organ, donating any payments she received to charity.[53] Bessy married George

Moore, an English-born soldier. They had the first four of an eventual 12 children before moving to Fiji, where George became the Commissioner of Lands and Crown Surveyer.[54]

Several of the Cazaly brothers became involved in local mining ventures. By the mid-1850s, most of Ballarat's shallow alluvial deposits had been played out, and attention shifted to the gold locked in 'deep leads' hundreds of feet below ground. These high-risk ventures were capital intensive, requiring the establishment of cooperatives.[55] In 1860, Owen was listed as one of 23 "sleeping" shareholders in the Koh-i-Noor Gold Mining Company.[56]

A further shift to quartz reef mining began in the late 1850s. These ventures required even larger amounts of capital and equipment so cooperatives were replaced by limited liability companies, often with hundreds of shareholders.[57] A local mining exchange opened and Owen became an accredited share broker and one of 14 agents who formed the Ballarat Incorporated Brokers' Association in 1865.[58] Henry, an accountant, invested in several local mining companies. In 1866 he, Owen and Peter bought shares in the Newington Freehold Gold Mining Company. Perhaps they thought the company name, with its echoes of their London home of Stoke Newington, might bring them luck.[59]

The Cazaly brothers also became active in Ballarat's sporting circles. In January 1861, Peter placed a newspaper notice appealing "to all lovers of cricket" to join him in forming a club in West Ballarat. A public meeting subsequently appointed him and Owen to a provisional committee, the latter serving as secretary and treasurer.[60] Three of the brothers took part in the first intra-club match the following month and James took seven wickets for 54 and top scored in a game against their rivals from Ballarat.[61] Games against Wendouree and a team of bank employees followed. In one match against Creswick in 1862, Owen and James took all 20 wickets between them for a total of 54 runs.[62] In March that year James' form was rewarded with selection in a Ballarat District 'Twenty-two' which played a visiting 'All-England Eleven' side. He batted at number 16 in both innings, scoring a duck in the first and two runs in the second.[63] Owen played for Ballarat when another touring English Eleven visited the district in 1864. One of the English players was Edward Grace, older brother of the more famous 'W.G.'.[64] In 1867, Owen played for a Ballarat Eleven against a visiting team of Aboriginal players captained by famed cricket and Australian Football pioneer Tom Wills.[65]

The Cazaly brothers also competed in track and field events but their most successful sporting pursuit was rowing.[66] James was an early member of the Regatta Rowing Club, which changed its name to Ballarat in 1864. In May that year he figured in the first races held on Lake Wendouree, when he teamed with club captain Ned Williams to win a pairs race. He also won his heat in the single sculls before fading light brought proceedings to an early close.[67] In June, James accepted a challenge by a Mr Wilson of the Prince of Wales Club in Melbourne to row any amateur in Ballarat and he won easily in front of a large crowd.[68] In October John, James, Ned Williams and Henry Golightly defeated a visiting Melbourne crew, the prize being four silver cups.[69] Then two days before Christmas James Cazaly and Ned Williams defeated a rival pair in a race postponed from the previous month's Learmonth Regatta.[70]

More local rowing clubs were soon formed and the first regatta held on Lake Wendouree in February 1865 attracted crews from Melbourne and Geelong. The Ballarat club won the Senior Fours, with a crew that included James, John and Peter Cazaly. The following month James defeated Ned Williams in a sculling race over two miles and later that year John won a sculling race against a Mr Petrie from the Alabama club for a £10 prize.[71]

For the best part of the next 20 years, no local regatta was complete without an appearance from one or more of the Cazaly brothers. Such was their dominance that one contemporary later joked they had slept in miniature boats instead of cribs as babies and cut their teeth on tiny wooden oars.[72] James and John were part of winning Ballarat crews at five local regattas between 1866 and 1872. They also competed at other regattas, winning races on the Yarra at Melbourne and the Barwon at Geelong.[73]

Just before Christmas 1866, a two-mile sculler's race was held on Lake Wendouree between James Cazaly and William Bell of the Alabama club. The local press described them as "the principal oarsmen of their respective clubs" and the prize was a trophy worth £20. After James won his backers hosted a celebration at St Mungo's Hotel and presented him with an inscribed silver pocket watch.[74]

Peter, the most prominent rower of the family, was a tempestuous character. After captaining the Ballarat City Rowing Club for 12 years he abruptly resigned and then complained loudly when he was presented with a "scrubby sheet of note-paper" acknowledging his service instead of the inscribed parchment he felt he was due.[75] Away from the oars Peter was an amateur musician and baritone who sang at many civic and charity events. In July 1866 he petitioned the Ballarat West Council to acquire a "Peal of Bells" for the town and chaired the subsequent fundraising committee.[76] Peter was also the first paid secretary of Ballarat's Benevolent Asylum, a charitable institution founded in 1860 to care for the district's poor and destitute.[77] He was an active administrator for many years but was suspended in 1886 and later dismissed after an audit found a series of "irregularities" in the Asylum's accounts.[78]

James, being younger and still making his way in the world, attracted far less public notice than his siblings. As a result his activities can be traced, not through the business and social pages of the local newspaper, but via its sporting columns and, on one occasion, its police reports. In August 1863 the *Star* reported that "the residence of Mr James Cazaly, in Ascot Street, was recently entered by some thief, who stole a silver quart cup stamped RTNR over 1856, a pair of new black trousers, a black cloth vest, four shirts, a silver medal, and two pairs of wellington boots."[79] The silver cup was the one James had won at the Royal Thames National Regatta; the medal was probably another rowing prize. The report did not mention James' occupation but others living in his street at the time included 24 miners, six quarrymen, three blacksmiths, two stonemasons and a bricklayer.[80] It therefore seems likely he was working as a miner or labourer.

In the winter of 1868, James and Owen went prospecting for gold in Gympie, Queensland.[81] Many of the 400 who sailed from Melbourne aboard the steamer *Hero* were fellow miners from Ballarat.[82] The brothers were among a party of 12 but Gympie's outlook had been exaggerated and the gold was petering out. One Ballarat miner wrote home with a warning:

> This is not a place for a man to come to without money, for the people here are very different to the people in Victoria. They would not give you a feed if you were starving.[83]

Owen wrote to a friend in August, gloomily stating that "the prospects of Gympie are not favourable."[84] By the end of November he and James were back in Ballarat.

When Ballarat was proclaimed a city in 1870 it boasted 40,000 residents, 477 hotels, 56 churches, 50 miles of gas mains and 13 breweries.[85] But gold yields from the deep leads were declining sharply, creating uncertainty about the city's future. A number of mines closed and many men left for other Victorian fields or to new ones springing up in New Zealand.[86]

James Cazaly left Ballarat too, not to search for gold this time but to move to Melbourne. His motives are unknown but they can be guessed. Unlike his brothers and sisters, he was not bound to the city by marriage ties, commercial dealings or cultural pursuits. Now aged 29, he may have found Ballarat constricting and wished to broaden his horizons. Most of his siblings would eventually be drawn to the capital too. Some, like John, would go looking for a new life. Others, like Peter, would seek to escape an old one. For now, though, James was striking out on his own.

3

BOOM AND BUST

MELBOURNE, 1871-93

As a newcomer to Melbourne, James Cazaly gravitated to what he knew best and threw himself into the city's rowing scene. Local regattas had begun in the capital during the mid-1860s, first on the lower Maribyrnong (or Saltwater) River near Footscray, then on the upper Yarra.[87] In January 1871 James was described as having "recently joined the Melbourne [Rowing] Club" when he defeated Joseph Bennett in a two mile sculling race.[88] Melbourne was one of the city's oldest clubs, and its boathouse lay alongside Princes Bridge on the south side of the Yarra.[89]

In April James rowed stroke in a Melbourne four that took on a Richmond crew for the Gardiner Challenge Cup at the Melbourne Regatta. The stroke is the most important position in a crew, their task being to set the pace and use their strength and judgment to adjust tactics during a race. At 12 stone four pounds James was heavier than the average stroke, but he more than compensated with his fitness and technique.[90] Previewing the race, the *Australasian* described him as:

> ... one of the best oarsman on the Yarra, [with] straight arms, straight back, good reach and powerful pull, any amount of strength and any amount of energy. He will lead his men a lively dance if they will but follow him.[91]

Richmond were pre-race favourites, having won the previous two years, but the Melbourne crew prevailed after Cazaly set a "long, powerful and swinging stroke" which saw off Richmond's quicker but less effective stroke rate.[92] Richmond reacted to their loss by lodging an appeal with the regatta committee. Cazaly, they alleged, was not an amateur because he had accepted money from a bookmaker after his win over Joseph Bennett three months earlier. The committee dismissed the protest but it was not the last time a Cazaly would be drawn into a debate between sporting amateurs and professionals.[93]

When the Richmond Club's Joseph Hood again questioned James' bona fides later that year, Peter Cazaly angrily defended his brother in print, pointing out that James had rowed as an amateur in England and informing his "kid gloved" critic that "Mr Cazaly belongs to as respectable a family as his own, and perhaps more so." Peter also gave an insight into James' financial circumstances, revealing he had "received a good education, but, in consequence of his father's death, he left England at an early age, and like many others in this colony, has not prospered as he wished."[94]

In early 1873 James was chosen in a combined Melbourne clubs crew to compete against crews from Ballarat, Sydney, Hobart and Geelong in the first ever Intercolonial Fours Championship. The Melbourne crew trained hard for two months before the event. After a change to their line-up, the *Australasian*'s rowing correspondent 'Cloanthus' (Matthew Byrne) reported that "Mr Cazaly is now stroke … I think all will agree with me when I say that to the hands of this crew we may safely entrust the honour of Victoria."[95]

The Intercolonial race was conducted over a four-mile course on the lower Yarra. Thousands of spectators lined both banks of the river, with some even climbing the rigging of anchored ships to obtain a better view.[96] The Sydney crew were firm favourites and began well, but the Melbourne crew overhauled them after the first bend and won by four lengths. Ballarat City, which included John Cazaly and was coached by Peter Cazaly, finished second, with the Sydney crew third.[97]

The result sparked heated debate in colonial rowing circles over the definition of what constituted a genuine amateur. The Victorian Association did not admit those who competed for prizemoney whereas New South Wales clubs were more concerned with excluding labourers, believing they had an unfair advantage over office workers. The captain of the Sydney crew, Arthur Fitzhardinge, attacked the Ballarat crew on these grounds, arguing three of their rowers would not be considered amateurs in Sydney. After responding that their stroke—a miner by employment—was the only one they could possibly object to, an irascible Peter Cazaly countered Fitzhardinge's argument by claiming that "a man working underground in bad air, gunpowder smoke and water, is placed at a disadvantage rather than otherwise."[98] The *Australasian* weighed into the debate, pointing out that each colony had agreed to row under their own definition of amateur and that the Sydney crew had ample opportunity to raise any objections before the race.[99]

Amid the inter-colonial posturing, James' own rowing reputation was assured. One sporting correspondent crowned him "a veritable Triton amongst the minnows" and a Victorian rowing historian later described him as:

> In the opinion of many the best man on the River, either as an oarsman or a sculler. In sculling he looked a picture of strength properly applied to the propulsion of a boat.[100]

James must have been working for the warehouse firm Watson and Sons around this time, because there are press reports of him rowing for them in December 1873 and playing for the company's cricket team that summer.[101] The firm was one of many established to meet Victoria's growing demand for miners' supplies and domestic goods. Founded in London in 1830 by merchant William Watson, his sons Robert, Alfred and Edward had opened the Melbourne branch in 1853. The following year they were selling linens, umbrellas, brandy, Havana cigars, hats, gloves and "watertight boots" from their premises in Flinders Street East.[102] By 1859, they had moved to 101 Swanston Street, one of 53 warehouse firms operating in the busy streets adjacent to Melbourne's wharves.[103] The company flourished and the Watsons became prominent businessmen and outspoken advocates of unfettered free trade.[104]

After several years at Swanston Street the firm opened a warehouse at 41 Little Collins Street around 1865.[105] Newspapers carried company advertisements seeking milliners, haberdashers, sales assistants and general hands, often including the provisos "must know the trade thoroughly, be unmarried, Protestant."[106] By 1874 the business had expanded to a large bluestone warehouse in Flinders Lane, complete with hydraulic lifts to haul goods between floors.[107] John Cazaly joined the firm as a packer after he too moved to Melbourne; the company would have provided the brothers with stable work as it rode the prosperity of Victoria's booming economy.

Little Collins Street, circa 1875

It was around this time that James met Elizabeth Jemima McNee. Elizabeth was born in Edinburgh, the fourth of an eventual 10 children born to Daniel and Euphemia McNee. Elizabeth was only a few months old when her family emigrated from Glasgow aboard the Aberfoyle in 1852.[108] Daniel had been a tailor in Scotland and Elizabeth became a dressmaker, though she also trained as a nurse, midwife and herbalist.[109]

James and Elizabeth were married by a Presbyterian minister five days before Christmas in 1873. James had just turned 33, Elizabeth was 21. The nuptials took place at her parents' home in Carlton rather than a church, possibly because Elizabeth was already eight months pregnant.[110]

The newlyweds lived just off Little Collins Street, three blocks north of the Yarra and close to the warehouse owned by James' employer. Little Collins, as its name implies, is a narrow thoroughfare running parallel to Collins Street between Spring and Spencer Streets. The surveyors who laid down Melbourne's grid pattern of streets in the 1830s planned the 33-foot-wide "little streets" as back entrances to the city's grander buildings, but each developed a life of its own during the economic boom which followed the discovery of gold.[111] By the 1870s Little Collins was a jumble of modest shops and dwellings sandwiched between more substantial offices, banks and hotels. Many narrower laneways branched off Little Collins and James and Elizabeth's neighbours included bootmakers, locksmiths, cabinet makers, wine merchants, a cordial factory and an oyster saloon.[112] It was in these confined and chaotic surroundings that their first child James William was born in January 1874.[113]

James jnr was joined by seven siblings over the next 15 years: Daniel, William (also known as Harry), Sydney, Albert (better known by his middle name George), Lenore (known as Lena), Ernest and Florence. Surviving records show the family moved several times during this period, first north to Carlton and then east to neighbouring Fitzroy. James' occupation was variously described as warehouseman, carter, storeman and labourer.[114] It is also believed that he supplemented his income as a physical instructor, teaching his own training techniques to rowers, runners, wrestlers and boxers.[115] According to one 1876 newspaper account James was certainly capable of decisive physical action when required:

> An act of bravery was displayed on Friday afternoon by Mr James Cazaly, well known in rowing circles. A pair of horses attached to a carriage containing a party of ladies, accompanied by a gentleman, bolted over Prince's Bridge. Mr Cazaly, with remarkable coolness, jumped boldly on to the box seat, and then made his way on to the pole of the carriage, seizing the reins. He was thus enabled to pull the frightened animals up before any damage was done.[116]

James continued rowing throughout the 1870s. In December 1874, he and his brother John made up half of the Watson and Sons crew which won the annual Stevenson Challenge Cup for warehouse crews.[117] The *Argus*' rowing correspondent noted that there had been "less interest in the event than usual", mainly because the presence of the Cazaly brothers had "somewhat dampered the ardour of rowing aspirants."[118] James and John were also part of a Warehouseman's crew which won the Grand Challenge Senior Fours at the 1875 Melbourne Regatta.[119]

Later that year, and after much feverish speculation in the press, James accepted a challenge by champion sculler John Christie to race any amateur over two miles. At stake was the Victorian amateur sculling championship and a trophy worth £25. Most bookmakers offered odds favouring Cazaly and a large crowd followed the race aboard a chartered steamer. The race was exceedingly close throughout. Cazaly led for most of the distance but Christie caught him a hundred yards before the finish line and won by less than a boat length.[120] In 1879 Cazaly defeated Robert Wing for a £25 wager and there are reports of him arranging further challenges as late as 1881, when he was 41.[121]

Melbourne continued to grow steadily as Victoria's post-gold rush generation came of age. The city's population nearly doubled between 1881 and 1891 and its inhabitants felt confident enough to host two international exhibitions during the decade to showcase their growing maturity to the world.[122]

By 1890, when their ninth child Edgar was born, James and Elizabeth had moved across the Yarra to a four-room terrace in Brooke Street, Albert Park.[123] The suburb was one of South Melbourne's newer subdivisions and the house was typical of many built by speculators to entice families from the crowded inner city. A number of manufacturing industries were also relocating to South Melbourne, offering labourers such as James the prospect of close and regular employment.

Other Cazalys were already living in the area. James' sister Bessy lived for a time at nearby St Vincent Place, an older and much more affluent part of South Melbourne.[124] Another Cazaly was a member of the South St Kilda football team and a Lou Cazaly—probably Louis, one of Peter Cazaly's sons—was an active member of the South Melbourne Rowing Club.[125]

By the early 1890s, Melbourne was at the tail end of a property boom which had lasted almost two decades. Fueled by British capital and speculative lending, the city's property values had reached unsustainable levels. A number of land and investment building societies collapsed during 1891-92 and the Federal Bank of Australia went into liquidation in early 1893. Within six weeks, 13 banks had shut their doors.[126] While most were eventually restructured and re-opened, consumer confidence was shattered and the damage to Victoria's economy lasted the rest of the decade.

Accurate jobless figures were not kept during this period but perhaps one in five of Melbourne's breadwinners were thrown out of work. Many men left the capital to seek work in rural areas or on the Western Australian gold fields.[127] In the absence of government social security, thousands of destitute families were forced to rely on churches and benevolent societies for handouts. The *Government Gazette* listed scores of bankrupts and newspapers carried regular reports of despairing men who had committed suicide.[128]

South Melbourne's large number of resident labourers meant it was hit hard by the Depression.[129] A dramatic fall in local manufacturing caused widespread unemployment: an 1893 survey of South Melbourne's 10 largest factories found only 700 men working where 3000 had been employed three years earlier.[130] The local population fell by 5000 during the five years from 1891, and one in every seven dwellings sat empty.[131]

One of the many businesses that failed was Watson and Sons, which went into liquidation in 1891 with debts exceeding £100,000.[132] John Cazaly had left to work for another warehouse company around this time but it is unknown if James was still employed at the firm when it collapsed.[133]

According to a family story, James had invested in property during Melbourne's boom but lost everything when the land bubble burst. The veracity of this story cannot be confirmed but his humble circumstances suggest his means were fairly modest to begin with. There was, however, one saving grace: Elizabeth's medical skills meant she was able to supplement the family's income as a nurse and midwife.[134] By the time their 10th child was born on Friday 13 January 1893, James and Elizabeth were renting a small timber cottage in O'Grady Street, Albert Park, from a local blacksmith.[135] For Roy Cazaly, it was a rather unpromising beginning.

4

A CHILDHOOD BY THE LAKE

Albert Park, 1893-1911

As the youngest of 10 children, Roy grew up in a long shadow cast by his older siblings. Years later, his daughter Pat recalled family stories that he was born with a liver complaint and had been a sickly child, fussed over by his mother and mollycoddled by his sisters.[136]

According to one story, Roy's brothers arrived home one day and were horrified to find that Florence and Lena had dressed him up in girls' clothes. Their response was to take him in hand and train him in various sports.[137] Their father James had converted an old stable at the rear of the house into a gymnasium and it was here that Roy learned the basics of boxing and wrestling.[138] His brothers also taught him ball sports and he displayed an early ambidexterity by batting, bowling and throwing left handed when playing cricket but preferring his right foot when kicking a football. The young Roy thrived on every sport he tried and would later say of his upbringing:

> I was in anything bar a wash. I was a bundle of energy. I was always looking for something to do to get rid of it.[139]

Roy developed an early fondness for animals and decided he wanted to become a vet. One day a neighbourhood dog had a leg broken by a milk cart. Refusing to allow the animal to be put down, Roy took it home, splinted the leg and spent several weeks carefully nursing it back to health.[140] He also

A CHILDHOOD BY THE LAKE

kept and trained pigeons. He once fell out of a tree and as he lay winded on the ground one of his brothers asked if he could have his pigeons if he died.[141]

Such scrapes aside, Roy doesn't appear to have got into any serious trouble, unlike his brother Ernest. When Ernest was 11, he and three accomplices were arrested after breaking into an Albert Park shop to steal money and sweets. Ernest had been the look-out during the robbery and the South Melbourne Court was told he had a previous conviction.[142]

Roy's early sporting development was profoundly shaped by his parents' decision to move from Fitzroy to South Melbourne not long before he was born. The family home may have been cramped but its proximity to nearby parklands and Port Phillip Bay provided ideal opportunities for a growing boy wanting to hone his sporting skills.

South Melbourne's 40,000 residents were fortunate to have the broad expanse of Albert Park on their doorstep. The park had been set aside for recreation during the early days of European settlement and it was progressively fenced from the late 1850s. Despite having sections periodically excised for housing, schools and other purposes, Albert Park in 1903 still sprawled across more than 450 acres of South Melbourne, with another 106 contained within the boundaries of the adjacent St Kilda City Council. By contrast, the hemmed-in residents of Collingwood had direct access to just 39 acres of public parks.[143]

Albert Park's centerpiece was its wishbone-shaped lake, which had been deepened and transformed during the 1870s and 1880s from a large, reedy swamp into an aquatic playground.[144] Local recreational pursuits included rowing and sailing on the lake, and swimming in the nearby bay and at the public baths along its foreshore. The Albert Park Swimming and Lifesaving Club was one of Victoria's first such clubs, having been established in the 1870s.[145]

Australian Football was another popular pastime in the district. Various forms of football had been played as a winter game in Melbourne since soon after European settlement and its distinctive rules began to be codified from 1859. During the 1860s and 1870s South Melbourne was home to several local clubs, including Albert Park, Emerald Hill (the original name for South Melbourne) and Cecil, which changed its name to South Melbourne soon after being established in 1874.[146]

Albert Park and neighbouring St Kilda were both foundation clubs of the Victorian Football Association (VFA), the premier competition, when it began in 1877. Other local clubs which subsequently joined included South Melbourne, Williamstown and Port Melbourne.[147] South Melbourne and Albert Park merged in 1880, retaining the former's name and adopting the latter's red and white colours.[148] South Melbourne shared its home ground, the Lake Oval, with the cricket club at the western end of Albert Park Lake; its fierce rival St Kilda did likewise at the Junction Oval at the lake's eastern end.

South Melbourne enjoyed early success in the VFA, winning the premiership in 1881, 1885 and three times in a row from 1888. Their matches drew large and enthusiastic crowds and champion players such as Henry 'Sonny' Elms, Peter Burns and Bill Windley became household names. In 1890 the club boasted almost 700 financial members, a number that dipped to 528 two years later as the Depression took hold and many could no longer afford the 10 shilling season subscription.[149]

By the late 1880s VFA clubs were formally classed as either 'senior' or 'junior' teams and each had to play at least 18 matches against senior teams to be eligible for the premiership. In 1892 there was an uneven number of teams so three clubs played 21 games, nine played 20 and Collingwood—in its first season in the VFA—just 19.[150] The scoring system during this period was also somewhat haphazard. Goals counted towards the final score but not behinds, resulting in a large number of drawn games.[151]

In 1893, the year Roy was born, the VFA consisted of Carlton, Collingwood, Essendon, Fitzroy, Footscray, Geelong, Melbourne, North Melbourne, Port Melbourne, Richmond,

South Melbourne, St Kilda and Williamstown.[152] Essendon won its third straight premiership and South Melbourne finished fourth.

As well as the VFA there was a thriving Metropolitan Junior Football Association (MJFA). The MJFA ran competitions ranging from 'first rate' down to 'fourth rate' which encompassed almost 100 clubs across Melbourne.[153] The plethora of local junior teams during Cazaly's youth included Union Jack and Marylebone (based in South Melbourne), Napier Imperials, Dundas and Leopold (Albert Park), Pembroke (Middle Park) and Alma (Port Melbourne).[154]

The sheer number of clubs suggests district football was in a decidedly healthy state but the same couldn't be said of the VFA, which had become unwieldy and fractious by the mid-1890s. Disagreements over rules, player payments, unruly spectators and the formula for sharing gate revenues came to a head after the 1896 season, when eight of the stronger and better financed clubs formed a new competition, the Victorian Football League (VFL). South Melbourne and St Kilda were part of the breakaway league. Port Melbourne, Williamstown and three other VFA clubs were not invited to join and the League and the Association became bitter rivals for most of the next century.

Melbourne was becoming increasingly urbanised. By 1903, 42 per cent of all Victorians lived within a 10-mile radius of the city's centre.[155] That year, most of the Cazaly family was still living in the rented five-room weatherboard cottage in O'Grady Street. They were typical of many working class families who lived cheek-by-jowl in the inner suburbs and toiled in nearby factories and businesses.

Roy's father, James, was a labourer, as was his brother George. Of his other siblings, Daniel was a butter churner, James jnr was a wool scourer and Sydney and William were both working for Skehan's, a butcher's shop on the corner of Park and Clarendon Streets.[156] The brothers later opened their own butchery in Hambleton Street, Middle Park, where their advertised specialities included sausages and corned beef.[157]

By 1906, most of the family had moved several blocks north to a six-room brick cottage in Glover Street. Lena was listed on the electoral roll as a rubber worker, as was George, who lived three streets away in Brooke Street. Lena and George worked for the Dunlop Rubber Company, which had recently built a huge new factory on reclaimed marshland in nearby Montague.[158] Consumer demand for Dunlop's products had surged during the early years of the new century and the factory's workforce grew accordingly. In 1906 more than 800 employees made car and bicycle tyres and a large range of domestic products including rubber boots, garden hoses and hot water bottles.[159]

Life seems to have been harder for Roy's ageing father, who was forced to trade on his past sporting triumphs to find work. In late 1907, readers of *The Age*'s 'Situations Wanted' column learned—between advertisements from unemployed carpenters and charwomen—that "James Cazaly, ex-champion oarsman and sculler, wishes situation as caretaker or watchman, urgent."[160]

Roy was enrolled at Albert Park State School in Bridport Street at a time when it was undergoing rapid growth. The school had first opened in 1873 with 654 pupils but almost 1500 were attending by 1885.[161] The opening of a new school in neighbouring Middle Park in 1887 helped ease enrolment pressures but by the turn of the century Albert Park's average daily attendance was still 1200. Some students were taught in corridors, others were crammed into the church hall next door and the local newspaper thundered that the tardiness of the authorities in neglecting to connect the school to the sewage mains "might almost be represented as amounting to criminal neglect."[162]

Overcrowding and questionable sanitation aside, Albert Park could boast two advantages over other Melbourne schools. The first was its proximity to the swimming baths of Port Phillip Bay. In 1891 Albert Park had become the first Victorian state school to establish its own swimming clubs.[163] By 1900 there were 247 pupils in the boys' swim club and 187 in the girls'.[164] Roy enjoyed swimming and spent many weekends at the beach during his youth.[165] May Cox, one of the pioneers of Victorian swimming instruction, taught at Albert Park during Roy's time there, and he probably came under her influence.[166]

One of Roy's school mates who excelled in the water was future Olympian Frank Beaurepaire.[167] Frank had learned to swim as a six year old, when his father tied a rope around his waist and threw him into the water at Stubbs' Baths. Frank couldn't always afford the two pence admission to the Baths so he would train in Port Phillip Bay while Roy followed behind in a rowboat. Cazaly later recalled that

> I rowed many a mile down the choppy waters of the bay after him. No sea was too rough for him. He had the heart of a lion.[168]

Albert Park School's other advantage was its strong football pedigree. From 1904, schools across Melbourne participated in an annual football championship run by the State Schools Amateur Athletic Association.[169] Albert Park played in the southern district, along with schools from South Melbourne, Port Melbourne and South Yarra. Its football uniform was a navy-blue jersey with a diagonal gold sash, white shorts, blue socks with gold hoops and a blue cap.

Albert Park defeated Carlton's Faraday Street to win the inaugural schools championship in 1904. They then played the visiting Petersham team from New South Wales in a curtain-raiser before the VFL Grand Final between Carlton and Fitzroy. Petersham won easily, although *The Referee* noted their average age was 16, compared with just 13½ for the Albert Park boys, and that "heights and weights were correspondingly unequal."[170] Clifton Hill Primary were school premiers in 1905 but Albert Park regained the title the following year.[171]

Roy began playing school football around this time, alongside his friends Frank Beaurepaire, Emil Fleiter, John Treloar and Stan Veale. Beaurepaire and most of the team were 15 years old; Cazaly and Veale were two years younger.[172] More than seven decades later, Veale remembered Cazaly as "a most pleasant, placid, modest bloke, a good footballer, and very popular" with his teammates.[173] Roy also proved to be an all-rounder at cricket, often singled out in match reports for both his bowling and batting prowess. During a semi-final loss to North Fitzroy's Alfred Crescent in 1906 he

[AUSTRALIAN WAR MEMORIAL COLLECTION]

Albert Park State School's victorious 1908 football team. Roy is standing on the far left.

claimed four wickets for 14 and scored 66 runs for the match.[174]

Sports such as swimming, football and cricket were seen as ideal training to prepare boys for military life. Albert Park had formed its own cadet unit in 1890 under the influential command of Major Sam Barclay and a number of Roy's teammates went on to have distinguished military careers.[175]

Albert Park's academic records from this period have been lost, but one fact concerning Roy's education is known. Before starting school he had taught himself to write left-handed, but his teachers made him use his right. This was a common practice at the time, based on the belief that left-handedness indicated a learning difficulty requiring correction or a defiant personality which needed to be curbed.[176] The stress of being forced to switch writing-hands caused Roy to develop a stutter. According to a family story, he cured himself by secluding himself in a room, reading aloud and breathing deeply from his diaphragm so his words came out slower. It was an elocution technique he later taught to other stutterers.[177]

Roy did not progress beyond primary school. Under Victoria's education system children only had to attend school until they were 14, and many regularly skipped classes.[178] The state had recently begun to offer secondary education but the South Melbourne Technical School—which might otherwise have given Roy some vocational training—did not open until 1918.[179] His friend Frank Beaurepaire went on to the prestigious Wesley College, but only because its headmaster Lawrence 'Dicky' Adamson had recognised his swimming prowess and offered him a half scholarship.[180] For most local families, further education was simply not a consideration.

Roy didn't have to look far to find work. The exact chronology of his early employment is sketchy, but it is known that he helped in his brothers' butcher shop delivering customer orders by horse and cart and worked as a motor mechanic. He found he was good with his hands and taught himself how to strip down and reassemble a car engine.[181]

South Melbourne's economy had recovered strongly during the early years of the new century and its rejuvenated industries provided thousands of jobs for local residents.[182] By late 1908, Roy was working alongside his siblings Lena and George at the Dunlop Rubber Company. For the active teenager, work was simply something that filled in the time between sporting activities. One of his workmates later recalled that:

> Lunch time intervals found us all trying to stop Cazaly from getting a touch of the rag and paper ball made from lunch wraps. By employing every means known in wrestling, six or seven of us were successful in keeping him out of the play.[183]

There was no shortage of leisure options for Roy and his mates once the working week ended. During the summer of 1908/09 he played cricket for Dunlop's company team in the second grade of the Victorian Junior Cricket Association. He featured regularly in the bowling reports and his figures included hauls of seven for 27 and five for 31.[184]

Australian Football still provided the main sporting outlet for Melbourne's youth each winter. Details of fixtures took up many newspaper columns each week and parks echoed to the dull thud of boot on ball every Saturday. As well as the VFL, the VFA, the Metropolitan Amateur Football Association and the Victorian Junior Football Association there were competitions organised according to district, trade and religious affiliation. The Boyle and Scott Association, for instance, fielded 74 teams across several divisions, and was reputed to be the largest football competition in Australia.[185]

During the winter of 1910, Roy played for the Nelson Rovers in J K Smith's Competition, which included both suburban and church-based sides.[186] The competition had two sections: one for juniors and an 'Open 18½' division. The Rovers competed in the open division, which meant 17½-year-old Roy was competing alongside men at least a year older. In one game against the eventual premiers Seddon Star "R Cazaly" was named best player on the ground.[187]

Roy also took up rowing around this time, no doubt introduced to the sport by his father James. He proved a natural and during the spring of 1910 took part in several races with the South Melbourne Rowing Club, which had been a fixture beside Albert Park Lake since 1878.[188] Rowing technology had improved dramatically since James Cazaly had started in the sport in the 1850s. Boats were now much lighter, thinner and stronger and sliding seats had replaced fixed seats. But while the equipment had changed, the training fundamentals remained the same. James would have taught his son that rowing in a crew required a disciplined subjugation of the self quite unlike other team sports. Writing in 1908, an English rowing coach explained the difference:

> [A] man who rows in a crew cannot hope to gain applause by individualising himself. The cricketer may make his brilliant strokes in his own way, and run up his special century; the footballer may tackle or kick or pass in his own particular celebrated style but the oarsman who does his work in a crew must be content to subordinate his individuality, to lose even his name and to be converted into a number as one member of a successful crew.[189]

Roy would learn to apply this principle of placing team cohesion ahead of individual ambition to all his sporting endeavours. He also kept up his football, and by the winter of 1911 was playing for the Middle Park Wesleys, a Methodist team competing in the open age division of the Protestant Churches' Association.[190] Several of his former Albert Park School teammates played alongside him, including Stan Veale.

Roy's specialist role for the Wesleys was as a follower. Followers have played a key role in Australian Football since the sport's early days. Their task, as the title suggests, is to pursue the play around the ground rather than remain in a set position. Then, as now, a good follower required strength, stamina and good all-round skills. As early as 1876, *The Footballer* recommended they should be:

> ... the strongest, lithest, most active and enduring, and best tempered men in the team—men who will last ... play for the ball and be always on it, good drop and punt kicks with both feet ...[191]

1910 St Kilda lapel badge.

Roy later credited his father with teaching him a rowing breathing technique—"in through the nose, out through the mouth"—which helped him to follow for long stretches during games. He believed he could do so without tiring because he was working with his lungs rather than his heart.[192]

The other type of player who made up the following division, or ruck, was the rover. Usually the smallest player on the ground, the rover worked closely with the followers at centre bounces and stoppages to help clear the ball downfield. The ruck was essentially a team within a team, working together to set up attacking opportunities and prevent the opposing ruck from doing the same. They were the engine room at ball-ups and boundary throw-ins, spearheading forward thrusts and helping stem opposition attacks. Each ruck originally had three or even four followers and two rovers but this led to congested play so from the late 1890s they were scaled back to two followers and one rover.[193]

As the 1911 season continued Roy was regularly named among the Wesleys' best players. His colleagues did not always display the same dedication: the team almost had to forfeit to the Northcote Methodists when several players decided to go and watch South Melbourne play St Kilda instead. The Wesleys, chastened, regrouped to trounce Carlton's Church of Christ the following Saturday by 87 points to nil.[194] Roy kicked a goal and was again among the best players but it was to be his last game for the club: his ruck skills and consistent form had come to the attention of St Kilda's scouts.

5

A RAW COLT FROM THE PADDOCK

St Kilda, 1911-12

For many years, it was thought that Roy Cazaly had played his first game for St Kilda in 1910, or even as early as 1909. In fact, the first Cazaly to represent the club was his older, somewhat wayward brother Ernest.

Ernest had a habit of making Melbourne's sporting pages for the wrong reasons. In May 1906 he was playing for Leopold in the Metropolitan Amateur Football Association when he was charged with deliberately tripping an opponent. He failed to appear at the tribunal hearing and was suspended for two seasons in his absence.[195] In 1907 he played for a South Melbourne team in the Wednesday Football League, a trades-based competition founded in 1896 to take advantage of a new mid-week half-holiday. The games were often rough affairs and a local newspaper described what happened after Ernest came to blows with St Kilda Wednesday's ruckman and local butcher Bill Woodcock:

> A relative of one of the St Kilda players jumped over the fence, and struck Cazaly, and several blows were exchanged in quick succession ... while several of the cooler headed players endeavored to quell the fight, several spectators jumped the fence, and nearly all the players rushed to the scene, followed by a couple of hundred spectators from the grandstand.[196]

The umpire and two police constables eventually restored order but Ernest was reported and suspended for the rest of the season.[197] He played for the South Melbourne Wednesday side the following year, and was again suspended. His chequered Wednesday League career ended in 1909, when the mid-week half-holiday was replaced with a Saturday half-holiday and the club was wound up due to financial problems.[198]

Ernest transferred back to the Leopold club, and it was there that he came to St Kilda's notice.[199] His name is included among a list of players in the back of a 1908/09 minutes book but he didn't make his League debut until the first round of the 1910 season. It is this game against University which many writers later wrongly attributed to his brother Roy.[200] St Kilda was without several key players when Ernest was called up.[201] Little is known about his performance but soon after his debut St Kilda wrote to him and teammate Gower Ross demanding "the return of [their] costumes and boots."[202] The terse letter was necessary because the two players had transferred to VFA side Brunswick. Ernest played several games for Brunswick during 1910, usually in defence, but he was a fringe player and did not take part in that year's finals. He later transferred to Port Melbourne.[203]

St Kilda, meanwhile, was undergoing one of its periodic bouts of internal strife during 1910. Dissention within the administration came to a head at a fiery committee meeting at the end of June. The meeting passed a motion of no confidence in its match committee, triggering the resignation of two of its members.[204] George Morrissey became the Saints' fourth captain for the season and the club finished last, their only win coming in the final round against a depleted Carlton. In desperation, the club had tried 60 players during the season, including 29 recruits.[205]

St Kilda's 1911 season was characterised by further on-field inconsistency and off-field instability. After a win against Geelong in the first round, St Kilda's season turned into another *annus horribilis*, with nine consecutive defeats. Press reports chronicled growing dissension between the players and administrators as the losses mounted. Trivial incidents were triggered and then magnified by spite, distrust and petty officialdom. Committee members were upset by "abusive language and disparaging remarks" by the players, and further angered when the players organised a picnic and then a dinner at the home of captain Harry Lever without inviting them.[206]

The situation reached crisis point before a match against Melbourne, when the committee withdrew the dressing-room passes previously issued to players' relatives and past players. The players were particularly incensed over the removal of the pass issued to former captain and life member Joe Hogan. Hogan refused to comment publicly but Lever added fuel to the fire by declaring:

> I don't want to strip for St Kilda if they are going to treat a good supporter like this. I am going to speak to the other players before the match on Saturday, and see what action we will take.[207]

The Argus compared the charged atmosphere at St Kilda that week to a political crisis.[208] The players met to discuss the pass matter while their Melbourne opponents waited on the field for some time after the scheduled start. St Kilda eventually appeared but according to one report most of them:

> ... might just as well have been 'over the fence,' looking on, for all the good they did. So half hearted did some of the tricolours play that the spectators indulged in many sarcastic remarks.[209]

Lever had to be physically restrained from jumping the fence after the match to remonstrate with the jeering spectators.[210]

Club secretary Herb Stoddart sought to explain the committee's actions after the game, stating the committee had decided to withdraw the guest passes and restrict future numbers due to the "very poky" nature of the rooms.[211] With the committee refusing to back down, the players met again after training the following Tuesday and affirmed their position. When 18 players told the club they would be unavailable for any more matches during the season they were told to hand in their uniforms.

Stoddart sought to put a brave face on the calamity, declaring the club had been inundated by junior players willing to "fill the breach" for its round 15 match against Carlton.[212] After further mediation involving Joe Hogan and the St Kilda mayor, the players offered an olive branch: having made their feelings clear they would continue to play provided there were no recriminations. The committee replied that they could not accept the players' offer without punishing the instigators.[213]

It was against this backdrop of intransigence and instability that Roy Cazaly was plucked from the Middle Park Wesleys for his first VFL game. It was July 29, 1911, and he was 18½ years old. He later recalled the suddenness of his selection:

> I was a raw colt from the paddock. They came for me on Saturday at lunchtime to play. It was naturally my big opportunity and I wanted to make good.[214]

Cazaly was not exaggerating about the lateness of his call-up: St Kilda had invited about 50 "stout looking lads" to assemble at the Carlton ground and they selected their team just minutes before the match.[215] Some of the recruits were such novices that the umpire felt it necessary to give them a run-down on the rules before the game.[216]

Only six regulars were present when the St Kilda side ran out. Just three of the team had played more than 10 League games and nine were making their VFL debut.[217] By contrast, 10 of Carlton's line-up had played more than 50 games each. The difference in games played between the two sides was massive: 1166 to 168.[218]

One of Cazaly's opponents was Carlton captain and shepherder Fred 'Pompey' Elliott. Elliott was in his final VFL season, having begun his career with Melbourne in 1899. The previous month he had become the first to have played 200 League games.[219] It is hard to imagine a more uneven match-up: the "raw colt" Cazaly against the wily Elliott, who had played more senior games than the entire St Kilda team.

Despite the mismatch, or perhaps because of it, Elliott took kindly to Cazaly. After Cazaly responded to Elliott's vigorous checking by lashing out at him, he expected an instant reprisal:

> Sparring up and waiting for him to come back at me, I was surprised when he grabbed my arms and said, 'Good on you son, don't take all they give you, but don't hit or out you'll go.' I cooled down in a moment.[220]

Inaccurate kicking by Carlton kept St Kilda in the game to half-time, but the Blues scored 12 goals to one after the long break to win by 114 points.[221] *The Argus* listed Cazaly as one of St Kilda's better players and *The Age* reported he provided "a few bright patches of play". The *Sport* was more fulsome in its praise, noting that:

> Cazaly, from the Middle Park Wesleys, gave every indication of developing into something good for St Kilda. His high marking and ruckwork were very promising in his first League match.[222]

Cazaly had shown enough promise to retain his place in the side but most of his new teammates were not as fortunate: six of his fellow debutants never played another League game and the other two managed just three games each.[223]

With the season's hopes gone and the players' dispute continuing, St Kilda's committee named further juniors for their next match. Large losses were becoming a depressing regularity, and one St Kilda member called for action to resolve the impasse between the officials and the senior players:

> Surely the time has now arrived for the members of this club to take a hand in the dispute between the players and the committee. I purchased a season ticket to view matches played with the best available talent, but, as matters are turning out, we are not receiving much for our membership.[224]

The situation turned even worse for St Kilda when they lost to Essendon by 125 points on their home ground. *The Age* described the game as "nothing more than a practice match" in which Essendon scored "with a wearying regularity".[225] Round 17 saw the Saints travel to Punt Road, where Richmond defeated them by 87 points. It was Cazaly's first game starting in the ruck, where he played alongside Charlie Taylor and rover Aubrey Hart and kicked his first VFL goal.[226]

St Kilda's final match of the season was at home to Collingwood. The off-field differences that had caused the players' strike had been papered over, at least temporarily. Harry Lever and four other senior players were recalled—no doubt feeling vindicated—but it was another lopsided encounter with Collingwood winning by 57 points. St Kilda's disastrous year ended with just two wins. The club had experimented with 62 players during the season, a record for any club in the first hundred years of the VFL/AFL.[227] They had lost the four games Cazaly had played by a total of 383 points. Amid such turmoil, his future in the side was far from assured.

Cazaly resumed rowing with the South Melbourne Rowing Club during the spring of 1911 and was part of a crew which won the Maiden Eights at the Albert Park Lake Regatta.[228] In October, he led a fours crew to victory in an intra-club competition which was followed by afternoon tea, a musical program and a dance at the boatshed.[229] Later that month the South Melbourne crew of Cazaly (bow), Les Bligh (2), Roy Johnson (3), Hughie Dixon (stroke) and N Worrall (cox) defeated 10 other crews to win the Maiden Fours at the Henley-on-Yarra Regatta.[230]

A family tragedy occurred on Boxing Day when Roy's brother Edgar was killed by a train on a railway crossing near Blackburn station. Edgar, recently turned 21, had spent time in the Kew Asylum for the Insane before being discharged several months before the accident. A coronial inquest heard evidence from an Asylum hall porter and a witness who had been on the train. The coroner, Doctor Cole, confirmed Edgar had been killed by the train but found insufficient evidence to show why he had been on the tracks.[231]

Later summaries of Cazaly's football career often stated that he played his entire time at St Kilda without pay. Apart from a period during World War I, when St Kilda's players voted not to receive match payments, this is almost certainly wrong.

The 1911 season had begun with a vigorous debate within the VFL about player payments. Football was bringing in larger crowds and bigger gate takings but the clubs seemed unwilling or unable to address their financial windfall in a consistent manner. While direct and indirect payments were explicitly banned under rule 29, it was an open secret that some clubs paid their best players and offered inducements for others to sign up or transfer from other clubs.[232] Such "under the lap" payments were often procured from wealthy benefactors and disguised as other expenses in club accounts or the funds set aside for end-of-season trips. As a result, some of the better players were paid, others who asked for payment were denied it and others still refused to accept it in order to maintain their amateur sporting status.

The League's reluctance to address this clearly unworkable status quo was cynically dubbed "shamateurism" by the *Sport* newspaper.[233] The need to acknowledge the game's inevitable professionalism was later pragmatically argued by St Kilda's champion forward Dave McNamara:

> The vast amount of money entailed in the upkeep of the game will necessitate the conduct of it on strict business principles. It has become a business, and that being so it must, and no doubt will, be conducted as such. Charges for admission to the matches have been made, and as easily exacted. Where is the money to go? It must follow that the major portion of it will go to the men who produce the pleasure and excitement for the subscribing public.[234]

The clubs, however, remained divided over the payment issue in 1911. Some, such as Melbourne, maintained they had never paid players and wanted to uphold the League's amateur status.[235] Other, more hard-nosed clubs such as Richmond believed payments would continue regardless of the League's stance and it was preferable to make them transparent.

The original motion to abolish rule 29 was supported by most clubs but was lost because a three-quarter majority was required. A subsequent proposal by Fitzroy and St Kilda to set a fixed maximum player payment of 30 shillings a week was also defeated because the weaker clubs couldn't afford it and the stronger clubs didn't want their hands tied. The League eventually agreed to abolish rule 29 after Fitzroy and St Kilda softened their stance.[236] Despite a renewed push by St Kilda to cap player payments, no serious attempt was made to limit the amount they could be paid until the passing of the Coulter Law in 1930.

The end of rule 29 meant player payments were now legal and could be openly reported for the first time. In June 1911, for example, it was revealed that St Kilda had secured the services of country player Kenny McKenzie by offering him a £14 guarantee, £3/10 per match and a weekly train ticket between Mooroopna and Melbourne.[237] Given such largesse, if Cazaly was not paid during his early days at St Kilda, he certainly would have been in later seasons as his value to the side increased.

The VFL introduced several changes prior to the 1912 season. On-field stewards were hired to help umpires control games and report players for infringements. Player numbers were introduced for the first time and the fledgling *Record* was given the exclusive right to publish player names and numbers for each game. Cazaly was happy to wear the number 13 jersey but at least one superstitious player at another club negotiated a swap with a teammate to avoid having to wear the dreaded "Devil's number".[238]

St Kilda sought a clean break from their disastrous 1911 season by making changes to their committee and recruiting several promising players. One of the most influential as far as the young Cazaly was concerned was brilliant centreman Louis William Schmidt, lured from Richmond for £2/10 per match. 'Billy' Schmidt could delight and frustrate supporters in equal measure: he had an innate ability to weave his way downfield but a tendency to run too far with the ball.[239] The two became firm friends. Schmidt would hone his footwork by dodging pedestrians in the street and Cazaly later revealed how he taught him to evade opponents:

> He gave me more individual coaching than any other man. He would run me out into Albert Park and set me running full belt at a tree. Just as I was about to take the tree on the run I had to do a blind turn. After I had hit those trees once or twice, I could turn on a threepenny bit. Schmidt would put a ball down and I would have to pick it up at full tilt and turn at the same time. This was a wonderful exercise for loosening up the hips.[240]

Cazaly retained his place in St Kilda's side for the start of the season, but some of the match committee's decisions were puzzling, leading one supporter to write to the *Sport* to "respectfully request" an explanation.[241] Cazaly appears to have been a victim of the club's erratic selection policy.

Starting in the centre and then on a half-forward flank, he played in four of the first five games but there was no mention of him in the published team lists after round six. Keen readers of the sporting papers soon found his name under a different column: he had transferred to Carlton District in the Metropolitan Amateur Football Association (MAFA):

> Roy Cazaly, late of St Kilda, played his first game with Carlton against Hawthorn and shaped well. He should be a decided acquisition to the team.[242]

Whether Cazaly was dropped by St Kilda after a falling out or left of his own volition is unknown. It is noteworthy, however, that he chose to play for a feeder side for Carlton's VFL team rather than with Leopold, the South Melbourne-based team which had won the MAFA premiership the previous season. He probably saw it as a chance to help fulfil his boyhood dream of playing for Carlton in the VFL.

Cazaly played as a follower for the rest of the season, and was often named among Carlton District's best. In early July he was injured when he fell awkwardly during a match against Beverley, Richmond's junior team. He completed the game up forward but missed the next two rounds, returning to help his side defeat Caulfield. The *Sport* noted that "Roy Cazaly played his first game for three weeks with Carlton on Saturday, and, although he didn't bustle himself, found time to kick three goals."[243]

Cazaly kicked two goals in Carlton District's subsequent loss to South Yarra and then two more in an easy home win against the Collegians. No VFL games were scheduled that day, resulting in a larger than usual crowd at the Carlton Cricket Ground. The team's players, officials and supporters took advantage of a bye the following Saturday to hold a picnic and intra-club social match at Doncaster in Melbourne's north-east.[244]

Rowing resumed in early spring and Cazaly's crew won the South Melbourne Rowing Club's Challenge Fours on Albert Park Lake.[245] Carlton District won their last two games against Leopold and University to finish in second place, but bowed out of the finals after losing to South Yarra on the Richmond ground. They ended their season with a creditable 14 wins from 18 games.[246] St Kilda, meanwhile, finished eighth in the League, with just seven wins for the year. There was little to herald the turnaround in fortunes that would come their way the following season.

6

A PREMIERSHIP
THROWN IN THE AIR

St Kilda, 1913-14

Keen to put another disastrous season behind it, St Kilda began training earlier than other VFL clubs in 1913. Harry Lever was again elected captain, with Dick Harris as vice-captain. Cazaly was recalled to the side, where it was reported that he was "a much improved player."[247]

St Kilda's hopes took an early blow when champion goalkicker Dave McNamara was refused a transfer from Essendon's Association team back to St Kilda, which he had left after a dispute in 1909. McNamara had kicked 188 goals and been the VFA's leading goalscorer during the previous two seasons, and he bitterly concluded that the Association felt his absence would affect their crowds.[248]

Cazaly played on the backline during the Saints' round one loss to South Melbourne. One reporter noted that St Kilda's second ruck was badly beaten and "it would not be a bad thing to give Cazaly a run on the ball."[249] He played forward the following week where his high marking was a feature in St Kilda's strong win against Fitzroy. By the time St Kilda defeated Melbourne in round five, Harry 'Vic' Cumberland and Cazaly had teamed up in the ruck, "the latter's shepherding being first-class."[250] Cazaly admired

Cumberland's dogged persistence and said later he had learned the finer points of ruck-play by observing him closely.

> He was the perfect physique of a man and taught me all I knew about ruckwork. Cumberland never wasted the ball and always passed it on to a teammate. He was a big man and a big-hearted footballer.[251]

After a loss to Carlton in wet conditions, the *Sport*'s correspondent noted that:

> Cazaly, for St Kilda, put in a lot of solid work throughout the day. Once he and [George] Challis met like two railway truck buffers, and the tricolour went down in the mud. George is not so slim as he used to be.[252]

St Kilda then defeated Essendon and Geelong but lost important games to Collingwood, South Melbourne and Fitzroy. By mid-season they seemed anchored to sixth spot but they finished strongly with six wins from their last seven games, including a one-point victory over Carlton in round 15. The home-ground win came following a goal by Billy Schmidt after the final bell and was their most thrilling for the year. Schmidt, who some St Kilda supporters had accused of "playing dead" to that point, was carried from the ground as "girls and women screamed; boys and grown men and old geezers roared and cheered."[253]

Wins against Collingwood and Essendon followed, with one reporter noting that "Cazaly, though not a brilliant and showy player, is nevertheless one of the most consistent men in St Kilda's team."[254] At the end of the regular season, Cumberland was named *The Argus* newspaper's player of the season and University's full-forward Roy Park had scored the most goals, with 53. It was an achievement made even more impressive by the fact that University had lost all of their games.[255]

Despite a final-round drubbing by Geelong, St Kilda had done enough during the second half of the season to secure fourth spot and claim a semi-final berth against South Melbourne. Fitzroy, meanwhile, had finished in top position and they entered the finals as very warm premiership favourites. St Kilda easily accounted for South Melbourne in the first semi-final, thanks largely to a cohesive team effort and six goals from nippy forward

Ernie Sellars. A week later Fitzroy overcame Collingwood in the second semi-final to set up a final with St Kilda.

No one knew the pain of St Kilda's history of losses better than their coach George 'Sugar' Sparrow. Sparrow had played for them during the early years of the VFL; now, as coach, he sought redemption for his beleaguered Saints.

A record crowd of almost 55,000 people gathered at the MCG. Even some with grandstand tickets were forced to stand "like herrings in a barrel" and plainclothes policemen were on hand to catch anyone passing their tickets to friends outside the gates.[256] The game was hard fought throughout and the *Record* described players who "met like battleships crashing into each other".[257] George Morrissey and Cazaly both scored three goals as St Kilda outplayed Fitzroy in the second half to win by 25 points.

Roy Cazaly, as he lined up for the 1913 Grand Final.

In later seasons St Kilda's win would have secured them the premiership but under the rules of the time Fitzroy as minor premiers had the right of challenge. St Kilda selected the same team; Fitzroy made two changes. A new record crowd of almost 60,000 turned out to see if St Kilda could break their premiership drought. As added incentive, a group of their supporters promised the players £180 to share, a gold medal each and a celebratory dinner if they won the flag.[258]

Fitzroy jumped St Kilda early in the Grand Final. The woefully inaccurate Saints did not register a goal in the first half and by three-quarter time Fitzroy led 5.11.41 to 1.10.16. The game looked to be all over but St Kilda regrouped to kick four goals in the final term to close within a point of Fitzroy's score. It was here that the Saints lost their nerve when Des Baird, who had marked within kicking distance, paused and then inexplicably handballed to George Morrissey, who missed the goals with a hurried snap.

The Saints' momentum was lost and Fitzroy's greater composure showed through as they steadied to win their fifth VFL flag by 13 points.

It was a shattering end to St Kilda's season and their players were still debating exactly what went wrong and who was to blame more than two decades later. Cazaly put the loss down to a combination of big occasion nerves and the lingering effects of a bout of influenza which had swept through the team in the week before the game. "If ever a premiership was thrown in the air, St Kilda threw that one," he later remarked.[259]

Cazaly had missed just two games for the year and had played a key role in the club's first final win over Fitzroy. His future in St Kilda's line-up now seemed assured, a prospect reflected by the fact that its committee twice discussed efforts by one of their members to help find him more secure employment.[260]

The 1913 VFL season was the last before Australia and much of the world was plunged into the horrors of the Great War. Several who played in the Grand Final subsequently enlisted and Fitzroy's Jack Cooper and Arthur Harrison were to make the ultimate sacrifice on the battlefields of the western front. But war still seemed a long way away in September 1913. As St Kilda's players and officials set off on an end-of-season trip to Tasmania, they would have consoled themselves that they had what it took to make another Grand Final. Sadly for them and their long-suffering supporters, it would be another 52 years before they would do so, and 53 before they would finally win their first flag.

Off the field, Roy had been courting a young woman named Agnes, the fourth child of Patrick James Murtha and Delia Ann Pettis. Patrick was born in Ireland's County Clare and had been a sailor before migrating to central Victoria. He appears to have lived an eventful life as he boasted of serving as a British Navy midshipman alongside the future King George V and to being feared by members of Ned Kelly's bushranging gang.[261] Delia was much more unworldly, the Ballarat-born daughter of American James Washington Pettis and Ann McGuire from Ireland. When Patrick and

Delia married in 1881, he was 50 and she was just 19.²⁶²

Agnes, or Aggie as she was better known, was born in Pyalong, 60 miles north of Melbourne, on Valentine's Day 1894. Roy would later describe Aggie as his companion, his inspiration and a shrewd authority on football:

> My wife was never far away when I was playing, and much closer when I was off the field. She became a great judge of the game and my keenest critic. After a year or two she had sized up players of other sides and could give me tips on how their efforts could be minimised. Her enthusiasm spurred me on, her nursing put me back in the game quickly after injuries, and her general care has kept me in the game for so long.²⁶³

The Protestant Roy and the Roman Catholic Aggie were married on Caulfield Cup Day, 18 October, 1913 in the five-room weatherboard house Roy's parents were renting in De Carle Street, Brunswick.²⁶⁴ His father and Aggie's mother had to give their written consent to the union as both bride and groom were still under 21. Aggie (who was 19 years old) and Roy (who was 20) lived alongside his parents and several of his siblings for the next two years.²⁶⁵

In February 1914, Roy's 34-year-old brother Sydney slashed his throat with a razor and died later in the Melbourne Hospital. A married father of three, Sydney had given up his work as a butcher several months earlier and he and his wife Ethel were staying at De Carle Street. Ethel told the subsequent inquest that Sydney had suffered from nerves and insomnia, and the coroner ruled his death was self-inflicted.²⁶⁶

Football resumed. Several key St Kilda players had departed, including George Morrissey and Ernie Sellars to Western Australia, but the long-anticipated return of Dave McNamara to the line-up sounded an early note of optimism. The players voted to retain Harry Lever as captain and chose McNamara as his deputy.²⁶⁷

Cazaly played in 15 of St Kilda's 18 games, often being praised in reports for his consistent and useful work. His usual position was on the half-

R. Cazaly, St. Kilda.

Cazaly's first photographic appearance in the *Record* came in round five, 1914.

forward flank, with occasional spells in a forward pocket or in defence. Influenza swept through the team mid-season and there was doubt whether Cazaly would be able to play against Carlton in round 11. He recovered in time but St Kilda lost a close game by three points.[268] Despite injuring a wrist he was able to take his place the following Saturday in a drawn game against Essendon.

St Kilda easily accounted for University in the last round but they had failed to live up to the promise they had shown the previous season, and the team finished seventh. Their low point came in the penultimate round, when Dave McNamara was reported for elbowing, tripping and rough play during a spiteful loss to Geelong. Cazaly, who was himself cautioned by stewards after a "fierce charge" which injured his opponent's collarbone, spoke on McNamara's behalf at the tribunal. It was to no avail and McNamara was suspended for 10 matches. To make matters worse, Billy Schmidt was reported for striking during the same match and was outed for nine weeks.[269]

The final rounds of the VFL season were overshadowed by the outbreak of the Great War in Europe. St Kilda now found itself in the invidious position of having the same black, red and white colours as Germany's flag. A committee meeting considered changing the team's colours and decided the players would pin Union Jacks to their chests as an interim measure.[270]

The last months of 1914 saw a rush to army recruitment centres by volunteers keen to enlist—so many in fact that some were turned away after the initial quota set by the Australian Government was exceeded. As they began their military training, a generation of young men who had never experienced the horrors of war thought they were embarking on a grand adventure. It was the relative calm before the firestorm of Gallipoli and the carnage of the western front. For now, civilian life continued much the same in South Melbourne, where a program of charity football events went ahead as planned.[271]

Cazaly maintained his involvement with the South Melbourne Rowing Club. In August, his four-man crew retained the club championship when they defeated two other challenge crews.[272] The following month he won the club's foot race around Albert Park Lake, completing the three-and-a-quarter mile circuit in 16 minutes and 58 seconds.[273] A photo of the club members taken in front of the rowing shed in late 1914 includes a long-limbed, square-jawed 21-year-old Cazaly in their midst.[274]

It was around this time, however, that Cazaly decided to end his involvement with rowing. He later explained that its training schedule overlapped each end of the football season, making it impossible for him to give proper attention to both sports. In reality, his decision was probably hastened by a letter the rowing club had sent St Kilda the previous year asking about his amateur standing. There is little chance he could have retained his amateur rowing status while being paid to play football.[275] James Cazaly was disappointed by his son's decision to quit rowing. There is even a family anecdote that he was so upset that he refused to ever watch him play football again, but this may be apocryphal.[276]

Just before Christmas came the grim news that Aggie's older sister Lucinda Pugsley and her three young children had been killed on their farm near Katamatite in the Goulburn Valley. The murders were committed by a local hawker who had been on friendly terms with the family until he became delusional and convinced they were trying to poison him. Cazaly journeyed to Katamatite to support Aggie's grief-stricken family during the funerals and subsequent inquest.[277]

It was a sombre end to 1914. The next four years would bring far greater challenges for the Cazaly family, organised football and the nation.

7

FOOTBALL DURING WAR

ST KILDA, 1915

In February 1915 Aggie gave birth to the couple's first child, a daughter they named Elizabeth Florence (and called Bessie) after Roy's mother and sister. The family was still living at De Carle Street, Brunswick, along with Roy's parents and several of his siblings, but they would soon move back to South Melbourne.[278]

The St Kilda committee's first order of business before the season began was deciding which colours the team would wear in place of imperial Germany's black, red and white.[279] A combination of 'khaki and scarlet' was briefly considered, before a motion that the team adopt Belgium's colours of black, red and yellow was carried unanimously. St Kilda became colloquially known as the 'Belgians' as a result.[280]

A 1915 St Kilda membership card featuring the club's new Belgian colours (black, yellow and red).

The first football casualty of the war was the ailing University team. Their final-round loss to St Kilda in 1914 proved to be their last game in the VFL and they withdrew from the competition. Many of the team's members and officials enlisted in the Australian Imperial Forces (AIF) while others, including champion goalkicker Roy

Park, transferred to Melbourne.[281]

There was speculation that the VFA's North Melbourne or Footscray could be invited to take University's place in the League but nothing came of it. In mid-March one of Melbourne's delegates proposed that the competition be abandoned due to the war but the motion was defeated by 13 votes to four.[282] The 1915 VFL season therefore began with deep misgivings within some clubs over whether organised football should continue. Everyone hoped for a swift end to the war but when news came through of the early heavy casualties at Gallipoli it was clear this would not be a short, sharp conflict.

Cazaly's old school in Albert Park established an honour roll in early 1915 to record the names of its 'old boys' who were enlisting in the AIF. By July it included 228 names—already thought to be a record for a Victorian state school—and 276 by early August.[283] South Melbourne's residents threw themselves into the war effort, contributing to local patriotic funds and supporting relief organisations such as the Red Cross and a Women's Welcome Home Committee. The council established its own honour roll, invested £10,000 in war loans and flew the Town Hall flag at half-mast each Sunday in honour of the fallen. Almost 3000 South Melbourne residents would enlist before the end of the war, including Mayor Levi Tate.[284]

Australia's military contingent during World War I was an entirely volunteer force, a fact that made it almost unique among the nations that participated in the conflict.[285] The absence of conscription—which would have essentially removed the question of individual choice—meant every able-bodied man aged between 18 and 44 had to decide whether to enlist. Cazaly, who had turned 22 in January 1915 and would almost certainly have passed the military's medical exam, chose not to.

Cazaly was not alone. By the time of the Gallipoli landings in April 1915 only around 13 per cent of the previous season's VFL and VFA players had joined up, compared with an overall enlistment rate of almost 39 per cent of eligible Victorian men by the end of the war.[286] Enlistment rates among footballers varied widely, however; they were often higher in the amateur and country leagues where players were more likely to be younger, single and keen to join up with their teammates *en masse*.[287]

In other respects, however, Cazaly's background mirrored many of those around him who were volunteering. He had been a rower, and almost 1400 rowing club members across Victoria enlisted during the war.[288] He was also a Protestant, and recruits listing their religion as Church of England comprised around half of all enlistments, no doubt reflecting their English birth or heritage. South Melbourne's Protestant churches contributed many men to the war: 196 parishioners from St Luke's joined up, as did 261 from St Silas'.[289]

In addition, the majority of enlistees were, like Cazaly, tradesmen or labourers.[290] Cazaly was still working at Dunlop Rubber, which was now South Melbourne's largest employer.[291] The company did not have its own wartime honour roll and it is unknown how many employees enlisted, but there would have been many. It cannot be argued that Cazaly was working in an essential industry because, unlike Britain, Australia did not mandate exclusions from military service based on occupation. In any case company records suggest that Dunlop, while certainly busy meeting domestic needs, was not involved in pressing war-related work. Its secure employment conditions may have deterred some from enlisting but—somewhat unusually for a private firm—it paid an allowance to the families of those who did to help meet any shortfall in pay and guaranteed employment preference to returning soldiers.[292]

On the other side of the vexed enlistment question, Cazaly was the youngest of his family and the youngest man often stayed home. He was also newly married with a child, and more than 80 per cent of AIF volunteers during the war were single.[293]

The whole issue was soon brought into sharp focus by Australia's declining enlistment rate. At the start of the war, the number of men joining up had kept pace with Australia's commitment to Britain of five battalions, peaking at a national total of 36,575 for the month of July 1915. Enlistments dropped sharply from then on, however, and continued to fall steadily.[294]

Alarmed by the widening gap between pledged reinforcements and actual enlistments, the Australian Government launched a Call to Arms Appeal. Almost a million surveys were sent to men of military service age asking if they were prepared to enlist straight away. Those who answered no were asked if they would enlist at a later date and, if not, why not. The returned surveys were thought to have been destroyed after the war but around 10,000 responses were rediscovered in an archive more than eight decades later. They make fascinating and sobering reading. An overwhelming majority of respondents said they did not plan to enlist because of family responsibilities, farm or business commitments, the pressure of debt and mortgages or conscientious objections. The responses show the vast majority who had not joined up by 1916 had no intention of doing so, and they help explain the continued slide in military enlistments. Beyond this, however, they also illustrate the conflicting responsibilities many men felt to their country and their families as they weighed up their decision.[295]

Whether Cazaly or his brothers received a letter from the Call to Arms Appeal is unknown but, like many others, they would have debated, argued and agonised over the best contribution they could make to the war effort. Ultimately it was Roy's brother George, 34 years old and single, who left his job at Dunlop's to volunteer.[296] Those eligible men who stayed behind would continue to be confronted by the enlistment question for the rest of the war.

As Australia's war casualties mounted, athletes and officials found themselves in the middle of an increasingly bitter public debate on the role of organised sport during wartime. Attitudes depended on whether people viewed it as a harmless recreation or a "proving ground" for military life. Footballers were an obvious target for those who believed sportsmen were "shirking" their national duty. For trenchant loyalists, nothing less than a cessation of all football and wholesale enlistment by its players would suffice. It was a view summed up by a letter to *The Argus* from 'Patriot':

> I was pleased indeed to learn from your football notes in "The Argus" of today that three of the leading members of the South Melbourne Football Club are going to stand down from the game until the war is over. The other 15 players would be forced to do likewise if the public would withhold their

patronage from the game, as I am doing. I am sure footballers would be more admired hereafter if they had a team to chase Germans and Turks, instead of chasing a bag of wind.[297]

While many such as 'Patriot' wanted to see senior football halted, the army used matches as a platform to drum up enlistments. Recruiting officers spoke at games and enlistment posters urged athletes to join up and "show the enemy what Australian sporting men can do."[298] Football players and crowds were a recurring motif on such posters, leading to protests by elements of the sporting press that football was being unfairly singled out as unpatriotic while other popular sports such as horse racing and boxing were largely ignored.[299]

Adding further fuel to the debate, those who opposed the game's growing professionalism, such as Wesley College headmaster 'Dicky' Adamson, used the war to accuse the organised leagues of doing the enemy's bidding. In a display of florid rhetoric, Adamson told his students that:

> Every 6d you pay to see a professional football match helps clubs to indirectly induce men to stay away from the fighting line. All that patriotic Germans need to do is subscribe to the funds of our professional football clubs, and so support our paid gladiators to perform in the League or Association Circus, instead of joining the colours. Deutschland uber alles! Why not iron crosses for the premiers instead of medals?[300]

In deference to such attitudes the VFA clubs voted to end their 1915 season early and later suspended the competition.[301] The decision pleased many and placed further pressure on the League's clubs to follow suit. Melbourne's sporting papers were also sensitive to demands that football be curtailed or scaled back during wartime. In response, *Sport* began publishing a progressive tally of footballers who had volunteered and the *Winner* regularly printed photos, profiles and letters home from footballers serving abroad.[302]

Having decided to continue, the VFL was eager to be seen to be playing its part in the war effort. Some club officials walked an uneasy tightrope of encouraging both organised football *and* military enlistment: Melbourne's president Dr McClelland told his members that "footballers make admirable soldiers" and St Kilda's secretary George Inskip became a representative on the Sportsmen's Recruiting Committee, which helped raise recruits under the 'Sportsmen's Thousand' banner.[303]

In June, St Kilda took advantage of a bye to play a combined Ballarat League side to aid Belgian and Serbian relief funds. "The Belgians will invade Ballarat" is how the *Punch* newspaper irreverently previewed the match, while *Sport* noted pointedly that "the players are paying their own expenses on the trip. Yet some people say that footballers are not patriotic."[304] Cazaly played and St Kilda won a close game in slippery conditions by 11 points. The players held a meeting the same week and unanimously agreed to forgo any allowance or expense claims for the rest of the season.[305]

In mid-August, Cazaly played in a St Kilda team that took on reigning VFA premiers North Melbourne in a fundraising match to aid wounded soldiers. Players and officials donated their time, a crowd of 10,000 people attended and more than £250 was raised but as a public relations exercise it backfired. Relishing an opportunity to prove its credentials for a possible future entry into the VFL, North Melbourne included several players from other teams and won a spiteful contest marred by numerous fights. The *Australasian*'s headline summed it up: "Patriotic match. A large attendance. A foul game". Writing in *The Argus*, Reg Wilmot declared:

> I have not seen so much punching in a game for years, and altogether most of the spectators, and many of the players, were heartily sick of it long before it was over. The financial side of it was the only one that was satisfactory; as an exhibition of football it was a disgrace.[306]

Cazaly had a consistent year with St Kilda. He started in defence but by the end of the season was playing on the half-forward flank and occasionally in the ruck. He played every game, chalked up his 50th League appearance and was often listed among the Saints' best players. St Kilda finished eighth and Wels Eicke was named their best player.

By late 1915, there were 372 names on the Albert Park School Honour Roll and headmaster Alfred Opie chose 'Conscription versus Voluntary Enlistment' as the topic for the Dux of the School essay competition. The winner was 14-year-old Roy Smith, who weighed up the pros and cons before concluding:

> It is all very well to talk of British freedom, but when that power is threatened we must have men to protect it. By all means let us have conscription if that is the only way to arouse these men to a sense of duty.[307]

The young scholar's essay was a foretaste of the bitter national conscription debate which would soon follow.

8

Recess and resumption

St Kilda, 1916-18

Cazaly began taking an interest in the conditioning and fitness techniques used by his trainers after suffering various injuries early in his career. It was while recovering from an injury to his right knee that he had changed his preferred kicking foot and soon found he could kick further with his left.[308] Sports therapy was an emerging science, and more football clubs were hiring trainers and masseurs to prepare their players for matches, keep them in peak condition and help them recover from injuries.

In 1909, a feature article in *The Argus* described a typical training session at reigning premiers, Carlton, and included photographs of players exercising with punching bags and skipping ropes, and being rubbed down in the rooms.[309] A *Sport* journalist observed another club's post-training regime two years later:

> Perspiring, panting, enervated players return to their dressing rooms, some limping, others leg weary or bodily distressed. The trainer is the man who fixes them up, harnesses up the muscles again, brings vigour to the constitution once more, builds up the stamina. He is in reality the personification of a medical practitioner, a masseur; has his liniments and his condiments, his bandages and bands.

The same journalist visited Stubbs' Baths on a Sunday morning where, amid the permeating smell of "concoctions" and the sound of hissing steam, he watched footballers being treated for injuries suffered the day before.[310]

A coterie of health practitioners soon grew up around the football clubs. In 1913 Thomas Grosvenor, a "masseur and medical gymnast", advertised a variety of hot bath treatments while the 'Nuropathi Institute' at 121 Collins Street offered its services to clubs at "moderate terms", promising to cure sprains and stiff joints using "Hand, Electric and Vibratory Massage."[311]

Cazaly later attributed much of what he learned about human anatomy and physiology to St Kilda's masseur, the German-born Heinrich Best. Cazaly marvelled at the methods Best used to treat player injuries and resolved to learn all he could about his techniques.[312] 'Old Besty'—as he was known to generations of St Kilda players—provided "electro-masseur" treatments for sprains, rheumatism, lumbago and tissue inflammation from his rooms in Chapel Street, St Kilda. He was the first treasurer of the Victorian branch of the Australasian Massage Association and was Honourary Masseur at both the Melbourne and Alfred Hospitals.[313] Although engaged by St Kilda, Best was even-handed in his approach to treating footballers: on the eve of a St Kilda game against Collingwood *The Argus* noted that Collingwood's injured captain Dan Minogue:

> ... has made rapid progress under the care of Herr Best, the St Kilda masseur. Thus St Kilda is helping to make the Collingwood captain fit to help to confound St Kilda.[314]

In late 1915 Cazaly was evidently carrying an injury that was proving unresponsive to Old Besty's treatment because the club decided to send him to Daylesford.[315] The spa town lies 70 miles north-west of Melbourne in a region with mineral springs reputed to help relieve medical ailments. The restorative properties of the local water was widely publicised, with one advertisement for the Hepburn Springs boasting of its "valuable curative properties".[316] Cazaly's mineral treatment appears to have worked: St Kilda's committee members were told in the New Year that he "had been to Daylesford and was back at work."[317]

The war meant St Kilda, South Melbourne and three other VFL clubs decided not to play in 1916, leaving only Carlton, Collingwood, Fitzroy and Richmond to continue.[318] The prospect of just four teams playing each other did not excite many, and crowds fell sharply as a result. The season limped to a farcical conclusion when Fitzroy, which had finished the home and away rounds a distance last, rallied to win their three finals and claim the premiership. Cazaly, meanwhile, sought and received a mid-season transfer from St Kilda to Camberwell in the Victorian Junior Football Association. Match reports from the competition are sketchy but it wasn't a successful year for Camberwell, which won just three of their 15 games.[319]

Reminders of the war and its growing human toll were everywhere. One of the most prominent football casualties was George Challis, a regular on-field rival of Cazaly's and the hero of Carlton's 1915 Grand Final win over Collingwood. Despite his athleticism, Challis had been rejected as medically unfit when he first tried to enlist because two of his toes overlapped. The army's medical standards were later relaxed and Challis' next enlistment attempt was successful. In July 1916 he was killed in the trenches at Fromelles.[320]

Tragedy struck much closer to home in mid-August when Roy and Aggie's 18-month-old daughter Bessie contracted diphtheria, a serious upper respiratory bacterial infection. While Victoria's overall infant mortality rate had been falling the prevalence of infectious diseases was more cyclical and there had been a noticeable increase in diphtheria cases since 1910. There was no vaccination yet available and more than 5000 cases were reported across Victoria during 1916. Most adult patients recovered, but the mortality rate was high among young children.

Bessie was taken to the Queen's Memorial Infectious Diseases Hospital in Fairfield, where she died five days after contracting the infection. Aggie and Roy buried her two days later. Today the only tangible reminders of Bessie are her grave in the Presbyterian section of the Coburg General Cemetery and a small photograph of her with her parents in a family album.[321]

In October 1916 Prime Minister William 'Billy' Hughes put the divisive question of overseas military conscription to a referendum. Victorians voted yes by a small margin but the nation just as narrowly voted no. Hughes declared the conscription issue dead, but he would revive it again a year later. By November, the Albert Park School Honour Roll contained the names of 540 enlisted old boys, including 32 who had died.[322]

Cazaly played cricket for Dunlop's over the 1916/17 summer. The club won the Victorian Junior Cricket Association second grade premiership and Cazaly was later presented with a trophy for most catches taken during the season.[323] In February 1917 Aggie gave birth to another daughter, Agnes Dorien, who became better known as Dorrie.

When football discussions recommenced, St Kilda's committee resolved to remain out of the VFL competition, having decided that "the impact of the war is just as serious as it was 12 months ago." The club urged the League to consider suspending the season "in the hope that by so doing it may bring home to players and supporters of football the urgent necessity of providing reinforcements for the overworked lads at present at the front."[324] In contrast, South Melbourne and Geelong decided to resume, resulting in a six-team competition.

The differing stances taken by the clubs underscored both the lack of consensus on the issue and the local influences at play. The conscription referendum had revealed a community almost evenly divided on the issue and the clubs, reflecting their own constituencies, were equally conflicted on whether organised football should continue in such circumstances.

The debates about football and enlistment were usually led by politicians, press men and preachers, but sometimes the voice of the ordinary person was heard amid the clamour. Wally Laidlaw, a tea blender from Park Street, had played two games for South Melbourne before the war. He enlisted in March 1915, was wounded at Gallipoli and was evacuated to Malta suffering from dysentery. By early 1917 he was serving in France. Writing home to his family, he outlined conditions in the trenches before turning to a more familiar topic:

Things were fairly quiet a week ago, so we had a football match between a couple of picked teams. We played in mud about six inches deep. After the first quarter it was hard to distinguish the difference between the players, as all were caked in mud. Our side won by seven points after the hardest day's toil I've done for a long time.[325]

In another letter home, Private Laidlaw noted that enlistment numbers were still falling, but he didn't blame organised football:

I am glad to hear South are again taking part in football, as they have done their share and it won't interfere with recruiting. I will be looking forward to the football results ...[326]

With St Kilda continuing to sit out the VFL competition, Cazaly could probably have sought a transfer to South Melbourne but he chose instead to play for South Melbourne Districts in the Victorian Junior Association (VJA). The team had begun life as the Pembroke Juniors in 1895 but subsequently had "different names, different colours and played on any old ground."[327] From 1910, it took part in the VJA as the Prahran Juniors, then as the Brighton Juniors and finally as South Melbourne Districts from 1914. The team enjoyed regular success and many players graduated to senior clubs. Wartime enlistments decimated the team, however, with more than 40 players volunteering by the end of March 1917.[328]

The team lost more players when South Melbourne re-entered the VFL so the availability of someone of Cazaly's calibre was opportune. He was appointed captain and coach of the team, which began with a good away win against Ascot Vale. Districts had a solid season but narrowly missed the finals, despite winning 10 and drawing one of their 17 games. Cazaly led from the front and was regularly named among their best players.[329]

The war dragged on. Enlistments among the old boys from Albert Park School had slowed but still reached 648 by June 1917. When South Melbourne's *The Record* published the names of all those from the district who had enlisted the paper quickly sold out and the issue was re-printed.[330]

A national wave of industrial disputes broke out in August. A strike over working conditions at Sydney's rail workshops quickly spread to docks, coal mines and timber yards across the eastern states. Many Melbourne firms were soon affected because coal was in short supply and vital raw materials were held up on the wharves. More than 1200 employees from Dunlop's Montague factory joined the strike in early September after refusing to handle rubber which had been unloaded by 'scab' labour brought in to replace striking dock workers.[331] Management's response was to employ more than 500 'loyalists' to take their place.[332] The general strike collapsed in October and Dunlop's workers voted to accept the company's settlement terms, which included having to re-apply for their old jobs.

One unexpected casualty of the Dunlop strike was the demise of the company's cricket team prior to the 1917/18 season. The publicly stated reason was the "recent industrial trouble", but exactly how one event precipitated the other is unclear.[333] Cazaly and several Dunlop teammates transferred to Middle Park in the first grade of the VJCA. He made 20 not out to help win a game against Brunswick and top scored with 42 in a draw against Richmond City but doesn't appear to have played in the finals.[334]

Australians again went to the ballot box on the divisive issue of military conscription five days before Christmas. This time, Victorians narrowly voted no and nationally the question failed by a slightly larger margin than the first vote a year earlier.

The VFA voted to resume for a shortened season in 1918 and St Kilda and Essendon elected to re-join the VFL, leaving Melbourne as the only surviving pre-war League club still in recess. Harry Lever resumed his role as St Kilda's captain, with Cazaly's friend and mentor Billy Schmidt as his deputy. The players voted to accept out-of-pocket expenses but not match payments, enabling the club to donate £360 in gate takings to various patriotic funds at season's end.[335]

Cazaly slotted straight back into St Kilda's line-up, one local paper noting that "his playing for South Melbourne District last year must have been beneficial to him".[336] After St Kilda's narrow round-one win against Fitzroy, *The Argus* described Cazaly as "the lion of their ruck", the *Sporting Judge* said he "towered" over his opponents and the *Record* noted that he had "developed into a great ruck player."[337]

Cazaly played the whole of the 1918 season as a follower for the first time in his League career. Vic Cumberland had enlisted the previous year so Cazaly usually teamed up in the ruck with either Reg Berry or Roy Ostberg and with Jack James, who he later described as one of the best rovers he ever played alongside. Consistently positive reports suggest Cazaly had found his niche, and had evolved from a useful utility player to a key positional one.

St Kilda performed well after their two-year hiatus, winning more than half their games and finishing the regular season in fourth place.[338] Their best win came in round four, when they inflicted South Melbourne's only defeat of the season. Veteran Dave McNamara, now 31, kicked three goals in the Saints' scrambling five-point victory. St Kilda's run ended when it was defeated by Collingwood in the first semi-final in front of almost 30,000 people, the largest football crowd seen in Melbourne since the start of the war. In a thrilling game St Kilda led by seven points at the last change but eventually lost by nine.[339]

In early August, Roy's brother George sent a photo of himself home from France, where he was serving with the Seventh Battalion's Second Infantry Brigade.[340] Three weeks later he was shot and wounded in battle, fracturing his right leg and foot. He was hospitalised in England for several months before being repatriated home to Melbourne.[341]

The Great War finally ended with an armistice on 11 November, 1918. Of a total Australian population of less than five million, 417,000 had enlisted and 332,000 had served overseas. Of these, more than 60,000 died and another 156,000 were wounded, gassed or taken prisoner. South Melbourne lost 421 of its citizens and the final tally of old boys recorded in the Albert Park School's *Great War Honour Book* was 694, including 73 who had died.[342]

At season's end South Melbourne's *The Record* named Cazaly among the League's best followers.[343] His St Kilda teammates voted him their best player, the committee awarded him an engraved medal as champion of the season and his name was added to the club's A M Taylor Memorial Shield.[344] James Cazaly, now 78, was stricken by heart disease a month after the war ended. Roy later recalled rushing to Melbourne Hospital to show his gravely ill father the champion's medal he had just received. "To my sorrow he never saw it, as I found him unconscious, and he died."[345]

Whoever registered James' death got several details wrong, including his place of birth, his father's name and his mother's maiden name. But these were mere trivialities. More poignant was the fact that in the column for 'offspring' were listed all of James' and Elizabeth's 10 children, including the deceased Edgar and Sydney, and their current ages had they all survived.[346] In a year that had seen the end of a conflict which had cost millions of lives worldwide one family was reunited, if only on a page in a registrar's book.

9

PEACE AND INSTABILITY

ST KILDA, 1919-20

Aggie and Roy's only son, Roy Lionel, was born in January 1919. The family was living in a seven-room brick terrace in Merton Street, Albert Park, at the time, along with Roy's mother Elizabeth.[347] Cazaly's sister Florence and his brother George (now returned from the war) were still working at Dunlop's but Roy had become a fitter with the railways. His occupations over the next decade would include labourer, mechanic and stevedore.[348]

Cazaly played district cricket for Port Melbourne's First XI over the summer. In one game against Caulfield he bowled unchanged from one end and took six wickets for 19 runs on a day where the temperature reached 106 degrees in the shade. In March he took seven for 48 against Brighton and match figures of nine for 28 against Elsternwick. In April, Port Melbourne and Hawthorn played off in the final, and the latter won in a match interrupted by rain. Cazaly's batting average for the season was modest but his consistent bowling performances saw him finish third in the club totals, snaring 24 wickets at an average of 10.8.[349]

The Melbourne side returned to the VFL's ranks in 1919. St Kilda was boosted by the return home from military service of Bill Cubbins and Bill Lowrie but a number of other enlisted players had been killed, including Claude Crowl, Lou Holmes, Bill Madden, Harold Parker, Hugh Plowman and Jack Walker.[350]

Cazaly missed six games early in the season, first due to a leg injury and then after contracting Spanish Influenza, one of 3000 cases recorded in South Melbourne between February and September 1919. The disease had been brought home by soldiers returning from Europe, and Victoria was declared infected in January. Most who contracted it recovered but it was still responsible for more than a quarter of all deaths in South Melbourne during 1919/20.[351] Influenza wards were set up across Melbourne, patients were quarantined and many schools, halls and theatres were closed in an attempt to contain its spread. Football was allowed to continue because authorities believed the disease was unlikely to spread via outdoor events, but teams struggled to replace players who contracted it.[352]

When Cazaly recovered and returned to the side he played in the ruck. A *Weekly Times* profile written by 'Rover' during the season listed several qualities which stamped him as an effective follower, including his speed to the ball, his deftness at gathering it with either hand and his ability to twist and turn through a pack to create opportunities for his teammates. Intriguingly, the same article revealed Cazaly thought too many goals were being scored, and had proposed a rule change to make goalkicking more challenging:

> He would like to see a bar introduced, from post to post, nothing to count unless the ball went over it, while behinds could, in his opinion, be advantageously ignored in the scoring.

Cazaly probably didn't realise it, but a similar, rugby-style cross bar had been used in early versions of the game played in South Australia during the 1870s and VFA delegates had debated its merits in 1896.[353]

In St Kilda's ruck Cazaly usually teamed up with the ever-reliable rover Jack James. His other ruck partner, however, varied from week to week in a revolving door selection policy which included Reg Berry, Gordon Dangerfield, Roy Ostberg and Bill Woodcock—Ernest Cazaly's old sparring partner from the Wednesday League. St Kilda never quite hit on a winning ruck combination and Cazaly candidly admitted some years later that the team had a "weak ruck" during this period.[354]

Roy and his brother Ernest played their only VFL game together in round eight, when Ernest was named in the back pocket to play Fitzroy at the Junction Oval. Amazingly, more than nine years had elapsed since Ernest's only other game for St Kilda in 1910.[355]

It was an unsuccessful year for St Kilda, which won just seven matches and finished ahead of only Melbourne and Geelong. Their season highlight was a rare win over eventual premiers Collingwood at Victoria Park in round two; their nadir came in round 12 when South Melbourne kicked 189 points against them, including 17 goals in the last quarter. It was a record League score for a single quarter which still stands today.[356] Cazaly received a personal tribute after the final round, when a group of St Kilda supporters presented him with £13 in appreciation of his efforts during the year.[357]

After St Kilda's season ended Cazaly was invited to coach South Warrnambool during the lead-up to their finals campaign. The local competition had been revived after the war and consisted of six teams. The records are incomplete but it is known that Cazaly played several games for South Warrnambool and led them to a narrow loss against Koroit in the final.[358]

While at South Warrnambool Cazaly discovered a brilliant young Technical School student named Colin Watson, who had played several games for Port Melbourne in the VFA before contracting influenza and returning home. Cazaly later wrote that "there sprang up between the two of us a friendship of master and pupil." Watson would join St Kilda the following season on Cazaly's recommendation.[359]

Cazaly again played cricket for Port Melbourne's First XI over the summer, where he often opened the bowling attack. When football training resumed his leadership skills and years of loyalty at St Kilda were rewarded when he was appointed captain and chosen as one of the four player representatives on the committee.[360] His deputy was rover Jack James.

In a year that closely echoed Cazaly's first with the club, St Kilda's 1920 season was wracked by on-field woes and internal divisions. This time, however, disputes flared between the players as well as with club officials. The lightning rod was Cazaly's friend Billy Schmidt, whose pre-season application to transfer back to Richmond was approved by St Kilda but denied by the League's permit committee.

St Kilda's 1920 Senior team, with Cazaly (seated centre holding ball) as captain.

In June the committee decided to recall Schmidt to the line-up, prompting half the players to declare they would not play if he was selected. Most were eventually placated but Wels Eicke, Bill Cubbins and Percy Jory refused to back down and were subsequently cleared to play for the St Kilda Juniors.[361] Coach 'Sugar' Sparrow resigned and Cazaly and club officials were forced to scour the suburbs for recruits to shore-up the team before their round six match against Collingwood.[362] Veteran player Vic Cumberland, now 43, excited supporters when he turned out for the first time since the war but even his presence couldn't lift the dispirited Saints.[363]

Newspaper accounts from this era didn't usually discuss on-field captaincy tactics but one report of the Collingwood game mentions Cazaly's attempts to plug the gaps in a weak side. With St Kilda trailing by eight goals at the main break he made a number of positional changes which had an immediate effect. St Kilda still lost, but they closed the margin considerably and managed to restrict Collingwood to just one goal after half-time.[364]

St Kilda's off-field dramas worsened as their on-field losses mounted.

After a 35-point loss to South Melbourne in round seven, *The Australasian's* correspondent paraphrased Abraham Lincoln, noting that "a house divided against itself must fall, and it is many years since St Kilda has been a happy family."[365] St Kilda lost nine of their next 10 games by an average of 53 points.

Towards the end of the season Cazaly, Schmidt and their teammate George Noonan took part in a 'cloak and dagger' country match near Bendigo. In what became famous as a 'ring-in' game played for high stakes, local team Elmore smuggled the trio into town by train for a challenge match against arch rivals Colbinabbin. Other Elmore ring-ins included South Melbourne's Mark Tandy and Jock Doherty. Equally determined to win the match, Colbinabbin had recruited a number of prominent VFA footballers to play under assumed names, including Hawthorn's Pat Dooley and Arthur Fehring. Both sides realised what their opponents were up to just before the bounce but the game went ahead in good spirit. Cazaly, Noonan and Tandy formed Elmore's ruck and Schmidt dominated in the centre. Elmore won the match, each ring-in was paid £5 plus expenses and the Colbinabbin president reputedly lost £50 on the result. Cazaly later described it as the funniest match he'd ever played in.[366]

It was an amusing diversion in an otherwise dismal year for Cazaly and St Kilda. The team finished last, with just two wins and 14 losses. In desperation it had called on 53 players during the season including 31 recruits, the highest number of debutants since Cazaly's first year with the club in 1911.[367] Most of the new men played only a handful of senior games but Colin Watson, the talented centre who Cazaly had scouted from South Warrnambool, would go on to win the club's best-and-fairest award in 1924.

After St Kilda's season ended, the team visited Sale where they defeated a combined North Gippsland side in a hospital fundraising match. Cazaly was among those who spoke at a smoke social after the game; it proved to be one of his last official duties as St Kilda's captain.[368] Dispirited by the continual ructions and heartsick by the schism between long-time friends, he had resolved to leave St Kilda. He later revealed the repercussions of the team's internal quarrels over Billy Schmidt and the personal anguish this had caused him:

Because I wanted to see Schmidt treated fairly the committee then in office set [against] me. I heard that my services would not be wanted so I thought I had better get out before I was put out. I asked for a clearance to South and it was granted. I did not like the trouble at St Kilda, and I wanted to be where there was peace. ... I felt no animosity toward any of them, but I did want to see Schmidt get a fair deal, and when he got it I was satisfied. Then the committee changed, and I could not help hearing that I was not wanted any longer ... No man could play League football unless he really likes the game. What he gets out of it is not the only consideration. During the war years I played at St Kilda merely for the game, but a man could not continue to play where there was no harmony among the players and officials.[369]

After 99 games with St Kilda, Cazaly crossed Albert Park to make a fresh start with South Melbourne.

10

'UP THERE CAZALY!'

SOUTH MELBOURNE AND VICTORIA, 1921

Writing about this turbulent period almost two decades later, Cazaly was keen to stress that he bore no grudges against his former club:

> Whatever has been said about that trouble let me add that I left St Kilda with sad feelings. There were no hard words between the club administrators and myself. Many good and trusted friends were left behind.[370]

With the benefit of hindsight, it seems obvious why Cazaly would want to join South Melbourne after leaving St Kilda. He had grown up in the district, gone to a local school and played junior football and cricket alongside many future South Melbourne players before and during the war. Cazaly and South seem such a natural fit that a more obvious question might be why he hadn't gone there years earlier. It is tempting to assume that Cazaly's sense of loyalty kept him at the club which had given him his start, and that he stayed until he couldn't stand the infighting any longer.

The actual story, however, is far less romantic. Some years later, Cazaly revealed that he had asked for a transfer from St Kilda seven times in eight years, not to South Melbourne but to Carlton, the team he had followed as a boy. St Kilda refused each request, and when it finally agreed to release him South Melbourne claimed him because he lived within their recruiting zone.[371]

Cazaly was hamstrung by a wartime change to the VFL's transfer policy. Prior to 1914, the rules governing the movement of players between clubs were relatively straightforward and transfers were usually granted provided both clubs agreed. During the war, however, the League introduced a new scheme in which each club was allotted a specific recruiting zone within metropolitan Melbourne.

The change annoyed those clubs already recruiting from beyond their immediate area and angered players who claimed it restricted their right to free movement. The temperamental Billy Schmidt had attacked the new scheme at St Kilda's 1918 annual meeting, complaining their officials had not consulted the players and the club had now lost access to its strong traditional recruiting areas of South Melbourne and Port Melbourne.[372] The scheme would later provide headaches for the League as it debated how to redraw the recruiting zones after it admitted new teams. In the meantime, Cazaly's residency in South Melbourne tied him to that club and prevented him from joining Carlton.

Talks to facilitate Cazaly's transfer to South began prior to the 1921 season. On 17 March the club's general committee agreed that the matter of "Cazaley [sic] of St Kilda be left in the hands of [player delegate] Mr Seedsman."[373] Turning their attention to the season ahead, the committee decided that 2000 members' tickets would be printed, training would start on 29 March and practice matches would begin four days later, provided the cricket season had ended and the ground was available.[374] Twenty-five-year-old Artie Wood was chosen as playing coach, defeating former premiership captain Jim Caldwell in a secret ballot of the committee.[375]

Cazaly's transfer was formally approved by the VFL's Permit and Umpire Committee and he was registered as a South Melbourne player with the League on 3 May. Two days later, the match committee selected him for his first game and he was allocated the number 1 jersey. That night in the gymnasium the players chose Carl Willis as their captain, with Wood as his deputy.[376]

Cazaly's first game wearing the red and white was, ironically, against his former club. It was his 100th League game and he played well, despite having suffered a bad reaction to an influenza vaccination earlier in the week.³⁷⁷ Cazaly kicked the winning goal just minutes before the final bell and South Melbourne won by a point.

Hopes were high that the team would recapture the form that had seen it win the premiership in 1918. As it transpired, South Melbourne had an inconsistent season but Cazaly was regularly named among its best players. He played so well in one come-from-behind victory against Geelong that a group of supporters awarded him a prize as their most effective player.³⁷⁸ Off the field, he threw himself into club matters, just as he had at St Kilda, and the players elected him to fill a casual vacancy on the club's committee.³⁷⁹

Cazaly's high marking had been noted from his first game at St Kilda, but this feature of his game was beginning to attract more attention in the sporting press. Against his old team, The *Age*'s 'Pivot' (Fred Ricketts) reported that "one mark by Cazaly right over Eicke's head, who had also leapt high, was particularly brilliant." *The Herald*'s 'Kickero' (Tom Kelynack) praised his "beautiful" high marking against Essendon, *The Argus*' 'Observer' (Donald MacDonald) enthused that he took many "very fine" marks against opponents taller than himself, and *The Australasian*'s 'J.W.' (former VFA player and Carlton coach John Worrall) noted that "Cazaly marked amazingly" during a game against Collingwood.³⁸⁰

Cazaly's aerial feats were gaining notice during a golden era for high-flyers. Despite being the most distinctive characteristic of the modern game, marking—and especially high marking—was not a key feature of Australian football during its formative years. The game's early laws allowed for a mark and resulting free kick but kicking was not a large part of general play, which largely consisted of congested packs (or "scrimmages") interspersed with downfield rushes by individual players. An early football guide assessed the running, charging and dodging finesse of prominent players but only singled out a handful for their kicking or marking skills.³⁸¹

Players during this era usually marked the ball on their chest with their feet firmly planted on the ground. The rules did not specifically protect those attempting a mark and a bid by several clubs in 1874 to outlaw pushing from behind while a player was marking was defeated.³⁸² South Melbourne's champion Peter Burns later recalled that opponents could shove a marking player in the back without fear of penalty:

> Think of the golden opportunities presented! There was the opposition high mark just settling under the dropping ball when you gave him all you carried right plumb in the small of the back. The busters were indescribable.³⁸³

Leaping into the air for a mark under such circumstances was considered foolhardy and was strongly discouraged. In 1876, football writer Thomas Power warned players that "Jumping for marks is dangerous. I pray you avoid it."³⁸⁴

Despite the risks, more players began springing into the air to meet the ball earlier and gain an advantage over their opponent. The high-marking trend continued during the 1880s as football manufacturing improved, general play became more open and players began to kick further and with greater accuracy.³⁸⁵ One of the most daring footballers during this era was Essendon's Charlie 'Commotion' Pearson, who regularly thrilled spectators with his high leaps and fingertip marks. *The Australasian* later said of him that "no better high mark ever lived."³⁸⁶

By 1891, the laws of the game were finally providing greater protection for high-flyers. Rule 17 now specifically outlawed pushing a player "when a player is in the air going for a mark" or "Slinging, deliberately Charging, or Throwing a player" after he had taken one.³⁸⁷

Growing public interest in the exploits of individual footballers was aided from the turn of the 20th century by the publication of player heights, weights and occupations, diagrams showing players in their field positions and photographs of players in action.³⁸⁸ Collingwood's champion full-forward Walter 'Dick' Lee was the most celebrated aerialist either side of World War I; an image of him taking a spectacular mark against Carlton in 1914 is one of football's earliest and best known action photos.³⁸⁹ Lee became one of the game's biggest stars and delirious Collingwood supporters would greet his leaps with cries of "Dick! Dick! Dick-e-e-e!":

> That final "Dick-e-e-e!" was a scream of triumph or the fluttering pulse of disappointment as his fingers wrenched the ball from those other groping hands, or as he crashed without it …³⁹⁰

By the 1920s crowds were loudly urging their favourite players to leap for high marks, with cries of "Clover!" for Carlton's centre half-forward Horrie Clover and "Freakie! Freakie! Freakie!" for Fitzroy's full-forward Jim Freake.[391] Now the most admired feature of the game, marking was regularly referred to in match reports and its best exponents were held in awe by spectators.

Cazaly was not a tall man, standing just 5 feet 10½ inches, but he was blessed with a phenomenal leap. According to later reports, he could consistently jump 22 inches straight up without bending his knees.[392] Cazaly had practised marking as a youth by stringing a ball up in the old stable behind his house and leaping at it from different angles. Sometimes he would use a specially greased ball to simulate wet and slippery match conditions. When he met the ball, he would wrap his large hands around it and bring it safely to earth.

But Cazaly knew that successful marking depended on more than a natural spring and a sure grip. He perfected his jump by observing the flight of the ball closely, carefully judging his leap and controlling his breathing. Cazaly had been taught what he called "the art of breathing" by his father when he was learning to row, and he later claimed it helped him gain extra height when marking. He had a five-inch chest expansion—from 41 to 46 inches—and he estimated that the extra deep breath he took just before he jumped enabled him to gain additional height.[393] Split-second timing was also crucial, and many observers remarked on his tendency to "hover" or "float" in the air just before the ball arrived. After one South Melbourne game against Essendon the *Record* noted that:

> His marking was one of the features of the game. At times he seemed to hang in the air before getting the ball.[394]

Cazaly later advised younger players that vision, timing and control of the body in the air were all essential components of a successful mark:

> Never take your eyes off the ball as you run through your preliminary. Then, in a stride, jump, throwing the chest at the ball and with your legs trailing, even if slightly bent under you. The hands should not seek the ball until the body has been thrown into the air and is floating ready for the action of the

hands and arms. This is all important, for if you try to raise the hands too soon they are apt to come in contact with another player.³⁹⁵

By combining each of these elements, Cazaly was able to consistently mark over much taller opponents. "I admit I've climbed on other fellows' backs to get higher, and toppled right over," he once said. "But I used to watch the flight of the ball perhaps more than the other fellow did, and perfect timing, that deep breath and a natural spring used to get me above him."³⁹⁶

Cazaly's aerial techniques also gave him an advantage in ruck contests. His following skills, first developed in junior football and sharpened alongside Vic Cumberland and Jack James at St Kilda, were further honed at South Melbourne. A profile penned by *The Herald*'s 'Leander' (Charlie Gardiner) mid-way through the 1921 season provides insight into his skills, strength and stamina:

> He is not a big man for a follower, measuring only 5ft. 10 1/2in. in height and weighing 12 stone, but he brings a keen intelligence to bear on all his play. This is apparent by the manner in which he hits out in the pack. He invariably finds his rover, but should the rover not be in his place Cazaly does not hit out and take a chance. He tries to take the ball himself and break through, rather than risk the other side gaining advantage ... One of the reasons why Cazaly has been an important factor in the South team is his ability to follow throughout the whole game, if necessary. He has actually done so without showing any signs of tiring. He states that he is never affected in the wind, and he attributes his staying powers to the fact that he does not carry any surplus flesh.³⁹⁷

Cazaly had the right combination of skills to be a great follower, but he also knew from his years at St Kilda that an effective ruck depended on three players able to work closely together. Richmond premiership captain, coach and follower Percy Bentley understood that successful ruck play required a combination of skill, strategy and good communication. He later explained that:

> The ruck is the driving force of the football team. Perfect understanding must be developed between the two followers. Remember the cardinal rule for the ruckman is to make the place men, and the smaller men of the side, play around him. In this he is both a battleship and a supply ship. Know where the rover is and try to give him the ball ahead of him so that he can break away towards the goal. That type of understanding brings fast, odd man exchanges that are the soul of good teamwork.[398]

All of the individual and team skills that Bentley advocated came together in South Melbourne's ruck trio of Cazaly, Manfred 'Fred' Fleiter and Mark Tandy. Fleiter was born in Carlton in 1897, the son of a German-born father and a Tasmanian mother, and grew up in Albert Park. His older brother Emil had played football with Cazaly at school. Fred gained the nickname 'Skeeter' as a junior footballer because he had thin legs like a mosquito, and it stuck with him throughout his career. As a youth, he was also a talented cricketer and a champion swimmer with the South Melbourne Open Sea Bathing Club. Cazaly was also a member, and the pair had performed as 'grotesque lifesavers' in a comedy routine during the official opening of the bathing season in December 1917.[399]

Fleiter's solid football form with South Melbourne Districts soon brought him to the attention of South Melbourne, but his senior debut was delayed when he fractured an arm during a pre-season practice match in 1919. He recovered in time to play three games that year and every match of the following two. A newspaper profile described him as a "tall, hefty shepherd" who stood six feet tall in his socks and weighed 12 stone 10 lbs.

> Occasionally he plays at half-back, but he follows for the greater part of the game and likes it better than watching from a place. He is fast for his size, and his bodily strength is backed by a ready intelligence and a clear perception of where his duty lies to his team when the game is on. Fleiter, like the "shepherds" of other teams, knows his work and is quite unconcerned about what people outside the fence think. 'My idea of football is that a man must do his best for his side no matter where he is placed. I am in the team to play my hardest, and I am prepared to do it.'[400]

"Fleiter was a great fellow to work with," Cazaly later recalled.

> He made every sacrifice for me. He took hard knocks [and] he fought his way through formidable packs so that I could get a clear run at the ball. 'Skeet' was a great footballer. Something more than the shepherder in the accepted sense of the term. Skeet had football brains.[401]

Mark 'Napper' Tandy had played on the wing when he first joined South Melbourne from Yarraville in 1911, and played a key role in their narrow premiership win over Collingwood in 1918. He was quick, cunning and easily spotted on the field due to his mop of sandy hair. Tandy worked at the Metropolitan Gas Works in West Melbourne. He kept fit and trained hard, although one contemporary profile euphemistically noted "he is no faddist, and enjoys the average luxuries an Australian man indulges in." A renowned joker both on and off the field, he was famous for performing his "sword dance" at club social outings.[402]

Cazaly later said that 'Napper' Tandy was the best rover he ever saw. He gave him his nickname because of his tendency to "go to sleep" on the field:

> He was the most complacent rover I ever rucked to. I would stir the soul out of him if we were being beaten ... He would just shake his head, smile, and say, 'Well, you're boss,' or 'Have it your own way.'[403]

Cazaly and Fleiter first played in the ruck together against Melbourne in round 4 of the 1921 season, and Tandy joined them as rover the next week. Over time, the trio developed a close understanding of their roles and a sixth sense of one another's whereabouts on the field. "We practised night after night," Cazaly later recalled.

> We had to work for it. Finally we were so accustomed to each other that it was like mind-reading. We were a true ruck team in every sense.[404]

Football writers began to write in glowing terms about South's dominant ruck combination, even in games where the rest of the team were well beaten. After a loss against Collingwood, the *Record* noted that:

> Cazaly, Fleiter and Tandy, South's first ruckmen, were a fine trio. Cazaly all day was a prominent man. His marking was brilliant. He met the ball one-handed on occasions, and gathered it in for the mark with great skill. Tandy was one of the best on the ground.[405]

(AUTHOR'S COLLECTION)

Cigarette swap cards of Roy Cazaly, Mark Tandy and Fred Fleiter issued in 1921

Similarly, *The Australasian's* John Worrall remarked after a loss to Essendon that "although South Melbourne were woefully handicapped in the ineffectiveness of their battery, their play in the outer field, and in the ruck, where Cazaly, Fleiter and Tandy were acting in concert, was of such a character that the match was a fine one to witness."[406]

The trio achieved a further measure of fame during 1921 when they were included in a series of cigarette swap cards issued by the Schuh Tobacco Company.[407] They would continue as South's first ruck combination until a knee injury to Fleiter part way through the 1922 season forced a change to the team's line-up. While they would occasionally reunite later on they were at their most potent during this relatively brief period between early 1921 and mid-1922.

It was during the 1921 season that the 'Up there Cazaly' call was coined. The use of 'Up there' in football parlance was not new. It had been used in reference to other players before and—on at least one occasion—to an entire team.[408] Now, however, the expression became synonymous with just one player: Cazaly. Fred Fleiter was the author of the phrase and in subsequent years Cazaly never tired of explaining how it originated:

> We used to nominate who was going for the ball. With a kick coming from either end, Tandy would take the short ones, Fleiter the middle length ones, and I the long ones. When I was to go, Fleiter would yell, 'Up there Cazaly' and up I'd go. Then the crowd began to catch on to the system and they'd yell the same thing.[409]

Exactly when crowds began to "catch on" and use the phrase is unknown. In all likelihood it was a South Melbourne supporter near the boundary line who heard Fleiter's cry, repeated it, and was soon joined by others whenever the ball was in the air and heading towards Cazaly.[410]

Cazaly's and Tandy's consistent form saw them both selected in the Victorian team for the fourth Australian National Football Carnival in Perth in August 1921.[411] The triennial carnivals were designed to include teams from each state but high transport costs meant only Western Australia, Victoria and South Australia competed at the first post-war carnival. It was Cazaly's first representative appearance for his state and Tandy's fourth.

Victoria's first match was against South Australia at Fremantle Oval, and resulted in an easy 35-point win by the Victorians. Cazaly, who kicked a goal and was among Victoria's best, started at half-forward before moving to the ruck while Tandy played on a wing. The Victorians' second game, against Western Australia at Subiaco four days later, was much more evenly matched and ended in a narrow loss to the home team by five points. The West Australians then defeated South Australia to win the round robin series.

South Melbourne's committee must have asked Cazaly to scout for possible recruits during the carnival because their minutes record he'd "watched the play of Iron [sic] very closely and in his opinion the player named was too slow and would not be suitable for our team."[412] Cazaly was referring to Fred 'Fat' Ion, Western Australia's bullocking ruckman. Ion was also known as the 'Glaxo Baby', after the well-nourished mascot of the Glaxo baby food company. He was six feet tall and weighed more than 16 stone but Cazaly's assessment may have been harsh because a contemporary account described Ion as a "solidly built but nimble and very fast shepherding ruckman."[413] South had probably asked Cazaly to look for a follower to recruit. If so, Cazaly might have shrewdly downplayed Ion's abilities, knowing a more effusive appraisal could jeopardise his mate Fred

Fleiter's future in the side.[414]

South Melbourne finished the season in seventh position, with five wins, one draw and 10 losses. Cazaly had played every game and was the team's leading goalscorer, with 19. Among the club prizes he was named 'Best all round' player, with Fleiter 'Most improved' and Tandy 'Most consistent'.[415] One South Melbourne official who had known Cazaly when he was with St Kilda later marvelled at his transformation "from novice to weight-for-age company" at his new club.[416]

Cazaly coached South Warrnambool again during the 1921 finals and the team defeated Koroit for the district premiership. One of their stars was vice-captain Colin Watson, who had returned to his home town the previous year after the internal ructions at St Kilda. There is less ambiguity about Cazaly's role this season than in 1919: a photo of the premiership side includes him standing in the middle of the back row.[417]

At the end of the VFL season, *The Herald* newspaper held a readers' poll to determine the competition's best positional players. More than 14,000 people voted and when the entries were tallied Cazaly was declared the League's best follower.[418] His turnaround in fortunes from just a year earlier at St Kilda was complete.

11

An unhappy coaching stint

South Melbourne, 1922

Cazaly played several matches for the South Melbourne Cricket Club's Second XI over the 1921/22 summer. His highest score was 58 and he took eight wickets at an average of 20.[419] He also continued to be a willing worker around the football club. He was re-elected as one of the four player representatives on the committee, was part of a sub-committee to help raise funds to sewer the ground and was on a selection panel to find a new club secretary.[420]

Cazaly was also an applicant for coach to replace Artie Wood, and in mid-March the committee resolved that he be appointed, "subject to a satisfactory arrangement with the Finance Committee." Agreement was reached two days later. Meanwhile, Cazaly's brother Ernest was one of several hopefuls who successfully applied to be an assistant trainer with the club.[421]

South Melbourne was feeling the pinch financially. It was carrying a debt of £300 but when the committee asked the membership to approve a two shilling increase in the cost of a season ticket they rejected the proposal. The committee responded by calling a special meeting to restate their case. More than 500 members attended and new coach Cazaly spoke about the economic need for the increase, which was then ratified by a large majority.[422]

Training began in April with 38 on the playing list, subsequently whittled down to 30 and then to 25. On 4 May a player's meeting elected Cazaly as captain, with Mark Tandy as his deputy. Cazaly, Tandy and Fleiter formed the match committee, along with club vice-presidents Killingsworth and Wagstaff.[423]

League football was enjoying a surge in popularity. Crowd numbers had grown steadily since the war, checked only temporarily by the Spanish Influenza outbreak of 1919. Average crowd sizes were increasing and total season attendances grew from 1.53 million in 1922 to 1.65 million in 1924.[424] Melbourne's extensive public transport network made going to the football easy and inexpensive. From Flinders Street railway station, supporters could take a train to any one of seven suburban grounds for between two and eight pence return.[425] More spectators were also travelling to matches by car and increasing traffic congestion eventually led the League to stop scheduling home games for South Melbourne and St Kilda and Richmond and Melbourne on the same day.[426]

The public's appetite for football news was voracious, and the Herald and Weekly Times newspaper group capitalised by launching *The Sporting Globe* in July 1922. Known to subsequent generations of readers as the 'pink paper' because of the colour of its newsprint, it quickly captured an eager readership by providing match reviews, player profiles, action photos, columns by specialist writers and opinion pieces by current and former players. The birth of the bi-weekly *The Sporting Globe* was followed by the launch of a new morning newspaper, *The Sun News-Pictorial*, two months later. The increased press coverage raised football's profile even higher and helped turn more players into household names.[427]

But while players were becoming more widely known, the clubs themselves remained closely tied to the suburbs where they had been formed. For South Melbourne's players and supporters, the club provided an enduring identity stretching back to the time before 1883 when the district had been known as Emerald Hill. As *The Sporting Globe*'s 'Leander' (Charlie Gardner) noted:

> South Melbourne have a habit of attracting to their team players who are imbued with a strong sense of local patriotism. It is this spirit that has made for their strength in the past, and will do so again.[428]

Many of South Melbourne's 1922 squad had been recruited from local junior sides such as Leopold, Middle Park, South Melbourne Districts and the South Melbourne Catholic Young Men's Society. There was a sprinkling of players recruited from country teams but only two—the Laird brothers, Chris and Frank—had played their first football in another state. The practice of systematic recruiting from interstate leagues was still a decade away.[429]

South Melbourne's deep local roots were reflected in their administrative structure. The club president was Robert Cuthbertson, part-way through a term that would stretch from 1920 until 1928. A prominent businessman, patron and local councillor, he would later win the Legislative Assembly seat of Albert Park for the Nationalists in 1927.[430]

The club's new secretary was Likely McBrien, who had been born in South Melbourne and schooled in Middle Park. A footballer and committeeman before the war, he would serve as secretary for six years, take over from Cuthbertson as president in 1928 and become the VFL's first secretary the following year.[431]

South Melbourne's head trainer was Jack 'Twister' Marshall, who was in his 35th year with the club.[432] Known for his bawdy sense of humour, Marshall used to tell new players about the amorous feats of 'Murphy's dog', a local canine Casanova famous for holding on to his conquests long after the task was complete.[433] A champion all-rounder in his youth, Marshall's years spent training boxers, wrestlers and footballers gave him unique insights into the human condition. He advocated five golden rules for success: train hard and regularly; don't be seduced by public applause; live a clean life; take all pleasures in moderation; and save your football money for the future.[434] Cazaly later said Marshall taught him "when I might feel like giving in, to fight back the hardest, as it was then that the other fellow was most likely to be feeling the same."[435]

South's physical culture instructor was Billy Meeske, a champion wrestler who had been a weightlifter, swimmer and cyclist before the war.[436] The club's two medical officers were the much-loved Joseph Milton D'Amer Drew, who practised in South Melbourne for more than four decades, and his son Joseph Harold D'Amer Drew. A keen motorist and amateur cricketer, Dr Drew snr was also the Cazalys' family doctor.[437]

The property steward was Bill Windley, who had played for South

Melbourne while it was still in the VFA and captained its League side in 1900. Windley was an expert in the art of the place kick and was responsible for distributing old footballs to local junior clubs.[438] Frank Killingsworth, club official for 26 years and a League delegate for 15, was a local jeweller described as "a 100 per cent South Melbournite in every sense."[439] Even the club's boot studder, Albert Latchford, had a proud local pedigree as the son of Harry Latchford, a South Melbourne player and trainer who had been born in the suburb in 1855.[440]

South Melbourne's committee minutes from this period provide further insights into the club's close relationship with its players and the local community. Officials cooperated with the cricket club on ground improvements, fielded requests from local sporting clubs to use the gymnasium, arranged wedding gifts for players, and organised testimonials for past champions fallen on hard times. Many of their decisions sought to improve the players' health and welfare, such as the purchase of a new bath for the change rooms and the trial use of trainers on Sunday mornings.[441]

John Counihan was a local supporter and would often take his young son Noel into the rooms after training. Noel's favourite players were Roy Cazaly and Mark Tandy; decades later he still recalled the sight of Tandy in his jockstrap, the players being "slapped and pummelled" by the trainers and the overpowering smell of eucalyptus oil.[442]

South Melbourne's ruck combination began the 1922 season where they had left off in 1921. After a narrow round-two win over Collingwood, in which Cazaly defied Doctor Drew's advice and played with an injured elbow, a journalist remarked:

> It is difficult to separate Fleiter and Cazaly when picking out South's most consistent player. Fleiter I consider to be one of the best ruck men playing, and though Cazaly's style is the more spectacular, by reason of his wonderful air work, I doubt if his value to the side is any greater than Fleiter's. With Tandy roving, the Scarlet Runners have a first ruck that will more than hold its own.[443]

After a loss to Essendon it was stated that "Cazaly was a magnificent worker among the stars and on terra firma."[444] Describing a round-five win against Carlton, the *Record* noted:

> Tandy was "on his own." He is a little champion, and was the best man on the ground. He always took full advantage of Cazaly's hitting out, and invariably made the best use of his opportunities. [Cazaly] is improving with age. It is marvellous how he plays in the ruck, for he is not nearly as big as the majority of the men he meets there. He capped his performance off with three good goals.[445]

Perhaps the most poetic description of Cazaly's repertoire of skills during this season was provided by 'Onlooker' in the *Referee*:

> Not tall but not short, thick and powerfully built, Cazaly has a bull strength that helps him in his springs through the soaring rucks, and as the forest of outstretched arms topped leaping figures, when Cazaly went after the ball, he mostly got it. A beautiful set of gripping fingers completes his equipment as a marking marvel, while his loping stride and great left foot kicks are other factors contributory to his reputation.[446]

But South Melbourne's problems were not with Cazaly or their ruck but with the rest of the team. "Too much is expected from their captain," observed one critic after an early season loss. "If he were properly supported, especially by the forwards, South would, I think, be more successful."[447] After losing to Richmond in round seven, *The Age* noted that "those in attack for South failed badly" while the *Record* remarked:

> It is not a difficult matter to name the best men on South's side! They were few and far between. Without Tandy and Cazaly they would be a poor team indeed. This pair show out consistently every match, but their good work is wasted owing to the lax methods of the forwards, who do not 'get into it' as other forwards do.[448]

In June, Cazaly and Tandy were selected to play for Victoria against a visiting South Australian team. When the players' votes for Victoria's captain were tallied Melbourne's George Haines and St Kilda's Bill Cubbins had tied so Cubbins withdrew his candidacy. When Cubbins and Cazaly then tied for the vice captaincy, Cazaly graciously withdrew in favour of Cubbins.[449] Victoria won in a quagmire. Cazaly, Tandy and Melbourne's Bert Chadwick were chosen as the second ruck for the return match against South Australia in Adelaide. Cazaly played well but the Victorians lost a thriller by six points after Dick Lee missed a place kick for goal just before full-time.

By mid-season, South Melbourne had lost six of their first eight games. Critics were quick to offer free advice, even if some of it was contradictory. After a heavy loss to Geelong, South Melbourne's *The Record* advocated that "the only hope for South now seems to be the encouragement of young players" but also urged the match committee to "try and keep as near as possible to the one side and not effect so many changes from week to week."[450]

In round 10, South Melbourne were well beaten by Melbourne after leading by 11 points at three-quarter time. The local paper's 'Wingster' was scathing of Cazaly's captaincy, reporting that he'd resorted to a defensive line-up in the last quarter which had unsettled the team:

> Immediately the whole side became disorganised because the players could not adapt themselves to their new positions ... This was an example of a match won and lost.[451]

After a narrow loss to Collingwood the next week Cazaly decided to take personal responsibility for the team's poor form and he resigned as both captain and coach.[452] South's committee considered asking him to withdraw his resignation before accepting it with regret. Cazaly stepped down from the match committee but retained his place on the general committee, assuring members he would continue as a player and "assist the club" any way he could. A special players' meeting elected Mark Tandy as captain and 'Tammy' Hynes to fill the now-vacant vice captain's role.[453]

Being relieved of the burden of leading his side seemed to give Cazaly a new lease of life. After South Melbourne's round 12 defeat of Essendon *The Record* noted that he "again played like a champion" and *The Age*'s Fred Ricketts reported that:

> Cazaly having resigned the position, Tandy captained South and the change appears to be beneficial all round. The former, free from worry, gave his

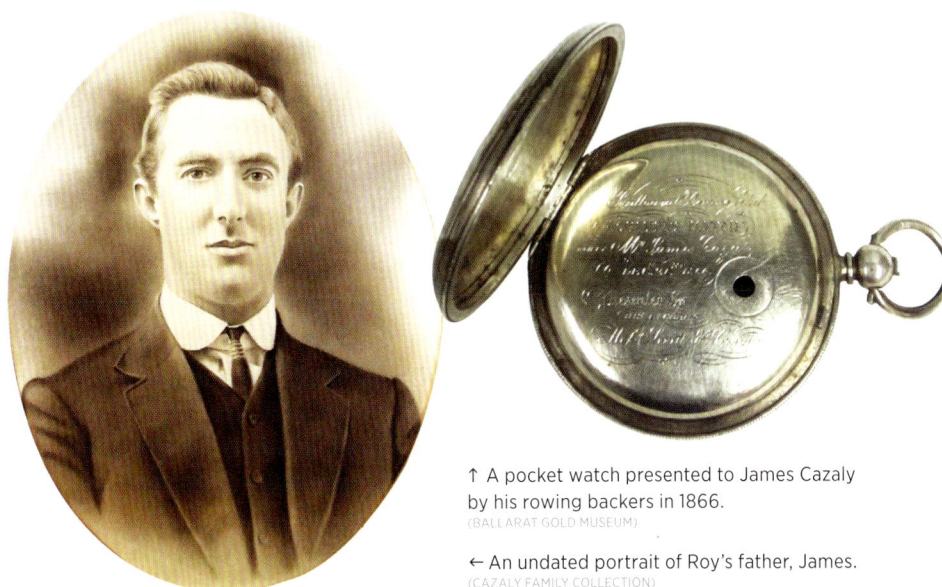

↑ A pocket watch presented to James Cazaly by his rowing backers in 1866.
(BALLARAT GOLD MUSEUM)

← An undated portrait of Roy's father, James.
(CAZALY FAMILY COLLECTION)

A formal photograph of the Cazaly family taken in South Melbourne, circa 1905.
BACK ROW: James jnr, Sydney, Ernest, Danny, William.
MIDDLE ROW: Florrie, Elizabeth, James snr, Lena. **FRONT ROW:** Edgar and Roy (CAZALY COLLECTION)

St Kilda's 1913 Grand Final side. Roy Cazaly is fourth from left in the front row. (RUSSELL HOLMESBY)

Proud members of the South Melbourne Rowing Club in front of their shed, December 1914. Roy (circled) is in the centre. (GRACE BLAKE)

The St Kilda team in Ballarat for a wartime charity match, June 1915. Roy Cazaly is circled.
(ST KILDA FOOTBALL CLUB)

↑ St Kilda's end-of-season outing to Maffra in 1920, with Roy Cazaly circled. His mate Billy Schmidt stands in front of him. (ST KILDA FOOTBALL CLUB)

← Cazaly in Victoria's 'Big V' strip. He represented the state 13 times between 1921 and 1926.
(CAZALY FAMILY. IMAGE ™ TRADE MARK NO. 1373860)

↑ South's famous ruck trio of Fred Fleiter, Mark Tandy (seated) and Roy Cazaly. (ROD TANDY)

→ Cazaly in his South Melbourne uniform. The 'SMFC monogram' strip was only used for the 1921 and 1922 seasons. (ROD TANDY)

The iconic image of Roy Cazaly in action against Essendon's Norm Beckton, *The Sporting Globe*, 16 July, 1924. (PHOTO BY NEWS LTD / NEWSPIX)

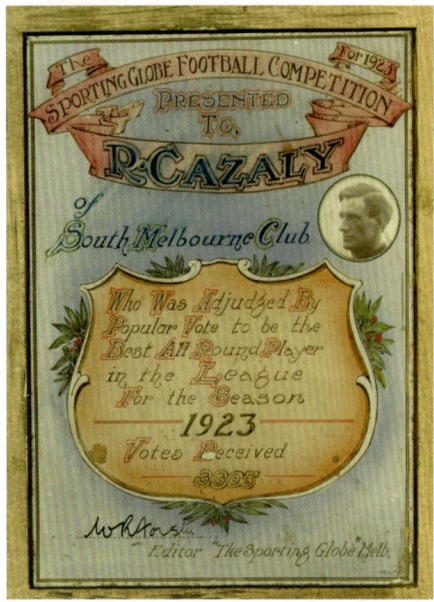 

The Sporting Globe award acknowledging Roy Cazaly as the League's best all-round player for 1923. (CAZALY FAMILY)

The hand-illustrated long-service award presented to Cazaly by South Melbourne in 1927 (CAZALY FAMILY)

Minyip's bustling Main Street during the local wheat growers' 50-year jubilee celebrations in 1925. Cazaly's Fruit Palace is on the far left. (MINYIP AND DISTRICT HISTORICAL SOCIETY)

↑ Roy Cazaly, circa 1928.

← Aggie Cazaly, circa 1928.

(CAZALY FAMILY)

The combined Northern Tasmanian team at North Hobart Oval, 1928. Roy Cazaly is at the front, Ernie 'Codger' Perrett is third and Harold Dilger is second from back. (CAZALY FAMILY)

← North Hobart's victorious 1932 premiership team. The suspended Cazaly is in the centre, wearing collar and tie.
(STATE LIBRARY OF TASMANIA)

best services, and was easily the best on the ground [and] capped a brilliant performance with four goals.[454]

Despite their first-up win under Tandy, South Melbourne performed no better than they had under Cazaly. They won just one more game for the season and drew another, finishing last. Cazaly was again South Melbourne's highest goalscorer for the year, with 28, further underscoring the team's lack of a key full-forward. Asked late in the season to name the best follower playing the game, Carlton's captain and champion forward Horrie Clover was emphatic:

Cazaly's 1922 *The Sporting Globe* award for best all-round player.

> Among the ruck men, Roy Cazaly comes first. He is only a small man, but that makes his ruck work all the more wonderful. Further, he is a good all-round footballer, and can mark and kick with the best.[455]

Clover was not alone in his assessment. At season's end, the fledgling *The Sporting Globe* invited the public to nominate the year's best League and Association players. In a shrewd marketing exercise, readers were invited to send in a voting coupon naming their best players across six categories. Cash prizes were offered to those whose selections matched those of the majority.[456]

The competition proved popular: almost 17,000 people voted and the paper hired a number of returned servicemen to sort the entries. After several days of tallying Cazaly was declared both the League's 'Best Follower', with 7520 votes, and 'Best All-Round Player', with 6634. He won both categories by a country mile, outpolling Carlton's Rupe Hiskins in the 'Best Follower' category by almost 6000 votes and his old St Kilda teammate Wels Eicke in the 'Best All-Round' category by nearly 5000. *The Sporting Globe* presented Cazaly with an inscribed gold medal and a handsomely framed certificate bearing his photo in recognition of his two awards.[457] It may have been a minor consolation after such a tumultuous season.

12

Trials and Tribunals

South Melbourne, 1923

Cazaly's consistent form meant it wasn't long before he was the subject of rumoured approaches from other football clubs and leagues. Stories began circulating during the 1922 finals, when the *Record* reported that VFA sides Port Melbourne and Hawthorn and an unnamed team from Western Australia were all keen to secure his services. Speculation was renewed during the 1923 pre-season when *The Age* noted that "there have been many rumours about R Cazaly", *The Herald* said country clubs had guaranteed him "big money" and *The Referee* reported he had been offered £10 a week, plus board and lodging, to coach St Patrick's in Albury.[458]

Cazaly did not speak publicly about these offers but in late April *The Sporting Globe* confirmed he would be staying at South Melbourne:

> Any doubt about Roy Cazaly playing for South Melbourne this season has been dispelled. He received an offer which amounted to £10 a week to go to Albury on a coaching engagement, but after some consideration, declined it. He will remain with South, but it should not be assumed from this that it was made "worth his while" to refuse the Albury offer. South officials say no special financial inducement was held out to him; on the contrary, the finance committee has not yet evolved its scheme for payment of players and, until it is done, no arrangement is being made with any player.[459]

The club minutes reveal that the finance committee had in fact discussed player payments six weeks earlier and agreed that all new players and "as many old players as possible" should be paid a flat fee per match. Existing players could accept a wage instead, but only on the understanding they would not share in any bonuses that may later be given to those receiving the flat fee.[460]

South Melbourne appointed Collingwood star Charlie Pannam as playing coach before the start of the 1923 season, but Collingwood refused to clear him as a player and he had to be content with coaching from the sidelines.[461] Paddy Scanlan was elected captain in his stead. Cazaly was good friends with Paddy's brother Joe, who also played for the club. The two had raced together at the South Melbourne Rowing Club and Joe later recalled the closeness between the players:

(WELLS FOOTBALL CARTOONS, SLV COLLECTION)

A 1923 caricature of Cazaly by *The Herald* cartoonist Samuel Wells.

> We were all mates, on and off the field. Eighty per cent of South Melbourne players lived in Albert Park in those days. We were all neighbourhood boys. I can remember Roy and I going off on a Sunday to go rabbiting with ferrets.[462]

Cazaly was a strong believer in the use of such jaunts to cement friendships off the field. "Clubs should get their players together as much as possible," he said later.

> Any excuse is good enough for an outing. Take your players into the bush, take them anywhere, so long as you break down the strangeness that helps to keep fellows apart.[463]

Football's popularity in Melbourne continued to grow. During 1923, an average of 80,000 people—or almost one in every 10 Melburnians—

attended a VFL game each week.⁴⁶⁴ Bigger crowds meant bigger gate takings, and even the umpires sought higher match fees.⁴⁶⁵ League clubs experienced strong growth and South Melbourne's membership reached 3490 during the season.⁴⁶⁶

The club at last found a class full-forward when Ted Johnson, a local recruit from Leopold, shone in a pre-season practice match against South Melbourne Districts.⁴⁶⁷ Johnson had previously played at half-back but his switch to the forward line brought immediate results and he kicked 44 goals to finish second on the list of League goalkickers.⁴⁶⁸

Match reports suggest Cazaly was out of form early in the year. After hurting a shoulder during the pre-season he was dogged by further injuries, suffering a poisoned arm, an injured thigh and then a broken toe.⁴⁶⁹ As a result, he was not included in the Victorian side which was heavily defeated by South Australia in Adelaide at the end of June. He was, however, chosen at half-forward for the return match in August after the state selectors swung the axe and dropped 11 players.⁴⁷⁰ Mark Tandy and Paddy Scanlan were also selected from South Melbourne. There was some press criticism that Cazaly and Tandy had failed to show enough form to justify their inclusion but both scored goals and had solid games as Victoria won easily by 40 points.⁴⁷¹

Cazaly's return to form coincided with a mid-season improvement in South Melbourne's fortunes. From last on the ladder after five rounds, the team climbed to fourth place after round 14 with their first away win against Geelong in five years. After the stirring victory, the train carrying the team arrived back at Spencer Street station at 9pm:

> Hundreds of South Melbourne supporters who had been unable to make the trip had gathered at the station, and as the train conveying the players entered the station round after round of vociferous cheering broke out from the mass of admirers. South Melbourne's mascot—a huge black cat—also came in for its share of cheers.⁴⁷²

A home loss against Carlton the following week proved only a temporary setback in South Melbourne's march to the finals.

Cazaly achieved two career milestones during a fractious game against

Richmond in round 17: he kicked five goals and he was reported for the first and only time in his VFL career. According to *The Age*'s John Ludlow the "rucks were having some strenuous duels, in which elbows were used freely ... The spiteful element came into the game early, leading to many open displays of fisticuffs." *The Argus* was more willing to apportion blame, telling its readers that:

> A "set" seemed to have been made against Cazaly, who was playing in his best form. He was subject to much mauling and jostling in the crushes, often before the boundary umpire was ready to throw in the ball.[473]

Several of these ruck clashes resulted in injuries, including one in which Mark Tandy had an eye gouged so badly that he couldn't see out of it by the end of the game.[474]

The incident that led to Cazaly and his opponent Frank Huggard being reported came in the third quarter, after Cazaly had kicked three goals. Both players fell heavily after a contest on the wing and Cazaly had to leave the field to have several stitches inserted in a gash above an eye. When he returned he played the rest of the game up forward and kicked two more goals as South Melbourne won by 45 points.

[SIMON HUGGARD]

Frank Huggard, who was suspended for six weeks for striking Cazaly.

Three umpires filed reports after the match. Field umpire Scott reported Huggard for striking Cazaly and Cazaly for retaliating; boundary umpire Stephenson reported Huggard for striking Cazaly; and goal umpire Gough reported Cazaly for striking Huggard.[475] The League's tribunal met the following Thursday night to consider the charges while a crowd of 500 waited anxiously outside for their verdict. South Melbourne's season hung in the balance: it needed to defeat St

Kilda to make the finals and Cazaly's suspension would make this task almost impossible.

Huggard and Cazaly both pleaded not guilty to the charges, and it was soon clear they would not be implicating each other. Huggard told the tribunal he had hit out in a pack but missed the ball and accidentally struck an unknown player. When asked why he had fallen to the ground he replied that his actions in attempting to strike the ball had presumably caused him to fall. Cazaly said he had been in the air with his arms up when he received a blow which temporarily blinded him. He did not know who had hit him but he had not struck anyone.

The three umpires gave their version of events, as did a spectator named Goddard who said he saw a player hit Cazaly but did not see him retaliate. After considering the evidence the tribunal found Huggard guilty and suspended him for six weeks, one of the season's heaviest sanctions. Cazaly was found not guilty, to the relief and loud cheers of those gathered outside.[476]

Cazaly's unblemished prior record no doubt counted in his favour but he was fortunate to escape a penalty. According to Frank Huggard's later version of events the match had been a strenuous one and Cazaly had elbowed him several times in the ribs to gain an advantage. After putting up with this for some time Huggard warned Cazaly he would "slug him one" if he persisted. When Cazaly again elbowed him Huggard had hit him hard above the eye.[477] Whether Cazaly retaliated is unclear—Huggard never spoke of it and Cazaly never publicly conceded it—but it is unlikely he would have passed up the opportunity. Throughout his career, Cazaly was disdainful of footballers who tried to unsettle an opponent by using "rough stuff" to injure or intimidate, but he felt it was justifiable to retaliate against an aggressor. As he later wrote:

> I have dealt it out, but I say honestly I have never been the first to start anything. With me it is a matter of redress. I had one infallible rule—if a player had a 'shot' at me, I gave him one back. It proved my best protection.[478]

Teammates later said Cazaly had perfected a quick left jab for such occasions. According to Joe Scanlan, he "had a pretty neat way of taking care of himself."⁴⁷⁹ Cazaly would have been acting true to form if he did retaliate against Huggard but he later insisted the tribunal had reached the right verdict:

> I was exonerated, and their decision was correct. I did not hit Huggard.⁴⁸⁰

Almost 50,000 people packed the Lake Oval two days later to witness South Melbourne's must-win match against St Kilda. It was a record crowd for the venue. The stands were full, thousands stood on the very edge of the playing area and hundreds more clambered onto the roof of the grandstand to secure a better view. The gates had to be closed early and several spectators were injured when a section of the fence surrounding the ground collapsed under the crowd's weight.⁴⁸¹

Cazaly and Tandy were still recovering from their injuries of the previous week. It was unclear if they would play but their appearance on the ground brought huge cheers from the home crowd. Cazaly, defying Doctor Drew's orders not to play, wore a special shield protecting his eye. Tandy was similarly myopic. A subsequent cartoon by Samuel Wells in *The Herald* showed a heavily bandaged Cazaly being carried onto the field on a stretcher and Tandy being led on wearing dark glasses.

St Kilda went into the game at full strength and refreshed after a bye the previous week but South Melbourne won an epic struggle by 20 points. Tandy and Cazaly were among their best, the latter collapsing after the match. Only players and officials had been allowed into the rooms before the game but afterwards, the *Record* remarked, "a regiment with fixed bayonets" could not have kept South's cheering supporters out."⁴⁸²

The results from other games meant South Melbourne finished the regular season in third place, and hopes were high that they would progress to their first Grand Final since 1918. They defeated Essendon in a semi-final highlighted by a seven-goal haul by Ted Johnson, but their season ended with a two-goal loss to Fitzroy in the preliminary final. Cazaly, an uncertain starter after injuring an ankle against Essendon, jarred his ribs early and then gashed his cheek in a collision with his opposite number 'Goldie' Collins. He was one of numerous South Melbourne casualties during the game.⁴⁸³

The Sporting Globe again ran a public competition to choose the season's best footballers across seven key positions, plus the best all-round player. Paddy Scanlan was selected as the League's 'Champion Centre Man', Mark Tandy was voted 'Best Rover' and Cazaly was again voted the 'Best All-Round Player'.[484]

13

CARNIVAL CAPERS

SOUTH MELBOURNE AND VICTORIA, 1924

Oh, Mr Gallagher! Oh, Mr Shean!
Have you ever seen South Melbourne Football Team?
With O'Connell on the wing—
He'll beat anything you bring!—
And Paddy in the centre—he's a King.
Oh, Mr Gallagher! Oh, Mr Shean!
Have you ever seen Mark Tandy?—he's supreme
And when Cazaly kicks the ball—
Well you can't see it at all!
Is it Carlton, Mr Gallagher?
No, South Melbourne, Mr Shean!

VAUDEVILLE COMEDY PARODY IN THE SOUTH MELBOURNE RECORD, 16 AUGUST, 1924

By 1924, Roy and Aggie were renting a four-room weatherboard house in Reed Street, Albert Park, for £12/6 shillings a week.[485] Their family had grown to six following the birth of Eleanor Isabel (known as Lena) in 1920 and Patricia Lilian (known as Pat) in 1923. Joan Olive would complete the family when she was born in 1926. Cazaly's expanding brood required transportation, and South Melbourne's finance committee agreed to lend him £40 at the start of the season to help him buy a car.[486]

Cazaly's need for a loan suggests a certain degree of financial profligacy as he was working as a tally clerk on the wharves and earning—as he later recalled—"big money" for the time.[487] Cazaly belonged to the Port Phillip Stevedores Association, the union whose members unloaded the large overseas ships which docked at Port Melbourne and Williamstown. The stevedores prided themselves on their superior cargo handling skills. They were known within the industry as the "bottom enders" and were considered the "aristocrats" of the port.[488] Dock work was lucrative: in 1924, a stevedore typically earned £1/3 for a nine-hour day shift and £2/5 for a 12-hour night shift. By contrast, manual workers in other industries were earning £4 or less for a full week's work.[489]

It wasn't easy to get work on the wharves and Cazaly probably owed his job to an influential South Melbourne supporter. William Bridgeman was a World War I navy veteran who was also on the wharves in 1924. Interviewed years later, he didn't sound impressed to have worked alongside prominent footballers:

> I worked with Roy Cazaly, up on the waterfront. And another big South Melbourne footballer called [Arthur] Hando. They were good footballers, that's all they were and nothing else.[490]

Bridgeman's dismissive comment further suggests the wharf work was a sinecure designed to provide employment for footballers at the club.

Collingwood again refused a clearance for Charlie Pannam to play the 1924 season so he remained as South Melbourne's non-playing coach. Paddy Scanlan and Mark Tandy were elected captain and vice-captain respectively.[491] Cazaly's name was linked to the coaching role at VFA club Brunswick during the pre-season but nothing came of it and he remained at the Lake Oval.[492] He was not as active in club affairs as he had been previously, but was appointed to a sub-committee to progress plans for an annual club ball.[493]

Early in the season Cazaly stepped down from the first ruck role to spend more time on the half-forward line, where he was particularly successful in feeding the ball to South's chief goalscorer Ted Johnson.[494] Harry Alexander took over the main following duties and Cazaly would often relieve him late in games.

A profile in *The Sporting Globe* by 'Jumbo' Sharland noted that Cazaly was "not fast, but often when he has taken the ball he will wheel around to the left and have a kick, and will leave a fast man bewildered."[495] Cazaly's deceptive nonchalance is a recurring theme: after one match *The Australasian* noted that he "rarely imparts the impression that he exerts himself to the full."[496] His laid-back attitude almost cost him a start one week: he had driven to Geelong to pick up teammate Bobby Allison from work and they arrived at the Lake Oval only just in time to take their places in the side.[497]

After a lacklustre start to the 1924 season, South Melbourne began playing with greater speed, skill and purpose. Cazaly's mate from the wharves Arthur Hando achieved some notoriety during their round-nine match when he vigorously shook a goalpost while Geelong's rover Arthur Pink was kicking for goal.[498] The ball hit the swaying post, registering a point instead of a goal, and South Melbourne went on to win by three points. Geelong

A 1924 South Melbourne Football Club membership ticket and match fixture.

protested afterwards, claiming Hando's deliberate action had cost them the game. After hearing evidence from the goal umpire, Hando and several other players, the League's investigation committee found him guilty, but let him off with a reprimand "in view of his past good sportsmanship".[499] Cazaly dubbed Hando 'the Pole Wobbler' from then on.[500]

South Melbourne won other matches in more orthodox fashion. By the time they defeated Essendon in round 12 they had won six games on end and were second on the ladder behind Fitzroy. Cazaly injured his chest during the Essendon game and *The Argus* remarked that "it was like a casualty dressing station to see [head trainer] Jack Marshall binding him up after the game."[501]

That same match provided what was to become the iconic image of Cazaly in action when a photographer snapped him leaping straight up, his left arm fully extended and cradling a football in his fingertips. Essendon's ruckman Norm Beckton is shown alongside Cazaly, looking up at him from a much lower height.[502] The photo was first published in *The Sporting Globe* on Wednesday, 16 July, pinpointing the game as South Melbourne's round -12 match at the Lake Oval four days earlier. The caption accompanying the photo read:

> Cazaly (Sth. Melb.) pulled down this wonderful one-hand mark against Essendon last week. Beckton (No. 3 Essendon) was quite nonplussed.

Despite the caption—and a reported "recollection" of the incident by Cazaly some years later—the photo probably depicts not a mark but a ruck duel or boundary throw-in, with Cazaly about to palm the ball to a waiting teammate.[503] The entire photo, rarely published, shows 'Skeeter' Fleiter crouching near the two ruckmen, closely observing the contest. In subsequent years, Fleiter was usually edited out of the scene, adding to the perception that it depicted a mark. In addition, Beckton is almost standing on the ground in the original photo whereas in later versions his left foot is blurred or cropped, implying that he and Cazaly are higher off the ground than they actually were. Even as a ruck tap, however, Cazaly shows an impressive athleticism as he has jumped at least two feet off the ground to outstretch Beckton for the ball.[504]

Cazaly's consistent form during 1924 saw him named as a half-forward and first-change ruckman in the Victorian team for the fifth Australian Football Carnival in Hobart. Mark Tandy (in his last outing for Victoria), forward Bobby Allison and centre Jack O'Connell were South Melbourne's other inclusions and Cazaly's former South Warrnambool protégé Colin Watson was selected from St Kilda.

The Victorians arrived in Burnie by ship on 5 August and travelled to Hobart for their first match against the host state two days later. Cazaly marked well and kicked two goals in Victoria's 39-point win, but Tandy was overshadowed by his opposite number Horrie Gorringe, the best Tasmanian player never to play in the VFL.[505]

Victoria's second game, against Western Australia, proved to be their toughest of the carnival. Both teams were evenly matched throughout a hard-fought game characterised by several clashes between Cazaly and the West's rugged follower Jack 'Fat' McDiarmid.[506] Some years later, Cazaly candidly admitted that the two had engaged in a feud throughout the match:

> Let me make no bones about it, I hit McDiarmid and he hit me throughout that game. I should know for I was at the business-end of those knocks whichever end you view them from.[507]

Rain fell for much of the game and the last quarter was played in fading light so bad it was impossible for the 15,000 spectators to distinguish the players, or the timekeepers to read their own watches. In the gathering gloom Victoria managed to hold on to win by eight points.[508] Cazaly later described the game as the best he'd ever played in:

> The men on both sides were in perfect physical condition, and it was natural that, with tension so great, no quarter could be asked and given. It was a game that will be spoken of for many years.[509]

For the Victorians, the result was a measure of revenge for their defeat by the westerners at the 1921 Perth carnival. After the game, the teetotaller Cazaly was alone in the Victorian rooms while the rest of the team were out procuring drinks for a celebratory binge. There was a sudden knock at the door:

'Come out Cazaly!' Outside were 'Fat' McDiarmid, [George] 'Staunch' Owens, [Western Australia's coach] Phil Matson and a man named Thomas. I looked over at the bunch and thought to myself 'Here's hoping I can still run.' I really thought the brawl was to start over again. The Vics were out and I did not like the prospect one bit. Mac burst out laughing. 'We've come to drink your beer,' he said. The Vics came back [and] that party ended at 5am.[510]

Three days later Victoria defeated New South Wales by 80 points in a game marred by drenching rain. All interest in the match as a contest vanished by half-time and the game degenerated into what *The Advocate* called "a burlesque on football":

Members of the opposing teams took a hand at throwing the ball in. Others were engaging in afternoon tea between the goalposts. Players gradually left the ground until there were only 10 men on the field altogether, which was unprecedented in carnival games.[511]

If that was "burlesque", then what occurred during Victoria's next game against Queensland can only be described as high farce. Cazaly was acting captain for the game in place of Paddy O'Brien. From the first bounce the Victorians toyed with their opposition, allowing them to run the length of the field and score at will before occasionally kicking a few goals of their own. After a while, Cazaly decided to turn the game into a training drill.

Every man was given a run on the ball to loosen up for the big game with South Australia on Saturday ... the Victorians practised playing to one man in front of the sticks, and as soon as that individual obtained a goal he was transferred [to] full-back.[512]

By midway through the last term 16 of the Victorians had kicked at least one goal each and only Mark Tandy and Ernie Wilson were yet to open their account. By the time they had, the final scoreline read Victoria 31.23.209 to Queensland's 17.12.114.[513] *The Age* described it as "one of the most interesting and humorous matches of the carnival" but the local paper was less impressed, calling it "one of the most farcical football matches ever witnessed in Hobart."[514]

The championship, which had effectively been decided after Victoria's defeat of Western Australia a week earlier, ended in anti-climax when Victoria easily accounted for South Australia by 53 points on the final day.[515] Reviewing the performance of individual players at the carnival, Western Australia's coach Phil Matson singled out Cazaly for his skills, 'Jumbo' Sharland described his form as "wonderful" and the *Record* noted:

> He must have been in the very pink of condition, for he wanted to be in the play all the time. Many Tasmanians considered Roy the best all-rounder in the carnival games. [His] marking and kicking amazed everyone.[516]

When the VFL competition resumed, South Melbourne continued their mid-season momentum and finished the home-and-away rounds in second place behind Essendon. The League trialled a new finals system in 1924 based on a format it had used only once before, in 1897. Under this system, the four leading sides at the end of the regular season played each other once during the finals, the premiers being the team that accumulated the most points and highest percentage.[517]

South Melbourne and Cazaly's form were both below par during the finals. The team won just one of their three games and Essendon claimed their sixth League flag, despite losing their last match in an indifferent display against Richmond. The round-robin finals system was unpopular with players and spectators alike and the experiment was quietly shelved.

Another League innovation from 1924 which proved more enduring was the awarding of the first Brownlow Medal to the League's 'fairest and best' player. The medal was struck in honour of former Geelong official and VFL president Charles Brownlow, who had died at the beginning of the year. Unlike the present 3-2-1 voting system, only one vote was awarded by the central umpire after each match. Geelong's Edward 'Carji' Greeves won the inaugural Brownlow Medal, with a total of seven votes. Melbourne's Bert Chadwick and Essendon's George Shorten were joint runners-up, with six votes each. Among the South Melbourne players, Tandy received three votes and Cazaly two.[518] Cazaly was South's second highest goalscorer for the year (after Ted Johnson) and the League's sixth highest, with 32.[519]

The Sporting Globe again invited the public to select the season's best League and Association footballers. More than 85,000 votes were cast across all categories, and the ballots took four weeks to count. When the results were finally announced Cazaly was again voted the League's 'Best All-Round Player', polling 3646 votes, from Carlton's Maurie Beasy, with 772. As further evidence of his versatility Cazaly also finished third in the 'Best Half-Forward' poll (behind Carlton's Clover and Duncan) and fourth in the 'Best Follower' poll (behind Beckton, Beasy and Fitzroy's 'Goldie' Collins). Tandy easily won the vote for 'Best Rover' and Ted Johnson polled third in the vote for 'Best Forward'.[520]

Prior to the 1925 season, the VFL pondered the most significant change to its composition since the admission of Richmond and University in 1908. The withdrawal of University at the end of 1914 had left the League with an uneven number of teams and the nine clubs had for some time considered admitting a 10th in order to eliminate the weekly bye. League officials were also keen to counter the influence of the rival VFA in Melbourne's growing outer suburbs.

North Melbourne were considered a warm favourite for inclusion, as were reigning VFA premiers Footscray, whose mayor and town clerk had attended a South Melbourne committee meeting earlier in the year to plead their case.[521] After considering applications from a number of teams, the League surprised most observers by admitting not one, but three new clubs for the 1925 season: Footscray, Hawthorn and North Melbourne.[522]

The changes were the most far-reaching since the VFL's formation in 1897. Cazaly, however, wouldn't get the opportunity to play against the new clubs for a while: he had decided to play some football in the country.

14

A SPELL IN THE COUNTRY

MINYIP, 1925-26

The town of Minyip lies in the centre of a vast wheat plain, 200 miles north-west of Melbourne. Squatters began running sheep in the district in the 1840s and closer settlement began in earnest following the passing of the 1869 Victorian Land Act.[523] Some early pioneering families were native Victorians while others emigrated from England, Scotland and Ireland. The area also attracted Lutheran farmers from South Australia, their surnames reflecting their German origins: Boschen, Petering, Huebner and Schurmann.

Football soon became part of the district's social fabric. A local competition began in 1889 and the Wimmera Football Association was formed in 1902.[524] Although mechanisation was making inroads by the 1920s wheat farming was still labour intensive, and the large rural workforce provided plenty of footballers keen to compete against those from neighbouring towns. Rivalries were strong and inducements to sign up or change teams were common.[525] Cazaly's former St Kilda teammate and mentor Billy Schmidt became the Wimmera's first paid coach in 1922 when he was hired by Warracknabeal while visiting relatives in the area.[526]

By 1925 the Wimmera District Football League consisted of eight clubs: Stawell, Horsham, Dimboola, Nhill, Rupanyup, Minyip, Murtoa and Warracknabeal. The towns were some distance apart so the league chartered special trains to transport teams and their supporters to matches.

The trains were popular: cars were unaffordable for many and in any event the district's unsealed roads were often dry and dusty in summer and boggy in winter.

Record wheat yields and prices brought prosperity to the Wimmera. In 1925, an estimated million bags of grain were harvested within a 10-mile radius of Minyip. Growers harvested an average of 25 bushels per acre and received 5 shillings a bushel, representing a gross income of around £2000 for a typical 320-acre farm.[527]

The money pouring into the Wimmera meant its clubs were able to entice high-profile coaches. From February 1925, the cashed-up clubs began advertising for playing coaches in the Melbourne papers. Applicants for the Minyip position were asked to write to club secretary Anthony Zahnleiter "stating salary required."[528] At the club's annual meeting, president Fred Keys reported with satisfaction that they had received 60 applications.[529]

Cazaly was one of the hopefuls. Now 32, he probably felt he was coming to the end of his VFL career, and the money on offer must have seemed attractive to a man with a growing family to support. Within days of Minyip's annual meeting he was appointed playing coach for an agreed £12 a week.[530]

Under a new rule adopted the previous year, Cazaly was required to obtain both a clearance from South Melbourne and a permit from the League before he could take up his new appointment.[531] The first condition proved a formality: Cazaly had shown himself to be a loyal servant, he was not seeking a clearance to a rival VFL club and it would have been churlish to refuse his application. South Melbourne's consent was probably also given on the understanding that he would only be away a season or two and then rejoin the club if he chose.

Obtaining the League's permission proved slightly harder. At a permit committee meeting on 1 April, South Melbourne's delegate explained that Cazaly was moving to Minyip for business reasons and that the club did not intend bringing him to Melbourne each week to play. Some delegates took exception to Cazaly not being present to answer questions, but after being told he had left for Minyip that morning they approved the permit in his absence.[532]

Cazaly settled his family in Market Street, one block from Main Street, and Aggie enrolled Dorrie, Lena and Roy jnr at the nearby primary school. The head teacher was Tom O'Neil, a strict man fond of using the leather strap.[533] An exhaustive round of pre-season social activities began, including a Euchre party and dance in the Memorial Hall and a players' dinner at Selkirk's Hotel. Even the local tailors entered into the spirit, announcing they would provide a "Complete Gent's Outfit" to Minyip's most unselfish player, as voted by the public.[534]

Training under Cazaly's guidance began on Tuesday and Thursday afternoons. The core of the Royal Blues had played together for several years, including Herb 'Choc' Boschen, Billy Dial, Ernie 'Codger' Perrett and Tom Wood. Cazaly was not the only player with VFL experience: former coach Ted Power had played alongside him at South Melbourne and rover Frank Strawbridge, the local grocer's clerk, had played 32 games with Fitzroy during the war.[535]

A curious public came to watch Cazaly put his charges through their paces. Ten-year-old Joffre Hewitt lived in Petering Street near the football ground; he could still recall Cazaly's booming drop kicks 85 years later.[536] Another who came to learn was Eric Zschech, who lived next door to Hewitt. A "sturdily built youth", Zschech captained the cricket and football teams at school and joined the Minyip Seconds at 15 years old. He often trained with the Seniors, and was inspired to set his sights on VFL football.[537]

The season began in overcast conditions on 9 May, when Minyip was defeated at home by Nhill by a single point. Cazaly scored two of Minyip's nine goals. The *Minyip Guardian* noted that Minyip's preparations had been hampered by the fact that many of their players were from country areas,

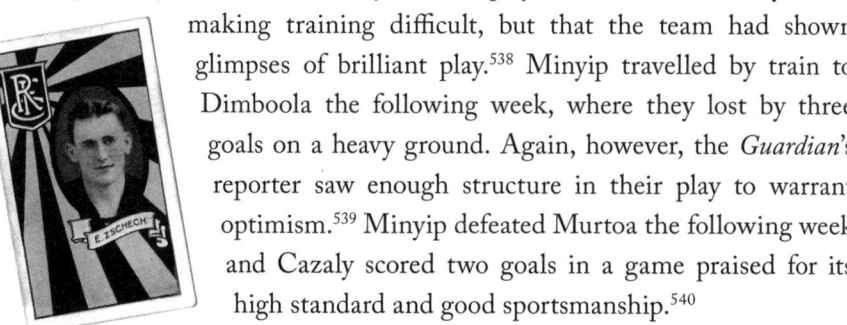

making training difficult, but that the team had shown glimpses of brilliant play.[538] Minyip travelled by train to Dimboola the following week, where they lost by three goals on a heavy ground. Again, however, the *Guardian*'s reporter saw enough structure in their play to warrant optimism.[539] Minyip defeated Murtoa the following week and Cazaly scored two goals in a game praised for its high standard and good sportsmanship.[540]

At the end of May Minyip travelled to Horsham, where they lost a closely fought game by 14 points. The *Guardian* apologised for being unable to provide a detailed account of the match: their reporter had bogged his car on the way to the ground and he didn't arrive until the last quarter.[541] Fortunately, *The Horsham Times*' correspondent provided a comprehensive description of a game that was fast, evenly paced and free from spite. He also highlighted weaknesses in the Royal Blues' side. Minyip, he noted:

> ... has a splendid individual team, but their play lacked the system necessary for victory. They were at times brilliant in the air, but they played like a team that has not practised together very much, and time after time flashes of good team work were broken at a weak spot ... Cazaly must have been out of form, as it was only on rare occasions that his form was conspicuous. No doubt, when he gets used to the style of game played here he will give much better exhibitions and show some of his Melbourne form.[542]

Minyip produced an upset win over Stawell the following week, overhauling a 15-point three-quarter-time deficit to win by seven points.[543] A minor sensation occurred after the game when Stawell's Robert Stewart was charged by police and later convicted of assaulting Minyip's Frank Strawbridge.[544]

Minyip was only just able to muster a team for their next game against Rupanyup, and had to include Strawbridge, who was still suffering the effects of concussion. Minyip did well to get within two points late in the match before the home-team kicked a steadying goal. Cazaly was listed among Minyip's more consistent players.[545] On 20 June, Minyip journeyed to Warracknabeal, where the home side kicked 8.1 in the first quarter and were never troubled, winning by 40 points. The *Guardian*'s football scribe began his report by asking "What was wrong with Minyip?"[546] It must have been a commonly asked question around town. By halfway through the season Minyip had won just two of their seven games on the field, and a further two following successful protests against opponents who had fielded ineligible players.

The second round of Wimmera League matches began on 27 June, when Minyip were defeated by Nhill. The match featured high marking but poor kicking, the sides scoring 11.32 between them. Cazaly kicked two goals and *The Nhill Free Press* correspondent named him as best on ground.[547]

The following Tuesday was the night of the Minyip footballers' dance. The Memorial Hall was decked out in royal blue and white and the team's 1922 premiership pennant hung above the main entrance.[548] Its presence must have been an omen, for Minyip defeated Dimboola at home the following Saturday by 22 points. Cazaly's marking and kicking were a highlight— quite a feat considering he had broken two fingers the previous day while repairing a car.[549]

During the 1925 season Cazaly also played mid-week football for Litchfield-Carron, a small farming hamlet 20 miles north-east of Minyip. The team was part of the North Western District Football Association, a competition based on the railway towns of Birchip, Cope Cope, Donald, Litchfield, St Arnaud and Watchem.[550] As with the Wimmera League, local pride was at stake and there are anecdotal accounts of side bets and even match fixing.[551]

On 8 July, Cazaly led Litchfield-Carron to a hard-fought victory over Donald. The play was extremely willing, and *The Donald Times*' reporter noted that "Cazaly, although a player of first rank, appeared to cause disapproval at times for sundry little exhibitions of what might be called nastiness."[552] One of these "little exhibitions" resulted in Cazaly receiving a severe gash above his left eye and having his shorts torn off. Some years later, Cazaly described what happened next with a greater degree of humour than he probably felt at the time:

> With my forehead split and eyes full of blood, I stood, with one hand to my face and the other holding the remnants of what were my pants. I was dazed, but heard my wife calling out 'Roy, Roy, come off, come off.' The next I knew she was at my side with two safety pins. Just then the ball came. I dropped my hold of the pants and the safety pins. My wife was bowled over in my haste. She complains to this day she deserved a free kick.

Driving back to Minyip that evening in torrential rain Cazaly ran off the road and tangled his car in a wire fence. He and Aggie didn't get home until 4 am. "It was easily the most outstanding day—the worst day—of my football career," he later recalled.[553]

The following Wednesday, Cazaly sprained an ankle and chipped a bone while playing against Watchem. The injury sidelined him for two weeks and he was unable to play for Minyip in a game against Horsham. Despite his absence Minyip played like men possessed, winning by two goals. The *Guardian*'s reporter was unable to find any passengers among Minyip's line-up, praising each player in turn.[554]

After such a stirring win, it must have been disconcerting for the team and their supporters when Minyip crashed to their biggest defeat of the season the following week, losing to Stawell by 132 points. The game started late due to the delayed arrival of the train carrying the Minyip players and they were never in the hunt. Cazaly started the game at full-forward but switched to the ruck and then to full-back in a desperate effort to stem the tide of goals. In contrast to the previous game, the *Guardian* could scarcely find a good player in Minyip's side.

Cazaly's next match for Litchfield-Carron was a semi-final against minor premiers Birchip. In a "roughly conducted" and spiteful encounter Cazaly was involved in a "fistic dispute" with his opponent and *The Donald Times* again felt obliged to mention that Cazaly's value to the team "would have been considerably enhanced had he paid more attention to the ball than to the man."[555] Birchip held off a fast finishing Litchfield-Carron to win by eight points. It was the end of Litchfield-Carron's season and Birchip went on to defeat Donald for the local premiership.

With a place in the Wimmera League finals at stake, a large home crowd watched Minyip lose to Warracknabeal in their last match of the regular season. It proved costly, as a win would have enabled Minyip to edge past Rupanyup on percentage and play in the finals. Stawell went on to defeat Horsham in the Grand Final in front of 12,000 spectators.

It had been a disappointing season for Minyip. Hampered by injuries and illness, the team had been brilliant at times but woeful at others; winning some games against expectations and rallying late in others after the cause was lost. Only 'Codger' Perrett had cause to celebrate when he won the gentleman's outfit as the team's "most unselfish player".[556]

Some current Wimmera residents have their own theories about Minyip's inconsistent form during 1925. One remembers his father telling him there were "two camps" in the team: one based around the newcomer Cazaly and the other around former coach Ted Power. Another recalls that whether you played often depended on your family name and who was on the committee. The end result was team disunity and a selfish attitude among some players. Unsurprisingly, Minyip never realised its full potential on the field.[557]

Cazaly's own season had been solid, rather than spectacular. But beyond his form slumps and occasional injuries there were signs something more serious was amiss. Phil McCumisky, a teammate who was also the local doctor, later told *The Sporting Globe*'s 'Jumbo' Sharland that Cazaly had "seemed out of sorts and dispirited" while he was living in Minyip. His comment suggests a deeper malaise.[558]

Cazaly was spotted at the Lake Oval twice after the football season ended, sparking speculation about a possible return to South Melbourne.[559] Despite this, in early October he was selected in the Minyip cricket team which competed in the Wimmera District Association.[560] The more pressing question of how he would provide for his family during the off-season was answered when an advertisement appeared in the *Guardian*:

> ### R. Cazaly
>
> *Desires to inform the Residents of Minyip and District that he has taken over the Fruit and Confectionary Business from Mr F.G. Keys in Main street, and hopes to merit a fair share of support from the public generally. The best of Sweets and Fruits only stocked. Fresh Vegetables daily. Hot suppers every night. A trial respectfully solicited.*

The store's owner was football club president Fred Keys. The lease was no doubt discussed during Cazaly's negotiations to come to Minyip and it was probably the business venture that South Melbourne had referred to when it granted his clearance. Taking on the enterprise was a risk—despite Cazaly's undoubted local profile—because there were already two similar stores in Minyip. It was also the first time he had run his own business, and Aggie wouldn't have had much time to help while coping with the demands of four small children.

During October, the *Guardian* devoted considerable coverage to the Wheat Jubilee, a festival celebrating 50 years of wheat-growing in the district. Many of the celebrations occurred in Main Street, where Cazaly's store was ideally situated to entice the crowds of visitors. Advertisements for the business continued during November and December and into January, promoting Christmas hampers, sweets and cordials on ice.

Cazaly played cricket for Minyip during the summer, bowling his left arm medium pacers and batting at the top of the order. Playing against Horsham in early November, he made 52 in a game disrupted by a dust storm.[561] In January he top scored with 65 against Warracknabeal before scoring 73 not out against Longerenong.[562] In February he played for a combined Wimmera side against a team from Geelong, and in March Minyip won the Wimmera cricket final.

Cazaly was then part of a district side which participated in a Country Week series of matches played at suburban grounds around Melbourne. Teams from throughout Victoria took part in the competition, which used a limited-over knockout format. After winning their first four games, Wimmera lost to Corangamite in the final played at the MCG, Cazaly top scoring in Wimmera's total of 238. His scores across the five matches were 35, 33, 51, 71 and 69. His mate Billy Schmidt also played for the side, and compiled some handy scores.[563]

[WEEKLY TIMES]
ALL-ROUND SPORTSMAN

ROY CAZALY, the Minyip football coach, who was one of the most successful batsmen in country cricket week.

The Weekly Times, 20 March 1926.

As the cricket season gave way to thoughts of football, the Wimmera clubs decided that the coaching salaries previously offered were unsustainable. At Minyip's annual meeting, secretary Zahnleiter declared that local clubs were paying too much for their coaches. He added, however, that "Cazaly was certainly the man for the position at a reasonable price." The meeting agreed that Cazaly should be approached, with final negotiations to be left to the committee.[564]

Within a week the issue had been decided. Cazaly would not be staying. An advertisement for his store appeared on 16 March but Dorrie, Lena and Roy jnr were taken out of school the next day.[565] By the time the next advertisement appeared the following week, the family had already returned to Melbourne. The *Guardian*, which usually reported the comings and goings of Minyip's citizens in forensic detail, was strangely silent on the matter.

From a distance of more than 90 years the reason for Cazaly's sudden departure can only be guessed at. The probable cause seems to have been failure to reach agreement over a new coaching salary, coupled with some lingering resentment over his initial appointment and the club's disappointing performance the previous season. But in April came another clue: a small notice in the *Guardian* advising of "a meeting of creditors in the insolvent estate of Roy Cazaly".[566] The *Victoria Government Gazette* provided more details in the legal language of the day:

> Notice is hereby given that the estate of Roy Cazaly, of Minyip, fruiterer and confectioner, has been sequestrated, and that a general meeting of creditors in the said estate will be held at the Insolvency Court Offices, at Warracknabeal, on Thursday, the 22nd day of April for the election of trustees and for the other purposes mentioned in the 72nd section of the Insolvency Act 1915.[567]

In plain language, Cazaly had gone broke. Perhaps he had been led to believe that the business would be more profitable than it proved. Perhaps he was let down by someone he left in charge during his cricket commitments. Perhaps some customers, used to buying on credit and settling their account once the wheat harvest was in, had reneged on their debts. Or perhaps

Cazaly had no head for accounts and Aggie, her hands full with their children, didn't have time to help with the bookkeeping. Whatever the reasons, Cazaly's first venture as a business owner had failed.

The Minyip Football Club advertised for a new playing coach and ultimately appointed George 'Toots' Taylor from Ararat.[568] Cazaly, meanwhile, was back training with South Melbourne, preparing for what would be his 13th season of VFL football.

15

BACK TO THE LAKE

SOUTH MELBOURNE AND VICTORIA, 1926-27

> High marking at South opened the eyes and the lungs of the spectators, who cheered loud and long, especially after one effort by Cazaly, who went up and seemed to stay in midair for a while before bringing the ball down like a sky pilot fetching home an enemy plane.
>
> THE *RECORD*, ROUND 6, 1926.

South Melbourne's fortunes had slumped during Cazaly's absence. The team finished eighth in 1925 but officials were hopeful of better success in 1926, especially after Collingwood finally granted coach Charlie Pannam his clearance to play.

A pocket booklet issued to the players at the start of the season provides an insight into the club's inner workings.[569] Head trainer Jack Marshall remained in charge of the training room and Billy Meeske—recently returned from a wrestling tour of the United States—continued to attend to the players' physical development. Club veteran and property steward Bill Windley was available "to coach any player into the art of 'place' kicking." The club also retained the services of both doctors Drew as well as an honorary dentist, Tom Sealey.[570]

Players were asked to sign-on before each training session and to alert the secretary of any absence, as attendance counted towards team selection.

Two local cafes provided meals on training nights, and hot sea baths were available at Stubbs' Baths on Sunday mornings. The players were not formally notified of their selection for matches, but were advised to check the daily papers for team lists. They were also urged to take particular care of their uniform, especially their boots. This last piece of advice was not lost on Cazaly, who later advised young players that:

> Care of your boots is vital. Be properly shod in a well-fitting pair of boots, properly laced, and light to the feet. A bad boot might mean the poor kick that loses the game.[571]

Cazaly's early form was patchy, but improved as the season progressed. In June he was chosen in the second ruck for the Victorian team to play South Australia at the MCG. He kicked a goal and played well but South Australia won by 11 points in a rare away victory. The following month Cazaly was selected in the Victorian team for two games against Western Australia in Perth and one against South Australia in Adelaide. He hadn't been named in the original side, but was called up as centre half-forward and chosen as vice-captain following the late withdrawal of Melbourne's Robert Johnson.[572]

The Victorian touring party travelled across the continent by train, arriving in Perth after a laborious journey which took the best part of five days.[573] Both teams had scores to settle: the West Australians for their loss to Victoria at the 1924 Hobart Carnival and Victoria for their defeat by the West at the Perth Carnival in 1921. Cazaly told a team reception at the Savoy Hotel that he was looking forward to the coming fray:

> I can assure you we will do our utmost, if not a little more. I was here in 1921. We suffered a reverse on that occasion and I for one will be trying hard to wipe out that defeat. All the fellows will be of the same mind.[574]

The locals certainly remembered the roughhouse game of five years earlier: in its descriptions of the visiting players, one newspaper could only say of Cazaly that he was "a player we do not admire".[575]

As expected, the first match was a physical, bruising affair. Cazaly was shirtfronted 10 minutes into the game and knocked out for several minutes.

Later, according to one account, "McDiarmid, the heavy West Australian shepherder, and Cazaly revived a Hobart carnival argument and stood toe to toe, exchanged blows and wrestled each other before being separated."[576] It was a rugged encounter, and even the local press had to admit there were "traces of viciousness" which were "quite uncalled for."[577] Hostilities were resumed during the second game three days later, when Cazaly and the West's captain Albert Watts fought, and other players became involved in a prolonged brawl.

The home side narrowly won both matches, showing better pace, system and accuracy in front of goal. Victoria's football journalists were mystified by the lack of reports and some of the rule interpretations made by the local umpires. Nonetheless, they consoled their readers that the close results would add further interest to the next national carnival.[578]

Cazaly, who had injured an eye in the first game and a shoulder in the second, arrived in Adelaide with an arm in a sling, and didn't play in Victoria's easy win over South Australia. When the team returned to Melbourne, a reporter asked him what he had thought of Victoria's second match against the West Australians. "It was just settling day for [the previous] Saturday," he replied. "They won the match but we won the fight."[579]

South Melbourne had begun the 1926 season poorly, losing five of their first seven games, but in an amazing form reversal they won nine of their next 10. Their sole defeat during this run came against ladder leaders Collingwood in round 17. After trailing by four goals at three-quarter time, they outscored Collingwood in the final term. In the last minute either Cazaly or Arthur Barlow (the reports differ) marked 45 yards out, but rather than kick for goal, attempted to pass to Ted Johnson at full-forward. The ball was intercepted and Collingwood held on for a six-point win.[580]

The loss proved costly because South Melbourne went into the last round needing to defeat Essendon by at least 30 points to overhaul them on percentage and scrape into the finals. South won a hard-fought game, but the margin was only three points and they missed the final four.[581] Cazaly kicked three goals in what turned out to be Paddy Scanlan's last game for South Melbourne.[582] The season's end also saw the retirement of Mark 'Napper' Tandy, after 206 games and 15 years of sterling service to the club.[583]

Cazaly's 1926 best-and-fairest award.

The Sporting Globe did not run a readers' poll in 1926. Instead, 'Leander' (C H Gardner) named his own best positional players. While noting that Cazaly remained a "formidable follower" and "a match winner on his day" he nonetheless named Collingwood's Syd Coventry ahead of him as the League's best follower.[584] Cazaly was awarded two Brownlow votes by the umpires during the season and voted most consistent player by his own teammates.[585] His prize was a silver tea and coffee service worth 30 guineas, which was presented during a club dinner and smoke concert at the Café Francais.[586] The club today recognises this as their first best-and-fairest award and Cazaly—who was 33 years and 260 days old at the time—remains their oldest player to have won it.[587]

Over the 1926/27 summer Cazaly captained the South Melbourne Footballers cricket team, which competed in the third grade of the Victorian Junior Cricket Association. One newspaper profile described him as a good defensive batsman with a "nice variety of strokes", and whose left-arm deliveries "often include a ball turning back a little". He averaged 60 with the bat and took over 100 wickets with the ball. In one extraordinary bowling effort against Union Jack he took all 10 wickets in the first innings for 19 runs and followed this up with seven for 11 in the second.[588]

Roy's mother Elizabeth died at the family home in Bridport Street at the end of January, aged 74. The listed causes of death were 'hyperpiesis' (persistent high blood pressure) and 'senile decay' and the attending physician was the South Melbourne club doctor Joseph Drew snr. Secretary Likely McBrien attended Elizabeth's funeral on behalf of the club and the flag at the South Melbourne ground was flown at half-mast in a mark of respect.[589]

South Melbourne's 1927 squad took on a new look following the retirement or transfer of several long-serving players. The most promising recruit was Austin Robertson, a champion schoolboy athlete from Xavier College. Charlie Pannam was again elected captain, with Herb Sutton as his deputy, and Cazaly was again chosen as one of four players on the general committee.[590] During the lead-up to the annual meeting, and again at the meeting itself, Cazaly scotched rumours he was preparing to leave the club to coach North Melbourne.[591]

Cazaly's pre-season preparation was severely hampered by what 'Jumbo' Sharland of *The Sporting Globe* described as serious gastric trouble. "I saw Cazaly recently, and he was looking far from well," he reported in late March. The *Football Record* also remarked that Cazaly had "been in bad health for a long time."[592] His lingering illness frustrated him and he proved an obstinate patient. In early May the local paper reported that "'Caz' could not resist the temptation of having a kick at practice, until the doctor arrived, and he then had to take his 'medicine.'"[593]

Doctor Drew finally gave Cazaly permission to train after South's one-point win against Carlton in the opening round "but he is to carry out no strenuous physical effort, and so he is perfecting his handball, and gradually working back into his best form." A week later, it was reported that Cazaly "appears to be in perfect form, and practically all his left-foot drop kicks and long shots at goal have been particularly well judged."[594]

Cazaly ended up missing the first four matches of the season, returning to a side that lost to Footscray by a goal. Injuries, suspensions and form slumps had taken their toll during his absence and South Melbourne decided to trial several juniors, including Len Thomas (son of pre-war champion Bill 'Sonna' Thomas) and local District player Cecil Pettiona. Both became long-serving players for the club.[595]

Cazaly missed a match against Fitzroy in mid-June due to influenza, then returned and kicked three goals at half-forward in a 15-point win over Essendon. But his form, like South Melbourne's, was inconsistent and when the Victorian squad for the sixth Australian National Football Carnival in Melbourne was announced his name was missing for the first time in several seasons.[596]

He was chosen instead to captain a combined VFL side against a team from the Wimmera. The match in Horsham was one of several representative games arranged to coincide with the carnival. Cazaly, who played in the ruck alongside Essendon's Joe Hammond, was one of five South Melbourne players named in the team.[597] It was a return to old haunts and a reunion with several of his former Minyip teammates, including Ted Power, Artie Wood and Eric Zschech. Both sides provided a hard-fought contest but the VFL team had too much experience and stamina, eventually winning by 28 points. The winners were gracious in victory: at a banquet that evening Cazaly proposed the toast to the Wimmera League and suggested it send a representative team to play in Melbourne every year.[598]

By late in the season Cazaly had regained the strength and form that had deserted him earlier in the year. In an article discussing the longevity of various players, 'Jumbo' Sharland noted that the average League player's career lasted only five seasons. Cazaly, by contrast, was "the marvel of Victorian football."

> He is defying Father Time and can ascribe his long service to his clean life. He does not drink or smoke and generally looks after himself as regards regular sleeping hours. Cazaly is a man who has his own methods of training. Roy believes that he is the only man who can determine his own physical fitness ... Cazaly carefully watches his diet in the football season. About Thursday he starts to eat lightly. On Friday he eats very little, and practically drinks no liquid beyond a glass or so of water. On the morning of the match he may have a couple of biscuits and some cheese several hours before the match but he has no liquid refreshment. He enters the field feeling very fit and has 'dried out'.[599]

Sharland's description of Cazaly drying out before a game is intriguing because the practice is counter-intuitive to everything we know today about diet, fluid loss and rehydration. Cazaly later described the habit as common among boxers but he probably learned it from his father James, who would have practised it during his rowing career.[600]

Many 19th century rowing coaches placed great faith in restricting the intake of liquid. Rudy Lehmann, who trained Oxford and Cambridge crews during the 1890s, thought rowers drank more during training than their bodies needed. His strict diet regime permitted only small intakes of fluid each day and none at all between meals.[601] Wilbur Bacon, who trained crews and rowed stroke for Yale, set an "absolute limit" for his oarsmen of one glass of water for breakfast, two for dinner and one for supper.[602] Such austere training techniques seem harsh—even dangerous—but they were the accepted methods of the time. It is worth speculating whether they caused or exacerbated the serious gastric illness Cazaly suffered at the start of 1927.

South Melbourne's last game was at home to Geelong. A large crowd saw them lead by more than five goals at half-time, but the visitors overhauled them with a 10-goal third-quarter burst, and won by 10 points. Cazaly was among South's best, and showed his usual pace and high marking. Now aged almost 35 and easily the oldest player on the ground, he kicked his 167th and last goal in the VFL.[603]

The South Melbourne team for 1927, Cazaly's last season playing senior VFL football.

Cazaly did manage to taste premiership honours in 1927, not with South Melbourne but with the Waterside Workers in the Wednesday Football League (WFL). The mid-week competition, which ran from the early 1920s until 1934, comprised workplace-based teams whose players had to be an employee of the company and a member of the relevant union.[604] WFL membership waxed and waned, but at various times included teams from the wharves, the Railways, the Fire Brigade, the Police, Post and Telegraph and taxi companies. The Fire Brigade and Railway teams dominated the competition most years, reflecting the large number of players they could draw on from their workplaces.[605]

To prevent the competition being swamped by League and Association players, each team was restricted to a maximum of six senior players, later reduced to four.[606] Prominent League players who also played in the WFL included Richmond's George Rudolph (Yellow Cabs), Essendon's Syd Barker (Fire Brigade) and South Melbourne's Cazaly, Arthur Hando and Peter Reville (Watersiders). The wharfies' home ground was next to the Kitchen and Sons soap and candle factory in Port Melbourne. Other match venues included the Motordrome, a speedway track which hosted several VFA finals (and one farcical attempt at ostrich racing) during the mid-1920s.[607]

Richmond's Jack Dyer played a number of WFL games for Yellow Cabs and later included some colourful recollections in his autobiography:

> The [Wednesday League] teams were full of cut-throats and criminals. You could pick a more honest team at Pentridge Gaol than some of the teams in the competition. One of the meanest and toughest bunches I have ever played against was the Watersiders. Each side had to appoint their own goal umpires. The wharfies had a beauty. You had to put a goal straight through the middle or he would signal a point.[608]

Even allowing for some typical Dyer hyperbole, WFL games could be rough and violent affairs. Reports were common—one Police player was banned for an entire season for kicking an opponent—and umpires were often abused by players during matches and by spectators afterwards.

Eventually the VFL, which provided the umpires, threatened to withdraw them unless the Wednesday League took steps to ensure their safety.[609]

Injuries were also common, which presented a problem for VFL clubs forced to find a substitute and pay the sidelined player for lost earnings. South Melbourne's finance committee decided this was an unacceptable risk as early as 1922, ruling they would no longer compensate any player injured playing mid-week football. Cazaly, Hando and Reville were therefore taking a financial as well as a physical gamble by playing in the WFL.[610]

Match reports were sketchy during 1927, but Cazaly played a number of games for the wharfies from late May after recovering from his gastric illness. He was often named among their best players, and after one win against the Police a delighted supporter presented him with a new hat.[611] The Watersiders dominated the season to finish the home and away rounds undefeated. They then unexpectedly lost the final to Railways and suffered a further setback after their captain and vice-captain were suspended for striking. The game was also notable for a fight between opposing trainers, and clashes between spectators in the stands.[612]

Despite their loss, the Watersiders were entitled to challenge Railways to a Grand Final because they had finished the season on top of the ladder. The game was played at the MCG and eight policemen were stationed on the boundary line to ensure the brawls of the previous match were not repeated. An estimated 7000 spectators attended—the largest WFL crowd for the season—and the match was broadcast on radio station 3LO. Delegates to a Waterside Workers Federation conference adjourned their deliberations to cheer on as the wharfies clinched the premiership by 12 points. Stand-in captain Cazaly kicked a goal and he and Peter Reville were among the best players.[613]

Cazaly would play another Wednesday League season with the Watersiders in 1931. In the meantime, a new challenge beckoned.

16

ROAST CHICKEN EVERY SUNDAY

CITY, TASMANIA, 1928-30

Cazaly again played cricket for the South Melbourne footballers in the Victorian Junior Association over the summer of 1927/28, where he often opened the bowling and batted at number three. His best batting figures included 74 not out in a match against Glenhuntly just before Christmas. Bowling his left-arm medium pacers, he took 4 for 36 against Balwyn in February, 1928.[614]

One Saturday Cazaly arrived home, still in his cricket whites, to find someone waiting for him. Ron Tyson was secretary of the City Football Club, one of the teams that made up the Northern Tasmanian Football Association (NTFA). Established in 1880, City was a proud club but it had been five seasons since it had last won a premiership. "City finished bottom of the ladder in 1927," Tyson recalled years later, "so the club gave me an open cheque to go to Melbourne and find the best man I could to coach the side." Tyson struck up an instant rapport with Cazaly, recalling:

> I can't remember if I suggested it, or he did, that he be paid £12 a week for 20 weeks. Nothing was signed—we just shook hands and that was it. He told me later that I looked such a thin little chap, but very sincere, that he couldn't refuse me.[615]

Roy, Aggie and their five children arrived in Launceston in early March aboard the steamship *Nairana* and moved into a house in West

Launceston.[616] Their home in Stone Street was half a mile from the city centre and about two miles from City's home ground at York Park.[617] Aggie enrolled the children at the nearby Wellington Square State School. Roy and Aggie made an immediate impression on the locals. City official Hugh Cameron's daughter Ailsa later recalled Roy as a "tall, lanky thing" who stood very straight and Aggie as a "little firebrand" who had it in for opposition coaches.[618]

Cazaly was formally appointed captain on March 12, with defender Bert Iles as his deputy. Training began the following week and Cazaly's official clearance from South Melbourne was approved by the VFL at the end of the month.[619] Ron Tyson would often take his 10-year-old son Des into the rooms to hear Cazaly address the team. "He never ranted and raved," Des later recalled. "The players had a tremendous respect for him."[620]

Ron Tyson may have been sent to Melbourne with an "open cheque" to secure a coach, but the club was in financial stress, having outlaid £600 the previous season but receiving only £160 in gate receipts. Cazaly was not the first Victorian to coach in Launceston but players of his calibre were rare and his arrival excited great interest. Hopes were high that his presence would draw bigger crowds through the turnstiles and boost City's coffers.[621]

The majority of City's team were continuing players from the previous season, but high-marking forward Lyall Burrows from Hobart's Lefroy club and rover Hec Brooks from North Hobart were among the new recruits. Half-back Ernie 'Codger' Perrett, Cazaly's teammate from Minyip, was another notable addition. City's most distinctive player on the field, however, was Bernard 'Mannie' Grenda. An excellent mark and champion runner, he wore thick glasses which he would tie behind his head with string when he played.[622]

But all the local talk was about Cazaly. Previewing the season, *The Mercury*'s 'Onlooker' predicted his presence would benefit not only City, but northern football generally:

> I believe that Cazaly's methods are startlingly different from those to which the City players have become accustomed. He is after a team of footballers in every sense of the word. The new man's coaching should "make" the City club.[623]

Launceston's population in 1928 was just 28,400, which was 20,000 fewer than South Melbourne's at the same time, but its football crowds were just as vocal and knowledgeable.[624] Tasmanians had been early enthusiasts of the Victorian code of football. Teams were formed in Hobart and Launceston as early as the 1860s and most quickly adopted Victoria's rules.[625] Three local competitions soon emerged based on Tasmania's main population centres. The forerunner of Hobart's Tasmanian Football League (TFL) began in 1879, the Launceston-based Northern Tasmanian Football Association (NTFA) in 1886 and the North Western Football Union (NWFU) in 1910.[626] Local rivalries were set aside several times each season for a triangular series of matches between combined northern, southern and north-western teams.

The most eagerly anticipated games on the football calendar came when the northern team took on the southerners. Tasmania's fierce north-south rivalry—which has no real parallel in any of the mainland states—stretches back to the earliest years of European settlement. Hobart and Launceston were founded as two separate colonies and each had its own lieutenant-governor until 1812 when the administration was consolidated in Hobart. Northerners became increasingly resentful that the state's political power lay in the south, especially when the north's total population overtook Hobart's.[627] The divide manifested itself in many ways but never more starkly than during the annual series of North-South football matches. The South almost always won, which simply added to the North's list of grievances.[628]

With Cazaly as captain and coach, the North defeated the South for the first time in nine years, sparking scenes of jubilation. 'Codger' Perrett, the North's best player, was praised for his aerial feats:

> Perrett marked in great style, so much so that somebody started the cry of "Hinkler", and many in the open stand took it up.[629]

A few days later the NTFA chairman presented Perrett with a watch and Cazaly with the match ball at a ceremony hosted by the Majestic Theatre.[630] Cazaly had helped restore pride to local football and he was promptly appointed coach of the northern team for the remainder of the season. The City club may have been paying for Cazaly's services, but the whole of northern Tasmania was reaping the benefits. As *The Examiner* noted:

> [Cazaly's] advent has transformed the game for the association. He galvanised his own club and drew out the best in the others. The administration had something to do with this, but Cazaly has been the star executive.[631]

The match ball presented to Cazaly after his Northerners defeated the South, in 1928, for the first time in nine years.

Journalist Raymond Ferrall wrote a column for Launceston's *The Daily Telegraph* under the byline 'Pivot'. He came to know Cazaly well, and later attributed his superb physical condition to the fact that he was an unhurried player, seemingly always in the right place at the right time:

> Cazaly had everything. Apart from his great physical skills and fine judgment, he had the perfect temperament of the true professional. He never got excited or shouted at his men, his control was superb, and if one of his men was having an off day or not performing well, [he] could work wonders with a few simple words. They looked up to him and admired him, and if one of them was unfairly attacked, retribution from Cazzer was fast and with little mercy.[632]

Ferrall witnessed a classic example of Cazaly's "retribution" during one of the famous North-South contests after South's captain Jack Dunn had flattened one of the northerners:

> Shortly afterwards, Cazaly placed himself near Dunn, and as it so happened they both went for the ball together. Then the game flowed on and Cazzer loped laconically away, but Dunn was a crumpled mess on the ground and had to be carried off. It was done so neatly and with such lightning speed and precision I really don't think anyone saw it, except Dunn ...[633]

Arch Flanagan was born the son of a railway worker in 1914 and grew up at Cleveland in Tasmania's midlands. At 14 he went to high school in Launceston on a scholarship and boarded with a family of North Launceston supporters. The father would dismiss Cazaly as "the old man with all the kids", but young Arch was a staunch City barracker.[634] Cazaly came to Arch's school one day to give the students a football lesson. He stressed two fundamentals: always mark with your fingers spread wide and kick to space in front of the leading player.[635]

Focusing on the fundamentals must have also worked at City because the team won most of their matches during 1928 to finish equal first with North Launceston. A sensation occurred at the end of the season when Cazaly and teammate Lyall Burrows were reported for striking during a come-from-behind win over Longford. There were echoes of Cazaly's report against Richmond's Frank Huggard at South Melbourne five years earlier, as a suspension would prevent him playing in the Grand Final. Four hundred City supporters waiting anxiously outside the tribunal cheered loudly after Cazaly and Burrows were found not guilty.[636]

The next day a record crowd watched City defeat North Launceston by 16 points to claim their first NTFA premiership in six years. A week later, City took on TFL premiers North Hobart at York Park to decide the state premiership. North Hobart were a formidable side and most pundits expected them to win. It was a close contest early but City then dominated play to such an extent that North Hobart scored just five behinds after half-time. Cazaly, who tangled with North Hobart's captain Jack Dunn several times in the ruck, kicked five goals and the bespectacled 'Mannie' Grenda scored three.

Dunn had attracted the crowd's ire during the game and a small knot of hostile City supporters surrounded him after the match. Cazaly sensed the mood and immediately went over to Dunn, offered a hand and helped escort him to the rooms, thereby defusing a potentially ugly situation. Ironically, Des Tyson later remembered the state final for another reason: an altercation between Aggie Cazaly and Jack Dunn's wife which involved umbrellas.[637]

It was the first time an NTFA club had won the state premiership in 20 years and the whole of northern Tasmania celebrated.[638] City treated their players to a social at the York Park club rooms, Cazaly was presented with an inscribed gold watch and, to quash a rumour that he would be departing for Hobart, it was announced he had been re-appointed for the following season.[639] Other end-of-season activities included a trip to Fingal where City's players took on a local side and attended a concert and dance where Cazaly provided the piano entertainment.[640]

City finished the season with a much healthier balance sheet and the club was only £92 in debt. Given that £72 of this was due to bonuses given to City's players no-one at the annual meeting begrudged the deficit.[641] Australia was, however, heading into a Depression and two anecdotes illustrate the stark differences in people's circumstances. North Launceston's Harold Dilger played alongside Cazaly in several matches for the north against the south. While Cazaly was being paid £12 a week at City things were starkly different at North Launceston where Dilger received no match payments, "not even the bus fare to get to training."[642] Noel Atkins was a young lad in Launceston during Cazaly's time as coach. His father Les played for City and he later recalled him saying:

The 1928 NTFA and state premiers.

> We have roast chicken at Easter and Christmas. Roy Cazaly has roast chicken every Sunday.[643]

One of the worst floods in Tasmanian history struck Launceston just before the start of the 1929 NTFA football season. Raging floodwaters washed away bridges, destroyed the Duck Reach power station and inundated the working-class suburbs of Invermay and Inveresk. Those living in the flood path were safely evacuated but 2000 homes and buildings were damaged or destroyed and 4000 people were left homeless.

The Cazalys' home was on a hill well above the flood peak, and their daughter Pat recalled them storing several families' possessions until the waters receded.[644] The Launceston Council subsequently distributed almost £70,000 to help the hardest hit residents repair their houses and replace furniture, clothing, fencing and livestock.[645] The flood's devastating effects on the local economy were felt for many years afterwards.[646]

The flood inundated York Park and delayed the start of the northern football season. When it finally began it proved disastrous for the reigning premiers who won just one game for the season. An obvious pointer to the poor result is the fact that 20 players—or more than half City's playing group—had either retired or transferred at the end of the previous season.[647] The more significant losses included vice-captain Bert Iles, centre Harry Wade and forward Reg Cullen. Rover Hec Brooks had returned to Hobart and 'Codger' Perrett went back to Melbourne.[648]

In response, City tried 31 debutants during the 1929 season and 54 players in total.[649] Of the new players, ruckman Jock Connell from Avoca made an immediate impact and would go on to play more than 200 games with the club. Another notable recruit was Stan 'Snowy' Joolen, a clever rover who had played for Leopold in South Melbourne before joining Port Melbourne in the VFA.[650] Most of the other debutants, however, played only a handful of games.[651]

With many of the new recruits failing to fire, Cazaly's main task was to strengthen the remnants of the side and look to the following season. At the annual City players' dinner he acknowledged the committee for their continued faith in him, thanked the players for their friendship and predicted they would regroup and win the next premiership.

On the same day that North Hobart defeated Launceston for the 1929 state premiership, Cazaly led a combined City-North Launceston-Longford team against a visiting Collingwood team. Collingwood were the reigning VFL premiers, so spectators were surprised and delighted when the locals raced to a five-goal lead early in the game. The visitors recovered their composure, however, and wore their opponents down with pace and stamina, eventually winning by 40 points.[652]

Cazaly resumed his cricket involvement with Crescent, a new club in the East Launceston Association. He was chosen as team captain and fellow City footballers Stan Joolen, Lyall Burrows and Jock Connell were other notable members. During one innings Cazaly and Joolen opened the batting for Crescent and then took all 10 wickets between them in the field.[653] Late in the 1929/30 season Cazaly was selected for South Launceston, which played in the first grade of the Northern Tasmanian Cricket Association (NTCA).[654] A teammate later described him as a useful middle-order batsman and a handy stand-in wicket keeper.[655]

In early April, South Launceston played Esk in their final match of the season. Esk were not in contention for the premiership but South would overhaul Tamar and claim the pennant if they could defeat Esk outright.[656] The match was played over two Saturdays and the result came down to the final session. South Launceston required 129 runs to win but had just 40 minutes to score them in rapidly fading autumn light. Because the Esk players didn't want Tamar to win the premiership they chose not to appeal against the light and their fielding became questionable at best. After lusty hitting from the top order Cazaly literally ran to the crease with his team requiring 10 runs to win from five balls. He and his partner Clarrie Lee reached the total in near darkness and South Launceston had won their first NTCA premiership.[657]

City's 1930 football season proved to be a near-repeat of their 1928 success, further underlining why 1929 had been such an aberration. Many of the players who had been with the club during 1928/29 stayed on and the line-up was more stable as a result, with just 33 players used in total.[658]

City's star recruit for the season was Laurie Nash. Nash's father Bob had captained Collingwood and coached Footscray before relocating his family to northern Tasmania in 1929 to run a hotel. Laurie had inherited his father's sporting skills and he soon made an impression as both a cricketer and footballer. Cazaly heard of Nash's prowess and telephoned club secretary Ron Tyson prior to City's first match to suggest they include him in the side. The 20-year-old Nash made an immediate impact at centre half-back and he played every game during the season.[659] Nash was fearless and full of confidence. As Des Tyson later recalled:

> Laurie was as mad as a hatter. He could fly above everybody else and it didn't matter if there were two or three City fellers going for the ball Laurie would still go for it and knock the City fellers flying.[660]

Cazaly knew that self-confidence was a key asset in any player. He later said that Nash "would go on to the field with the feeling that he was the best player, and his great energy and self-confidence helped him to carry off the part he always determined to play in a game."[661] Laurie's older brother Robert also made his debut for City in 1930. Taller and less flashy than Laurie, he kicked a number of goals at full-forward.

In July, Cazaly was chosen in the Tasmanian team for the seventh Australian National Football Carnival in Adelaide. Seven other players were selected from northern clubs—including Laurie Nash, Lyall Burrows and 'Snowy' Joolen from City—with three chosen from the north-west and the remainder from southern clubs.[662] Now aged 37, Cazaly was at least 10 years older than his state teammates and easily the oldest player at the carnival.[663] Many northern observers assumed that Cazaly's experience meant he would captain the Tasmanian side, so there were dark mutterings when the selectors instead named Allan Leitch, son of TFL chairman William Leitch, with Cazaly as his deputy.

Tasmania had a disappointing carnival. In their five games they defeated only Queensland and lost heavily to Victoria by 102 points, Western Australia (59 points), South Australia (71 points) and even New South Wales (75 points).[664] One Tasmanian sporting paper noted gloomily that the carnival "has given Tasmania cause for anxiety, and the form displayed certainly suggests that we have definitely slipped."[665] It may be churlish to speculate whether Tasmania would have played better had Cazaly been captain but it is hard to imagine how they could have performed much worse.

The triangular series of intra-state games held during the 1930 season were evenly split between the three sides. Cazaly led the NTFA to a win over the TFL in June, a loss to the NWFU in July and a win against them in August. At the end of that month 9000 spectators gathered at North Hobart to watch the North take on the South. Cazaly led the North and his opponent was the Tasmanian captain Allan Leitch. Cazaly (with four goals), Joolen (three) and Robert Nash (two) were the North's main goalkickers but the Southerners won an epic struggle by 22 points.[666]

At the end of the NTFA season City easily defeated Launceston for the local premiership, spurred on by a seven-goal haul from Les Moir and three from Joolen. City then soundly defeated TFL premiers Lefroy by almost 10 goals the next week to claim their second state title in three years. Robert Nash kicked five goals, Joolen three and Cazaly two.[667] It was a fitting end to City's 50th anniversary year and the club held a grand Victory Ball to celebrate. Cazaly was once again the toast of northern Tasmania but his thoughts were returning to Victorian football.

17

Depression football

Preston, 1931

Unusually for Cazaly, and despite contemporary reports to the contrary, he left Tasmania before he had secured a definite playing or coaching position on the mainland.[668] Back in Melbourne, he renewed his old associations with South Melbourne and played for their Footballers' XI in the first grade of the Victorian Junior Cricket Association. In April they defeated Richmond District in the final to win their first pennant since 1923.[669] Cazaly, meanwhile, moved his family back to Albert Park and into a four-room brick terrace in Dundas Place, which they rented for £1 a week.[670]

A clue to Cazaly's football intentions came when it was reported he was training with the Melbourne Football Club. He had played the second half of a practice match after hurrying to the ground from his cricket final and South Melbourne's *The Record* announced that he and another footballer, Bert Avery, had both signed to play with the club.[671] Within a week, however, it was revealed that South Melbourne would not clear Cazaly because Melbourne could not guarantee him work. He had, instead, been signed to captain-coach Preston in the Victorian Football Association (VFA).[672]

A 1931 Preston membership card.

Preston was a residential and industrial suburb

of Melbourne six miles north of the city's centre. Originally settled as a farming district during the 1840s, it grew rapidly after World War I, aided by an abundance of cheap land, the extension of the tramway and the electrification of the Reservoir rail line. From a population of fewer than 10,000 in 1921 Preston boasted 30,000 residents by 1930, having been declared a city in 1926.[673]

Organised football had been played in Preston since the 1880s and the local side achieved early success in the Victorian Junior Football Association during the early years of the new century. Admitted to the VFA in 1903, it returned to junior ranks after several years of woeful performances, including 29 consecutive losses during 1910/11. In 1926 the club was re-admitted to a VFA desperate to rebuild its fortunes after losing Footscray, Hawthorn and North Melbourne to the VFL the previous year.[674] Preston repaid the Association's faith by making the finals each season between 1927 and 1929.

Preston's long-serving president was Henry Zwar, a prominent businessman, sporting patron and politician who would serve a term as local mayor in 1933-34. Zwar owned a large tannery near the club's Cramer Street Oval which later produced the leather for the white 'Prestonite' footballs used for night training.[675]

Factories, brickworks and the Preston tram workshops provided steady employment during the 1920s but the onset of the Depression at the end of the decade threw many residents out of work.[676] The introduction of Victoria's Unemployment Relief Act provided 'sustenance' work for around 1000 local men during 1931 but the labour program was sporadic and usually only guaranteed a few days' work each week. There were 1800 men on Preston's official unemployment list that year, though the actual number was no doubt higher.[677] Football gate receipts and membership ticket sales fell sharply, leaving Preston with liabilities totalling £111 and nine pence at the end of the 1930 season.[678] Coach and player payments were the club's biggest ongoing expense, and it is notable that spending in this area was almost halved between 1930 and 1931.[679]

Cazaly was engaged as Preston's playing coach for a reputed £8 a week, a healthy sum considering it was the height of the Depression and the basic weekly wage—for those lucky enough to still be in work—was around £4/2.[680] Cazaly had not been the committee's original choice. Their first, North Melbourne ruckman Norm Lewis, was found to be under a long-standing suspension imposed before North Melbourne had joined the VFL. Their second, Charlie Dibbs—recently married and living locally—led pre-season training for several weeks before being refused a clearance by his club Collingwood.[681] As a result, Cazaly's appointment was hastily arranged and confirmed just three days before the start of the season. The players unanimously elected him captain, with Jack Monohan as his deputy.[682]

Further unsettling Preston's preparations, Cazaly was forced to miss their first match after his clearance papers from the City club were delayed *en route* from Launceston. Even then, it took a heroic effort by one of Preston's officials to track down the paperwork at the Melbourne GPO and rush it to the VFA's permit committee in time for them to approve Cazaly's transfer the night before Preston's second-round clash with Coburg. As the VFA *Recorder* noted:

> After a lot of hard groundwork and some good airwork, Roy Cazaly's clearance arrived to the delight of all. The boys came into their own with the old saying 'Up There, Cazaly' ...[683]

In addition to Cazaly, Preston had a sprinkling of players with previous VFL experience, including full-forward Harry Davie (Melbourne and Carlton), followers Les Hughson (Collingwood and Hawthorn) and Danny Warr (St Kilda) and defender Bert Taylor (Fitzroy).[684] Preston's early form after their disrupted start to the season was indifferent. After narrowly losing their first match against neighbouring Northcote they proceeded to win and then lose games with frustrating regularity. One candid report in the *Recorder* noted that Preston's committee "were thoroughly disappointed with the display given by many of the players in the match against Prahran, and some plain talking was indulged in at the players' meeting."[685]

By the start of round nine Preston were languishing in eighth place. They were considered no chance of making the finals but Cazaly responded by trialling new players from the Seconds. Juniors who made their senior debut included forward Bob Cameron, winger Frank 'Dicky' Dowling, half-back Alex McEacharn, fullback George Smith and the Spargo brothers Frank and Pierce. Many would go on to have long careers at Preston or other clubs.[686]

It was during the 1931 season that Cazaly came to know journalist Hec de Lacy, who had joined *The Sporting Globe* as a football writer while Cazaly had been in Tasmania. Their alliance resulted in an opinion piece written by Cazaly for the *Globe* in which he set out the essential elements of good ruck play. It was the pre-cursor to a series of occasional articles he would write for the paper.[687]

De Lacy admired Cazaly as a player, tactician and leader and was proud to call him a friend. While it could be argued this friendship coloured his reporting, their closeness enabled him to write with insight and candour about Cazaly's complex and sometimes contradictory character.

De Lacy spoke to Cazaly at Preston soon after he had replaced several senior players with juniors. The journalist suggested he'd taken a huge risk which may backfire. "I'll take a chance," Cazaly replied.

> I've got 18 fighters behind me now, not one of these kids cares whether he is playing on the Preston ground or away from home. He'll go down fighting. I can do something with kids like that.[688]

The coach's changes paid off. Playing with better system, pace and stamina, Preston embarked on a remarkable streak which saw them win eight of their next nine games and draw the other. Cazaly, as usual, led from the front. During a win against Sandringham he kicked five goals and stayed on the field despite breaking a toe in his left foot early in the second half.[689] Reporters noted his steadying influence in the ruck or up forward, with one writing, after a narrow win over Northcote, that:

> It was not the work he did himself, but that which he encouraged his young side to do that made him so valuable. In the close finish Roy was worth two men to the younger players.[690]

Cazaly was also careful to look after the physical wellbeing of his young charges on the field. Hec de Lacy later recalled witnessing what happened after an opposition ruckman threw a punch at one of Preston's wingers.

> Cazaly left the forward line, ran the big fellow to earth, spun him round and with his open hand smacked him across the mouth. While this was going on, another opponent, and a former League man, ran up from behind, gave Cazaly a rabbit-killer and dropped him. He was up in a split second. The ball was kicked into a bunch, in which Cazaly and his assailant were the principals. Despite my closest watch, all I can report is that Cazaly came away with the ball, loping along in the long-striding way he had, while the assailant had his tongue hanging out over his cheek and was evidently seized suddenly with some sort of violent spasm. The rough stuff stopped in a trice.[691]

Preston were a very social club away from the field. Euchre parties, fortnightly dances, a picnic, a celebrity concert and a 'Popular Boy' competition were all held during the season, allowing players and supporters to mix socially and raise much-needed funds to help meet team expenses. Cazaly took part in the club's fox-trot dance competition and provided the piano interludes during one mid-season card night.[692]

By the end of round 17 Preston had climbed into the four and they went into their last match needing to defeat Coburg to be guaranteed a finals berth. In driving rain and before a partisan opposition crowd of 6000 they triumphed by a goal to finish the regular season third on the ladder. Cazaly exuded confidence before Preston's semi-final against minor premiers Oakleigh:

> We have a strong, young, well-balanced side, all players being seized with the importance of the big engagement. The youngsters at Preston have done everything I have asked of them. That is why I am so confident that we will defeat Oakleigh and then go on to take the pennant. They have been set some severe tasks, but have never flinched under the severest punishment, and have come back to take the honors. We will not have a quitter at Preston.[693]

Cazaly's confidence proved well-founded: after trailing by 10 points at half-time, Preston settled down to overhaul Oakleigh's lead and win by 23. Speaking after the game, Cazaly confessed he'd feared his young side would be rattled by their more experienced opponents:

> They were white with over-anxiety. I knew, however, that once they had started they would soon warm up. A semi-final in senior company is a big trial for a colt.[694]

Preston's win set up a showdown with their traditional rivals Northcote. Victory would see them play Oakleigh again in the Grand Final but Preston went into the match without their leading goalscorer Harry Davie, who was suffering from rheumatism, and experienced fullback Bert Taylor, who had pneumonia. Follower Lyall Seebeck, who had played every game during the season, was also absent as it was his wedding day.[695]

Preston kicked with the aid of a strong northerly wind in the first quarter but wasted the opportunity and could manage just 1.3 to Northcote's one behind. They were then kept scoreless against the wind in the second quarter while Northcote kicked 6.14. Despite kicking 5.6 in the third quarter Preston were unable to catch their opponents, who stretched their lead during the last quarter to win by 37 points. Speaking afterwards, Cazaly attributed the loss to the strong wind which had disrupted Preston's passing game and the fact that his young players had shown their inexperience on the day.[696] Preston's valiant run had ended and Oakleigh went on to defeat Northcote for the premiership.

Vice-captain Jack Monohan was named Preston's most consistent player and Seniors debutant 'Dicky' Dowling was runner-up. Cazaly himself had a solid season, kicking 25 goals and figuring among Preston's best in many games.[697]

Cazaly also played for the Waterside Workers in the Wednesday Football League (WFL) during 1931 alongside his former City teammate Stan 'Snowy' Joolen. The wharfies were making their reappearance after a two-year absence due to what *The Age* euphemistically called "waterfront troubles" but had in reality been a major national maritime dispute at the end of 1928.[698] Cazaly was captain and coach, but the team did not train so any coaching presumably took place during games.[699] Despite his leadership role it seems Cazaly only played a handful of matches, a puzzlingly small number even allowing for his occasional sidelining due to injury.[700]

The mid-week competition was drawing healthy crowds: in a paper he wrote to illustrate football's social and economic benefits, VFL secretary Likely McBrien estimated that it was attracting 11,000 spectators each week, placing it third in patronage behind the VFL and VFA and well ahead of the Saturday Industrial League, the Metropolitan Amateurs and the various sub-district and church-based competitions.[701]

The Wednesday league's make-up had changed since Cazaly had last played four years earlier. Teams from the Railways, Fire Brigade, Post and Telegraph and Yellow Cabs remained, but the Police, Air Force and Red and Checker Cab teams had all departed, replaced by sides from the Press, Telephone Exchange and Victoria Markets. The WFL's reputation for rough play and violence had not improved, however; if anything it had worsened.[702] The league averaged one serious outbreak of on-field violence each month. In early June, a torrid encounter between the Watersiders and Yellow Cabs resulted in four players being hospitalised. In response, Railways tried to have the wharfies expelled from the league and when their motion narrowly failed they forfeited their next match against them in protest.[703]

In July, a game between Victoria Markets and the wharfies was marred by several fights and an all-in brawl involving a thousand spectators who jumped the fence to join in.[704] The next month one of the Watersiders, Johnson, was disqualified for life after he kicked a Yellow Cabs opponent several times and then assaulted the umpire in the rooms after the game.[705] At a crisis meeting called by officials to discuss the continuing violence, the Watersiders claimed they were being victimised, Railways threatened to withdraw from the league and the Post and Telegraph delegate asked for police to be stationed on the ground at the end of matches.[706]

Preston's officials eventually grew tired of the WFL's violence, the injuries and the impact on their playing list. The committee banned its players from taking part in any further Wednesday games, but their edict must have been overturned or ignored because Cazaly played at least one further match for the Watersiders and Les Hughson continued to play for Post and Telegraph.[707]

One of the wharfies' better wins came against the Railways team at North Melbourne in early August. There were rumours it would be a rough match: resentment lingered over the Railways' earlier attempt to have the wharfies expelled and the two clubs had agreed on a side wager of £25. A large number of unemployed men broke down the gates to gain free admission but those expecting a violent game were treated to a display of "fast, open and clean football."[708] The Watersiders won half their matches for the season, finished equal fourth with the Fire Brigade team but missed the finals on percentage.[709]

The South Melbourne Footballers' XI had disbanded so Cazaly captained South Ports in the second grade of the VJCA over the summer, his team eventually losing to Victoria Brewery in the semi-final. He was third in the batting averages, scoring 249 runs at an average of 31.9, and topped the bowling averages with 43 wickets at 6.3.[710]

Preston advertised their coaching position as the 1932 football season loomed but Cazaly was not an applicant, despite intense speculation in the local paper and a general assumption among the public that the job remained his if he wanted it.[711] Perplexed by his lack of interest, the club re-advertised the role, received 16 applications and eventually selected Yarraville's captain-coach Harry Hunter.[712]

There was speculation Cazaly did not re-apply because he had sought the coaching post at Melbourne but there is no firm evidence to support this contention.[713] As with his previous clubs, it seems money or, more correctly, its absence during the Depression, was the sticking point. The local paper had reported it "doubtful that the Preston club are in the position to pay the fancy prices that have been paid previously, so whoever may eventually be appointed, it is only fair to assume that he will have to accept the position at a considerably reduced figure."[714]

Cazaly had decided to return to Tasmania. In early March the North Hobart Football Club advertised in the Melbourne papers for a "first-class playing coach", asking applicants to state age, qualifications and salary required. Cazaly applied and was appointed.[715]

18

FIGHTS AND A FLAG

NORTH HOBART, 1932-33

Cazaly's clearance from Preston was approved on 22 March, 1932. He and his family arrived in Launceston aboard the *Nairana* six days later and caught the train to Hobart, where they were met on the platform by North Hobart's president Charlie Dunn and other committee members.

North Hobart, one of four teams in the Tasmanian Football League (TFL), was a club whose players were conditioned to expect success. They had won eight TFL and four state premierships between 1902 and 1929 and had only lost the previous year's flag following a replay of the Grand Final. The team contained a mix of old hands, transferred players and raw recruits. High-marking half-back Stan Felmingham was returning to the side after a stint playing in Launceston, and one of the more promising new players was Alby Goggins, a rugged defender from Tasmania's Midlands known as the 'Bothwell Badger' for his determination when burrowing into packs.[716] North Hobart players had a habit of bestowing unusual nicknames on their teammates: others in the 1932 side included Len 'Sox' Powell, Alfred 'Oxy' Pratt, Burnell 'Sugar' Edwards and, more obviously, Len 'Apples' Pye.

Cazaly's opposition coaches were Collingwood star and 1929 Brownlow medallist Albert 'Leeter' Collier—who was halfway through a two-year stint with Cananore—former Port Adelaide captain Vic Johnson at Lefroy and former West Adelaide vice-captain Chris Bennett at New Town.[717]

Training began on 5 April and the club held a welcome social for Cazaly at the rooms the following evening. He called for the members' support, asked the players to give their best and expressed confidence that the team had the right material to win the premiership.[718] In mid-April Cazaly led his charges in a narrow practice-match loss against Lefroy, one reporter noting that "his form, even though not extended, was sufficient to indicate his days as a first-class player are by no means numbered." North defeated Cananore in another practice game the following week, but the much anticipated match-up between Cazaly and Collier failed to materialise after the latter was sidelined by an attack of boils.[719]

North Hobart opened the season proper with a solid victory over Lefroy and proceeded to win their next nine games in a row. A four-point loss to Cananore in round 11 provided only a momentary setback and was followed by five wins on end. Cazaly played the majority of these games at centre half-forward, with occasional spells in the ruck. He was regularly among the goalscorers, and commentators were quick to praise his shrewdness, judgment and on-field leadership. Following a win against New Town the *Sporting Record* remarked that:

> The ex-South Melbournite provided a model of position play in attack where he led the suburban defenders a merry dance in their occasional attempts to keep him covered. His anticipation and fine marking on innumerable occasions put the Reds in a scoring position, and with astute coaching, the players further in followed his example and ran out to receive his passes with unfailing regularity. Apart from obvious control over his team as a leader, no man did more to make victory so decisive.[720]

In June, Cazaly was vice-captain of a combined TFL team that played a VFL side in front of 7000 fans at North Hobart. It was the first time a representative VFL side had visited Tasmania since the 1924 Carnival. 'Leeter' Collier captained the TFL team and Cazaly's former St Kilda teammate Bill Cubbins led the Victorians.[721] North Hobart's Alan Rait—who Cazaly later nominated as the best full-forward he had seen since Dick Lee—kicked nine goals for the TFL but the home side were outplayed, losing by 37 points.[722]

When the local competition resumed North Hobart continued winning. Then a sensation occurred on 20 August when they overhauled a 28-point deficit early in the last quarter to win a spiteful encounter against Cananore. The match was interrupted by several brawls and at one stage during the second quarter a policeman entered the field to help umpires calm proceedings. *The Mercury* was scathing in its description of events:

> The disgraceful conduct of players in the Cananore v North Hobart match on Saturday disgusted a crowd of over 6,000 who paid admission money in the belief that they would witness a game of football, but were forced to watch incidents more in keeping with a street brawl. It was a degrading spectacle and it is doubtful whether its equal has been witnessed in Hobart in League matches which are supposed to be under strict control.[723]

Cazaly was involved in several of the clashes and was reported by the umpires for charging and elbowing Cananore's centre Pat Hartnett and for charging 'Leeter' Collier. North's ruckmen Stan Ryan and Frank Smith were reported for similar offences against Harry Sutton and Russ Johnston.[724]

Almost forgotten in the aftermath of the fracas was the fact that North Hobart had secured the minor premiership. There were just three more matches before the finals and Cazaly must have cast his mind back to the two previous occasions, at South Melbourne in 1923 and City in 1928, when he had found himself facing a judicial hearing at the tail-end of a season.

A large crowd gathered outside the tribunal hearing the following Thursday to await the verdict. Cazaly, who vigorously proclaimed his innocence, was cleared of charging Collier but found guilty of charging and elbowing Hartnett. In a harsh sanction, he was suspended for the rest of the 1932 season and the first six matches of the next. Stan Ryan's penalty was almost as severe while Frank Smith was disqualified for three matches.[725]

Despite his suspension Cazaly was allowed to continue coaching from the sidelines. Vice-captain 'Sugar' Edwards assumed the captaincy role and 'Sox' Powell and Bill Hawkes moved to the ruck. At the first game after the tribunal hearing the crowd roundly booed the umpires and greeted Cazaly "with a roar of cheering and applause" each time he strolled past the pavilion.[726]

The tribunal affair had an extraordinary sequel several days later when the police charged Cazaly and Cananore's Harry Sutton with having disturbed the peace by fighting during the match. Cananore supporter Arnie Walters later recalled the incident which led to the police charges:

> It was a bit of a grudge match really, there was a lot of bad feeling between the players and early on in the game there were a few fights. Anyway, the ball was bounced and another brawl started in the middle, a fair dinkum brawl, fists flyin' everywhere and Cazaly and Sutton was in it, as well as others, and Sutton, well he was a bit of a hot-head, and he was gettin' stuck into Cazaly. I think Cazaly was down, like, on his knees, and Harry was gettin' stuck into 'im and other players was draggin' them apart.[727]

The police charges against Sutton and Cazaly were listed for separate mention in early October. After hearing the evidence against Sutton, Police Magistrate Horace White found the fighting charge proven and fined him £1 with a further 11 shillings in costs. Cazaly was represented in court by prominent barrister and future Labor Premier Albert Ogilvie. Under questioning, Cazaly said he had been struck several times while on the ground and that he'd merely tried to smother the blows. After Ogilvie called several eyewitnesses supporting Cazaly's version of events Magistrate White said he was satisfied he'd been defending himself and dismissed the charge.[728]

Between Cazaly's criminal charge being laid, heard and dismissed North Hobart progressed to the TFL Grand Final against Cananore and won easily by 52 points. The suspended Cazaly and Stan Ryan are included in a photo of the victorious premiership side, easily identifiable as the only two players wearing civilian clothes.[729] A week later North Hobart lost the state final by a goal to Cazaly's old team City.[730] North's 'Apples' Pye won the William Leitch Medal for the TFL's fairest and best player, and full-forward Alan Rait was the competition's leading goalscorer for the fifth season in a row, with a haul of 102.[731]

Over the summer, Cazaly captained the North Hobart Footballers in the Tasmanian Cricket Association's B grade. In March, he led the side in a tour match against the City club in Queenstown, taking all six top-order wickets for 34 runs. While on the west coast he also gave one of his famous blackboard lectures to an appreciative gathering of players from the Mines' United Football Club, premiers of the Queenstown Football Association.[732]

After moving to Hobart the Cazalys had lived in West Hobart, but during 1932 Roy set up his home and a masseur business opposite the Royal Hobart Hospital. The large three-storey sandstone building on the corner of Argyle and Collins Streets had been built by Hobart merchant Sir Elliot Lewis in 1846 as a residence and commercial warehouse.[733] The Cazalys lived on the top floor, and daughter Pat later recalled the old bell pulls which had been used to summon servants, and the dark corners where her brother Roy would hide in wait to scare his sisters.[734]

Cazaly's treatment rooms, which included massage tables and a gymnasium, were on the floor below. Here he practised Swedish massage and the muscle treatments he had learned from Harry Best at St Kilda and Jack Marshall at South Melbourne. Injured footballers provided much of Cazaly's early business: in May 1933 it was reported that "as a masseur, players have great confidence in him, and he not only attends to those of his own club, North Hobart, but the other teams send players needing attention to him."[735] Roy jnr, now 14, was his offsider in the rooms and he proved a quick learner.[736]

Massage techniques were undergoing important changes. Previously, massage was essentially a passive remedy in which the patient was pummelled and prodded by the masseur. Greater attention was now being given to exercise therapy and muscle re-education as part of a more interventionist approach to injury treatment and pain management.[737] The use of "electrical treatment" to stimulate muscles and increase blood circulation was also becoming more common and it was under this heading that Cazaly advertised his services in Hobart's Post Office directory.[738] He would have observed 'Old Besty' using electrical therapy on St Kilda players—and no doubt underwent it himself—but it would have been a novel experience for those who now came to him for similar treatment.[739]

Cazaly's re-appointment as North Hobart's coach in 1933 was not a *fait accompli*, despite him having delivered a premiership the previous season. North's committee members were still unhappy with the severity of his playing suspension. They felt his long absence from the field had been disruptive and they blamed it for the team's narrow loss to City in the state final.

After considering cancelling the remainder of Cazaly's contract the committee decided to retain him because of his value to the team.[740] It appears, however, that they didn't pay him during his suspension because his salary—which had totalled £247/5 in 1932—fell by more than half to £115 during 1933.[741] As the new season began, Cazaly sought remission for the remaining six weeks of his sentence, telling the league in a personal appeal that it was the first time he had ever been disqualified from playing and that it had resulted in "serious financial loss". The league's investigation tribunal was unmoved, however, and his suspension stood.[742]

North Hobart began pre-season training without two of their best players after Len 'Apples' Pye left to play with Fitzroy, and champion forward Alan Rait decided to play with Footscray. Rait had been courted by six VFL clubs and Footscray's additional guarantee of employment—which North Hobart had been unable to match—was a deciding factor in his decision.[743] The method of his departure stung North Hobart and Cazaly joined a growing call for local clubs to be compensated for the loss of key players to the VFL:

> For years clubs in Tasmania have been paying high prices for the services of Melbourne coaches, in the hope of improving their players, but what do we find? As soon as a young player's capabilities have been developed, at considerable expense to the club, he is induced to go to Melbourne. It can hardly be said that the club is not entitled to some return for the money it spent on teaching him to play the game.[744]

The departure of Rait and Pye, Cazaly's continued absence through suspension, and injuries to others resulted in a side that was unsettled for much of the season. When Cazaly finally returned to the field for the start of round seven on 10 June he played one game at full-forward before alternating between ruck and centre duties. His form improved towards the finals and a number of his positional changes were successful but Cananore swept all before them, winning 13 of their 16 matches. North Hobart easily accounted for New Town in the semi-final but were overwhelmingly defeated by Cananore in the Grand Final. Within days there were whispers that Cazaly would not be staying at North Hobart.[745]

19

FROM UGLY DUCKLINGS TO PREMIERS

NEW TOWN, 1934-36

Despite the rumours, there were no immediate signs Cazaly was planning to leave North Hobart. He was master of ceremonies for several club social functions and captained their cricket team to a pennant in the Metropolitan Cricket Association over the summer.[746] He attended and spoke at North Hobart's general meeting in January but later that month a Melbourne newspaper reported that he had applied for the coaching position at Footscray.[747] Nothing came of his bid but in March it was revealed that North Hobart had appointed former North Melbourne ruckman Max Pitchford as coach and Cazaly would be coaching neighbouring team New Town.[748]

The exact circumstances surrounding his departure from North Hobart are unknown but there was probably lingering ill-feeling on the club's part over his 1932/33 playing disqualification and on Cazaly's part over the committee's refusal to pay him during his suspension. Whatever the reasons, it is notable that Cazaly continued to provide massage and electrical treatments to North Hobart players even while coaching their cross-town rivals.[749]

Cazaly's new club had none of North Hobart's pedigree and premiership tradition. Although a football team had been formed in New Town during the 1870s it had spent most of its life in junior ranks, only earning promotion as the TFL's fourth team in 1921. Its subsequent form had been underwhelming, making the Grand Final just twice in 13 seasons and losing both.[750]

With Cazaly in charge New Town's supporters now looked forward to the new season with uncharacteristic confidence. The *Sporting Record* noted "if Cazaly can knock some sense and system into the players while hope is still fresh and enthusiasm unchilled, New Town will be a particularly hard side to defeat". The *Mercury* remarked that he was "the right type to take charge of a side whose weakness has during several seasons been its lack of a strong and clever leader."[751]

New Town began the season with three straight losses. Then Cazaly broke several ribs during a match against his old team North Hobart and was sidelined for a month. New Town's rover Gerald James assumed the captaincy role and Hilton Buckney, who had captained Lefroy the previous season, was brought in as acting coach while Cazaly recovered.[752]

New Town's form was indifferent during Cazaly's absence. His return to the ruck in round eight helped spark a solid win against Cananore but such victories were few and far between as New Town looked to be maintaining their reputation for under-achieving.[753] The team's long-suffering supporters may have taken consolation from the fact that Cazaly was seeking to strengthen his side via positional changes and judicial promotions from junior ranks. The problem, as one critic pointed out, was that New Town had been "team-building" for a decade and "as it has been practising the art in each succeeding year it should have attained some degree of proficiency."[754]

Off the field, the whole family threw themselves into the fairs, dances and card nights that comprised the club's fundraising activities. In May, Dorrie was crowned New Town's 'Social Queen' and Lena, Pat and Joan were among her attendants.[755] The children were now old enough to help their father with his training and match-day preparations. Roy jnr later said his father "brought all his family into his sport with him" and that everyone played a role:

> Mum did the cooking, was his greatest critic and dietician and treated his injuries. Saturday night after a match was spent in getting Dad ready for the next week's match. I looked after his boots and footballs, my sisters looked after his football clothes. We were his trainers, masseurs, lackeys and we loved it.⁷⁵⁶

Ten-year-old Pat and seven-year-old Joan went to their first football game during the 1934 season. Their father had previously discouraged them from attending by claiming there were too many "rough people" in the crowd but Pat wanted to satisfy her own curiosity about what took place. Roy relented and asked Aggie to "get the girls outfitted, so they'll be nice and warm." Years later, Pat remembered her mother's fierce barracking during the game:

> My mother, who always spoke very quietly! I thought, 'that's not my mother!' Oh yes, she was very one-eyed. I think she went to every match my father played.⁷⁵⁷

Towards the end of the season New Town were showings signs of improvement. Going into the last round they had to defeat North Hobart and hope that Lefroy defeated Cananore in order to make the finals. New Town won but their effort was in vain after Lefroy lost their match. North Hobart went on to win the premiership.

In February 1935 club members debated changing New Town's colours from green and gold to black and white. Supporters of the new scheme, including Cazaly, argued the traditional colours faded over time, and a black and white strip "would make the players look big, fit and smart." The motion received majority support but failed to achieve the necessary two-thirds margin required to change the club's constitution.⁷⁵⁸

New Town began their season with a solid win over Cananore. Two days later, Roy and Aggie flew to Melbourne to fulfil a commitment to captain a team of past South Melbourne players against current players in a fundraising match. Crossing Bass Strait by air in 1935 was not without risk: a de Havilland airliner had crashed near Wilson's Promontory the previous year with the loss of 12 lives and the same plane on which the Cazalys travelled crashed near Flinders Island several months later, killing all five on board.[759]

Roy and Aggie were scheduled to arrive in Melbourne several hours before the match but their flight was delayed by heavy fog, leading to shouts of "Where's Cazaly?" from among the 7000-strong crowd as the players ran on.[760] They eventually arrived at the ground at half-time and Roy was given the honour of leading the past players out for the second half. He kicked four goals in two quarters but the current players defeated the "old timers" by 23 points.[761] After the game Cazaly spoke of his pleasure at being asked to take part:

New Town's 1935 membership badge.

> I have been away from South Melbourne for so long that frequently I have wondered if South people ever remembered me. It came as a delightful surprise to receive this invitation to take part in the match thereby affording me the opportunity of meeting so many of my old pals.[762]

Cazaly trained twice with his old side over the following days before he and Aggie returned to Tasmania by ship. Arriving in Burnie on Saturday morning and seasick after a stormy crossing, their car suffered a puncture and Cazaly was forced to change the tyre in pouring rain, using a fence post as an improvised jack. They arrived back in Hobart just in time for Cazaly to lead New Town in a win against North Hobart. Fittingly, it came at the club's home ground, which was being used for the first time in two seasons following extensive improvements.[763]

Cazaly played the whole season in the ruck, alongside follower Hedley Rooke and rover Athol Paul. In June Cazaly, now 42, was selected to captain the combined TFL side in a match against their traditional rivals from the NTFA. It was his first time leading the southern team and they won easily by 70 points.[764] Later that month Cazaly was hurt during a loss to Cananore, re-injuring two of the ribs he had broken the previous season. He had previously worn a home-made shield to protect his ribs but had

The program for the smoke social held to honour Cazaly's long career.

lent it to another player before the match. Fortunately the new injury didn't prove too serious and he was able to play in New Town's win against North Hobart the following week.[765]

A more unusual injury occurred soon afterwards while Cazaly and several other New Town players were on a hunting trip in the Ouse district. Winger Len Goodluck, scouting separately from the rest of the group, was shot in the leg when someone mistook him for a rabbit. Luckily he was not seriously hurt and missed just one game as a result.[766]

In late July Cazaly was chosen to captain a combined TFL team against a touring St Kilda side. A match-day profile described Cazaly as retaining "the pace and stamina of youth", despite his advancing years:

> A fighter of tremendous capacity, he has abilities that are distinctive; his graceful marking, beautiful kicking, and clever turning making him one of the greatest players of all time. The men who were associated with him in his early football days have closed their careers; Roy has outlasted them all.[767]

That evening Cazaly was honoured at a smoke social organised by the New Town club to celebrate his long football career. Guests at the function included St Kilda's coach Dan Minogue, their masseur Harry Best (now a sprightly 72), South Melbourne official Jack Rohan and former local teammates and opponents Horrie Gorringe, Allan Leitch and Jack Dunn. Part of the evening's program, complete with speeches, toasts and musical interludes, was broadcast live to Tasmanian homes via radio station 7ZL.[768]

The 1935 TFL competition was extremely close-fought throughout. After winning eight of their first 10 matches New Town lost several games mid-season—including one in which Cazaly insisted on playing despite an injured shoulder—but then rallied to win their last three.[769]

A sequence of unfortunate events befell the team in the lead up to the finals. The first occurred when back-pocket player Herb Hitchens was hit by a train at the Hobart rail yards and suffered a serious head injury. Then Cazaly was reported for attempting to strike North Hobart's full-back Trevor Richardson in the second-last round. The incident no doubt sparked feelings of *déjà vu* but unlike 1932 the charge was dismissed by the league's investigation committee. Finally, rover Athol Paul was reported for elbowing an opponent and suspended for two entire seasons.[770]

Despite these substantial setbacks, New Town managed to defeat Lefroy in the last round to claim the minor premiership for the first time. North Hobart then narrowly overcame Lefroy in the semi-final to set up a Grand Final showdown with New Town. In a game in which the lead changed several times, Cazaly and Hedley Rooke dominated in the ruck, Ted Ferguson starred in defence and Jim Langford kicked seven goals. New Town twice steadied when it seemed North Hobart would over-run them and they eventually won by 14 points. Club secretary Ted Freeman later recalled that "it was the astute brain of the dynamic Roy Cazaly that won the day."[771]

The club had won their first TFL premiership and jubilant supporters invaded the ground amid scenes of wild celebration. As the *Sporting Record*'s 'Kickero' reported:

> The New Town supporters were delirious with joy. The legions emitted a roar that could be heard half a mile away; they stormed the ground to carry their heroes to the dressing room. All the disappointments at New Town failures in previous finals were swept away.[772]

Speaking after the win, Cazaly stressed that his main coaching challenge during the season had been a psychological one:

> When I took over the club the players seemed to be suffering from an inferiority complex. So many times had they failed in their ambition to secure a premiership that there appeared to be an atmosphere of futility. It was a hard job to knock that out of them, and make them realise that they were as good as, if not better than, the other teams. They, however, gave me loyal support, and this season I could see that they were imbued with a fighting spirit that would pull them through any match.[773]

Sixteen-year-old Roy jnr played in a premiership side on the same day as his father, part of the Macalburn team which won the State School Old Boys' Association pennant.[774] A week later, Cazaly snr led an unchanged New Town team against Launceston to decide the state premiership. Arch Flanagan, by now a teacher in Hobart and occasional player for North Hobart, later said it was the best game of football he ever saw:

> Launceston opened up an early lead. Cazaly "plugged" one of them to put them off their game, but the Launceston players were very disciplined.[775]

New Town were competitive during the first two quarters but Launceston kicked 10 goals to three after half-time to win their third successive state premiership.[776]

Asked what his future plans were, Cazaly denied a rumour that he would soon be coaching at South Melbourne, but beyond that was non-committal:

> My plans for 1936 are indefinite. I do not know if I will still be in Hobart; much depends on my business and on what way it will expand within the next six or eight months.[777]

As it turned out, Cazaly did apply for the South Melbourne coaching position, along with players Len Thomas, Lindsay Richards and several others. Jack Bisset, coach for the previous three seasons, was eventually reappointed.[778]

Prior to the new TFL season Cazaly announced he would no longer take the field but would continue as New Town's non-playing coach.[779] Ted Ferguson was chosen as captain, with Hedley Rooke as his deputy. Stan 'Snowy' Joolen joined Cazaly at New Town, making it the fourth club they had been at together since the Waterside Workers in 1927. Former Richmond and Victorian follower George Rudolph also transferred to the club and played several useful games at half-back.[780]

Changes were afoot at Hobart's other clubs too. Rumours that a local club had approached Fitzroy champion and triple Brownlow medallist Haydn Bunton came to nothing, but Cazaly's former protégé at Minyip, Eric Zschech, was appointed Lefroy's new captain-coach; Richmond ruckman Fred 'Fritz' Heifner took over at Cananore, and former South Melbourne player Cecil Pettiona took the reins at North Hobart.[781]

Cazaly's decision not to play the 1936 season lasted exactly one week. After watching his team's heavy opening-round loss to Lefroy he played the following week to fill in for a sick player. *The Mercury* reported his reappearance as a one-off measure but from round four he played the rest of the season, usually in the ruck but occasionally at centre half-forward.[782]

A social highlight occurred mid-season, when New Town took advantage of a bye to play a combined team from the Tasman Peninsula Association. The match, played alongside the historic Port Arthur penitentiary, resulted in an easy win for the visitors. Afterwards, the *Sporting Record* reported:

> Roy Cazaly got half-a-dozen of the local team to change guernseys with the same number of New Town men, and took the opportunity of explaining how to make a break, demonstrating with both teams. Much improvement was soon evident in the teamwork of the home players. It was a sporting gesture on the part of Cazaly, and favourably commented on by local residents.[783]

Back in Hobart, Cazaly sought to lead from the front but it was a disappointing season for the reigning premiers, which won just two games and drew another. New Town's season ended abruptly after 15 rounds, leaving the other teams to fight out the premiership.[784] The club's annual report attributed the team's form slump to injuries, disqualifications and the loss of key players, but their failure to make the finals must have been keenly felt by their supporters.[785] Cazaly polled equal third in the umpires' vote for the league's best-and-fairest player, behind Lefroy's Eric Zschech and North Hobart's 'Apples' Pye.[786]

Away from football, Cazaly was beginning to take a close interest in breeding and training greyhounds. Greyhound racing, also known as speed coursing, was enjoying a surge in popularity thanks to the legalising of on-course betting by the Ogilvie Government and the construction of a new track, complete with lights, on Hobart's Domain. Going to the dogs soon became the social highlight of the week, and crowds of several thousand spectators were common.[787]

Cazaly, "bewitched" by the sport, borrowed £16 to buy his first racing greyhound, called Antique.[788] He won three trophies at the Tasmanian

Kennel Club's 1936 show and in December was elected the inaugural president of the Southern Tasmanian division of the Owners, Breeders and Trainers Association, which soon represented almost 90 per cent of those involved in the sport.[789]

20

LAKESIDE LAMENT

SOUTH MELBOURNE, 1937

In early 1937 Cazaly made it known that he wanted to return to a coaching role in Melbourne. The two League clubs most interested in talking to him were Fitzroy and his old club South Melbourne. Fitzroy great Haydn Bunton had just coached his team to their first ever wooden spoon while Jack Bisset, South's captain-coach since 1933, had lost the confidence of his administration.[790]

The South Melbourne and Fitzroy committees met on February 9 to discuss their applicants and—unbeknown to each other—both selected Cazaly as non-playing coach. It was reported that when a South Melbourne committee member learned of Fitzroy's decision he quickly telephoned Cazaly to formally offer him a three-year contract. Cazaly simply said he'd been negotiating with both clubs, and that South had been the first to accept his terms.[791]

A series of social functions and farewell tributes were hastily arranged. It seems Cazaly was not planning an immediate return to Tasmania as he advertised several fishing nets, a lounge suite and other items of furniture for sale in *The Mercury*'s classifieds. He resigned from his greyhound commitments, taking one dog with him to Melbourne, and appointed friend and teammate Stan 'Snowy' Joolen to take charge of the masseur business during his absence.[792]

South Melbourne had experienced something approaching a golden age while Cazaly had been in Hobart. Under president Jack Rohan the club had embarked on an audacious recruiting campaign during the early 1930s to secure star players from other clubs and leagues. The VFL's Coulter Law prevented clubs from paying each player more than £3 a week but clubs with wealthy benefactors were able to attract players with the additional guarantee of employment.

Western Australia had been hit hard by the Depression and a number of prominent footballers were lured east by the prospect of a VFL career and a secure job. South's star recruits included Johnny Leonard—who became captain-coach in 1932—Brighton Diggins, Johnny Bowe, Jim 'Brum' O'Meara and Bert 'Blue' Beard. So many players crossed the Nullarbor during this period that Hec de Lacy began referring to South Melbourne as the 'Swans', after Western Australia's faunal emblem. The nickname stuck and a swan soon became the club's mascot.[793]

South Melbourne's recruiting drive was bankrolled by Archie Crofts, a prominent businessman and local councillor who took over as president from Jack Rohan at the end of 1932.[794] Crofts owned a chain of eponymous grocery stores across Victoria which provided employment for many of the interstate recruits, who were quickly dubbed the "foreign legion". Soon his stores employed 24 South Melbourne players.[795] The experience of Subiaco half-back flanker Bill Faul was typical. After being unemployed throughout 1931 he accepted South Melbourne's offer of a place in the team and a job in one of Crofts' stores. Faul won South Melbourne's best-and-fairest award in 1932 and was runner-up for the Brownlow Medal.[796]

Other members of the foreign legion recruited during 1932-33 included South Australia's Hans 'Ossie' Bertram and Wilbur Harris and Cazaly's former protégé Laurie Nash from Tasmania.[797] Not all the new talent came

from interstate: among the home-grown players, forward Len Thomas, pocket forward Herbie Matthews, goalkicking phenomenon Bob Pratt and champion athlete Austin Robertson helped round out an impressively talented team.

South Melbourne made it as far as the first semi-final in 1932 before winning their first premiership in 15 years the next season. Jack Rohan had masterminded the recruitment strategy while Archie Crofts had provided the cash. Speaking after the Grand Final victory, Rohan candidly declared that:

> This year, a dangerous and costly policy has been carried out successfully. It cost a king's ransom to bring players from Western Australia, but every one of them was worth it.[798]

South Melbourne's 1933 premiership should have heralded the start of a new era but the Swans were runners-up the next three seasons. Part of this can be attributed to bad luck—Bob Pratt was knocked down by a truck two days before the 1935 Grand Final, and injuries plagued the 1936 side—but South's stellar playing list and overall record during this period suggests they should have won more flags.[799] There was something about the Swans' star-studded line-up during this period that didn't quite jell at crucial moments, recalling the adage that a team of champions will always be beaten by a champion team.

Cazaly's appointment as coach made front-page news in South Melbourne's *The Record* and he took the opportunity to lay out his manifesto for the coming season, declaring that individual brilliance was not enough to win premierships:

> It is essential that a complete balance be obtained—every player must be taught to realise that he is only a cog in a machine that must work smoothly. It needs only one cog to slip to smash that machine, and my first objective will be to guard against that danger. South Melbourne players will have to realise that there can be only one boss, and they will find me firm, but just, if there is too much individualism.[800]

Hopes were high that the new coach would find the formula to recapture the Swans' premiership form, but the South Melbourne of 1937 was a shadow of the team from four years earlier. Retirements and transfers had taken their toll, recruitment efforts had stalled and just seven members from the 1933 premiership side remained on the books.[801] The League had tightened the residency requirements for interstate signings and the club's benefactor, Archie Crofts, had become more focused on a parliamentary career and a string of champion racehorses.[802]

Prior to the new season it was announced that Cazaly would be in charge of both the Firsts and the Seconds, in order "to have all South's players under the eye of the expert coach."[803] There was speculation that star player Laurie Nash might forgo football to concentrate on making the Australian cricket team for its next tour of England but in the end the lure of playing on proved too great.[804]

Nash was a frontrunner for the Swans' captaincy, as was Brighton Diggins, the champion half-forward and loyal deputy to departing captain-coach Jack Bisset. Diggins, who had also applied for the coaching position, believed he was on a long-standing promise that he'd be made captain once Bisset retired.[805] When Cazaly and the committee chose Nash instead, Diggins resigned as vice-captain and then walked out of the club after the committee dropped him for the opening match.[806] There was now a distinct air of uncertainty about South's prospects, as the team continued pre-season training and Cazaly busied himself trialling ruck replacements for the departed Bisset and Diggins.

South Melbourne began the season with a 70-point thrashing by Carlton at Princes Park—their biggest defeat in five years—followed by a 55-point home loss to Collingwood. It was a disastrous start, best summed up by a newspaper cartoon showing a trio of doctors examining a bedridden swan and diagnosing "internal trouble".[807]

The Sporting Globe, 5 May, 1937.

Rumours soon began circulating that Cazaly was willing to come out of playing retirement to provide a steadying role on the field. Cazaly had foreseen this possibility at the start of the season, although under his scenario injuries rather than poor form would have sparked his return.[808] For several weeks he did nothing to dispel talk of a playing comeback, remarking that "if a settling influence is felt by the committee to be necessary, I may be useful there."[809]

There is little doubt Cazaly could have proven "useful" on the field. Journalist Percy Millard went to watch South Melbourne train around this time and was amazed by what he saw:

> Here was a man, past 43, and with something like a quarter of a century of strenuous football behind him, marking, kicking and dodging in the manner of a class footballer in his prime. It was astounding. His long-running left foot drop kicks for goal were accuracy itself, finding the target nearly every time. His marking bore the unmistakable imprint of a champion. His long, baulking turn was a masterpiece of strategy. In short, 'Cazzer', despite his age, looked what he undoubtedly still is—a polished footballer … Should South find it necessary to play him later, it is a safe bet that he would more than hold his own on the field, especially in a forward pocket.[810]

Talk of Cazaly's return grew louder when he sought a transfer from his previous Victorian club Preston—the necessary first step in applying for a playing permit—but eventually South's officials put an end to the comeback speculation.

Cazaly found a playing outlet of sorts when he captained a South Melbourne past players' team in a charity match against a crop of current players led by Laurie Nash. Sadly, there was no reunion of South's famous ruck trio: Fred Fleiter was absent and Mark Tandy was taking part in a stay-in strike at the Gas Works. Instead, Cazaly partnered 'Butch' Matthews and Bill Condon in the ruck and kicked two goals as he led his veterans to an entertaining nine-point win.[811]

Cazaly teamed up with his friend Hec de Lacy during the winter to write a series of football reminiscences for *The Sporting Globe*. Over several weeks, he wrote about his early influences, memorable games he had been involved

in and the players he most admired. He concluded the series with a list of practical tips for junior players.⁸¹²

Two photos accompanying one of Cazaly's articles provide glimpses into his sometimes unorthodox training techniques. In the first, he is shown kicking a football into a bed sheet draped over a wire, a drill he'd designed to help players improve their kicking accuracy while on the run.

In the second, he holds a long fishing pole with a football suspended from it. Half-back Jim Cleary is shown leaping for the ball from the side while Cazaly drifts the ball away from him. It was a technique he often used to show players how to "balance and float in the air."⁸¹³

During 1937, Cazaly and his family were renting a brick villa in Page Street, Middle Park, a short distance in the literal sense but figuratively a long way from the pokey houses and co-joined terraces Roy had grown up in. Their home was close to the South Melbourne ground and just a few blocks from Port Phillip Bay. World billiard champion Walter Lindrum lived across the street.⁸¹⁴ Pat Cazaly later recalled it being a busy time:

> Our house was always full of footballers. You know, all these big tall men coming in. They'd be there every night during the week, and then on Sundays; it was always full, and my mother would make all these salads.⁸¹⁵

One of the frequent visitors was ruckman Wilbur Harris, who one day presented Pat with a puppy he had concealed in his coat pocket.⁸¹⁶ She also remembered her parents giving Harris a heat treatment at their home:

> They had a tin baby bath, and they'd fill it with boiling water and put towels in it. And Mum would get one end [of a towel] and Dad the other, and Dad would wring one way and Mum would wring the other. And when they got all the water out, the towel would go straight on to where the injury was. In those days, that was how the footballers got heat on to their injuries.⁸¹⁷

During this period Roy and his brother George were both working for Johns and Waygood, a long-established engineering firm based at City Road in South Melbourne.[818] It was a secure time to be working for the company as the construction industry emerged from the worst of the Depression. Annual earnings had more than doubled between 1934 and 1937 and the company employed over 300 men manufacturing everything from maintenance lifts and roof trusses to oil storage tanks and radio transmitter masts.[819]

The Swans remained winless until round six, when they defeated lowly Hawthorn by three points. Contributing to their woes, champion full-forward Bob Pratt was beset by ankle problems and played just six games for the season. To add insult to existing injury, Pratt then asked for a clearance to Carlton, which had offered to find him work and pay him while he stood out of football. South refused his request point blank but Austin Robertson was a high-profile departure, reluctantly cleared by the club after he received a lucrative offer to play and work in Perth.[820]

By June, the writing was on the wall. Conceding their team had little hope of making the finals the committee announced it would focus on "team building", under which "young, promising players" would be included in the side for the remainder of the season:

> Roy Cazaly, who is under contract for three years, is to remain as non-playing coach, and over that period it is to be his task to build up a powerful side along the lines of the present Melbourne eighteen. It took the latter side five years to reach its present standard, and the Southerners are confident that they can equal that performance in less than three years.[821]

In essence, the committee were endorsing a methodical rebuilding strategy which Cazaly had practised at several of his previous clubs. Of the 10 players who made their senior debut during 1937, eight did so after round four.[822]

As so often happened under Cazaly's coaching, his changes began to bear fruit. Roy Moore, who took over from the injured Pratt at full-forward, proved a revelation, kicking 31 goals in seven matches before having to quit

after Archie Crofts suddenly and inexplicably appointed him manager of his Bendigo store.[823] Wins against North Melbourne, Footscray, St Kilda and Carlton revived hopes of a possible finals berth before injuries, form slumps and further retirements—including veteran fullback and dual best-and-fairest winner Ron Hillis—took their toll.

South Melbourne lost five of their last six games to finish the season in ninth place: the biggest fall from grace by a previous year's Grand Finalist since the advent of the 12-team competition in 1925. It had been, said 'Wingster' of South Melbourne's *The Record*, a fatal combination of "departures, domestic differences, retirements and injuries" which had brought about the Swans' calamitous situation.[824]

Amid the recriminations, South Melbourne's committee came under fire for allowing Bisset and Diggins to leave the club and for appointing Nash as captain, an inexperienced leader who had been unable to make the on-field adjustments required when match circumstances changed. Archie Crofts stepped down as president, members voted out the vice-president who had been chair of selectors, and the club was left with only a small operating profit after plummeting gate receipts wreaked havoc on its finances.[825] To make matters worse, Laurie Nash announced that South Melbourne had been unable to find him secure work and he would seek a clearance to St Kilda, who assured him they could.

Over the summer, Cazaly played cricket for Johns and Waygood in the B Grade of the Mercantile Association, which included many of Melbourne's industrial and engineering firms. In mid-November he took eight wickets for 53 against the Vacuum Oil Company. The following month he scored 86 not out and took five wickets for 20 against the foundry workers from John Danks and Son.[826] The cricket may have provided a welcome respite as he pondered what to do next with his South Melbourne charges.

21

THE LEGION OF THE LOST

SOUTH MELBOURNE, 1938-39

Several challenges arose from an unexpected quarter during the off-season after the VFA left the Australian National Football Council (ANFC) and instituted two changes which had an immediate impact on its fractious relationship with the VFL. Combined, they posed the greatest threat to the League's dominance of the code in Melbourne since the bitter split of 1896.

The first change was the VFA's legalisation of the two-handed throw, or 'throw pass'. Under a new rule, players were allowed to throw the ball to a teammate, provided they used both hands and kept their arms below shoulder height during the action. Supporters of the change argued it would speed up the game, eliminate scrambling play and end debate about how umpires should interpret the 'handball', 'holding the man' and 'holding the ball' rules. It's equally vocal critics believed it would alter the game beyond all recognition. Legalising the throw, they warned, would ultimately lead to the end of kicking and, therefore, marking.

Despite these dire predictions the Association's new rule was eagerly endorsed by a coalition of journalists, players, coaches and country leagues. Cazaly was one of its strongest advocates, arguing it would result in a faster, more open and hence more attractive style of play:

> The throw is an ideal rule. It makes men play the type of game that a coach

is always striving for. It makes them play on, opening out the game as they race on taking the pass that comes naturally with the throw.[827]

The Association's bold new rule caught the VFL flat-footed. The ANFC had previously flirted with the throw-pass idea and the South Australian Football League had even campaigned for its national introduction a decade earlier; now spectators had an opportunity to see it in action and make their own judgment.[828] The public voted with their feet. Numbers attending Association games surged during the next two seasons, culminating in a crowd of 47,000 for the 1939 VFA Grand Final between Williamstown and Brunswick.[829]

The second far-reaching decision made by the VFA was the unilateral scrapping of its long-standing agreement with the VFL requiring players to gain a formal clearance before transferring between League and Association clubs. VFA players had been crossing to the League for years but now any Association club with the resources could tempt a League player to defect without a clearance. Crucially, there was no equivalent of the VFL's Coulter Law in the VFA to constrain the amount their clubs could offer players.

A few Association players now crossed to the League but more high-profile players eventually went the other way, including Collingwood's Ron Todd and Brownlow medallist Des Fothergill.[830] Bob Pratt later transferred to Coburg but the first and most prominent League player targeted by the Association clubs was South Melbourne's captain Laurie Nash.

Nash's earlier plan to transfer to St Kilda had fallen through but he prevaricated about his future during the 1938 pre-season while the Swans made further attempts to find him work. Just when it seemed they had done enough to retain him Nash announced he was joining VFA club Camberwell, which had offered him £8 a match, a job on the local council and £3 a week to play for the local cricket club.[831] *The Record*'s front page headline that week read: "Nash Hurls Bomb at South". It was a body blow to the Swans' season hopes.[832]

Once they had recovered from the shock, South's officials sought to put on a brave face on the situation. Herbie Matthews and Bob Pratt were appointed as new captain and vice-captain. Cazaly spoke of his team

being "rich in young players" and said he was more optimistic about their prospects than he'd been at the start of the previous season. Several players, notably George Bryce, Jack Hacker and Reg Humphries, were said to be improving, and Roy Moore agreed to return after Cazaly and club secretary Dick Mullally visited him in Bendigo and Archie Crofts agreed to transfer him back to his South Melbourne store.[833]

Cazaly gave a blackboard lecture to South's juniors early in the season in which he outlined the finer points of the game, explained various plays and reviewed the strengths and weaknesses of each player, offering constructive advice to each in turn. The local paper reported that:

> The moves and counter moves on the field were portrayed on the blackboard for over an hour. The placing of the successful Cazaly-Fleiter-Tandy ruck was also demonstrated, and the round of applause at the conclusion evidenced the keen interest with which the lads had followed the workings of that famous Southern trio.[834]

Any South Melbourne supporters hoping for a return to those heady days were soon sorely disappointed. After a 29-point win over Footscray in round one, the club lost 16 of their next 17 games, a horrendous sequence alleviated only by a narrow win against Melbourne late in the season. Bad luck certainly played its part after Matthews and Pratt both suffered early injuries. Matthews played only four games for the year and Pratt's ongoing ankle woes restricted him to just seven late in the season. Their leadership roles were assumed by Len Thomas and Jack Graham.

The Swans' injuries and poor form led to renewed calls from despairing supporters for Cazaly to take the field. Writing to South Melbourne's *The*

Record on behalf of "umpteen" others, 'Unbiased' declared "I would wish some of our geese to be swans, and our coach a magician, but as neither are possible, the next best thing is to include him in our future experiments." Another correspondent described the team as "the legion of the lost" while 'Old Southerner' argued that Cazaly's presence would provide much-needed on-field leadership and attract more supporters through the gates:

> The main argument used by critics against 'Caza' returning to the game is that "the young players would 'kill' him". It must be remembered that Roy Cazaly is employed at manual labour. His muscles are hard, and he carries no superfluous flesh. As for the 'killing', personally I would not like to be on the receiving end of 'Caza's' return gifts.[835]

South Melbourne's committee eventually went public to scotch rumours that it was considering playing its coach. "Cazaly is 46," said one official, "and it is ridiculous to expect a man of that age, notwithstanding his great achievements in the past, to stage a comeback." The unnamed official went on to state that "I know Roy does not want to play again, but he is being pushed into it from another source."[836]

The remarks stung Cazaly. During a football lecture to the Christian Brothers' Past Pupils three days later he said he felt "wonderfully fit" and could achieve good results if he played again. He went even further during an interview with the *South Melbourne Record*, declaring:

> I am willing to stake my reputation on a playing comeback. Those who have relegated themselves to the armchair stage would perhaps scarcely realise how one can keep active, mentally and physically, and be keen to play—keen to fight on ... I have studied the game closely since coaching South, and feel sure I would, at least, not disgrace myself ... Those who criticise must remember I go through a course of preparation to keep fit before the season commences, so that I may be able to demonstrate the various moves on the field. The club is in such a position now that I feel I could mould the side together, if only for a game or two ... and even though I might not be playing the same as of yore, it would have a steadying effect. So, it is up to the committee. I am only the coach. I leave it to their judgment as to whether they think it a wise move, or otherwise.[837]

Cazaly must have known South's committee were unlikely to change their position: it is therefore difficult to interpret his comments as anything other than a calculated rebuke. In the midst of this public spat came news that South's leading ruckman Jack Graham had initially accepted, then turned down, a lucrative offer to transfer to Camberwell without a clearance.⁸³⁸ It was a narrow escape, but further proof—if any was needed—that the Swans had become fatally distracted by their own internal machinations.

Cazaly was involved in two workplace accidents at Johns and Waygood during the winter. In the first, a falling steel girder, which might easily have crushed his foot grazed his boot, leaving him bruised and hobbling. A few days later part of a metal rivet lodged in the corner of his eye, narrowly missing the pupil. The near-misses were probably the only pieces of luck to go his way all year.⁸³⁹

Late in the season, Cazaly met with South's committee and asked them to endorse changes to his coaching regime. Under the new arrangements, captain Herbie Matthews would train the Seniors under Cazaly's guidance while he would focus on correcting the faults of existing players, attend the Seconds' matches to observe their progress and help identify potential recruits.⁸⁴⁰ The committee agreed to the changes but they came too late to prevent a final-round loss to Geelong.

South Melbourne's supporters had stayed away in droves during the season. Gate receipts plummeted, revenue from members' tickets fell by £500 and the club lost money on every match.⁸⁴¹ The club's financial position must have worried the officials but Cazaly would have been more exasperated by his failure to instil the precise teamwork he had demanded of his players when he had taken on the coaching role. In one of his *Sporting Globe* columns he had written that "the potentialities of Laurie Nash, Bob Pratt and Austin Robertson could have been bewildering, but for some reason they never got down to that perfect team work that makes the deadly attack."⁸⁴² But this observation was mild compared with the frank criticism he later levelled at South's committee:

> If players think out their moves then it naturally follows that you have the whole side playing in unison with every player backing up each other. This is what I wanted at South Melbourne, but the committee did not back me and in turn the players acted otherwise. They attended training but that was as far as it went. We had 18 players with little sense of unity. So South stayed at the bottom.[843]

It had been a bitterly disappointing season, made worse by the fact that Brighton Diggins, who had walked out on the club in frustration the previous year, led Carlton to the VFL premiership in just his first season as captain-coach.

Cazaly had a year left on his contract but it was clear that further changes were required to the Swans' coaching arrangements. Prior to the 1939 season, the committee announced that captain Herbie Matthews would take full responsibility for the Seniors' training while Cazaly would focus on developing the juniors and recruits. In a formalisation of the measures introduced late the previous season, Matthews took charge of the Seniors on Tuesday and Thursday nights while Cazaly supervised the Seconds and recruits on Mondays and Wednesdays. To what extent Cazaly was consulted about the new arrangements is unclear, but it is noteworthy that the committee felt the need to confirm them with him in a formal letter.[844]

Freed from the responsibilities of coaching the Seniors, Cazaly set out to impart what knowledge he could to South's juniors. In mid-May, and after seeking formal selection through the match committee, he took the field to lead the Seconds in a game against Richmond. His friend Hec de Lacy was there to observe the result:

> 'Cazzer' went on to the field as playing coach, the idea being to direct and stimulate the youngsters by his presence. Starting modestly in a forward pocket, 'Cazzer' was soon in the ruck, stimulating the defence, or driving the ball forward with beautiful passes. Backing up their coach, South were a great little fighting side. At half-time, using a blackboard, Roy gave the finest

football lesson that it has been my privilege to listen to. It was practical, sound and sufficiently personal to impress his colts, not with ideas of blood and thunder, but with sound football fundamentals.[845]

Cazaly played in the Seconds for the rest of the season, sometimes at half-forward or a forward pocket but more often in the ruck.

Roy jnr, now 19, also played a number of games for the Seconds after transferring from local junior side South Melbourne United.[846] He had a smaller physique than his father, standing just 5 foot 6½ inches and weighing 10½ stone. He was a skilful player but he felt the public pressure of being Cazaly's only son, compounded by the fact that he shared his first name. He subsequently revealed that when his father was playing at South Melbourne he used to "fight his way to school and fight his way home."[847] In later years he confided to a journalist that it had been difficult "growing up the son of a legend [because] you try too hard".

> It would have been great if I was nearly as good as Dad, but I never got close. I wasn't big enough and, anyway, any dreams I had of being a big-time VFL footballer ended when war was declared.[848]

During 1939 Roy jnr was working at the Dunlop Rubber factory, just as his father had three decades earlier. It was here that he met his future wife Kathleen Brady, the daughter of a fireman who lived in Beach Street, Port Melbourne. Emily Davies, a family friend, worked alongside Roy and Kathleen making bicycle tyres on the factory's third floor. Emily could still recall the pungent smell of molten rubber more than 70 years later.[849]

On June 24, father and son played together for the first time in a match against Geelong. Roy jnr started in the backline while his father played up forward. The younger Roy was soon shifted to the half-forward line, where he played several more games alongside his father.[850] The presence of both men on the field sparked nostalgia among spectators and prompted *The Argus*' Percy Taylor to comment that "the day may not be far ahead when South Melbourne supporters will be shouting, 'Up there Cazaly, junior'."[851]

At the end of July Cazaly snr joined his former St Kilda teammates Dave McNamara, Jack James, Harry Lever and Roy Bence in a veterans' charity game against former Fitzroy players. He played in the ruck and scored a goal from a place kick as Fitzroy won an entertaining match by 12 points.[852]

Cazaly snr and jnr played a memorable game together in mid-August, the younger Roy kicking one goal and his father three as South Melbourne's Seconds defeated ladder leaders Footscray by 37 points.[853] Germany invaded Poland two weeks later and Britain and her allies declared war on Germany. Roy jnr, who was a member of the Naval Reserve, was called up into the Navy. Kath and his family would scarcely see him for the next six years.

Cazaly's three-year contract with South Melbourne expired at the end of 1939 and the following season found him without a playing or coaching position for the first time in his career. Despite this he remained outwardly optimistic, confidently declaring—like Mr Micawber in *David Copperfield*—that "something will turn up".[854]

22

AMONG THE WOWSERS

CAMBERWELL, 1941

Camberwell was never one of the VFA's powerhouse sides. Throughout the team's history its successes were few and far between and its troughs were long and deep.⁸⁵⁵

Part of the reason for this may be that the club had emerged from one of Melbourne's more genteel areas, where football passions were not as easily stirred as they were in the inner suburbs. Geographically, Camberwell was only six miles from the centre of Melbourne but culturally it was a world away from Cazaly's working-class roots. Compared to South Melbourne, Camberwell had fewer Catholics, more Presbyterians, fewer labourers and more small businesses. It also had a reputation for 'wowserism': in 1920 residents voted to prohibit alcohol sales within its boundaries.⁸⁵⁶

Like other localities in Melbourne's middle-suburban ring, Camberwell's population was boosted after World War I by new housing subdivisions, the extension of rail and tram networks, and a rapid rise in car ownership. The number of houses within the city doubled between 1919 and 1933 and a 'Souvenir of Camberwell' promotional booklet published that year boasted of tree-lined streets, spacious parks, fine churches and excellent schools.⁸⁵⁷

Comedian and satirist Barry Humphries was a young boy growing up just a few streets from the Camberwell Sports Ground when Cazaly arrived in 1941.⁸⁵⁸ Humphries' later poem 'An Ode to the City of Camberwell' captures much of the area's solid, respectable character:

Oh Camberwell! Your parks, your shops,
War Savings Streets and tramway stops;
Your famous Junction with its web
Of wires above; below the ebb
And flow of busy shopping mothers;
Braithwaite the Chemist, Adair Brothers ...⁸⁵⁹

Conservative leader Robert Menzies' famous wartime speech appealing to the "forgotten people" of Australia's middle class would have resonated with many Camberwell residents.⁸⁶⁰

The bitter rivalry between the VFL and VFA was still simmering in 1941. The 'throw pass' remained legal in the Association and a number of players lured from the League were bringing in large crowds, including Bob Pratt at Coburg and Ron Todd and Harry 'Soapy' Vallence at Williamstown.

Camberwell's president Dr Frank Hartnett had been instrumental in recruiting Laurie Nash from South Melbourne in 1938. Other League players who subsequently crossed to Camberwell without a clearance included South's Terry Brain, Hawthorn's Norm Hillard, Melbourne ruckman Harry Harley and Richmond follower Reg 'Hawk Eye' Henderson, who in working life was a detective famous for his photographic memory of suspects' faces.⁸⁶¹

Hartnett and most of his League recruits had departed by the time Cazaly came to Camberwell but Nash and Henderson were still there. Another making his mark was winger Reg Horkings, who had won Camberwell's best and fairest in 1940. The club finished eighth that year and Horkings later explained it had sought out Cazaly in the hope he could revitalise them with his ideas and methods.⁸⁶² Pre-season training began in late March with Cazaly and new president Gil Hendrie stressing the importance of teamwork rather than individual brilliance.

The impact of the war could be seen everywhere. A number of Camberwell's regular players were away in army camps, their places filled by local juniors.[863] Seven thousand local men enlisted during the conflict and Camberwell's citizens pledged more money to one war loan appeal than any other Australian municipality.[864] There was disagreement within the community over whether organised football should continue but discussions were tempered during the war's early days by a cautious pragmatism. The *Sporting Globe*'s Hec de Lacy probably encapsulated the feelings of most when he wrote:

> In proper doses football can be a great national tonic ... But let us not delude ourselves. Let us keep our sense of proportion. In the wider scope of man's planning the winning of the 1941 premiership doesn't matter two hoots. As soon as football interferes with our war efforts, football must be cut out of our curriculum.[865]

Cazaly and his family had been living in Bridport Street during his final year at South Melbourne but by 1941 they were renting a house in Bethela Street, Burwood, a mile and a half from the Camberwell Sports Ground. The brick and stucco home has since been renovated, but at the time it was a typical five-room suburban bungalow.[866] Roy jnr was away at the war. Dorrie was a clerk, Lena was employed by the Moran and Cato's grocery store chain, Pat worked in an office at Myer's and Joan, the youngest at 15, was still at school.[867]

Aggie's niece Edie Harrison came to live with the Cazalys for two years around this time. Eleven-year-old Edie had grown up in working-class Richmond and the Cazaly home in Burwood seemed a mansion by comparison. Edie, who dreamt of being an actress, loved dressing up in Aggie's furs and staging her own musical shows. She got on well with her cousins, later describing them in succinct terms:

> Dorothy was the boss, Lena was the lady, Pat was just beautiful and Joan was the tomboy.[868]

Aggie and Roy treated Edie as another daughter. More than six decades later her fondest memories were of helping Roy walk his greyhounds in a nearby park, and of him taking her to see a Betty Grable musical at Hartwell's Regal Cinema:

> I was allowed to go on a Saturday night, but not through the week because that was school and because he was busy down at training ... [He took me] because it was a musical and he knew I would like it. And he'd say 'This is for you, because you have been very good'.⁸⁶⁹

Camberwell started the season poorly, registering just one win from their first five matches. Laurie Nash was their one bright hope at centre half-forward and his early sequence of goals included hauls of four, nine, six and eight.⁸⁷⁰ Cazaly faced a situation similar to that at Preston a decade earlier and he responded the same way: by promoting local juniors. Within a few weeks, all but three of the 32 players on Camberwell's list were locals and only eight were aged over 24.⁸⁷¹

Cazaly was single-minded in his expectations. Reg Horkings later recalled that he "spoke to each and every player before the game and gave them specific instructions for the day, a one-on-one approach which proved successful". The coach was very clear about how his players should approach their task. According to Horkings:

> Cazaly played the game very tough and expected his players to do the same. If you hesitated to go through hard then you weren't picked in the side.⁸⁷²

Cazaly's skills as a masseur also came in handy. As Laurie Peters later recalled:

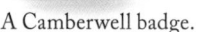

> He knew all about your pressure points; you wouldn't get a pro any better. I got injured one day at Camberwell and got hit on the neck near the shoulder. I was in tears and he said "There's a nerve there and you've been hit on that". He massaged it for a while and he said "You'll come good", and I did.⁸⁷³

A Camberwell badge.

Cazaly's positional moves began to pay dividends on the field. Camberwell lost their round-six game against Preston—despite another eight-goal haul from Nash—but they were beginning to play with better system and teamwork. The loss of experienced defender Jack Seelenmeyer, who had enlisted in the RAAF, came as a blow but the team was boosted by the mid-season transfer of veteran centre Stan Spinks from Hawthorn.[874] By round 14 Camberwell had won seven games in a row and climbed from 10th place into sixth. Asked about the club's turnaround in fortunes, Cazaly said the committee had given him free reign with the side and his young players were learning the value of strategic, coordinated play.[875]

Cazaly was confident his team would make the finals, but they lost three of their next five games to slip back to seventh. Despite this, the coach remained optimistic about the club's future prospects, declaring that:

> Camberwell will improve, which should be all to the good for 1942. We have several fine young players who should go far in the game. Give me the young local boy, for he is keen on the district and his club. He is always out to win.[876]

Realising Camberwell had missed their finals chance, Cazaly decided to take the field for the last two games of the season. He was now 48. Thirty years had passed since his first game with St Kilda and he now became one of the oldest, if not *the* oldest, to ever play in the VFA.[877]

Against Northcote in round 19 Cazaly moved Laurie Nash to full-forward and placed himself at centre half-forward. It was the first time the two had played a match together since City in 1930. Les Carbarns, a former teammate of Cazaly's at St Kilda, went to report on the game for *The Sporting Globe*.

> I had a word with Roy before the match and he told me why he was in action again. With Camberwell unable to make the four, he took it as a splendid opportunity to obtain first-hand knowledge of his team on the field. He has his own idea on non-stop play and, with Camberwell liking the open spaces, wanted to show them how to use those spaces. Roy wisely played quietly at half-forward with an occasional drop into the ruck for a few minutes, to spell Henderson. Some of his hit-outs distinctly showed signs of his old skill.[878]

Nash scored 13 goals in the victory over Northcote and went one better the following week as Camberwell ended their season with a seven-goal win against Sandringham.[879] Camberwell had won 12 of their 20 games and they finished in seventh place, two wins and several percentage points outside the final four. Nash polled fifth in the Recorder Cup, the trophy for the VFA's best-and-fairest player. His phenomenal goalkicking had kept Camberwell competitive in many games but his season tally of 141 goals was upstaged by Bob Pratt, who kicked 183 for Coburg.[880]

Cazaly's late season optimism and his decision to play in Camberwell's last two games suggested he was planning to stay at the club. Once again, however, he had been hedging his bets: within weeks the neighbouring Hawthorn Football Club announced his appointment as their non-playing coach for the 1942 VFL season.[881]

23

MODEST EXPECTATIONS

HAWTHORN, 1942

The circumstances surrounding Cazaly's appointment at Hawthorn were the exact opposite to those which had led to his previous VFL stint five years earlier. At South Melbourne, there had been high hopes that Cazaly would give the team the edge they needed to return to premiership glory; at Hawthorn the expectations were much more modest.

Hawthorn had joined the VFL almost by accident. Formed as a junior side in 1902 and invited into the VFA in 1914, the team's subsequent form was indifferent at best and it reached the finals just once, in 1923.[882] It was therefore a surprise inclusion when the VFL decided to expand their competition from nine clubs to 12 before the start of the 1925 season. In reality, the League's hard-headed officials were prepared to overlook the club's lacklustre record in order to secure a new team from Melbourne's rapidly growing eastern suburbs.

The 'Mayblooms'—or the 'Mustard Pots', as they were briefly known during the 1930s—did little to repay the League's faith. From 1925 until 1941 they finished last or second-last 10 times, and never higher than eighth. Tired of the club's 'easybeats' tag, president Dr Jacob Jona began his 1941 report to Hawthorn's members in blunt terms:

> [Y]our committee is greatly disappointed with the performance of the team, winning only three matches for the year. This state of affairs cannot be allowed

to continue; efforts must be made to strengthen the weak positions in the field and it is hoped that the team will meet with greater success in 1942.[883]

Hawthorn had already begun to ring the changes by the time Jona presented his report. Bert Mills, who had been captain and coach the previous two seasons, announced he would not be an applicant for either post, although he wished to continue as a player. A sub-committee charged with finding a new coach recommended Cazaly's appointment, subject to his appearance before the general committee and the agreement of financial terms.[884]

Cazaly met the committee, assuring them that "he would, with the cooperation and support of the committee, improve the premiership position of the club". After Cazaly left the room, Jona and secretary Vic Hocking reported that he had agreed to their offer of £4/10 a week, commencing from the first night of training. Jona invited Cazaly back to the meeting, congratulated him on his appointment and wished him every success. The new coach replied with an assurance that he would "do his utmost to bring the Brown and Gold further up the premiership ladder".[885]

Cazaly busied himself with recruitment strategies throughout November. At a committee meeting held on Remembrance Day he spoke of the need to find new players "at the earliest opportunity" and it was agreed that the match committee should meet to discuss tactics.[886] At the club's annual meeting, Jona spoke of his optimism and Cazaly presented the premiership trophies won by Auburn, the club's third 18 in the Melbourne Boys League. Jona, Hocking and Cazaly had reason to look forward to 1942 with enthusiasm.[887]

But storm clouds unrelated to football were gathering in the north. For the first two years of the war, Australia's military focus had been on its troops fighting in Africa and the Middle East. This suddenly changed in December 1941, when Japan's attack on Pearl Harbour brought hostilities to the Pacific and catapulted the United States into the conflict. The fall of Singapore and the bombing of Darwin in February 1942 had a deep psychological impact on the Australian people. As the battle for the Pacific intensified, football clubs and the wider public pondered the future of organised football under the shadow of a possible Japanese invasion of Australia.

A similar debate to that which had occurred during World War I now played out. Some demanded that organised sport be suspended in the cause of the greater war effort.[888] Others believed it boosted public morale and provided a welcome respite for the young, the elderly and those working in essential industries. Labor Prime Minister John Curtin, who had played for Brunswick in the VFA before World War I, favoured sport's continuation, provided it wasn't at the expense of the overall war effort:

> War must come before all other considerations and recreation must be for the purpose of promoting fitness for work. We have to score points against the Japs with a gun, and all our activities—and these include sport—must have that as our objective.[889]

Politicians left the final decision to local leagues and a number voted to go into recess, replaced for the duration by armed service or junior competitions. Jacob Jona was also senior vice-president of the VFL and his pragmatic views typified those held by many officials. On one hand, he felt that "young men who are able to play the bigger game should do so in preference to football." On the other, he believed that if the public wanted football and the government allowed it, it was the duty of clubs to provide it.[890] The Hawthorn committee considered the vexed issue at its first meeting for 1942, resolving that the competition should continue "provided it does not interfere with the national war effort."[891]

But beyond this dilemma, the clubs had serious logistical issues to consider. The military had resumed a number of sports grounds for army camps, and several clubs were forced to find alternative training and playing venues, including Melbourne (who relocated to Punt Road), St Kilda (Toorak Park), South Melbourne (Princes Park) and Footscray (Yarraville Oval). There was also the question of finding sufficient players. While some clubs gained recruits from the ranks of disbanded junior teams, those commencing pre-season training found their numbers depleted by military enlistments. Finally, the strict petrol rationing, which severely limited public travel, forced Geelong to go into recess.[892]

For a time it seemed these factors might all conspire to prevent the competition from continuing. In late March, the League wrote to the remaining 11 clubs asking if they wished to play on. Hawthorn's committee again debated the issue and even flirted with a motion—subsequently defeated—to merge with Melbourne.[893] Hawthorn, Melbourne and Collingwood eventually voted not to continue, although they agreed to abide by a majority verdict. When the other eight clubs voted to continue, the League drew up a fixture to begin on 9 May. Geelong's absence meant one club had a bye each week.

Cazaly was interviewed by his friend Hec de Lacy prior to the start of the 1942 season. The *Sporting Globe* journalist asked his opinion on two rule changes proposed by a retiring League official: introducing unlimited interchanges and allowing non-playing coaches on to the field to direct their players during matches. Cazaly emphatically agreed with both suggestions. Allowing unlimited interchanges, he declared, would avoid situations in which an injured player often stayed on the ground rather than force his team to play a man short:

> No injured man should be asked to carry on. A man who takes a knock hard enough to warrant medical attention should be retired in his own interests for a spell. There is no argument against that. It is just plain common sense.

Cazaly also thought unrestricted interchanges would enable greater tactical decision-making and result in more entertaining games. His only caution was that interchange tactics would have to be devised and overseen by just one person, namely the coach.

Cazaly's support for the idea of allowing non-playing coaches on to the ground during matches underscored the reasoning behind his decision to take the field for Camberwell late in the previous season:

> With a coach out on the ground all the wandering and scrambling will be eliminated. The idea that a coach cannot send out a message to his men is ridiculous. What is he there for, if not to instruct his side? If a non-playing coach were allowed on the ground he could remedy weaknesses and, by instruction, keep men in their correct positions.[894]

Cazaly's comments are instructive because they illustrate several key aspects of his coaching philosophy: his compassion for his players' welfare, his willingness to trial innovative methods to improve the game, and his strong belief that the coach—even a non-playing one—remained the unquestioned leader of his team.

Training at Glenferrie Oval began in mid-April with almost 50 players and recruits turning out for a light session.[895] The previous year's vice-captain Jack Carmody was elected captain and Cazaly's transfer from Camberwell was accepted by the League's permit committee.[896] Regulars at training included Andy Angwin, Jack Burke, Wally Culpitt, Bill Pavey, Phil Ryan and Bobby Williams, while recruits included Frank Curran, Harold Daly, Ron Harris, Jack Mathieson and Jim White.[897] Hawthorn's players were not paid during 1942 and there was no Seconds team.[898]

With the Japanese air force continuing to bomb Darwin, and its army advancing towards New Guinea, fears of enemy attacks were never far away, no matter how remote the possibility. The local council even turned down Hawthorn's request to use floodlights for night training on the grounds that it would be "unwise at the present time".[899]

Cazaly would have been preoccupied by thoughts of his son in the Royal Australian Navy. After serving on the heavy cruiser *HMAS Canberra* during the early months of the war, Able Seaman Cazaly had sailed to London in late 1940 to join the *HMAS Nizam*, a British N-Class destroyer on loan to the Australian Navy. After serving on hazardous escort convoys in the Atlantic and the Mediterranean, he returned to Australia, was posted aboard the destroyer *HMAS Arunta* and saw action in the Coral Sea.[900] In between tours of duty he took advantage of some rare shore leave in April 1942 to marry Kath Brady at St Silas' Anglican Church in Middle Park. Roy was 23; Kath was 21. The bride wore white lace over taffeta; Dorrie and Lena Cazaly were bridesmaids, and Mark Tandy and his wife, Lily, were among the guests.[901]

The League received a boost when the VFA decided to go into recess due to the impact of military enlistments and wartime restrictions.[902] When the Association granted players temporary clearances to cross to League teams a number from Camberwell followed their old coach to Hawthorn, including Bob Austen, George Bennett, Reg Horkings, 'Barney' Jorgensen and Laurie Taylor.[903] The club's biggest recruiting coup, however, occurred mid-season, when rover Tommy Lahiff transferred from South Melbourne. Lahiff had clashed with the Swans' committee over their selection policy and walked out in protest. Famous for speaking his mind, Lahiff provided experience, aggression and more than a touch of larrikinism.[904]

Enlistments, manpower restrictions and other enforced absences presented the coach and selectors with serious logistical challenges in naming a side each week. Eighteen players made their debut during 1942, the most since Hawthorn had joined the VFL in 1925 and a club record that still stands.[905]

Some regulars, such as centre Jim Bohan, worked in essential industries but were usually able to train and play, shift rosters permitting.[906] Laurie Peters worked for the railways and crammed in as much football as he could. He trained at Glenferrie on Tuesday and Thursday nights, played mid-week football on Wednesdays, turned out for Hawthorn on Saturdays and umpired on Sundays.[907]

By contrast, those serving in the armed forces usually had no advance notice of when they may be available. A written invitation to train was often returned with the advice that the player was now stationed elsewhere in Australia or "somewhere abroad". Bert Mills, Hawthorn's previous captain and coach, was away in the Army and played only one game all season. Defender John 'Peter' O'Donohue had grown up across the road from Glenferrie Oval but after joining the Navy he managed to play just two games during 1942. "They were the days where if you came home on leave or your ship was in port and you trained a couple of nights you'd get a game," he later recalled.[908]

Others who had enlisted were stationed closer to home, and Vic Hocking assured them they'd be considered for selection whenever they could obtain leave.⁹⁰⁹ One who usually could was Alec Albiston, the dynamic rover who had won Hawthorn's best-and-fairest award in 1941. Albiston was a Royal Australian Air Force (RAAF) radio mechanic but somehow managed to play 14 games during the season, despite being based 130 miles away at Sale.⁹¹⁰

League crowds were well down on the previous season: attendances at Hawthorn's home games never passed 5000 and averaged just half this number by season's end. Football reporting was noticeably reduced, even in the local papers, which gave more coverage to preparations for possible enemy air raids.⁹¹¹

During the war Cazaly was still working as a mechanic at the heavy engineering firm Johns and Waygood. The company's main workshops in South Melbourne were engaged almost solely on defence contracts, manufacturing wireless radio masts, army equipment, lifts for hospital ships and tools for defence factories. During 1942, a separate plant making mortar shells and bombs employed 400 people working three shifts each day.⁹¹²

According to one later account, the political activist Bertha Walker recruited Cazaly as a company spokesman for the 'Sheepskins for Russia' campaign.⁹¹³ The campaign, also known as the Russian Relief Fund, was established after Germany invaded the Soviet Union in June 1941. Despite initial Federal Government suspicion about its leaders' alleged communist sympathies the appeal gained widespread public support, raising £200,000 in donations over four years.⁹¹⁴

As he had at his previous clubs, Cazaly sought to encourage greater team cohesion off the field. He was invariably the instigator whenever a players' social evening or gala night was proposed, gave blackboard lectures and suggested that those not selected for Hawthorn games play for local clubs in social matches.⁹¹⁵

Despite a 16-point loss to Fitzroy in round seven, former Carlton great Rod McGregor saw signs of greater consistency among a side that the coach was "building from the base". He told *The Sporting Globe*'s readers that:

> The Cazaly touch was apparent in surer and more correct style marking, better co-operation and headwork and the moves in the game that make for united effort by an even distribution of the work involved. The change suggests the right man at the head of affairs—a coach who is not deluded by temporary success, but one whose own career reflects the belief that strategy and skill are essentials in high-grade football.[916]

One eyewitness to Hawthorn's round 10 encounter against South Melbourne was Tasmanian Dick Hemingway, who was on shore leave from the Navy. Writing home to his family, he told them that:

> I really went to see Roy Cazaly, who coached Hawthorn. He was just the same old "Cazza", living every kick of the game.[917]

It was not a memorable year for the club whose only real highlight came in round five when it defeated Collingwood at home by eight points. It was Hawthorn's first victory over the Magpies in 30 attempts and the players held a dinner the following week to celebrate.[918] But the club's most poignant story of 1942 was that of half-back Alex Nash. Home on leave from the RAAF, Nash was named as 19th man for Hawthorn's last match of the season, his only senior game with the club. Eighteen months later he was killed in a Beaufort bomber over New Guinea, aged just 21.[919]

Hawthorn's pre-season optimism had proven to be misplaced. The club lost all but one of their 15 games—the historic victory over Collingwood—and finished last. Despite this, Hawthorn's outgoing committee recommended Cazaly's reappointment, a proposal unanimously adopted by the new committee just before Christmas.[920]

The season's rigours had taken their toll on Cazaly's health. After a winter bout of flu he was absent from several committee meetings late in the year and did not attend the club's annual meeting in December. Secretary Hocking called at his home several times to see him without success and a letter he sent him confirming his reappointment as coach went unacknowledged.[921] Cazaly subsequently apologised for his absences, which he attributed to his recurring illness. He told the committee he was now "well on the road to recovery" and looking forward to a more successful season in 1943.[922] On this occasion his optimism was to prove well-founded.

24

FROM MAYBLOOMS TO HAWKS

HAWTHORN, 1943

Despite the continuing war the League agreed to carry on in 1943. Geelong remained in recess so it was decided the bottom side would drop out after round 11 to ensure an equal number of byes.[923]

Training at Glenferrie Oval began on 23 March and winger Bobby Williams was elected captain in place of Jack Carmody. Policeman Jack O'Keefe—a six-foot champion boxer and triple premiership player—brought some much-needed experience to the ruck when he transferred from Melbourne.[924] There were fewer new players than the previous season, but military enlistments and essential service commitments again took their toll on Hawthorn's ranks. Defender Peter O'Donohue was still serving with the Navy and managed just two games for the year while ever-reliable rover Alec Albiston was unavailable as the RAAF had transferred him to Darwin.

Others trained and played when they could. Winger and occasional half-forward Ken Feltscheer worked for the railways. "In those days we worked Saturday mornings, which meant that it became quite a frenzied time to have your lunch and then get to the ground," he later recalled.[925] Forward Alan Saker, a recruit from Williamstown, was an engineer at the Port Melbourne factory building Wirraway engines for the RAAF. His shift roster meant he could only train occasionally and he played just two games for the season.[926]

Cazaly had turned 50 in January, but he still led from the front during the team's training sessions. Feltscheer vividly remembered the coach's displays of fitness almost seven decades later:

> He was a magician. When you were training he would pick out a player and challenge them to lay a finger on him. It didn't matter how fast you were, he was able to wrong foot you and of course he was no longer a young man. He was very light on his feet and very evasive.[927]

Cazaly hadn't lost his knack of being able to inspire his players. According to O'Donohue:

> Roy was a great man to get to know and a man you had a lot of respect for. He never ranted and raved. When he spoke you were compelled to listen because what he was saying was in your best interest and the club's best interest too.[928]

Fellow defender Laurie Peters simply recalled that "Cazza was a damn good coach, one of the best I ever played under".[929]

Several of Cazaly's methods were somewhat unorthodox. Players interviewed for Hawthorn's official history told how he would put up posters in the rooms with motivational sayings such as "Brain beats brawn" and "The power of individual thought brings collective action". Captain Bobby Williams described Cazaly as someone who thought and acted differently to other coaches:

> He'd have you jumping for a ball on a stick, then he'd draw lines for the forwards, showing them by diagram how to attack the goals. He tried to teach us how to inhale and exhale. Really, he was before his time. He wanted to be a full-time coach, and he had the attitudes of a full-time coach, long before there was any such thing in football.[930]

Cazaly was also keen to try out innovations during games. In the days before runners could take the coach's messages to players, he would stand on the sidelines and shout instructions. Tom Lahiff later wrote that he used his booming voice to good effect:

> You had no trouble in picking up what he said—and neither did the spectators. Your eyes would really burn when he was paying out on you for something you had done wrong.[931]

During one game, Laurie Taylor was felled by a shirtfront from Richmond's captain Jack Dyer, only to hear Cazaly yelling at him to "Get up! Don't let them know they hurt you!"[932]

Cazaly's most enduring contribution to the Hawthorn Football Club came soon after the start of the 1943 season. The coach had been annoyed for some time by the team's 'Mayblooms' nickname. According to Andy Angwin:

> He was always crook on it. He kept saying we had to drop it, that it was too sissy, that it sounded as if we were a mob of girls. He felt it sometimes meant we were beaten before we went out.[933]

Cazaly decided to do something about the team's uninspiring tag. His daughter Pat was fond of relating what happened next:

> Dad came home one night and we were all sitting around the dinner table. He said 'You know, "Mayblooms", that's a sissy name for men' and he said 'Any ideas, girls?' We were going around the table saying different names and it came to my turn and I said 'Well, Hawthorn Dad, why not [the] Hawks?' He said 'That's not a bad idea. I'll put it to them'.[934]

It is a neat explanation, but it is not the only one that has been advanced. Some of the players later said the suggestion came from secretary Vic Hocking, who was inspired by his home town of Eaglehawk near Bendigo.[935] A third version says the name was decided upon at a players' meeting, but this conflicts with a later account from Laurie Peters, who recalled:

> It was one Thursday night and Cazaly and Vic Hocking said they were going into the committee room and they were going to rename the club. When they came out Vic said "we are now called the Hawks". The players didn't know anything about it [before that].[936]

Of course, one account does not necessarily negate the others. It is conceivable that Pat Cazaly suggested the 'Hawks' nickname to her father, who subsequently discussed it with Hocking and some of the players. What *is* beyond doubt is the matter-of-fact way in which the club's new moniker was officially adopted. Hawthorn's minutes simply record that "the coach informed the committee that he had suggested a new name for the club, the Hawks". There was no debate, no vote and the only action arising was a

The Hawks logo was first used on the cover of Hawthorn's 1943 Annual Report.

request for Hocking to find a stuffed hawk for the committee room.[937]

The new nickname became public when *The Sporting Globe* revealed that "Hawthorn's coach told the players [before their round-two game against Essendon] that in future they would be known as the Hawks".[938] Laurie Peters later recalled Cazaly's pre-match address, in which he urged the team to play like hawks, swoop in for the ball and soar forward like birds of prey.[939] Hawthorn lost that game but the club had made a symbolic break with its past: the insipid Mayblooms were dead and the Hawks had been born.

Exactly what role their new name played is debatable but Hawthorn won seven of their first 10 games and spent much of the 1943 season inside the unfamiliar, rarified atmosphere of the top four. Their undoubted star was defender Wally Culpitt who found his niche after Cazaly heeded his plea to be given a chance on the forward line. Culpitt kicked nine goals in his first game at full-forward, followed by hauls of six, six and five in successive games.[940]

Following a strong win against Collingwood in round 11 the Hawks stumbled against Essendon and Carlton but then defeated Richmond and

South Melbourne to remain in touch with the leaders. They were in fifth place going into the final round and the players knew they would make the final four if they could defeat last-placed North Melbourne.

Victory seemed almost certain, but Hawthorn went into the match without Culpitt, who had been unable to obtain leave from the RAAF.[941] His absence up forward soon proved costly, as Hawthorn failed to score a goal in the first two quarters and lagged by 25 points at half-time. Cazaly responded by moving centreman Jim Bohan to full-forward and he sparked a third-term revival which saw the Hawks kick six goals to trail by just three points at the last break.

The final quarter was a torrid affair, with Hawthorn continually peppering North Melbourne's goals but spraying the ball wide. By late in the term they had kicked an atrocious 1.8, with a further four shots going out on the full.[942] With five minutes remaining the Hawks were behind by a point with the ball bottled up in their forward line. Tommy Lahiff later claimed he was the only player who grasped what the situation required:

> Close to the end I realised that if we got just one behind, we'd earn two premiership points for the draw. That would be enough to get us into the final four. I kept singing out, 'Punch it through, punch it through', but they were trying to kick goals. Everyone seemed to get their hands on the ball bar me, and I reckon I was the only one who knew what to do with it. Cazaly knew, of course, but there were no runners in those days, and he couldn't get a message out. It was so frustrating.[943]

According to Jack Barker's later recollection, half-forward Jack King had a set shot from the edge of the goalsquare in the last minute but kicked into the man on the mark.[944] The ball was cleared downfield, the bell sounded and Hawthorn had missed their first ever finals appearance by a solitary point. Jim Bohan, who had kicked four of Hawthorn's seven goals, later said he cried all weekend.[945] Laurie Peters played for the Seconds that day, and was relieved in retrospect that he hadn't been in the Firsts:

> The committee went crooked on them [afterwards] and Bobby Williams—who was captain in '43—got scrubbed more or less the next year.[946]

It was a frustrating end to a season that, at times, had promised so much. For the first time in their history Hawthorn won more games than they lost and went within a whisker of their first finals appearance. In his season post-mortem, Hec de Lacy wrote that Hawthorn had shown they could beat any team when they were at their best. The problem had been the players' uneven temperament, which had fluctuated between stage fright and over-confidence, and their absence of tough finals experience:

> Hawthorn lack the background of premierships fought for—titles won and titles lost. That is an irreplaceable essential in the give-and-take of premiership winning. Some sweep on to greatness. Some learn the hard way. That is how it stands with Hawthorn today.[947]

Cazaly later maintained that the Hawks would have gone on to greater heights if they had reached the finals: "We had beaten every other team, and had we made the four that year, we would most certainly have won the premiership."[948]

It was an audacious claim but Cazaly could be excused his exuberance. He had, after all, helped engineer Hawthorn's best season, instilled some much-needed belief in his players and shown them a tantalising glimpse of what was possible.

Mayblooms no more: the fledgling Hawks in 1943

25

HOME-FRONT

BUSH LIFE IN LENAH VALLEY

Despite Hawthorn's willingness to re-engage him as coach, Roy and Aggie had already decided to move back to Tasmania. Daughter Pat later explained that they liked Hobart very much and wanted to return and resume their massage practice.[949]

Having decided it was impractical to live in the centre of town as they had done previously, Cazaly bought 20 acres of rural land at Lenah Valley. The property on Brushy Creek Road was in the foothills of Mount Wellington, in a gully surrounded by wooded slopes. The area had originally been settled by English emigrant Richard Hickman in 1845, when the district was known as Kangaroo Valley. Hickman had planted extensive fruit orchards and fermented his own wines.[950] One of his original weatherboard farmhouses became the main Cazaly family home, and Roy turned one of the old fruit-packing sheds by the creek into a garage for his car and a stable and tack room for horses.

Family stories and photos from this post-war period suggest a bush idyll verging on the rustic. Although the property was only three miles from the centre of Hobart, the Post Office directory listed just 25 other families living in Lenah Valley, including orchardists and farmers.[951] Brushy Creek Road was still a dirt track and town water was not yet connected so the family used the creek for all their cooking and washing. Aggie kept a cow for milk. Early communications were rudimentary, and the houses along the road shared one telephone line. Winters in the valley were cold, and Cazaly would use his draught horse Nobby to drag firewood out of the scrub.

Marjory and Colin Woolford moved to Brushy Creek Road soon after the war, when they bought another of the houses built by the pioneering Hickmans. The Cazalys were their nearest neighbours, and they became good friends. Marjory Woolford remembered Roy as somewhat reserved, but Aggie was always friendly and "ready for a chat". When the Woolfords moved in, Aggie was involved in a battle with the council to have town water connected. "When Colin told her he hoped to establish a small market garden on the flat beside the creek she was so happy," Marjory later recalled.

> She now had someone who needed water as much as she did. So they kept on at the council until finally all the houses had water laid on.[952]

Cazaly might have thought he'd left coaching behind when he left Melbourne but it wasn't long before he was dragged back into the fray. All three Tasmanian senior league competitions were suspended between 1942 and 1944 due to the war. To help fill a community need, football competitions were organised between armed forces and essential service teams. In early 1944, Cazaly was asked to coach the Southern Tasmanian Police team in the United Services Football Association. It was a strong competition as it included many men who had played senior football before the war.[953] Under Cazaly's guidance the Police overcame the Navy team to win the southern competition and then comfortably defeated the RAAF team (winners of the Northern Tasmanian Patriotic Association) to claim the state premiership by 33 points.[954]

Around this time Cazaly renewed his interest in training and breeding greyhounds. He began advertising "farm-reared" pups for sale in *The Mercury* classifieds and in October 1944 he was elected president of the Greyhound Owners, Trainers and Breeders' Association.[955] More than half the owners in southern Tasmania soon joined and Cazaly urged the rest to become involved. "We must be united, and every owner, trainer and breeder should join the association if our interests are to be fostered," he told one meeting prior to Christmas.⁹⁵⁶

The association flexed its growing influence three months later when it threatened to boycott an upcoming meet if the Greyhound Racing Club accepted entries from non-members. Cazaly was unapologetic about their tactics. "There is no charge against the club, and no bitterness, but we will not race with non-members," he told one reporter. Within days, Cazaly had helped negotiate a settlement with the club that received unanimous endorsement. By the time of its annual meeting in October 1945 the association had 300 members and represented more than 90 per cent of owners and trainers.⁹⁵⁷

Cazaly raced his own greyhounds with some success, but his focus increasingly turned towards training pacers. Living on acreage allowed him to renew his love of horses, which had begun in South Melbourne when he used them to make deliveries while working in his brothers' butcher shop, and was rekindled during his time in Minyip.

Cazaly's training career began with a horse called Slogger but his first real success came with Gale Derby, which won the 1½-mile Novice Handicap on Remembrance Day 1944 despite starting at long odds.⁹⁵⁸ Gale Derby went on to win seven races and later bred two fillies. Cazaly also trained Raidella, a classy mare he had leased from a Deloraine baker named Williams. Raidella won her first race in June 1946, and won five more over the next 18 months.⁹⁵⁹

Meanwhile, Cazaly had convened a meeting in late 1945 to establish the Southern Tasmanian Trotting Owners, Trainers and Drivers' Association and he was elected president.⁹⁶⁰ One of the association's first actions was establishing an insurance fund to cover the cost of damages to members' sulkies during races. Cazaly was also nominated to head a deputation to the trotting association to discuss concerns with the operations of the stipendiary board.⁹⁶¹ Over the next few years he led a number of delegations to trotting officials and state racing ministers seeking further reforms to the way the sport was run.

Away from Brushy Creek Road, the 'Up there Cazaly!' expression had taken on a life of its own. During World War II it was commonly used by soldiers of the Australian Imperial Force's 9th Division, many of whom had enlisted from the southern footballing states.⁹⁶² The soldiers took the phrase with them to North Africa in 1941, where *The Herald* war correspondent John Hetherington saw it chalked on a shell-torn wall at Sollum in the western desert.⁹⁶³ In October that year, ABC war correspondent Chester Wilmot even heard it being used by Scottish anti-aircraft gunners during the siege of Tobruk:

> When I first saw them play soccer here one evening, I was amazed to hear them calling out a famous Australian football war cry ... 'Up there Cazaly'. As a broad Scotch voice came out with this it didn't seem right that this essentially Australian catchcry should be shouted in a foreign tongue, a foreign game in a foreign land. But the Scotties had picked it up from some nearby Diggers with whom they used to play a friendly game.⁹⁶⁴

Several journalists working alongside Australian soldiers later wrote that the 9th Division even used 'Up there Cazaly!' during battle.⁹⁶⁵ Colin Pura, a 9th Division captain, even wrote of the expression being used as a "war cry".⁹⁶⁶ There may have been cases of this but it was not an official battle cry *per se*. The 9th's war cry was the more prosaic 'Hoh! Hoh! Hoh!' whereas 'Up there Cazaly' was more commonly used as a laconic greeting or expression of surprise, just as it had been before the war.⁹⁶⁷

The phrase was not confined to the 9th Division or even to North Africa. Keith Rossi, an artilleryman and radio operator with the 6th Division, heard fellow soldiers using it during games of two-up in Palestine and at Kakakog Ridge in New Guinea. Rossi later described it as a "civvy street expression" that "just rolled off the tongue, much better than, say, 'Up there Brown!'"⁹⁶⁸ It was also heard in other theatres of the war and barracking airmen yelled it during an Australian Football match between two Royal Australian Air Force teams played in London in early 1944.⁹⁶⁹

The war meant it was some time before all of the family could be reunited in Hobart. Joan, who was still only 17, moved from Melbourne with her parents but Lena stayed because she was a now manager for the grocery firm Moran & Cato's and spent much of the war relieving in stores across Victoria. Dorrie, the eldest, was already living in Hobart, having married Ernest Robins in 1943. Ernest had been an orchardist in Victoria but after they moved to Tasmania he became a stevedore on the Hobart wharves. Pat's fiancée Russell Whitecross was fighting with the Australian Army in New Guinea. They were married in September 1944—one of only two occasions they saw each other during the entire war—and Pat stayed in Melbourne until he was discharged.[970]

Lena Cazaly had met a returned serviceman, Desmond Ransley. They were engaged in May 1947 and married at Hobart's St David's Cathedral the following March.[971] Joan also became engaged in 1947 and was married in 1948 to returned Navy man Allan 'Nedda' Park.[972] A builder by trade and a champion footballer with Hobart, 'Nedda' had met Joan at the Belvedere dance studios in Argyle Street. One night when they were courting he embarrassed her by yelling "Joan Cazaly, I love you" across the crowded dance floor.[973]

During the latter stages of the war Roy jnr was serving in the Pacific aboard the heavy cruiser *HMAS Shropshire*. The British government had given the ship to Australia following the loss of *HMAS Canberra* and Cazaly was part of an early draft sent to England to refit the vessel in late 1942. The expedition was a hazardous one. After crossing the Pacific under destroyer escort, and travelling across the United States by train, the Australians sailed through U-boat infested waters to refit the *Shropshire* at the Chatham Naval Dockyard. England's ports were subject to heavy German bombing and the sailors endured numerous air raids, including one which destroyed the pub at which they often drank.[974]

The refit took several months, after which the *Shropshire* underwent sea trials off Scotland before sailing to Sydney via South Africa and Fremantle. Over the next year the *Shropshire* undertook several tours of duty in the Pacific supporting the United States' 7th Fleet at Milne Bay, the Admiralty Islands, Morotai and the Surigao Straits, scene of the last great sea battle of World War II.[975]

Acting Leading Seaman Cazaly made a lasting impression on many of the *Shropshire*'s crew. He loved reading comics, was a fiercely competitive deck-hockey player and had a "funny, twisted grin" whenever he was up to mischief, such as the time he hid a contraband bottle of whiskey in his sock beneath his bell-bottomed trousers.[976]

Cazaly was captain of the *Shropshire*'s portside anti-aircraft gun. The ship's Vickers Mk VIII heavy guns were officially called QF (for Quick Firing) naval two-pounders but they were colloquially known as 'pom-poms' because of the thunderous noise they made when in use. Each of the gun's eight barrels had its own 150-round magazine, enabling them to be fired continuously for more than a minute without reloading.[977] The threat of enemy action meant the pom-pom's 16-man crew were in a constant state of readiness, often eating and sleeping by their gun. Eric 'Slim' Curtis was one of the crew's ammunition loaders. He later described Cazaly as someone devoted to his task who had a tendency to "shoot first and ask questions later". Lieutenant Mackenzie 'Mac' Gregory recalled him as an "incredible shot" who often showed a stubborn streak during target practice:

> When the Captain desired the guns to cease fire he would ring the check fire bells. At times the port pom-pom would still keep going. Captain Nichols would send for Roy, who would appear on the bridge and salute his Captain to be told 'Cazaly, when I ring the check fire bells, you stop firing!', to which Roy would respond 'Sir, if I can still see them, I will keep on firing'. He would salute again and march off the bridge.[978]

By early 1945 the *Shropshire* was in the Lingayen Gulf providing naval bombardment support for the Allied invasion of Luzon, the largest island in the Philippines. Japan was fighting a desperate rearguard action and a number of vessels took direct hits from kamikazes, including *HMAS Australia*, the flagship of the Australian squadron. The suicide planes caused severe damage and loss of life to the Allied fleet.

In the late afternoon of January 6, Cazaly was at his pom-pom's controls when he spotted a kamikaze coming out of the sun and heading straight for the *Shropshire*. He quickly trained his guns on the plane and shredded it with a prolonged and accurate burst of fire. Large pieces of the plane fell either side of the ship but all on board escaped unscathed.[979] 'Mac' Gregory was officer of the watch on the *Shropshire*'s bridge at the time; he and many other eyewitnesses later said they owed their lives to Cazaly's quick reflexes and calm, deliberate action. Cazaly was typically modest whenever asked about the incident, simply saying "we were trained to respond in a certain way and I just did what I was trained to do".[980] He was later awarded a Distinguished Service Medal for his actions during the Lingayen Gulf campaign.[981]

The *Shropshire* was part of the Allied flotilla which took part in the official Japanese surrender ceremony in Tokyo Bay in September 1945. With the war finally over, Roy jnr crewed on ships bringing Australian troops home from Europe and the Pacific. He was eventually 'demobbed' in 1946 and he and Kath moved to Hobart the following year.

The Cazaly clan grew quickly as each of the children built their own homes on Brushy Creek Road. War service loans helped with the construction costs but the building program was sporadic and it was several years before each couple was in their own home. Children arrived at regular intervals: Barry Robins in 1943, Gail Robins in 1945, Teresa Ransley, Stephen Park and the twins Susan and Peter Whitecross in 1949, Roy Ransley in 1951, Cheryl Park and Anthony Whitecross in 1952, Rick Cazaly and Vere Ransley in 1953, Wayne Park in 1954 and Mark Ransley the following year.

Cazaly's grandchildren all called him 'Gagga', a nickname which arose from young Barry's early attempts to say 'Grandad'. Cazaly doted on each of his grandchildren and they idolised him in return. He would give them sweets and threepences and bring home gifts whenever he had been away. Often he would tease and confound them before revealing their presents by telling them "If you ask, you don't get; if you don't ask, you don't want."[982]

Unsurprisingly, given his own background, Cazaly insisted on a strict dietary and fitness regime for his grandchildren. He made them chew charcoal tablets to strengthen their teeth and lie on the floor to practise their diaphragm breathing.[983] He couldn't bear to see any of his grandchildren get sick and he and Aggie would often dispense herbal remedies: there was senna tea and prunes to aid digestion, and onions and sugar to relieve their coughs.

Pat's twins, Susan and Peter, were born prematurely and spent time in Calvary Hospital when they were just a few months old. One day Peter caught a chill because the ward's windows had been left open so Cazaly went and brought him home. "That was the finish for Dad, because nobody in his family got colds," Pat later recalled. Aggie massaged Peter's chest with warm olive oil and Roy made sure all his grandchildren took cod liver oil during winter from then on.[984]

Decades later, each of the grandchildren recalled little things about 'Gagga' with affection. For Barry, it was watching him train footballers and accompanying him to the dressing sheds. For Teresa, it was something as simple as brushing his hair. For Gail it was helping him with the horses and his commanding presence whenever he entered a room. For Wayne it was his huge hands and his sage advice that "even if you can't play the game, at least look like you can".[985]

Aggie was always seeking to improve the property during these post-war years, and would co-opt anyone she could to assist. Don Bratt was a family friend and regular visitor:

> Aggie made sure that any male that visited was charged with the responsibility of helping clean the place up. If you went out there, you'd end up with a pick or a shovel in your hand.[986]

Aggie was a keen gardener and was immensely proud of her roses and orchids. She would use horse manure to mix her own fertiliser in a huge drum and later won prizes for her flowers at the Hobart Horticultural Society show.[987]

Life on Brushy Creek Road retained some perils, despite Aggie's ongoing attempts to civilise the property. One day Anthony wandered off and was missing for some time until a frantic search party found him at the far end of Brushy Creek Road. Anthony later recalled another occasion when he played with matches and nearly burnt down the property, prompting a "quiet talking to" from his grandfather.[988] Life in the bush also meant snakes. Gail and Rick were both bitten by harmless whip snakes but one Christmas four-year-old Peter was bitten on the leg by a tiger snake. Pat carried him across the gully where her father calmly fetched a razor, cut the wound, sucked out the poison and drove him to the hospital. Roy jnr and Russell Whitecross dispatched the snake with an old military sword and a .303 rifle and Peter spent Christmas Day recovering in hospital.[989]

The grandchildren all attended the local primary school at Lenah Valley. They would usually walk there together but some mornings Cazaly would be out training one of his pacers and insist on giving one or two of them a lift on the sulky. The same thing would occur in the afternoon if Cazaly "just happened" to be driving one of his pacers past the school.[990]

There was always something to do on weekends and holidays, whether it was riding bikes around Lenah Valley or bushwalking in the surrounding hills. Roy jnr would take the boys rabbiting and if their hunt was successful the family would have rabbit stew for dinner. One year he built a rifle range and introduced an air-rifle competition for the local children.[991] Roy snr taught the boys how to perfect various football kicks and they wore out many footballs practising on Brushy Creek Road. Marjory Woolford's sons Ian, Tony and Graham played cricket and football with the Cazaly grandchildren, took part in Roy jnr's air rifle competitions and raced billy carts down the dirt track which led to Augusta Road.[992]

Cazaly made sure his grandchildren dressed in their best clothes once a week to attend a Sunday School run by the Baptists at the Lenah Valley Community Hall. Cazaly was not overtly religious, despite being a Freemason and saying Grace before meals.[993] He called himself a "believer", but felt he didn't need to go to church to show it.[994] His choice of the Baptists for his grandchildren's religious education was probably pragmatic: it was close to home and he knew the Sunday School teacher Andrew Lawry, who was a manager at *The Mercury*.[995]

Dancing was a popular family pastime. Roy and Aggie's children had learned to dance when they were young because they had been to so many footballers' dances.[996] On Saturday nights the whole family would go dancing at the Belvedere or the Community Hall. Dorothy was a state ballroom dancing champion and ran her own dance school upstairs at the Belvedere. Evenings at home were often spent singing and dancing while

Roy snr played the family's Steinhart piano. He had never had formal piano lessons but had learned the basics from his mother and taught himself to play by ear. As Pat later recalled:

> Dad was a really good pianist and he could just play anything. You could say to him 'Play this' and he'd say 'How does it go?' and you would hum the song and he would just play it.[997]

Musical ability ran in the family: Dorothy also played the piano, Joan was an accomplished organist and Roy jnr had played the guitar and the ukulele before the war. The Cazalys often invited their neighbours over for sing-alongs and Marjory Woolford later recalled "they always were a happy, noisy few hours".

> Mr Cazaly used to play the piano beautifully and a lot of the night was spent singing to his playing. New Year's Eve was always a big party with lots of people. Just before midnight everyone would go outside, link arms and on the stroke of midnight sing Auld Lang Syne at the top of our voices. That certainly did echo around the valley.[998]

Bush life enabled Cazaly to indulge his lifelong love of animals, which seemingly knew no limits. At various times he owned a black-and-white cat called Butch, another cat named Tiger, a silky terrier called Tiny and an English springer spaniel named Faithful, which he claimed had followed him home. Cazaly would also feed dozens of feral cats which lived in the bush at Lenah Valley. No one else would dare go near them but Cazaly would buy sheep heads from the butcher, boil them in a large copper drum and then call over each cat and feed it in turn.[999]

Cazaly couldn't bear to see any animal suffer. Aggie once asked him to kill one of the family's ducks for Sunday dinner but he couldn't bring himself to do it because it used to follow him around the property.[1000] When one of his horses became ill and had to be destroyed it was one of the few times Stephen ever saw his grandfather cry.[1001]

26

HEALING HANDS

POST-WAR PHYSIOTHERAPY

After returning to Hobart, Cazaly had re-established his consulting rooms in the basement of Tregear's Building in Argyle Street, opposite the Royal Hobart Hospital and close to his former rooms in Collins Street. He soon built a loyal clientele: a surviving record book shows he treated 29 patients in the five days leading up to Christmas in 1943.[1002]

Massage therapy had been undergoing important changes since Cazaly had last practised in Hobart. There were moves towards more formal accreditation and the term 'masseur' was starting to be replaced with the more encompassing 'physiotherapist'. World War II brought further changes to the vocation as medical technologies improved and practitioners began treating veterans for a range of battle-related injuries and illnesses.[1003]

Cazaly had long been known for his "healing hands", and he had a simple explanation for his success:

> What do you do when you hurt yourself? You rub the place, don't you? That's what I do, too.[1004]

Roy jnr soon developed a similar reputation as the two expanded the business together. There were only three other masseurs working in Hobart at the time, and the Cazalys were easily the most well known.[1005] Their rooms were the best equipped in Tasmania and they provided a mix of traditional and modern treatments including massage therapy, muscle manipulation, Turkish baths (or steam rooms) and electric diathermy. One advertisement for the business offered remedies for "Arthritis, Lumbago, Rheumatism, Sciatica, Fibrositis, and Other Circulatory Disorders".[1006]

Patients came to see them after suffering illnesses, workplace injuries or car accidents. Footballers came from throughout the state for physiotherapy, jockeys used the Turkish baths to keep their weight down and rowers sought help after jarring their wrists on the choppy waters of the Derwent.[1007] Even nurses came in for treatment after finishing their shift, despite the Hobart Hospital having its own physiotherapy department.

The rooms were open from 9am to 10pm, and as the business grew it was common for the Cazalys to treat dozens of patients each day. Details of each one's name, condition and treatment program were meticulously recorded on index cards.[1008] Depending on the ailment, a typical consultation would involve 30 minutes of heat treatment, 30 minutes of electrical diathermy and 30 minutes of massage and manipulation.

Cazaly snr prepared his own massage ointment by combining Capsolin anti-inflammatory cream with Vaseline on a large slab of marble. The resulting compound generated enormous heat when applied and was known within the family as 'hot stuff'. Aggie assisted by mixing up industrial quantities of pig's flare, another type of massage ointment made by boiling up pig fat, rendering it down and straining it through gauze into sterilised jars.[1009]

The Cazalys offered several different diathermy treatments. Depending on the ailment, electricity was applied using direct current, known as 'galvanic', or alternating current, known as 'faradic' and 'sinusoidal'. Direct current was used to relieve pain via circulatory change, while alternating current was used to stimulate the muscles and nerves.[1010] The cabinets plugged into the electricity mains and current was applied using wires or insulated electrodes. One smaller cabinet, which produced a blue spark, was useful for cauterising warts and the larger ones had to be moved around on castors. The machines hummed loudly when in use and to a nervous, first-time patient they must have seemed like props from the set of a Frankenstein movie.[1011]

In mid-1947, Hobart hosted the 10th Australian National Football Carnival and the Cazalys took the opportunity to advertise their services in a guide issued to coincide with the carnival, as well as in *The Mercury*.[1012]

Business was brisk as a constant stream of footballers visited the rooms for treatment and advice. Veteran sports commentator Norman Banks interviewed Cazaly during the carnival as part of a live broadcast carried by Tasmanian and Melbourne radio stations.[1013]

Cazaly used an industrial sewing machine to make knee braces for injured footballers. The leather braces had internal chamois padding, a hole for the knee cap and eyelets at the sides for laces. One day New Norfolk footballer Gordon Triffett injured his knee during a practice match and took a teammate's advice to "go see Cazza". A strenuous regimen of massage, heat treatment and exercise sessions followed, spread over half a dozen visits. One day Cazaly showed Triffett his own knee brace and offered to make him a similar one. He agreed, and Triffett wore it during matches from then on.[1014]

John and Jim Thompson took their father, Don, to see the Cazalys in 1950, after a stroke had left him paralysed down one side and unable to walk. After six months of weekly massages, manipulation and heat treatments Don was showing signs of improvement. After 12 months he was able to walk with the aid of a stick. Cazaly and his son taught the brothers how to massage Don's limbs and how to build him a rudimentary exercise bike. John says his father benefitted greatly, not just from the Cazalys' caring treatment but also from the camaraderie he gained from mixing with other patients:

> After his stroke he was ready to throw in the towel. They gave him something to live for.[1015]

Rosemary Nichols was another who sought help. A self-described "nervous first-time mother", her young son Mark had feet that turned inwards. After an

ROY CAZALY as he was when coach of City (Launceston). He is showing how to place a ball for a place-kick, which these days is almost a lost art.

ROY CAZALY
Hobart Turkish Baths
Massage and Electrical Treatment
For SCIATICA
LUMBAGO
RHEUMATISM
and ARTHRITIS

Tregear's Buildings
30a ARGYLE STREET, HOBART

174

The Cazaly business advertisement which coincided with the National Football Carnival in Hobart. [1947 Tasmanian Football Guide. Author's collection]

orthopaedic surgeon dismissed her concerns a friend suggested she take him to see Cazaly snr. He recommended regular massage and advised her to put Mark's shoes on the wrong feet for a while. The deceptively simple treatment worked but Cazaly refused to take any payment from the relieved mother.[1016]

A number of poliomyelitis sufferers also came to the rooms seeking treatment. Polio is a viral disease that attacks the nerve cells, causing fatigue, stiffness and muscle weakness in its milder forms, and irreversible paralysis in its worst. Originally known as infantile paralysis, polio's indiscriminate and highly infectious nature caused widespread fear during several worldwide epidemics in the 20th century. For reasons that are still unclear, Tasmania recorded the world's second-worst *per capita* polio epidemic during 1937-38. More than 1000 cases and 81 deaths were reported, with several smaller outbreaks occurring in subsequent decades.[1017]

Cazaly had witnessed polio's devastating effects while he was coaching at South Melbourne.[1018] He was a follower of Elizabeth Kenny, a self-trained Queensland nurse who had developed her own treatments during the Depression. Most doctors ordered that polio sufferers be splinted during the disease's early acute stage in order to rest their weakened muscles and prevent future deformities. After this initial confinement, the patient usually underwent rehabilitation exercises designed to rebuild their muscles.[1019] Kenny, by contrast, believed immobilisation was useless and even harmful because it slowed circulation, caused muscle wastage and added to the patient's feelings of helplessness. Kenny argued that the patient's muscles and joints needed to be regularly manipulated through an intensive exercise regime which included hydrotherapy and heat compresses. She also placed great importance on establishing empathy with patients, believing this encouraged a natural impulse to want to move their damaged limbs.[1020]

Kenny's unorthodox views and criticism of conventional treatments alienated her from the mainstream medical fraternity but won her many followers among polio patients and their desperate families. Her methods struck an intuitive chord with Cazaly because they mirrored his compassionate approach to treating patients and his belief in promoting physical activity to repair muscle damage.

Mary Guy contracted polio in 1950, when she was eight. As a young girl she spent considerable time at Wingfield House, a children's residential facility in New Town.[1021] Patients at Wingfield were strapped and splinted, in keeping with the orthodox thinking of the day, but one day Mary's mother overheard someone talking about Cazaly's treatments and took her to see him. Three times a week, Cazaly would carry Mary down the nine steps from her parents' car into his Argyle Street rooms. He would gently say "Up there, Cazaly" whenever he lifted her, and for a long time Mary thought he'd invented the saying just for her. "I loved him," she said later. After a year of intensive massage and muscle treatment, Mary eventually regained some use in her right hand and was able to sit up unaided.[1022]

Another of Cazaly's patients was Margie Bryce, who was diagnosed with Still's Disease, also known as juvenile rheumatoid arthritis, when she was 11. The disease has no known cause and begins with fatigue, fevers and skin rashes, leading to joint pain and chronic arthritis. Doctors told Margie's mother to keep her at home and make her comfortable as she'd either die within two years or be crippled for life. Refusing to accept this prognosis, she took Margie to see Cazaly. Like Mary Guy, Margie knew nothing about Cazaly's past life as a footballer when she first met him:

> I couldn't understand why so many people greeted him with 'Up there Cazaly'! The kindness and gentleness of this person was a revelation. I must have attended his physiotherapy rooms every day, five days a week for at least 18 months. He asked what was hurting the most that day—treated me with heat and gentle massage—never got angry if I couldn't do what he asked of me. He put me on a very strict diet and generally got me through a very traumatic time. As far as I am concerned, he saved my life.[1023]

While Cazaly and his son were the public face of the physiotherapy business, the whole family played their part in keeping it running. Joan, Dorrie, Russell Whitecross and Ernest Robins all worked in the rooms at various times as masseurs, physiotherapists and trainers. Aggie would look after the bookwork and she and Joan spent long hours at Brushy Creek Road washing and drying mountains of linen. It was common for them to wash 25 loads each weekend and granddaughter Cheryl later recalled three clothes lines which were always full.[1024]

The Cazaly grandchildren would often visit the rooms after school. Gail remembered the staff's starched white uniforms and the overpowering smell of liniment; her brother Barry recalled there were always footballers coming in to receive attention for an injury or just to have a yarn with 'Cazza'.[1025]

State governments were beginning to require physiotherapists to meet greater accreditation requirements and in 1951 the Tasmanian Parliament passed the Physiotherapists' Registration Act. By law, all providers of physiotherapy services had to be registered and keep detailed records of their patients and the treatments provided. In early 1953 Cazaly, his son and Russell Whitecross were among the first Tasmanian physiotherapists to be formally registered.[1026] The Tasmanian Government also established a five-member Physiotherapists' Registration Board to oversee the industry and Roy snr was appointed as a practitioners' representative.[1027]

Not every patient could come to them for treatment so Cazaly snr would visit them in their own homes. His grandson Stephen often accompanied him on trips to the rural Huon Valley south of Hobart. If money was scarce grateful patients would pay for their treatment with eggs, fruit and vegetables.[1028] The rooms were closed on weekends, but Barry Robins recalls visitors coming to Brushy Creek Road seeking urgent treatment from his grandfather.

> There would hardly be a Sunday go by that someone wouldn't want to come up and talk to him or have some form of injury treated. I remember a bloke come up with a slipped disc once and he couldn't walk. My uncle [Roy jnr] was there as well as my grandfather. They manipulated his back and got him so he could walk.[1029]

Other visitors came not for treatment, but to borrow money. Cazaly would invariably agree but Aggie would insist on recording the loan details in a little black book. One day, Don Bratt found himself in financial strife when a hire car he had rented was damaged by a mate and he was held liable for the £50 excess. "I didn't have 50 shillings, let alone £50," he later recalled. After Bratt plucked up the courage to ask for a loan Cazaly gave him a lecture about personal responsibility and then wrote him a cheque. Bratt paid him back at the rate of one pound a week over the next year. He never forgot Cazaly's generosity—or his lecture.[1030]

27

RETURN OF THE PRODIGAL SON

NEW TOWN, 1948-50

Away from the physio rooms Roy jnr was making his mark on the football field, resuming a promising career abridged by his six years in the Navy. He played for New Town's Seconds during 1947, and was named their best-and-fairest at the end of the season.[1031] Hobart's Tasmanian Football League (TFL) had been restructured along district boundaries after the war. North Hobart and New Town survived but Cananore and Lefroy were replaced by Hobart and Sandy Bay, and new teams joined from Clarence and New Norfolk. The expanded league proved popular and was soon attracting the largest per capita crowds of any senior competition in Australia.[1032]

New Town had not won a premiership since Cazaly had taken them to their first in 1935 and its committee decided it needed to become more professional in its approach. Under new president Les Fyle and vice-chairman Keith Dickenson, members voted to set aside money to pay its players and to improve New Town's ground and facilities.[1033]

Late in 1947, the club asked Cazaly if he would consider returning to coaching. A deal was soon done and he was signed as non-playing coach for the following season for £8 a week. The prodigal son had returned home.[1034]

Pre-season optimism was high. The club ran out of

membership badges and supporters at a social dance cheered when told champion forward Allan 'Nedda' Park had been cleared from Hobart to play for his father-in-law's team.[1035] He became the club's leading goalkicker for the season.

The other mainstays of New Town's attack were ruckman Jack Rough and rover Bobby Parsons. Rough, a fast and brilliant follower, had been New Town's best-and-fairest the previous season. Parsons, who was nicknamed the 'Mighty Atom', was an on-field dynamo and an off-field larrikin in the style of Mark 'Napper' Tandy.[1036] Other stalwarts included Roy Witzerman at fullback, captain Bill Tonks in the back pocket, Les Patterson and Harold Loring on the half-back line and Roy Brain and Bill Kelly on the wings. Roy jnr was promoted from the Seconds early in the season. He played a number of games in a forward pocket but had to miss three matches after being found guilty of striking a New Norfolk opponent.[1037]

Cazaly snr was an imposing presence during training sessions. As he had at his previous clubs, the coach barked his orders from the middle of the oval. Parsons later described him as "a giant of a footballer as well as a man. He was well into his 50s then but he could do anything the players could."[1038] Sixty years later half-back flanker Kev Orpwood recalled:

> I can see him now standing in the centre of the New Town ground. Firstly we would run about four laps. I'd feel somewhat puffed out and he would purposely say 'Go Kevin!' and he'd tease you by pretending he was going to kick it and all the time he was shouting 'Go!'. When he finally decided to kick, it was so accurately done he'd always find your chest—his left-foot drop-kick was super.[1039]

Keith Welsh was *The Mercury*'s chief football writer. He would often talk with Cazaly during training nights, later recalling him as being "very strict, yet persuasive. Many other coaches were 'fire and brimstone' but he wanted players to think about what they were doing."[1040]

> He'd get the rucks and rovers together and explain to them what he wanted them to do ... there had to be an understanding between them. And when the rovers or rucks got the ball he expected it to be kicked to a certain position. He concentrated on forward play ... driving the ball low and making

a man run to position, he made each man adopt play-on tactics until a goal was kicked.[1041]

Adrian Collins remembers watching Cazaly run training sessions during this era. "Most other teams at that time would simply run a few laps and practise kicking between the forwards and the backs, but Cazaly did a lot of one-on-one work with the players."[1042] When 'Nedda' Park went through an inaccurate patch with his goalkicking Cazaly spent time with him at training to help correct his running approach to goal. 'Nedda' kicked six goals against New Norfolk the next match.[1043]

New Town's 1948 playing list was notable for its stability. Cazaly used just 54 players in total for the Firsts and Seconds, and the vast majority played 10 games or more. His steady line-up allowed him to spend less time training recruits and more time addressing his existing players' strengths and weaknesses. Half-forward Doug Scott later said the coach "knew every player's ability, mentality, character and behaviour. While we were getting changed he often sat near a player and talked to him about what to do and about his opponent."[1044]

The coach was always prepared to try something new during matches, particularly if his side was losing. Sometimes he would simply swap the two wingers but he would also switch players between defence and attack to rectify a structural weakness that had become apparent. Scott later recalled that such moves "always paid off" and it is notable that New Town regrouped to win a number of games after trailing at half-time.[1045] Coaches were not allowed to use runners to send out messages so Cazaly began using a megaphone to bark instructions from the boundary line, often yelling at his rover to "get out of the packs, Parsons!" When opposing coaches complained that the tactic was distracting their players the league banned it.[1046]

New Town was the TFL's most improved team for the season, winning 10 of its 15 home-and-away games and drawing another. Their main opponent going into the finals was Sandy Bay, which had finished the home-and-away rounds as minor premiers. Sandy Bay had provided some close contests during the season but New Town accounted for them by 16 points in the second semi-final to set up a Grand Final against North Hobart.

After an even first half marred by injuries to full-forward 'Nedda' Park, centre half-back Harold Loring and centre half-forward Stan Barwick, Cazaly made several positional changes among his forwards which had immediate success. Playing with better system and pace New Town gradually increased their lead and held off a late charge by North Hobart to win by 16 points.[1047] Half-forward Doug Smith kicked five goals, including four in the last quarter. The *Voice* noted that "as an exhibition it fell short of expectations; as a contest it had everything but a tight finish".[1048] Cazaly praised his side's tenacity after the match, and the walking wounded who had fought out the game: "We had six injured men, and I have never seen such magnificent fighting".[1049]

The club completed the premiership trifecta when its Seconds and its affiliated junior side Buckingham won their respective Grand Finals.[1050] Among the club trophies presented the next day Bobby Parsons was named 'Most Consistent', Roy jnr was awarded 'Most Unselfish' and ever-reliable fullback Roy Witzerman was 'Best and Fairest'.[1051]

New Town faced North Launceston a week later to decide the State Premiership. The northerners were firm favourites to win, particularly after Park and Barwick were ruled out due to their injuries. New Town's prospects took a further blow during the first quarter when captain Bill Tonks had to leave the field to have several stitches inserted in his upper lip. With his team trailing by 21 points at half-time Cazaly made five positional changes in a bid to improve their centre and forward lines. *The Mercury*'s Keith Welsh reported that "the result was amazing":

> New Town, for the first time, won across the centre. Rough dominated the ruck and Parsons roved better. New Town was constantly in attack, and four goals were added, while its superb defence kept North down to 1.2.[1052]

The lead changed several times during a torrid final term before New Town rallied from 17 points down to win its first State Premiership by two points. New Town's best players were ruckman Jack Rough and stand-in full-forward Doug Smith, who kicked seven goals despite an injured right hip. Cazaly was full of admiration for his men after the match, telling the crowded dressing room their situation had been "very, very bad" at half-time but he had "seen nothing finer than your finishing effort. I congratulate you, and thank you from the bottom of my heart."[1053]

In early October more than a thousand guests attended a celebratory State Premiership Ball at Hobart City Hall, a glittering occasion which saw the unveiling of the premiership flag. A club Premiership Dinner held prior to Christmas featured a performance of the can-can by a chorus line of players dressed in drag. The celebrations were a fitting end to Cazaly's first season back leading his old club and he confidently predicted that 1949 would bring further success.[1054]

New Town's side remained largely intact at the start of the next season. Three exceptions were winger Roy Brain, who transferred to Launceston, forward Doug Smith who moved to Scottsdale to help run his father's store and defender Bill Tonks who was granted a clearance to Hobart.[1055] Jack Rough was appointed as New Town's captain, and promising follower Bill Fox joined him in the ruck to establish a formidable partnership.

Kev Orpwood later recalled his first game in 1949 with chagrin. He hadn't trained much as the cricket season had just ended and he'd fumbled the football a lot as a result. Orpwood recalled that at training the next Tuesday Cazaly had told him to: "roll the ball along in front of me and chase it until I dropped". The simple but gruelling drill boosted both his skills and his confidence. Orpwood vividly remembered another lesson he learnt from the coach:

> A lot of players, including me, used to hesitate when confronted with an opponent. At one training session Cazaly said he'd heard some of our supporters calling us 'squibs' and would rectify that. He took six or seven of us aside and told us to put an arm out in front and try to get the ball with the other. When our opponent saw your arm it made him hesitate. It was so simple, but it worked wonders.[1056]

Cazaly liked to keep oppositions guessing about his final field placings until the very start of each game, a tactic that extended to the media. As journalist Keith Welsh later recalled:

> 'Cazza' was obstinate. He was the only coach who would not give me the placed players. Every other team would give us 'backs', 'half backs' and so on. Roy just gave me 20 players. That's why I always put 'New Town' and, underneath it, 'unofficial placings'. I'd probably have 16 right but Roy always ensured I had a couple wrong.[1057]

New Town had another consistent season. Under Cazaly's strict instructions the side continued its open, fast-paced approach, which relied on players making space to receive the ball from a teammate and play on at all costs. Winger Maurie Oborne spent much of the season sitting on the bench next to Cazaly as the team's 19th man. He later described him as a "second father", recalling that "I learned a lot about football from him but I learned more about people."[1058]

By the end of the regular season New Town had won 11 of its 15 roster games, finishing with a healthy percentage of 136.5.[1059] Several players were carrying injuries late in the season, including Bobby Parsons, Roy Witzerman and Harold Loring, but all recovered in time to play in the finals.[1060]

New Town's "hoodoo" team was Hobart, which had defeated them three times during the season and finished 12 points clear of them on top of the ladder. Hobart were therefore deserved favourites going into the second semi-final but New Town came from 16 points down at the last break to defeat them by two goals. Their main casualty from the game was ruckman Bill Fox, suspended for four matches after striking Hobart's captain-coach Jack Sullivan.[1061]

Hobart defeated North Hobart in the preliminary final to set up another showdown with New Town to decide the TFL premiership. On the eve of the Grand Final Jack Rough stated that "if fitness, teamwork, comradeship and the spirit of loyalty fostered in New Town by coach Roy Cazaly count for anything, we will be premiers".[1062] Cazaly, continuing his practice of not revealing his final side until the last possible moment, surprised many when he named fringe player Brian Kelly as Bill Fox's replacement in the ruck.[1063]

His tactics paid off. New Town outclassed Hobart to win the premiership by 32 points, despite suffering injuries to Rough, half-forward Stan Barwick and winger Bill Kelly. Stand-in ruckman Brian Kelly repaid Cazaly's faith by being named best on ground.[1064]

It had been another successful season for New Town, tempered only by the Seconds' loss to North Hobart in their Grand Final and the Firsts' subsequent defeat by North Launceston for the state title.[1065] Full-forward 'Nedda' Park was the TFL's leading goal scorer, Bill Fox was club best and fairest and junior side Buckingham won the State School Old Boys' premiership. New Town had now won three senior premierships since 1935—all of them under Cazaly's coaching—and their supporters were further cheered when he confirmed his re-appointment for another season.[1066]

Early in the new year Cazaly was approached by powerbrokers within the Liberal Party to stand for state parliament. Under Tasmania's Hare-Clark electoral system, voters elect several representatives from each electorate rather than a single member. The number elected has varied since the system was introduced but in 1950 voters in each of Tasmania's five electorates elected six MPs.

Supporters of the Hare-Clark system argue it is inherently more democratic than single member constituencies. But while it is designed to better reflect voter intentions, it also increases the chances of a hung parliament in which neither major party wins a majority of seats. Such was the case before the May 1950 election, when Premier Robert Cosgrove's Labor Party held office with the tenuous support of independent Bill Wedd. Cosgrove, Wedd and the Liberals' leader Rex Townley all represented the Denison electorate and the Liberals saw an opportunity to improve their electoral chances by running a prominent candidate in the tightly contested seat. They also sought to capitalise on Cazaly's statewide profile by pledging to establish a Recreation Division, which would seek his advice when establishing sporting facilities around the state.[1067]

While the Liberals' motives in approaching Cazaly are understandable, his decision to stand for them is at first puzzling. He had, after all, grown up in working-class South Melbourne, laboured in factories, played football with the watersiders and been a workers' representative at Johns and Waygood. His nomination must have surprised many who assumed that if he ever chose to stand for politics, it would be for the Labor Party.

When Noel Counihan asked Laurie Nash about this apparent contradiction some years later, Nash replied that Cazaly had always maintained a "working class outlook" and Counihan concluded that his decision must have "reflected a change in prosperity".[1068] This may be partly true but, given his willingness to take on causes, he was probably driven more by personal altruism than political ideology. Cazaly later said he was motivated to stand by a lack of integrity in public life and decided to "have a go" at helping straighten things out. His comment further suggests an essentially non-partisan outlook.[1069]

For Cazaly, the election was poorly timed. The campaign came at the start of the football season and time usually spent preparing his players was now taken up with stump speeches, town hall meetings and radio broadcasts. The day before the election, he and Rex Townley were addressing a group of workers on the Hobart wharves when a fight broke out in the crowd. One account said the fracas was sparked by political differences but it was later reported that a heckler had called Cazaly a "twister"—a derogatory term for a masseur—prompting others to take offence on his behalf.[1070]

In Denison the key battle was always going to be between Labor's Robert Cosgrove and the Liberals' Rex Townley; the real interest lay in which of the other 13 candidates would be elected on their surplus votes.[1071] Cazaly polled poorly. He was eliminated early in the count and was one of five candidates to forfeit their £15 electoral deposit. The vagaries of the Hare-Clark system meant that Horace Strutt, a sitting Liberal who received only 124 more primary votes than Cazaly, was re-elected on Townley's surplus.[1072]

Cazaly took his defeat philosophically. When his grandson Barry accompanied him to a football match in New Norfolk soon after the election two local wags chided Cazaly that he couldn't go fishing anymore because he had "lost his sinker", or electoral deposit. Cazaly was able to appreciate the humour. "I had to laugh," he admitted later.[1073]

RETURN OF THE PRODIGAL SON

New Town's star recruit for the 1950 season was 19-year-old Rex Garwood. A freakishly gifted athlete, Garwood had captained Buckingham to four State School Old Boys' premierships in a row. He had lined up in many positions but senior football was a step up in class and Cazaly set out to appraise his talents. At the start of the season he told Garwood:

> I'm going to find out where you can play and where you can't. I'll test you out and I don't want you to complain. If you just do the job I give you you'll be of real value to our team this year and you'll get a game every time.[1074]

Cazaly was true to his word. During the season Garwood usually played at centre half-forward or centre half-back, but also had spells in the second ruck and at full-forward. He was selected for every game and was named New Town's best first-year player at the end of the season.[1075]

Garwood soon discovered that Cazaly had hard and fast rules that he expected his men to follow during games. "We had our set positions and you weren't allowed out of your area," he later recalled. "You never handballed unless you got caught and you never kicked backwards." According to Garwood, Cazaly expected his players to set their own performance standards and live up to their own expectations:

> He always said forwards and followers and centres are judged on their possessions and how they use them. Backs are not judged on their possessions, it's how many kicks the opposition gets. You set yourself a standard before the game of how many kicks you wanted to get—if your opponent got more, then you're below your standard and you're looking at going out [of the Seniors] next week.

Garwood also learned that Cazaly almost never went to his star players straight after a victory, preferring to speak to those that were on the "border line" of selection each week.

> He'd be very quick to praise them and encourage them quietly. My God he got a lot out of them, even those who had no brains whatsoever. He was a shrewd old bugger.[1076]

The coach would often join his players for a post-match celebration. As Doug Scott recalled:

> He didn't drink but came to the hotel. He would move around the various groups while he had a soft drink but didn't talk much about the game. He liked to listen to a joke and had a great sense of humour [but] he would not tolerate bad or loud behaviour.[1077]

Cazaly did, however, have a strict ban on his players going to pubs late in the week before a match. When he learned that Jack Rough had been into Cooley's Hotel the day before a game he dropped him for one match, even though Rough hadn't had a drink and New Town's place in the top two was on the line. To Cazaly it was the principle that mattered.[1078]

The 1950 TFL competition proved more even than the previous two years, mainly due to Hobart's continuing good form and the resurgence of North Hobart. After a lacklustre start to the season in which they won only two of their first six games New Town settled down to win 11 of their next 14. They finished the regular season in third position, behind Hobart and North Hobart.

New Town easily accounted for Sandy Bay in the first semi-final and North Hobart in the preliminary final to set up a premiership showdown with Hobart. In a game generally acknowledged to be the best TFL Grand Final for many years, New Town stormed home from three goals down at the last break but Hobart scraped home by two points to deny them their third successive premiership. There was some consolation, however, when Cazaly coached the Seconds to a premiership against Sandy Bay and the state title against Longford.[1079] Ruckman Bill Fox again won the Seniors' best and fairest and *The Mercury* named him as the TFL's best player.[1080] When Cazaly agreed to remain as coach for the 1951 season the club's future remained in steady hands.

28

ONE LAST HURRAH

NEW TOWN AND TASMANIA, 1951-54

New Town lost Jack Rough and Bobby Parsons as captain-coaches to North Western Football Union (NWFU) clubs prior to the 1951 season. The loss of a captain and two-thirds of a winning ruck trio might have caused instability in other teams, but Cazaly calmly and methodically restructured his line-up. Roy Witzerman became the new captain, forwards Charlie Aiken, Gerry Flint and Harold Loring took turns alongside Bill Fox in the ruck and centres John Chick and Jack Conway shared the roving duties until star rover Bob Cranfield transferred from New Norfolk midway through the season.[1081]

Chick, a 19-year-old centre, had joined the Seniors from the Glenorchy Under-19s. He and teammate Rex Garwood both attended Hobart Technical College and would run to beat the tram to the New Town Oval and begin training before anyone else arrived. "No other team trained like we did," Garwood later recalled. The sessions under Cazaly were tough but "if you'd done your bit you knew you'd be right the next Saturday when he put your name on the board."[1082]

At the end of July, Cazaly played in the ruck during a curtain-raiser for a charity match at Glenorchy. Afterwards he amazed and delighted spectators by completing all four quarters of the main charity game. Playing on the ball and in a forward pocket, he scored a goal and had a hand in three others kicked by 'Nedda' Park.[1083] He was now 58.

The 1951 TFL competition was the most even in years, with many close results. New Town finished the regular season equal with Hobart and North Hobart on top of the ladder but ahead of both on percentage. Having safely steered his team into the finals for the fourth time in as many seasons, Cazaly flew to Melbourne to play for a *Sporting Globe* team in a Children's Hospital charity match. More than 40,000 spectators flocked to the Junction Oval to watch Cazaly and a number of other well-known sporting personalities take part, including retired footballer Jack Dyer, former boxer Ambrose Palmer and professional wrestler Chief Little Wolf.[1084]

If New Town needed further incentive to win one more premiership under Cazaly, they received it the following week when he told the club he was thinking about retiring from coaching to "give a younger chap a go". He candidly admitted that:

> The job takes a lot of my time and has started to worry me a little lately. It takes a lot of time and work to get to understand the little idiosyncrasies of both Firsts and Seconds players.[1085]

Following an easy 50-point second semi-final win against Hobart, the club presented Cazaly with a petition. Signed by every registered player, it thanked him for his work as coach for the past four years and urged him to postpone his retirement for at least another season. Cazaly was deeply moved by the gesture:

> There are times when one is lost for words, but I will treasure this all my life. Of all the football trophies I have received there is none more dear to me than this.[1086]

New Town went on to defeat North Hobart for the 1951 premiership in emphatic style, winning by 71 points after leading by 32 points at quarter time and 10 goals at the last change.[1087] Ruckman Bill Fox was the club's best and fairest for the third season in a row. Centre half-forward Rex Garwood was its highest goalscorer and he won the William Leitch Medal as the league's best player in just his second season in senior football.[1088] The New Town Seconds also won their Grand Final and Buckingham claimed their fifth premiership in six years. New Town under Cazaly had become a well-oiled machine, its dominance so complete that rival clubs began complaining that its district boundaries should be redrawn.[1089]

New Town celebrated their triple premiership at a special club dinner, where Cazaly took the opportunity to rebuke those claiming its recruiting district was too large. "New Town is no better than any other club", he said. "The only difference is that we have united ourselves. We have built together." Cazaly also spoke candidly about the importance of football to him in his adopted state:

> I have seen the best footballers in Australia and played against the best, and I say this, right from my heart: this is my home of adoption. There are no better players in Australia than those in Tasmania.[1090]

Prior to Christmas Cazaly confirmed his earlier intention to retire from coaching.[1091] Despite this, he often watched New Town's training sessions the following season, filled in for new captain-coach Bill Fox when asked, and advised local district side Glenorchy. He ran school football clinics and played in a past champions' charity match at Latrobe, aged 59.[1092] He simply couldn't stay away from football.

In March 1953, a profile in *People* magazine painted a picture of a man still in robust health:

> Though Roy Cazaly was born in 1893 and has 10 grandchildren he doesn't look his age. His hair is greying, but his tall frame has a spring to its step, his blue eyes are bright in a face ruddy with health, his mouth and chin have the same old determined look and his friendly handgrip is powerful.[1093]

Hec de Lacy flew to Hobart two months later to renew their old friendship and interview him for *The Sporting Globe*. The journalist stayed at Cazaly's home and observed him settling disputes between his grandchildren, treating patients in his rooms and training his pacers. The photos that accompanied his article perfectly illustrate these three abiding passions: Cazaly walking with his grandchildren in Lenah Valley, working alongside his son to treat an injured schoolboy in their rooms, and driving the training sulky behind one of his horses.[1094] Hec de Lacy concluded his profile on a poignant note:

> I've known Roy Cazaly for the better part of 30 years, and I told him I've often been confused by the cross-streak of violence—call it aggression if you prefer it—which is so strangely blended with the highest idealism, and above all a passionate love of kids and animals. So there you have Cazzer: philosopher, fighter, family man, healer. He's still the man you like to call a friend.[1095]

Hec de Lacy couldn't quite believe Cazaly when he told him he was finished with football coaching, and he was right. In 1954 Cazaly agreed to come out of retirement to coach the southern representative side in their annual triangular series against the north and north-west sides.[1096] He also agreed to take on the much sterner task of coaching the Tasmanian state side in a make-or-break game.[1097]

Tasmania's football pride was on the line following a poor performance at the 1953 Australian National Football Carnival in Adelaide, where the side had lost all of its games and finished last. The state now faced relegation to the second division at the next carnival unless it could defeat a combined Australian Amateur team for the final place in the first division.

The decision to engage Cazaly as the state side's first non-playing coach signaled a clear break with past practice. Keith Dickenson, New Town's delegate to the TFL, had recommended that Cazaly be appointed coach during the lead-up to the 1950 carnival in Brisbane. His motion had been defeated but officials finally realised the gravity of Tasmania's situation after their woeful 1953 carnival performance.[1098] Speaking after his appointment, Cazaly declared:

> I have always believed that with representative teams it is necessary to have someone over the fence who has no club interests. When we can develop a State, rather than a club, outlook, we will have gone a long way towards becoming a power in interstate football.[1099]

Tasmania drew its representatives from three separate and evenly matched competitions. As City-South player Geoff Long later recalled, regular intrastate games meant that:

> You played several games a season against the other best players in the state. You had former VFL players playing, and then you had the best Tassie players who didn't go to the mainland, and so the two combined made up a fairly skilled side.[1100]

Athol Webb

Having coached the TFL side, Cazaly was in an ideal position to assess the players from each region prior to the state team being selected. The side ultimately chosen to play the Amateurs comprised nine players from the south, six from the north and five from the north-west coast. There were several current and future greats among them. Team captain Gordon Bowman from Sandy Bay had played half-forward in Melbourne's 1948 premiership side; Burnie's captain Ray Stokes had played 93 games for Richmond; Ulverstone's captain-coach Arthur Hodgson had been Carlton's best and fairest in 1950 and 19-year-old full-forward Athol Webb would later feature in Melbourne's 1956 and 1957 premierships. Several others were leaders or best and fairest winners at their respective clubs.[1101]

Arthur Hodgson

It was a star-studded line-up but the players had only a short time to train together once the side was chosen. The Amateurs, by contrast, had already played a practice match against a Victorian side and then defeated Queensland to earn the right to play Tasmania.[1102] Laurie Moir, a winger from City-South, says the players knew the pressure was on. "The feeling was that 'we've got to win this'", he later recalled.[1103]

Ray Stokes

The southern-based members of the team had a training run on the Wednesday before the game. The five players from the north-west coast arrived in Hobart that night and the six Northern Tasmanian Football Association (NTFA) players drove down the next day in Athol Webb's red Zephyr.[1104] The full squad trained at North Hobart that afternoon, where Cazaly focused on forward, ruck and rover work.[1105] Speaking to journalists before the session, he hoped that "once the boys get together and become accustomed to each other's play they will quickly fall into the plan which I will put before them".[1106] According to Geoff Long it was an unusual training session:

> After we did a few of the normal things—circle work and training drills—Roy called us together and said, 'Now in a game there's a lot of mis-kicks and you've got to be ready. I want you to go around the circle again and when you get the ball I don't want you to look for anyone at all, just kick it anywhere', and the person further up the field had to anticipate where that ball was going.[1107]

Launceston rover Noel Atkins was the team's vice-captain. Interviewed years later, he recalled Cazaly urging his players to use intense vigour to win every contest and to dispose of the ball to the maximum advantage of their teammates:

> Cazaly believed that every contest presented a unique, often unanticipated, opportunity. Rather than conforming to a pre-determined mould he emphasised initiative.[1108]

Atkins said that Cazaly adopted a simple, three-pronged approach, which the players could "readily visualise and understand".

> With steadfast purpose he aimed to lift the level of fitness, the level of skill and the level of confidence. As a counter coach he would first attack the third element. By lowering the confidence level of opposition chief playmakers, he knew psychologically that their levels of fitness and skill would slip away. He knew the slippage would become infectious. Consequently, Cazaly invariably made his most telling moves after half-time. He could turn an imminent defeat into victory.[1109]

Tasmania's preparations suffered a last-minute hitch when North Hobart's champion ruckman John Leedham was sidelined with suspected appendicitis. Sandy Bay follower Mike Clennett was named as his replacement.[1110] In the rooms before the game the trainer giving Geoff Long a rub-down told him he was in "absolutely superb" physical condition. Long—who went on to be Tasmania's best afield—suspects the wily Cazaly had briefed the trainers to build up the players' pre-match confidence.[1111]

Despite the high stakes the game itself proved an anti-climax. It was a hard-fought contest but the Tasmanians were quicker, stronger in attack and defence and showed greater system and teamwork.[1112] The home side led throughout and pulled away after half-time to win comfortably by 53 points. As *The Mercury*'s Keith Welsh later remarked:

> The Amateurs were considered a sure thing [but] Cazaly had Tasmania going beautifully. They were superior from start to finish and they won easily.[1113]

It was a deeply satisfying result for Cazaly, whose first and only state coaching stint had helped save Tasmania from the ignominy of carnival relegation. Under captain Rex Garwood the state side went on to equal its best ever national carnival performance two years later in Perth, defeating both South Australia and the VFA to finish third behind Victoria and Western Australia.

29

Time on

1955-60

Retiring from coaching gave Cazaly more time to spend training his pacers at Lenah Valley. His son-in-law Des Ransley helped exercise them and often drove them in races. Cazaly doted on his horses. He fed them wheat and barley and a special home-made mixture of bran and molasses. His grandchildren would lick their fingers, plunge them into the sticky mess and then scoff it down; one day Gail choked on a mouthful and 'Nedda' Park had to put a hose down her throat.[1114]

Cazaly named several of his horses after his grandchildren, including Miss Gail and his most successful pacer Master Barry, the offspring of champion import Raider and the mare Ace High. Cazaly had bought the brown stallion as a yearling and he trained him throughout his career. Master Barry won his first race as a six-year-old in the Tasmanian-bred Maiden at New Norfolk in March 1951. Just like his trainer he improved with age and he was the leading stakes winner for the 1955/56 season with six wins, two seconds and a third.[1115]

Master Barry's stable name was Brazen and everyone who met him described him as stubborn and cantankerous. The younger grandchildren were scared of him, and Cazaly kept a close eye on him whenever he was being shod. When Master Barry lunged at Cazaly in the stables one day, he neatly sidestepped him and gave him one of his trademark left jabs. His daughter Joan witnessed the event:

It must have tried to do something to Dad, tried to bite or kick him. Dad had a fist as hard as a piece of brick you know. Anyway, he hit the horse on his nose and it went down on its knees.[1116]

In 1956 Master Barry was one of 55 nominations received from throughout Australia and New Zealand for the inaugural Tasmanian Pacing Championships. Driven by leading reinsman Jack Stamford, Master Barry won his two-mile heat and then outpaced nine other starters in the 1½-mile final to win comfortably.[1117] Master Barry had been the pre-race favourite and his victory was a popular one. Premier Robert Cosgrove presented the winner's trophy, after which Cazaly took the reins and drove the horse on a victory lap of the circuit, accompanied by shouts of "Up there Cazaly" from the cheering crowd.[1118]

Winning the Tasmanian championship gave Master Barry entry into the 1956 Inter Dominion Championships in Sydney. He won a Free-For-All race at Warragul before the championships but performed below his best during the Inter Dominion heats and did not make the final.[1119] There was some consolation, however, when Jack Stamford drove him to a brilliant victory in the £2000 Autumn Cup at the Melbourne Showgrounds several weeks later.[1120] Master Barry was later retired to stud in New South Wales where he sired 17 winners.[1121]

The 'Up there Cazaly' phrase had survived the war, no doubt given a renewed lease of life by the returning troops.[1122]

It crossed over to another field, the arts, in 1955, when playwright Ray Lawler included it in his *Summer of the Seventeenth Doll*.[1123] Often described as the first authentically Australian play, the *Doll* is set in a terrace house in working-class Carlton and its characters include a barmaid and two sugarcane cutters from north Queensland. Lawler, the son of a council worker, had begun acting and writing before the war while working in a factory alongside footballers such as Footscray's Joe Ryan. "On Saturday mornings Joe was a star", Lawler later recalled, "but from Monday morning till Saturday noon he was a welder who practised his shoulder bumps by

charging at any young fellow like myself whenever we crossed paths".¹¹²⁴

Lawler's exposure to everyday working life meant he was attuned to the language of Melbourne's pubs, factories and streets. Although he set the *Doll* in the 1950s, his use of 'Up there Cazaly' had its genesis in the 1930s, when its main characters had first met. He chose it because:

> It was the way people of my generation spoke ... the slang term was still in fairly common everyday use [in the 1930s]; by 1953, the year in which *Summer of the Seventeenth Doll* is set, it had become an affectionate rarity.¹¹²⁵

The *Doll*'s language, accents and themes struck an immediate chord with Australian audiences more accustomed to seeing foreign plays performed by overseas actors. After successful seasons in Melbourne and Sydney, Laurence Olivier's theatre production company took the play to London in 1957, where it provoked curiousity among the locals and nostalgia among Australian expatriates.¹¹²⁶ One of those who went to see the play was John Clark, a Hobart-born teacher and postgraduate drama student at Bristol University. Clark, coincidentally, had been coached by Roy Cazaly when he'd played half-back flank for the Tasmanian University side. For Clark, the *Doll* was a revelation:

> I thought, here's a play that's talking about people I know, it's a play dealing with Australian characters and Australian ideas and ways of thinking and feeling that I know about, and it inspired me to believe an Australian theatre was possible.¹¹²⁷

Clark returned to Australia in 1958 and was later instrumental in establishing the National Institute of Dramatic Arts (NIDA), becoming its director in 1969. Intriguingly, Clark believes elite footballers and actors have much in common:

> How they perform is determined by a series of emotional and intellectual responses. Great footballers and great artists are able to transform themselves, their minds and bodies working in harmony. It happens intuitively and they don't have to think about it.¹¹²⁸

Despite being NIDA's director for more than 30 years and helping foster the careers of many great actors, Clark still nominates "kicking a football with Roy Cazaly" as his greatest achievement.[1129]

By the time he turned 65, Cazaly was a picture of contentment enjoying life surrounded by his family on Brushy Creek Road. He loved nothing better than reading a good western or driving to the newsagent every Saturday night to buy the sporting papers. He was the first in the neighbourhood to buy a television set when they became available for sale, and the whole family would gather at his home to watch episodes of *I Love Lucy*.

Larry Noye was a sports writer with *The Mercury* and would often cross paths with Cazaly in Hobart's streets. Their subsequent football discussions usually concerned on-field events but one day in FitzGerald's department store the conversation turned to morality. Cazaly recounted an incident that had occurred decades earlier when he had been at a South Melbourne function. A young woman had flirted with him on the dance floor, telling him he could put his boots under her bed anytime. "You don't mean that", Cazaly chided. "I love you Cazzer" the woman insisted. Cazaly's response was blunt: "You don't love me, you're suffering from idolatry". It was an exchange that Noye recalled years later after a certain high-profile player's off-field indiscretions became public.[1130]

In February 1958, Roy and Aggie embarked on their first and only holiday abroad: an eight-month trip to the United Kingdom and Europe. After flying to Melbourne they spent a week visiting family and friends, including Aggie's sisters Blanche and Olive, Roy's last surviving sibling Lena and his old South Melbourne ruck partner Mark 'Napper' Tandy and his wife Lily.[1131]

In early March they boarded the *Strathnaver*, a Pacific and Orient passenger liner built in 1931 for the mail service run between England and Australia.[1132] Coincidentally, it was the same vessel that had carried their son to Liverpool in 1940 after it had been requisitioned for wartime service as a troopship. Roy and Aggie took turns writing a travel diary as the *Strathnaver* left Fremantle and passed through various ports on its voyage to England. Roy bought a slide projector in Aden, and the lengthy slide nights that took place on their return went down in Cazaly family folklore.

Roy sent an aerogramme home to his son at the end of March outlining the daily routine of shipboard life: Aggie had been seasick early in the voyage and Roy was tired of "doing nothing but eat and sleep". He asked how the physiotherapy business was going and revealed his anxiety about his grandchildren, especially young Rick. "Your mother worries over him more than the others on account of things as they are", he wrote. He was referring to the end of Roy jnr and Kath's marriage.[1133]

The *Strathnaver* docked in London on 8 April where, intriguingly, the incoming passengers' log listed Roy and Aggie's "country of permanent residence" as Tasmania rather than Australia. They stayed a fortnight at the Strand Palace Hotel in the West End and then a further month at a boarding house in South Kensington, taking in the sights of London. They also visited distant relatives of Roy's in Finchley before travelling to Scotland and Ireland. Returning to London they spent a further three weeks in the capital, where Roy set out to hone his photographic skills with his new Kodak Retina, noting in their diary that he "took many snaps, some good, some indifferent because I was still in the raw state as a camera man".[1134] In early July he and Aggie took a ferry to Calais and travelled extensively throughout France, Spain, Italy, Switzerland and Germany.

Arriving back in Melbourne aboard the *Iberia* in late October, Cazaly was met on the docks by reporters keen to hear his impressions of English sport. Ever the innovator, he said he'd attended the Football Association Cup Final at Wembley Stadium and been impressed with one feature in particular:

> Before the match began, every one of the 70,000 spectators stood and sang *Abide With Me*. It gave the event a wonderful atmosphere. I'd like to see the same thing at Grand Finals here. Our big match has everything else over the great soccer matches—colour, crowds and spectacular sport—and the hymn would add balance to the occasion.[1135]

Life resumed on Brushy Creek Road. Following his divorce Roy jnr had fallen in love with Geraldine Belz, a young woman from West Hobart who shared his passion for ballroom dancing. Geraldine often stayed at the Cazaly family home during their subsequent courtship, sleeping on the enclosed verandah outside Roy and Aggie's window. Cazaly snr's pride and joy was his black Ford Customline and Geraldine knew she had been accepted into the family the day they returned home from an outing:

> On arriving back Roy snr quietly showed that I was 'one of the family' by giving me his car keys and asking me to drive his car up to the house, with Roy [jnr] and his Mum still in it. They sat there with big smiles. They knew his simple action spoke volumes and told me so.[1136]

Roy and Geraldine were married at Hobart's Sapphire Ballroom in March 1959.[1137]

The following month Cazaly visited Melbourne to take part in a former players' charity match. Now aged 66, he captained a team of old St Kilda players against a team of Richmond veterans led by Jack Dyer.[1138] While in Melbourne Cazaly caught up with Fred 'Skeeter' Fleiter and Mark 'Napper' Tandy. The three reminisced about their playing days at South Melbourne and bemoaned much of what they saw in the modern game. Fleiter decried the lack of good kicking, Cazaly said players were not being taught how to play scientifically and Tandy complained that ruckmen were punching the ball rather than palming it to their rovers.[1139] It was the famous trio's last reunion.

Cazaly was easing into retirement, but he still spent a good deal of time in the family's physiotherapy business. Working in the rooms alongside his son enabled him to re-establish a close bond that had been disrupted by the war. Geraldine later recalled an incident in late 1959 that illustrated this closeness. It came after Roy jnr fell from a ladder while putting up Christmas decorations and broke seven ribs, punctured a lung and injured his back.

> He was in hospital only a couple of days when a nurse started to rub his back with methylated spirits without looking at it first. Well! Next morning his dad had him home. Every day he would carefully put oil on Roy's back and cover it with a large dressing. As his back started to heal his dad would massage him, often twice a day. This went on for three weeks until Roy decided to go

back to work. His dad had semi-retired but was now putting in extra hours to cover for Roy and this worried him. Looking back this showed the good, caring father-son relationship they had.[1140]

Roy jnr spent so many hours in the rooms treating patients that his own health suffered. His son Rick remembers being woken late one night by the sound of an incessant car horn. His father had just managed to drive home before falling asleep at the wheel, his head resting on the horn.[1141]

30

SIREN

1961-63

Football followers have long debated whether great footballers are born or made. In April 1961, *Sports Novels* published an article by Larry Noye in which Cazaly ruminated on the subject at some length. Reflecting on a lifetime spent playing alongside and coaching many of the game's best, he declared that great players were both born *and* made.

Cazaly listed three elements he considered vital in any great player: ability, incentive and development. He cited former teammates Fred Fleiter, Billy Schmidt and Laurie Nash, Carlton's Horrie Clover, Brownlow medalists Colin Watson, Ivor Warne-Smith, Haydn Bunton and Dick Reynolds, Melbourne's Ron Barassi and Tasmania's own Horrie Gorringe as champions who had the brains, the application and the tenacity to seek to continually improve their game. Each had their own particular skills, he explained, but what set them apart from merely good players was their "dynamic drive" to succeed:

> That dynamic drive is very important. It comes from the brain. It is not so much what we hear of as the 'killer instinct', but a mental message.[1142]

He could just as easily have been describing his own "dynamic drive" to succeed, a vital ingredient he recognised in others but didn't claim for himself.

Cazaly was beginning to slow down but he maintained an active interest in football and continued to accept invitations to speak at club functions and dinners. He'd invariably talk about football and how its virtues could help develop good citizens.[1143] In September 1961, *The Mercury*'s Keith Welsh invited him to a Sandy Bay training session to give kicking advice to a young forward, Tony Thiessen. Welsh later wrote that "the old master and his pupil spent some time together, and towards the end of the evening Thiessen's kicking had already improved". [1144] The "old master" was delighted when his old side Hawthorn reached their first VFL Grand Final that year, and was thrilled when they defeated Footscray to win their inaugural premiership.

In April 1962, Cazaly was interviewed by sports journalist Bill Barwick as part of radio station 7HT's 25th anniversary celebrations. During the interview, which survives as a recording, Cazaly explained the origin of the 'Up there Cazaly' cry, outlined his breathing and marking techniques, called for the reintroduction of the place kick, reflected on past great players and argued that modern footballers needed to prepare better for games.[1145]

Cazaly became seriously ill soon after. Roy jnr would later say that the illness destroyed his father's digestive system and that he subsequently had difficulty absorbing food.[1146] Cazaly's medical records no longer exist so the exact causes are unclear but his family believes he had contracted a virus after drinking untreated water in Spain in 1958. The root cause, however, may stem from the serious gastric ailment he had suffered more than 30 years earlier at the start of the 1927 football season.

Rick Cazaly believes his grandfather's illness may have been misdiagnosed and his condition made worse by stress or high blood pressure. Whatever the causes, Cazaly's health went into a sharp decline and he suffered a series of strokes. His deterioration was both puzzling and deeply troubling to his family, who had thought him to be indestructible. His daughter Pat visited him in Calvary Hospital after one of his strokes, when he was conscious but immobile and unable to speak. She fed him some chocolate and left the rest in a drawer, telling him she'd give him more when she visited again. The next time she came, his eyes went straight to the drawer.[1147]

After time spent convalescing at home Cazaly suffered a heart attack in December 1962 and was re-admitted to Calvary Hospital. Arriving for work at *The Mercury* the next day Larry Noye was told by his editor: "Roy Cazaly's entered hospital; write an obituary."[1148] By the new year, newspapers around Australia were reporting that Cazaly was seriously ill and close to death. A round of career retrospectives appeared, with one journalist writing that "Roy Cazaly is to Australian Rules football what Babe Ruth was to baseball and Don Bradman is to cricket".[1149]

Cazaly hovered in and out of consciousness for the next few months. The family maintained a bedside vigil and ensured there was always someone present.[1150] At times his condition would improve for a few days before deteriorating again. One of the Calvary nurses later said his face would light up during his more lucid moments whenever the conversation turned to football.[1151] By July 1963, and requiring full-time nursing care, Cazaly was moved to the Hathaway Nursing Home in Sandy Bay. From his playing weight of 12½ stone he had wasted away to just 7 stone.

Roy Cazaly died on Thursday, 10 October, 1963, a week before he and Aggie would have celebrated their 50th wedding anniversary. He was 70. Newspapers across Australia recorded his death with front-page tributes and career summaries. More than 500 mourners formed a mile-long funeral procession the following Monday outside St John's Anglican Church in New Town. Many of Cazaly's old friends and teammates came to pay their last respects, including Billy Schmidt, Mark Tandy, Joe Scanlan, George Rudolph and VFL umpire Jack McMurray jnr.

After the service Cazaly's casket was carried through an honour guard of past and present North Hobart and New Town players. Premiership pennants from both clubs covered his coffin as police escorted the cortège to the Cornelian Bay crematorium. Speaking afterwards, Tandy said he had never seen a footballer to equal Cazaly. His old friend and teammate Laurie Nash later told an interviewer he had never played under a better coach.[1152]

Cazaly's will, drawn up the previous year, was less than two pages long. In it, he had named Aggie as sole executor and bequeathed her his entire estate. In the event of Aggie predeceasing him he had appointed his son as executor, leaving him his share of the business and directing that everything else be sold and the proceeds divided equally among his children.[1153]

On Cazaly's death certificate Dr Athol Corney had listed the causes as cerebral haemorrhage and arteriosclerosis.[1154] His daughter Joan had a much simpler explanation:

> The little thermostats in the body just refused to function. I think he burnt his body out playing football. It was only his heart that kept him going and eventually it just gave up.[1155]

31

Post 1963

Aggie Cazaly spent her last years living quietly in Hobart. In 1973 she was guest of honour at the inaugural Truth Cazaly Awards and in 1976 the organisers presented her with a Cazaly statuette. Three years later, the Tasmanian Football League chose to honour her husband's legacy at the TFL Grand Final. As Up There Cazaly blared through the public address system Aggie, by now 85, sat proudly beside her daughters as they were driven around the boundary line in front of a cheering crowd of 25,000.[1156] Aggie died in a Hobart nursing home in 1987, aged 93. She had outlived her husband by almost a quarter of a century.

Roy snr's death coincided with the start of a new era for the family business as it adapted to changing patient needs. The Cazalys had always been open to new fitness trends: they had offered exercise classes for women during the 1950s and later installed ultraviolet lamps to help holidaymakers make an early start on their tans.[1157] After relocating from Argyle Street to Liverpool Street and then to 60 Collins Street in 1962 they provided physiotherapy, Turkish baths, a gymnasium, boxing ring and judo classes. The hours were long but the business did not bring in a large income.

Roy jnr didn't have a car during this period so he would catch trams around Hobart twice a week to visit patients in their homes. Washing clothes for the business and a young family was a full-time job and Geraldine recalls that finally being able to afford an automatic washing machine was "like winning Tattslotto".[1158]

While his father had focused mainly on the medical and rehabilitation aspects of the business, Roy jnr now expanded the fitness side for a wider clientele. Between 1968 and 1980 he extended the premises to include two squash courts and a larger gym. Women's fitness classes were introduced and clients were segregated: men used the facilities on Monday, Wednesday and Friday, and women on Tuesday and Thursday. As the children grew older the business became a family affair: Geraldine worked full time in the business, Rick joined as a masseur and exercise instructor in 1969, another son Brett began as a masseur in 1976 and daughters Teyana and Zena also worked there during the 1970s.[1159]

The 1980s saw a fitness boom among the general public. The Cazaly Fitness Centre, as it was now known, became a seven-day operation, offering memberships, which included access to three fully equipped gyms, exercise classes, a solarium, hydro spa pool, fitness assessments, Swedish massage and dietary advice. In 1980 an ambitious plan was developed to build a huge new Cazaly Fitness and Health Centre in a converted warehouse in Hunter Street on Hobart's waterfront. The centre would have included a large gym, physiotherapy rooms, indoor pool and an all-weather rooftop jogging track but the visionary proposal fell through amid council planning and approval issues.[1160] Rick says that his father was "driven to be successful in that business and he always had a dream of bigger and bigger things".[1161]

In August 1982 more than 300 people attended a dinner dance to mark half a century since Roy snr had started his Hobart masseur business. Two years later, the business expanded further when Rick opened a branch of the fitness centre in Devonport.[1162] He worked alongside his father as assistant director for several years before they divided the business in 1988. Roy, Brett and another son Carl opened a physiotherapy practice in Hobart's northern suburbs while Rick managed a new fitness centre in Bathurst Street.[1163]

Roy was also active among navy veterans and helped organise a number of reunions with his old *Shropshire* shipmates. His own experiences and his lasting friendships gave him unique insights into their state of mind after six years of war, as he revealed in an interview in 1984:

> The problem was that, by the time the war ended we were getting pretty good at it. Men build up resistance to the pressure of war. They grow used to it and miss it when it is removed. Some very good mates went to pieces. They had nothing to take the place of all the excitement they had been through. Work saved me. That and the influence of my father.[1164]

Rick Cazaly later recalled the ongoing effects of the war on his father:

> He spoke about it every single day in some respect. Other blokes internalised it and it damaged them [but] I think things happened that reminded him and he spoke about it. I reflect on how lucky I was that he did.[1165]

Roy's wartime stories were such a topic of conversation in the rooms that regular patient and renowned author Margaret Scott offered to help him write a book about his experiences. The book never eventuated because, said son Carl, "Dad would respond by saying 'everything we went through wasn't all that deserving of being written down—it was just what we did to survive'".[1166]

Roy continued running the family business until 1993, when he retired due to poor health. Like many of his former shipmates he had contracted mesothelioma, a rare and aggressive cancer, when stripping out the *Shropshire*'s asbestos insulation in England during the war. His close friendship with others who had the disease meant he recognised the symptoms only too well and knew what to expect. He died from its effects in September 1994, aged 75, a month before celebrations to mark the 50th anniversary of the *HMAS Canberra-HMAS Shropshire* Association. [1167] His ashes are interred at Ulverstone's Shropshire Naval Memorial Park, alongside those of many of his former shipmates.

Roy jnr's son Brett operated a massage business from the site of the physiotherapy practice for another decade before changing careers. Rick continued the fitness centre in Bathurst Street where Carl joined him in 1995 for several years before running his own personal training business. Rick sold the main business in 2006, but continues to deliver health and fitness programs via the Roy Cazaly Family Trust, which provides health and safety training and lifestyle coaching under the banner of Cazaly Sports Pty Ltd.

Roy and Aggie's other children are all deceased. Joan Park died in 1990, Lena Ransley in 2004 and Dorrie Robins in 2005. Their last surviving child, Pat Whitecross, died in 2009 aged 86. Although she had been in failing health for some time she stayed mentally alert, retained her love for Hawthorn and never tired of listening to Up There Cazaly being played.

Most of Roy and Aggie's grandchildren continue to live in Cazaly's adopted state of Tasmania, quietly proud of his achievements and fiercely protective of his memory. Many of their own children and grandchildren have excelled across a range of sports, a fact that may have something to do with their inherited genes.

All of Cazaly's closest teammates and most of those he coached are long gone. Mark 'Napper' Tandy retired in 1926 after playing 207 games for South Melbourne. By coincidence, he and Cazaly both represented Victoria 13 times, captained South Melbourne and were later inducted into the Australian Football Hall of Fame. Tandy had married Lily Ford in 1917 and they had one son, Mark jnr. Lily Tandy was Pat Cazaly's godmother, and Roy snr gave Mark and Lily's grandson Rod his first pair of football boots. Despite living in different states the Tandys and the Cazalys remained close friends in retirement.[1168] Tandy suffered from hypertension in later years and died at his Ferrars Street home in South Melbourne in May 1965, aged 73. At his funeral his coffin was covered in red-and-white wreaths, and the flags at the Lake Oval were lowered to half-mast.[1169]

Fred 'Skeeter' Fleiter played his last game for South Melbourne in 1925 and later coached the club for part of 1929. Off the field he worked with his brother Emil in the family tailoring business and later drove a fruit truck. In 1937 Fred married Iola Lockwood, a bookkeeper, at Middle Park's Carmelite Church.[1170] Iola's father, Bill, was the live-in caretaker at the South Melbourne cricket ground for 24 years from 1921. The club acquired a young white cockatoo as its resident mascot in 1937 and it was probably Bill who taught it to screech 'Up there, Cazaly' from its cage beside the caretaker's cottage. The cockatoo was still performing two decades later.[1171] In retirement Fred Fleiter lived at the family home in Withers Street, Albert Park, where nephews who visited remember him as an imposing but kindly giant of a man. He died following a heart attack in January 1973, aged 75.[1172]

Laurie Nash, Cazaly's protégé and friend at three different clubs, played his last game for South Melbourne in the famous 'bloodbath' Grand Final of 1945. After coaching two country sides to premierships he was appointed South Melbourne's non-playing coach for the 1953 season. He had a two-year contract but was controversially sacked at the end of his first year after South Melbourne finished eighth.[1173] Nash kept in contact with Aggie after Roy's death, and he always maintained that Roy was the greatest player and coach with whom he'd been associated.[1174] He died in 1986, aged 76.

Hec de Lacy's children Mavis and Dennis retain fond memories of visiting the Cazalys in Tasmania and of the times Roy stayed with them when he visited Melbourne after the war. Mavis says he would "fix us all up" with his physiotherapy and recalls one night when they went to the movies to see John Wayne and Maureen O'Hara in *The Quiet Man* and laughed all the way home. Hec de Lacy pre-deceased Cazaly by several years, dying in 1956. Four decades later he was one of the first media representatives inducted into the Australian Football Hall of Fame.[1175]

Most of the clubs Cazaly played for or coached are still in existence in one form or another. St Kilda has played in seven premiership deciders—including a replay—since Cazaly's Grand Final appearance in 1913 but has so far won just one, in 1966. The club left its Junction Oval home for Moorabbin Oval after the 1964 season but there have been proposals to move its training and administration facilities back to the historic venue.[1176]

St Kilda announced its Team of the Century in April 2001, but Cazaly was not included. The side featured nine players from their 1966 premiership team and just two—Dave McNamara and Bill Mohr—who played before World War II. Despite speculation, Cazaly wasn't included when the club announced their inaugural Hall of Fame inductees in 2003. The A M Taylor Memorial Shield, which includes Cazaly's name among its best-and-fairest winners, went missing for more than 50 years. It was rediscovered in 2004 being used as a prop by an amateur theatre company in Mordialloc and returned to a grateful club.[1177]

South Melbourne won their third premiership in 1933 but had to wait another 72 years to claim their fourth. In between, the club relocated from Melbourne to Sydney in 1982 and became the Sydney Swans. The club has played in four further Grand Finals since 2005, losing in 2006, 2014 and 2016 but winning their fifth premiership in 2012. After being used for some years as a soccer venue, the Swans' former home ground at the Lake Oval now hosts Melbourne's main athletics venue. The shell of the 1926 heritage-listed red brick grandstand has been restored and now houses the Victorian Institute of Sport.[1178]

In August 2003 the Swans announced their Team of the Century. Cazaly had been included in a shortlisted squad of 66 players—interestingly, as a forward rather than as a specialist ruckman—and there was a general expectation that he would be named in the final team.[1179] He wasn't, causing surprise on the night and in subsequent media reports.[1180] He was, however, included in the Swans' inaugural Hall of Fame when the club announced their first 26 inductees in July 2009.[1181] More than 90 years after the 1926 season, Cazaly remains both their first and their oldest best-and-fairest winner.[1182]

After missing the finals by one point under Cazaly in 1943, Hawthorn eventually reached the finals for the first time in 1957 and won their inaugural premiership under John Kennedy snr four years later. They have gone on to become one of the powerhouse AFL clubs of the modern era, winning a total of 15 premierships to the end of the 2016 season. Although Hawthorn played their last home game at Glenferrie Oval in 1973 and moved their training and administrative facilities to Waverley in 2006 the old "sardine tin" remains its spiritual home.

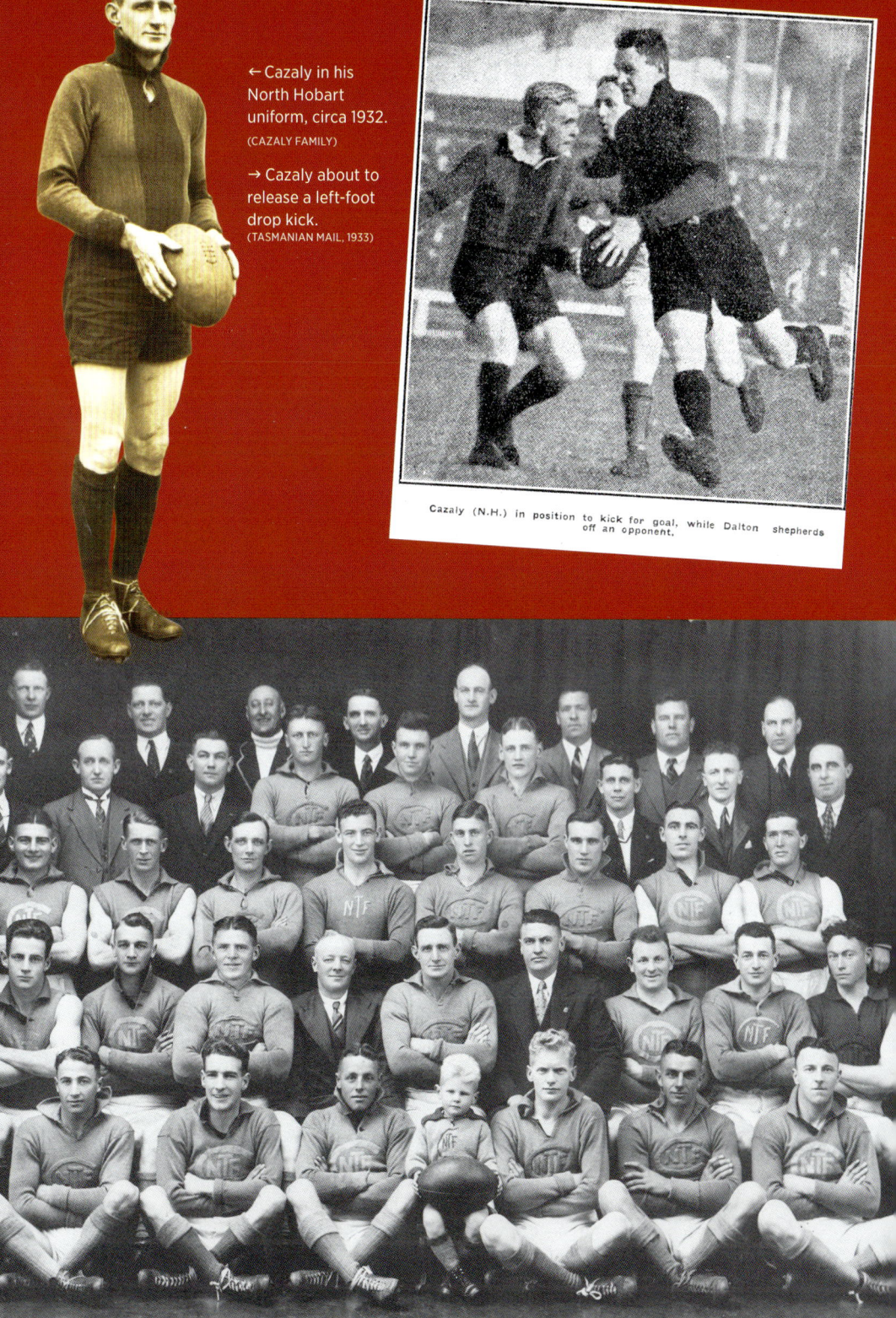

← Cazaly in his North Hobart uniform, circa 1932. (CAZALY FAMILY)

→ Cazaly about to release a left-foot drop kick. (TASMANIAN MAIL, 1933)

Cazaly (N.H.) in position to kick for goal, while Dalton shepherds off an opponent.

Cazaly (second row, centre) and his 1934 New Town team [DAVID JONES]

↑ A 1937 Alex Gurney *Herald* caricature of Cazaly, his South Melbourne players and officials (PAUL HARVEY)

→ Cazaly puts Jim Cleary through a marking drill (THE SPORTING GLOBE, 3 JULY 1937)

↓ The Swans' 1937 membership ticket (EDD GARRETT)

Cazaly and his daughters Dorrie, Pat, Lena and Joan at home in the Melbourne suburb of Burwood, circa 1941. (CAZALY FAMILY)

A wartime photo of *HMAS Shropshire* sailing under Sydney's Harbour Bridge. (CHRIS JOHNSTON)

Roy jnr's Pom-Pom battery crew aboard the *HMAS Shropshire*. (RON RUSSELL)

A homemade metal and leather knee brace made by Roy Cazaly snr. (CAZALY FAMILY)

New Town's winning 1948 TFL premiership side in front of the Argyle Street stand, North Hobart Oval. Captain Bill Tonks is at the front, followed by vice captain Les Patterson and Allan 'Nedda' Park. Roy Cazaly jnr is third from the back. (GRAHAM KELLY)

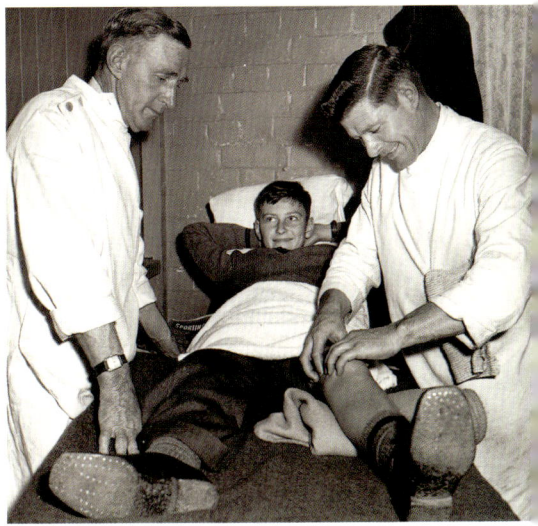

Roy snr and jnr attending to 13-year-old schoolboy Graeme Salmon in their rooms in 1953. (CAZALY FAMILY)

New Town's players presented Cazaly with a petition in 1951 pleading with him to stay on for another season. (CAZALY FAMILY)

Cazaly, (right) runs out for his last match, a charity affair, in 1959. The caption is all wrong: Cazaly was aged 66, and the player in the Richmond strip is not Jack Dyer. Unfortunately, not even the Richmond FC Museum can identify him. (CAZALY FAMILY)

Roy Cazaly and his grandchildren at Brushy Creek Road, Lenah Valley, in 1953. Left to right: Roy Ransley, Barry Robins, Peter Whitecross, Susan Whitecross, Roy snr holding Anthony Whitecross, Teresa Ransley, Stephen Park and Gail Robins. (CAZALY FAMILY)

Roy and Aggie during their cruise to the UK in 1958. (CAZALY FAMILY)

Cazaly drives his champion stallion Master Barry in a training trial. Master Barry won the inaugural Tasmanian Pacing Championship in 1956. (CAZALY FAMILY)

Cazaly and his granddaughter Gail Robins in 1953 with Miss Gail, the horse he named after her. (CAZALY FAMILY)

One last reunion for South's legendary ruck trio: Roy Cazaly, Mark Tandy and Fred Fleiter outside Tandy's South Melbourne home in 1959. (CAZALY FAMILY)

Of the two former Victorian Football Association (VFA) clubs Cazaly coached, Preston is still competing in the Victorian Football League (VFL). In 2012 they became the Northern Blues, having been previously rebadged as the Preston Bullants and then the Northern Bullants. Their current alignment with Carlton in the Australian Football League (AFL) means they have adopted a similar blue-and-white strip but they have retained their traditional red-and-white colours for their clash guernsey. Home games are divided between Carlton's Ikon Park (Princes Park) and their traditional ground at Preston Oval.[1183] In 1994 the electoral ward in the Darebin Council, which includes Preston Oval, was named after Cazaly.[1184]

Camberwell's record after Cazaly's one season in 1941 was modest. The club made the Grand Final in 1946 but struggled throughout the 1950s and were relegated to Division 2 in 1961. More competitive from the mid-1970s, Camberwell lost two Grand Finals before finally winning their first premiership in 1979. They were promoted to Division 1, relegated again the following year and won another Division 2 premiership in 1981. After several disastrous seasons, Camberwell were unable to field or finance a competitive team. They left the VFA and joined the Victorian Amateur Football Association (VAFA) in 1992, but disbanded two years later. The Camberwell Sports Ground is now the home ground of Old Scotch Cardinals, who compete in the Premier section of the VAFA.[1185]

Minyip continued to be a competitive side in the Wimmera Football League (WFL) after Cazaly's departure, winning seven flags after World War II. Coincidentally, Roy's nephew Syd was a rover for the team in the early 1950s and was the side's best and fairest in their 1952 premiership year.[1186] In 1995 Minyip merged with neighbouring team and former fierce rival Murtoa to become the Minyip-Murtoa Kookaburras. The team chose to combine the colours of the two clubs and alternate home games between the two towns. The 'Burras won three WFL premierships in a row between 1996 and 1998 but are yet to win another in a competition dominated most seasons by teams from Horsham.[1187]

In Cazaly's adopted home state of Tasmania, the City club have had a number of name and league changes since 1930. The team won Northern Tasmanian Football Association (NTFA) premierships in 1932, 1939 and

1941, and a string of flags during the 1950s. They changed their name to City-South in 1957, moved from York Park to the Youngtown Oval and won five local premierships and three state titles between 1959 and 1974.[1188] In 1986 City-South merged with East Launceston to become the South Launceston Bulldogs. They were one of the inaugural teams in the Statewide League that year but in 12 seasons they did not finish higher than sixth, and left the competition at the end of 1997. In 2002, Roy Cazaly was named at half-forward in the City-South Team of the Century.

After several years and two premierships in the NTFA the club agreed to join a revamped Tasmanian State League (TSL) in 2009. After several lean years, the Bulldogs won the premiership in 2013 under captain-coach Mitch Thorp. Despite this success, South Launceston's members voted to leave the TSL at the end of 2013 rather than accept AFL Tasmania's ultimatum to merge with another club.[1189] The team moved to the Northern Tasmanian Football Association (formerly the northern division of the Tasmanian Amateur Football League) and won the Division One competition in 2014, despite having none of their premiership players from the previous season.[1190]

North Hobart continued to enjoy continued success in the Tasmanian Football League (TFL) after Cazaly left the club in 1933. It won 19 premierships and 12 state flags between 1934 and 2003, becoming Tasmania's most successful football club.[1191] In 2000 Cazaly was named an assistant coach of North Hobart's Team of the Century.[1192] In 2009 North Hobart joined the new Tasmanian State League but disbanded in 2013 and was replaced by a new franchise, the Hobart City Football Club. Hobart City contain many of North Hobart's former players and officials, maintain their traditional red-and-blue colours and remain based at North Hobart Oval.[1193]

After their three TFL premiership victories under Cazaly between 1948 and 1951, New Town won three further flags during the 1950s. In 1957, the club merged with Glenorchy Rovers and relocated to King George V Oval. As the Glenorchy District Football Club they won five premierships between 1958 and 1985. Glenorchy named their best-and-fairest award after Cazaly in 1980. The team were an inaugural member of the TSL from 1986 and won two premierships, but were left without a competition when the TSL disbanded in 2000. Glenorchy were admitted into the Southern Football

League (SFL) the following year but had to relinquish their traditional black-and-white colours and magpie emblem because another team, Claremont, already had the same strip. Claremont's departure from the SFL enabled Glenorchy to revert to their traditional colours and emblem in 2004.

After winning SFL premierships in 2007 and 2008 Glenorchy joined the revamped Tasmanian State League in 2009 and are currently one of 10 teams in the competition.[1194] Cazaly was named coach of New Town's Team of the Century in 2000 and was inducted into Glenorchy's Hall of Fame in 2002.

32

THE LEGEND GROWS

> Roy Cazaly was the kind of footballer who induced the critic to delve deep among his adjectives ... Yet, in that strange manner in which we often show our greatest admiration, we strung together no superlatives. We paid our tribute to his prowess in the vernacular—in the phraseology of the man in the street.
>
> HEC DE LACY, 'UP THERE CAZZER!', *SPORTING GLOBE*, 9 AUGUST, 1941

'Up there Cazaly' survived the death of its namesake. In 1966 the linguist Sidney Baker wrote that, unlike more regional expressions, it had become a "national possession", alongside utterances such as 'Goodoh!', 'Whacko!' and 'You beaut!'[1195] But even then, the phrase might have slipped quietly into obscurity had it not been for the advent of the Truth Cazaly Awards in 1973. The publishers of Melbourne's *Truth* newspaper devised the awards as an alternative to the VFL's Brownlow Medal, which they saw as outdated. The *Truth*'s sports editor Brian Hansen later wrote it was "universally agreed around football circles that the Brownlow was a bit of a joke".

Umpires played favourites when it came to handing out votes. They didn't always give best afield votes to the best players—rather they gave them to the best-behaved player.[1196]

The Truth Cazaly Awards were the brainchild of Hansen and Southdown Press' managing director Brian Morris. Southdown published *TV Week* magazine and Morris was keen to develop a football award based on his successful Logie Awards format, which relied heavily on viewer participation.

Hansen oversaw the establishment of the awards but he credits Morris with devising the name after they had considered and rejected other suggestions including the 'Colemans' and the 'Dyerbolicals'.[1197] Carlton and United Brewers agreed to sponsor the awards and Channel Nine was the initial broadcaster. Launched with typical *Truth* fanfare in honour of "one of the greatest footballers ever", the awards were hailed as "the richest football bonanza in history".[1198] The VFL player awarded the most votes by the *Truth*'s panel of football writers during the season received the Gold Cazaly, a Perspex cube containing a statuette of its namesake frozen in his famous pose like an insect trapped in amber. The trophy also came with a cash prize: $2000 in 1973, which grew to $6000 by 1981.

Cazalys were also given for the season's best positional players, coach, captain and a host of other categories. A progressive vote tally was printed during the season but publication was suspended several weeks before the finals to maintain an air of mystery before the award presentations. There was also an element of public participation, with *Truth* readers invited to vote for their favourite player. The concept of having football writers and the sporting public select the best players was not unusual: a number of Melbourne's sporting media had been running similar competitions for years.[1199] What distinguished the Cazaly Awards were the sheer number of awards, the large cash prizes and the live televised ceremony to announce the winners.

The VFL publicly endorsed the Cazaly Awards, despite its obvious challenge to the Brownlow's title as football's pre-eminent award. The League's only stipulations were that an award not be given to the best umpire and that the presentations didn't clash with the Brownlow Medal ceremony.[1200]

The Cazalys were compered by Bert Newton and Ernie Sigley, assisted by retired players including Ted Whitten, Jack Dyer and Lou Richards. One player who benefited from their publicity was Geelong's John 'Sam'

Newman, who filled in as co-host one year after Dyer had a car accident on the way to the presentation.

With their live television coverage and celebrity status, the Cazaly Awards soon became the biggest night on the football calendar, attracting hundreds of players, coaches, wives and girlfriends to the ballroom of the Southern Cross Hotel. In 1973, Aggie Cazaly, now 80, attended the inaugural ceremony as a special guest to present Richmond rover Kevin Bartlett with his Gold Cazaly. Aggie said her husband would have been proud to know the awards had been named after him.[1201]

Several prominent VFL players won a Gold Cazaly who never won a Brownlow Medal, including Kevin Bartlett, Leigh Matthews, Sam Newman and Garry Wilson. Gary Dempsey, Graham Moss and Kelvin Templeton won both.[1202] According to Brian Hansen the Cazaly Awards eventually "outlived themselves" but the format of the modern Brownlow Medal ceremony, with its professionalism, glamour and celebrity, owes much to the blueprint they established.

The 'Up there Cazaly' phrase's final, most potent, lease of life came in April 1979 when Channel Seven decided to commission a promotional tune for its football coverage.

The Network's advertising agency asked musician Mike Brady to write a football anthem which might spark the public imagination in the same way as cricket's C'mon Aussie C'mon jingle had the previous summer for the Nine Network.

Brady had been a reluctant convert to Australian Football, having migrated with his parents from England as a soccer-mad 11-year-old in 1959.[1203] On his first day at St Joseph's convent school in Port Melbourne the school bully put him in a headlock and demanded to know which VFL team he barracked for. Brady chose Collingwood in a quick-thinking act of self-preservation:

> I was only a little Pommy kid; I'd only just got off the boat. What I found fascinating—and still find fascinating—was this obsession with football.[1204]

Twenty years later, and in the midst of a successful jingle-writing career, Brady's inspiration came after he recalled a "tough as boots" nun who used to yell "Up there Cazaly" in the school playground. Coincidentally, he'd also watched a televised version of Ray Lawler's *Summer of the Seventeenth* Doll trilogy two nights earlier in which the call was used several times.[1205]

Despite playing some football as a youth and that notional support for Collingwood, Brady hadn't taken much interest in the game since his days at St Joseph's. He had only a hazy notion as to who was Roy Cazaly, but he knew instantly that he had a good hook for a tune.[1206] The expression formed the basis for a song which took Brady just 25 minutes to write and required only minor changes to the lyrics once it was on the page:

> I wrote it straight down and it was so effortless that it was odd. And I knew the moment I'd written it that it was something a little bit special.[1207]

A deceptively simple song at first hearing, Up There Cazaly is actually quite complex because of its unusual key modulations. It begins quietly, almost reflectively, before building to the crescendo of the now famous chorus. Ironically, the mighty roar in the original recording, heard just before the chorus, was taken from an old soccer sound effects record.[1208]

The promotional tune and its accompanying video of spectacular marks was an instant hit with Seven viewers, who flooded the station's switchboard asking where they could buy a copy. Brady and his musical arranger Peter Sullivan quickly re-recorded the song as a single on the Fable record label, hoping it might sell a few thousand copies.[1209] It sold more than 250,000 copies by the end of that year and eclipsed Slim Dusty's Pub With No Beer as Australia's highest selling record.[1210]

The VFL asked Brady to sing the song at the 1979 Grand Final but the deal almost fell through after his manager asked the League for an appearance fee. The lyrics were distributed so the crowd could sing along but they were already so well-known it's unlikely anyone needed them. Brady has performed the song at numerous Grand Finals since 1979, sometimes alongside other artists but usually on his own:

> I always have a big smile on my face whenever I'm singing it because of

the irony of writing a song about football, which at the time I had no idea about.¹²¹¹

The song was used in the 1980 film version of David Williamson's football play *The Club* and has been covered by artists as diverse as Dame Edna Everage, the Red Army Choir and Richard Clayderman.¹²¹² Brady has reworked the lyrics for business and charity events, and the Swans even commissioned an Up There for Sydney version after the team relocated from Melbourne in 1982.¹²¹³ The song helps keep Brady in demand for corporate functions but he admits:

> There have been occasions when I've left it out because I was afraid of what might happen. Late in the season, guests at black-tie dinners take speccys on the dance floor or over tables.¹²¹⁴

In 2007 the AFL chose not to include the song at the Grand Final, a spokesman later saying League research had found people were "sick of it".¹²¹⁵ The resulting uproar on radio talkback and in newspaper letter columns left the League in no doubt about the public's feelings. It was reinstated for the game's 150th celebrations in 2008, and the League and Brady have since reconciled.

More than 35 years after it was released the song Brady jokingly refers to as his "superannuation composition" remains his signature tune. Beyond that, it stands as a joyous celebration of the national game, now regularly reprised as part of Grand Final celebrations.

The other enduring feature associated with Cazaly that continues to fire the public imagination is the 1924 *The Sporting Globe* photograph of his leap over Essendon's Norm Beckton.

The image has been reproduced numerous times since its first publication and is regularly included in lists of Australian Football's most iconic photos.¹²¹⁶ The unedited version was used to illustrate Percy Bentley's chapter on ruckwork in the *The Sporting Globe*'s 1946 *Football Book*, where it was captioned as a "perfect hit-out".¹²¹⁷ In 1972 *The Sun* featured it among

Australia's greatest sporting pictures and it was included in a book of *100 Great Marks* compiled by football journalists Scott Palmer and Greg Hobbs in 1974.[1218]

Mike Brady used the image to illustrate the sheet music for Up There Cazaly and in 1994 it inspired a set of 100 Cazaly Classics football swap cards issued by the *Herald Sun*.[1219] During the AFL's centenary year in 1996 the *Herald Sun* chose it as the frontispiece for its *100 Years of Footy* and the artist Robert Ingpen incorporated it in a huge tapestry commissioned to mark the Melbourne Cricket Ground's 150th anniversary in 2003.[1220] The following year, artist Hayden Dewar included the leaping Cazaly (and the accompanying phrase) in a 50-metre mural he painted on the side of Dimmey's department store in Richmond, strategically placing him between the cartoon character Ginger Meggs and the gangster 'Squizzy' Taylor.[1221]

Public fascination with the original photo means it generates discussion every time it is reprinted. In 1979 its reproduction following the release of Up There Cazaly sparked a readers' debate in several newspapers between those who thought it showed a mark and those convinced it was a tap. In 2008 its publication in the *Herald Sun* even created discussion about whether Cazaly's opponent in the photo was in fact Essendon's Norm Beckton or Carlton's Charlie McSwain.[1222]

Given the image's pervasiveness, it is ironic that Cazaly is barely identifiable in the original *The Sporting Globe* photo because his face is obscured by his upraised left arm. In an intriguing paradox, he remains both relatively anonymous and instantly recognisable.[1223] And a split-

second image captured in time has come to symbolise both the man himself and the very feature of the national game which makes it so identifiably Australian.

33

REAPPRAISING THE LEGEND

Almost since Australian Football's very formation, spectators and commentators have debated, compared and argued over its greatest players.

Many players from Cazaly's era ranked him among the best to have played the game. A number who played alongside or against him considered him *the* best all-rounder or follower they had seen, including Laurie Nash, former South Melbourne coach Artie Wood, Richmond defender Vic Thorp, Geelong rover Alex Eason and Collingwood champion Syd Coventry. Others, such as Coventry's brother Gordon, bracketed him with Fred Fleiter and Mark Tandy in the best ruck combination they had seen.[1224]

Sporting journalists of Cazaly's time were lavish in their praise. In 1923 *The Argus*' Reg Wilmot included him in a list of the best ruckmen from the previous four decades.[1225] Seven years later, *The Sporting Globe*'s Wallace 'Jumbo' Sharland described Cazaly as the best all-round player since Essendon champion Albert Thurgood, who had last played in 1906. Sharland had "not the slightest doubt" Cazaly would have won the Brownlow Medal at least once had it existed earlier in his career.[1226] In the same year, *The Referee*'s Harold Prider described Cazaly as probably "the greatest utility player in the game's history".[1227]

In 1942 experienced football writer Hec de Lacy set out to rank the best players he'd seen during the previous two decades. He first listed a number of qualifications:

> He must be a match winner. He must be able to turn the cause that seems lost. He must be dynamic—able to take advantage of every break coming his way in the game. He must be a stubborn fighter in the face of relentless opposition. He must have all the gifts—be able to mark and kick well, dispose of the ball accurately, have a good football head and afford a measure of protection for his teammates.

Using this criteria de Lacy assessed the merits of a number of players before rating Cazaly number one, ahead of dual Brownlow medallist Ivor Warne-Smith, Laurie Nash and Syd Coventry.[1228]

In 1958, football historian Cec Mullen took a longer view, including Cazaly in his list of the 13 best players in the first hundred years of the game.[1229] Mullen had been born in 1895 and followed the game his entire life, so his judgment can be said to carry weight.[1230]

The modern era saw renewed interest in the game's greatest players, with further attempts to compare and rank them. One of the first to do so was sports journalist and author Jim Main, who in 1977 compiled his own list of the best hundred footballers of all time. Main approached his task chronologically, starting with St Kilda's Vic Cumberland and concluding with Essendon's 1976 Brownlow medallist Graham Moss. He placed Cazaly at number four, between Dick Lee and Ivor Warne-Smith.[1231]

In 1981, the Herald and Weekly Times published a list of 240 VFL greats. *The Herald*'s chief football writer Mike Sheahan and *The Sporting Globe*'s Greg Hobbs reviewed the game's various eras, named its great players and selected the best ever from each of the VFL teams. Cazaly was included in an article contributed by *The Herald*'s former chief football writer Alf Brown and he was chosen as one of South Melbourne's best ever 20 players.[1232]

Cazaly was inducted into the Sport Australia Hall of Fame (SAHOF) in 1987. Athlete membership is limited to those who have achieved the highest honours in their sport and embody its values of courage, sportsmanship, integrity, mateship, persistence and excellence. To date, Cazaly is one of only 21 Australian Footballers among the SAHOF membership, alongside such greats as Ron Barassi, Kevin Bartlett, Peter Hudson, Leigh Matthews, Laurie Nash and Bob Skilton.[1233]

But Cazaly's highest sporting recognition was yet to come. As the centenary of the VFL/AFL in 1996 approached, the League's Chief Executive Officer Ross Oakley decided to establish an Australian Football Hall of Fame to recognise those who had made a significant contribution to the game since its inception. Oakley's vision was inspired by a visit to the National Baseball Hall of Fame in Cooperstown, New York.[1234] Established in 1939, it has grown to become a national institution and the template for many other sporting halls of fame around the world.

Oakley adopted the rigour of the Baseball Hall of Fame's approach to honouring their greatest players but departed from its model in two key respects. First, rather than establish a cumbersome series of selection panels, he appointed a single committee to consider candidates for the Australian Football Hall of Fame. In establishing the committee, he sought out people with a passion for the game and an understanding of its history across various eras.[1235]

Oakley's second departure from the Baseball Hall of Fame model was to ensure that eligibility criteria for the Australian Football Hall of Fame was not overly prescriptive. The number of games played, coached or umpired were important but candidates were also assessed on the basis of their ability, integrity, sportsmanship and character. This latitude allowed committee members to consider an individual's excellence and overall impact on the game—broader criteria more likely to stimulate useful discussion than a simple, black and white review of their career statistics.[1236]

The selection committee met several times from mid-1995 to decide who to recommend for the initial Hall of Fame intake. Those on the committee recall it being an intensive and exhaustive process. Nominations were made by clubs, leagues and committee members themselves. Clarifying information was sought on particular candidates when required and their suitability further discussed. Shortlists were drafted, compared, debated and rewritten. To help ensure a consensus, each nominee required the support of three-quarters of committee members in order to be endorsed.

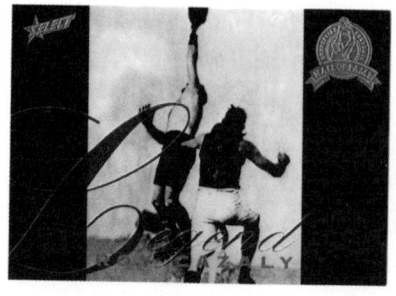
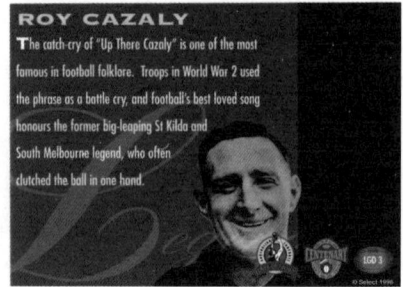

The committee eventually recommended 136 Hall of Fame inductees, of whom 12 were selected as inaugural Legends. To be eligible for Legend status, players must have made a significant and permanent contribution to the game.[1237] In choosing the inaugural Legends one committee member revealed that E J 'Ted' Whitten was the only automatic selection agreed to at their first meeting, a decision hastened by the fact that Whitten was very ill at the time.[1238] Another recalled that John Nicholls was not on the original shortlist but was added after another candidate was withdrawn. When attention turned to Cazaly, some on the committee were familiar with his career while others initially knew little beyond Mike Brady's song. One member later said there was no doubt the song helped but added that Cazaly had an impressive record and there was no question about his standing. His inclusion was unanimous.[1239]

The 12 inaugural Legends selected by the committee were Ron Barassi, Haydn Bunton snr, Roy Cazaly, John Coleman, Jack Dyer, Graham 'Polly' Farmer, Leigh Matthews, John Nicholls, Bob Pratt, Dick Reynolds, Bob Skilton and Ted Whitten.[1240]

The selection committee's broad criteria and the fact their decisions are made behind closed doors has led to occasional public debate about the judging process and the merits of various candidates. It has also caused controversy, most notably when Collingwood president Eddie McGuire and many fans campaigned to have Lou Richards elevated to Legend status during the lead up to the 2009 Hall of Fame inductions.[1241] Eventually, Ross Oakley went public to defend the Hall of Fame criteria and the integrity of its selection process:

> The title of Legend was established very clearly for on-field performance. It was reserved for the very best in the game, those who had a tremendous impact on the game on-field, and changed the game in some way for all time. If you look at the Legends nominated, they all fit that category.[1242]

Other recognition followed. In 1999, a dozen of the *Herald Sun*'s football writers marked the impeding millennium by ranking their top 200 footballers of the 20th century. Of the first 50 players selected, only Haydn Bunton, Dick Reynolds, Gordon Coventry, Bob Pratt, Laurie Nash, Ivor Warne-Smith, Jack Dyer and Allan Hopkins played before World War II. Roy Cazaly was named at number 56, ahead of such modern greats as Tim Watson, Gary Dempsey, Stephen Silvagni, James Hird, Gerard Healy and Paul Kelly. Among his contemporaries, Cazaly was listed ahead of Albert and Harry Collier, Syd Coventry, Dick Lee, Dave McNamara, Carji Greeves, Horrie Clover, Colin Watson and Vic Cumberland.[1243]

In 2008, football journalist Mike Sheahan took on an even more ambitious task: selecting and ranking the best 50 players from the game's first 150 years. He considered many factors when compiling his list but his "guiding principle" for inclusion was that a player had to have consistently influenced the game over a long period.[1244] Sheahan candidly admitted his task was next to impossible and "reckless at best". He knew his selections would prove contentious as they were based on the subjective analysis of just one judge. He also acknowledged the difficulty of assessing those who played before he was born.[1245]

As Sheahan predicted, his selections sparked controversy. Much of it related to his ranking of individuals from the game's modern era but there was also a side debate concerning the lack of representation from the period Sheahan's *Herald Sun* colleague Trevor Grant called the 'Dark Ages' of Australian Football. Grant noted that Sheahan's list included only nine players from the pre-World War II era and just four who played before 1930: Dick Lee, Gordon and Syd Coventry and Albert Collier. Essendon's Albert Thurgood, probably the greatest player from the game's formative years, was left out, as were Peter Burns, Horrie Clover, Vic Cumberland and Cazaly, who Grant described as an "unlucky omission".[1246]

In recent years, the criteria for selecting "best players" has been broadened and redefined to better acknowledge the contribution of players from different cultural backgrounds. A Greek Team of the Century was announced in 2004, an Indigenous Team of the Century in 2005 and a VFL/AFL Italian Team of the Century in 2007. In July 2013 the AFL named a Multicultural Team of Champions, the "best 22 VFL/AFL multicultural players" since 1896. In order to be considered, a player or at least one of his parents had to have been born overseas. Although this was probably not the intent, this criteria favoured players from the game's earliest years and from Australia's post-war era, the two periods when players or their parents were most likely to have been born overseas. From a squad of 50 nominees, Ukrainian-born Alex Jesaulenko was chosen as captain, Jock McHale (of Irish parentage) was named coach and Cazaly secured a "double guernsey" selection in the ruck, on the basis that his father James was English and his mother Elizabeth was born in Scotland.[1247]

In 2013, the Australian Football website invited Jim Main to review and update his 1977 list of football's greatest players, taking account of those who had emerged in the three and a half decades since he had compiled it. After careful consideration, Main 'delisted' and replaced 20 players from his original hundred, but retained Cazaly.[1248]

The quandary faced by Main, Sheahan and various Hall of Fame selection committees in assessing those they never saw play underscores both the difficulty of compiling such lists and the contrasting approaches taken. For historians such as Main, a close study of football history leads them to conclude that the enduring contribution of certain players will always guarantee them a place among the game's greats. Main included Cazaly in his 1977 list on that basis and retained him when he later revised it.

Many journalists and administrators take a different approach. The fact that most of them grew up during the television era has resulted in a preference for players from the modern era when selecting teams of the century and similar representative squads. Football writer and historian Adam Cardosi argues that this inbuilt bias has skewed the Australian Football Hall of Fame selection process:

With very few exceptions, the achievements and relative merits of the men of the pre-TV era are not canvassed, and their case for inclusion almost never made. That is because popular debate about footy history tends to be confined to living memory, which now stretches back no further than the war years. As such, it is widely assumed that because no one alive today saw the 'old-timers' play, can watch them on video, or can otherwise assess their contribution visually or by first-hand account, they are beyond assessment and therefore cannot be considered.

As a result, says Cardosi:

> If we take the HOF at face value, footy legends only started to appear in number from the 1930s, and reached a high point in the 1960s and 1970s ... Thus, according to the HOF's reckoning, the first 65 years of the game is worth one legend, while the next 65 years is worth 24 legends.[1249]

Another difficulty in comparing early players with their modern counterparts is the absence of detailed statistics from the game's formative years. While goals and, later, behinds were recorded from football's early days, it was not until the 1930s that newspapers began publishing the total kicks, marks, handballs and free kicks from each game. Detailed individual player statistics came even later and were not regularly recorded until the mid-1960s.[1250] The advent of Harry Beitzel's *Footy Week* magazine in 1965 ushered in a statistics revolution. For the first time, supporters could now read and analyse their favourite player's match statistics in detail each week. According to Carlton premiership player and latter-day statistics guru Ted Hopkins, it was the first time kicks, marks, handballs, scores, free kicks and tackles were available for every player, every round.[1251]

Hopkins, who founded the sports statistics company Champion Data in 1995, acknowledges the difficulty of assessing footballers from the distant past. But while noting the dearth of early statistics, he cites other criteria which can help identify great players from *any* era, including superb athleticism, fitness and conditioning; a pursuit of excellence in training and skills development; career longevity; and consistent performance at the highest level. For Hopkins, these are enduring yardsticks, which can be used to separate the approach of the professionally minded player from the "casual amateurism" of the rest.[1252] His benchmarks call to mind Cazaly's own description of that internal "dynamic drive to succeed", which he believed set great players apart from their peers.[1253]

Commentators, historians, statisticians and fans will continue to review, debate and rank Australian Football's best players. If we accept the premise that the stamp of greatness can be identified regardless of playing era then Roy Cazaly's continuing place among the game's champions seems assured.

34

AFTERWORD

> Sports do not build character; they reveal it.
>
> US SPORTS WRITER HEYWOOD HALE BROUN

In 1976, the artist and activist Noel Counihan was asked to write an entry on Roy Cazaly for the Australian Dictionary of Biography (ADB) project. Counihan had grown up in South Melbourne and was the young boy whose father had introduced him to Cazaly in South Melbourne's rooms during the early 1920s.[1254] Counihan was amazed by the extent of Cazaly's crowded life. After examining his life in detail he wrote—half jokingly, half pleadingly—to the ADB's editor Geoffrey Serle:

> Did you know what you were letting me in for when you made that blithe request? I know every writer must plague you for more space but really Cazaly's career is quite rich—a many sided versatile and exceptional athlete and more besides. One could go on for pages about this unusual bloke: he was a physical instructor, mastered Swedish massage methods, became involved in the study of muscular anatomy and of treating muscular injury, studied and practised Sister Kenny's methods during the polio epidemic ... He became an outstanding trainer of horses in Tassie and built up a big health clinic in Hobart ... So unless you're going to be content with a truncated, potted, cryptic catalogue of events—even then incomplete and unbalanced—I must have more words.[1255]

Counihan had discovered what others have learned before and since: that once examined in detail Roy Cazaly's life proves to be far richer than the sum of its parts.

One winter several years ago, I drove to Minyip in north-west Victoria. I chose the town because there had been very little written about Cazaly's time there in 1925-26 and I thought I might find clues to his character and temperament. What I learned was instructive. As he had at his previous clubs, Cazaly had thrown himself into the local community and been an active member of its football team, both on and off the field. He ran a store in the main street and played district cricket over the summer. And yet he was reportedly "out of sorts and dispirited" during his time there, his business went bankrupt and he left just as the football team was negotiating to reappoint him for another season.

As I researched Cazaly's life further I began to detect a theme. Although he was a man with many achievements, he seems to have taken setbacks to heart and been occasionally wrong-footed by them. Cazaly's circumstances at Hawthorn at the end of 1942 were similar to those when he left Minyip. Following a disappointing season he went to ground, avoiding the club secretary who called at his home to discuss his reappointment. He stayed on at Hawthorn but returned to Tasmania a year later, despite taking the team to within a point of their first final. In both cases, Cazaly retreated to the security of past experiences and the people and places he knew best. In 1926, he had returned to South Melbourne, the scene of many of his playing triumphs. In 1943, he went back to Tasmania, the state where he had recorded his best coaching results during the 1920s and '30s.

Could such episodes have induced moments of self-doubt, melancholia or even depression? There were, after all, cases of mental illness in his family and one (and probably two) of his brothers had committed suicide. This is of course mere conjecture. Cazaly appears to have confided in no one, there are no letters or diaries to elucidate his inner thoughts and depression was—until relatively recently—a largely undiagnosed and misunderstood condition.

What is not in dispute is that Cazaly overcame many personal and sporting stumbling blocks during his lifetime. As a schoolboy, he conquered a stutter by teaching himself a method of diaphragm control which slowed his breathing and his speech. As a young footballer he overcame an injury to his right leg by teaching himself to kick equally well, and eventually better, with his left. He was dropped by St Kilda in 1912 but worked his way back into the side via district football. He and Aggie lost their first child Bessie to diphtheria. He took a stand on the incessant infighting gripping St Kilda and left the club. In 1922, he took responsibility for South Melbourne's poor form and quit as coach and captain, but stayed on as a player. He regrouped from a poor season with City in 1929 to lead them to another local and state premiership the next year. His two seasons as South Melbourne's Senior coach in 1937-38 ended in failure but he remained in 1939 to mentor the Seconds and help rebuild the club's fortunes. After his failed bid for the Tasmanian Parliament in 1950 he swallowed his pride and got on with coaching New Town to another premiership the next year.

In dealing with each of these many setbacks Cazaly no doubt reflected on guidance he had often given others to help restore his own self-belief. It was advice he had learnt from South Melbourne's head trainer Jack Marshall:

> A man might be feeling down and out, but then is the time he needs to assert himself, and fight back for his place in society, and maybe his self-respect.[1256]

Many things made Cazaly a great player, but this determination to overcome adversity was his most enduring attribute. Late in life he said that a champion footballer was both born *and* made. He knew that while natural ability was an important prerequisite for success, willpower and self-belief could turn a very good player into a great one.

Cazaly showed his resolve in many ways. When he was young, he invented novel ways to practise his skills and reflexes. He would string a football from a rope and practise his marking from different angles. To improve his agility and evasive skills he would run straight at trees in Albert Park and dodge them at the last second. He strove to make the most of every opportunity. He knew it was largely by chance that he had been selected for his first game at St Kilda and he was determined to do all he could to stay in the side. As a young player he set out to learn from teammates and opponents alike. Throughout his career he sought to become the complete footballer and would work assiduously on what are now called the 'one percenters'.

He watched how the club masseurs prepared and treated players, and he developed his own regime to avoid and treat injuries. In the days before club clinicians he knew that a good diet was important. He never smoked, avoided fatty foods and didn't drink alcohol. "I am always keen to stress the need of perfect physical fitness and the care of the body", he once wrote. "I fussed over my injuries between matches, sparing no effort to be 100 per cent fit as a game started."[1257] He later applied what he had learned about fitness and human anatomy to become a successful physiotherapist.

Cazaly's meticulous approach to diet, fitness and training paid off. His VFL career spanned 17 seasons: in the first hundred years of the VFL/AFL only 34 footballers played more.[1258] If not for his occasional injuries, the two years that St Kilda spent in recess during World War I and his season at Minyip in 1925, he would have become the first footballer to play 100 games with two different VFL clubs.[1259] He got better with age and experience. He won South Melbourne's inaugural best-and-fairest award in his second-last League season, when he was almost 34. More than 90 years later, he remains the Swans' oldest best-and-fairest winner. His supreme fitness enabled him to play two games for Camberwell when he was 48, and he played in charity matches well into his sixties.

Although Cazaly had some coaching success in Victoria, his greatest victories came in Tasmania, where he took everything he had learned as a player and applied it to his coaching. He understood that players were motivated by different stimuli. Some responded well to team lectures, others learned best when taken aside individually. He spoke quietly but with conviction, in a way that made players lean in to listen closely to what he had to say.

He knew it didn't matter how many great players a coach had at his disposal, success can only come through unselfish teamwork and systematic play. He stressed the importance of each player knowing their role, and being ready to back up a teammate. He demanded they achieve and retain peak physical fitness. Anything less, he declared, was unfair to themselves, the team and their supporters.

He was a thinker and an experimenter. He studied the way the game was changing, and trialled new methods to give his teams an advantage over their opponents. During matches he rode every passage of play from the boundary line, revelled in his teams' victories and felt their losses keenly.

Cazaly had admirable moral qualities. He despised bullies and labelled them cowards. Teammates and opponents said he was tough but fair, a player who rarely started a fight but was prepared to finish one if necessary. Off the field, he was hailed for his essential decency. Fame did not swell his ego, or alter his moral compass. To many young men he was a *de facto* father; to many women he was their ideal of how a man should behave. His moral approach to life is best summed up by the advice he gave his children:

> Do right and right will come of it. Do wrong and no good will ever come of it.[1260]

Like many men of his era, Cazaly was taciturn in public and seemed reserved to those meeting him for the first time. And yet in private he showed enormous kindness towards his family and to his grandchildren in particular. He took strength from Aggie, his tough-as-teak companion who stood by him through all his endeavours, advised him on his opponents, nursed his injuries and kept the finances in order. Cazaly had spent his childhood and adolescence living in cramped houses so when he finally settled in Tasmania he chose a block of land large enough for his whole family. He and Aggie lived far enough away from their children to give them privacy but close enough to allow regular family get-togethers and celebrations.

Unlike other busy and successful men, he did not draw a demarcation between his sport, his work and his family. He included his children and later his grandchildren in all his activities, even something as simple as cleaning his boots or helping feed his horses. The physiotherapy practice, too, was a family enterprise in which everyone played their part. It helped Cazaly reconnect with his son after their six years apart during the war, and it allowed his daughters and sons-in-law to play important roles in its operations.

For a while I puzzled over how Cazaly went from being a unionist on the wharves to standing for parliament as a Liberal Party candidate. Noel Counihan thought this reflected his change in prosperity over time but I believe the real answer lay in his continuing belief in the power of collective action, whether working on the docks or organising greyhound breeders.[1261] For Cazaly, taking on advocacy roles was instinctual. He was a natural leader and others looked to him to state their case, run their meetings and help settle their disputes.

In many ways Cazaly was an uncomplicated man. He took pleasure in small things, such as training his horses or reading a good western. His family teased him for being a soft touch, whether it was feeding stray animals or giving a loan to a stranger. He could be hard-nosed when negotiating coaching contracts but beyond that money never meant as much to him as someone's word. He was humbled by simple acts. He had a sideboard full of sporting trophies but when New Town's players gave him a modest petition thanking him for his years of service he cherished it above all his other awards.[1262]

Cazaly finally retired from coaching after the 1954 Tasmanian state team victory, but he never really gave football away. He was always prepared to help out at a football clinic, give one of his famous blackboard lectures or provide advice to a junior player. In retirement he maintained loyal friendships with former teammates. They came to visit him at Lenah Valley and he sought them out whenever he visited Melbourne.

It seemed Cazaly would go on forever, which made his crippling illness and lingering decline all the more perplexing and distressing to his family. They took turns watching over him as he lay ill, and when he died they were bereft.

Time marches on. It is now more than 120 years since Roy Cazaly's birth and half a century since his death. Mike Brady's anthem is the only reason most present-day Australians have heard of Cazaly, but it would be churlish to argue, as some have, that he is only remembered today because of it. The reason there is a song is because there was a phrase that captured the imagination of men and women who incorporated it into their language. This everyday expression—sometimes used as encouragement, sometimes to express surprise or delight—remained part of our language throughout the 1920s, the Great Depression, World War II and beyond, until it eventually went the way of words such as 'cobber' and 'strewth'.

Even then Cazaly's name refused to die. Before Brady's song there was

AFTERWORD

Ray Lawler's *Seventeenth Doll* trilogy with its 'Up there Cazaly' references and the Truth Cazaly Awards, which for almost a decade rivalled the Brownlow Medal in acknowledging the game's best. While these events revived interest in Roy Cazaly, his story had never really gone away. It had simply lain dormant in the collective memory, waiting to be rekindled and heard by a new generation.

Appendix 1

LIFE AND CAREER HIGHLIGHTS

1893	Born in South Melbourne, the last of 10 children.
1913	Marries Agnes Murtha. They have six children, the first born in 1915.
1911-15 & 1918-20	St Kilda (VFL): 99 games, 39 goals. Plays in 1913 Grand Final. Best and fairest winner in 1918 and captain in 1920. Coaches Camberwell (VJFA) in 1916, South Melbourne District (VJFA) in 1917 and South Warrnambool (WDL) in 1919 finals.
1921-24 & 1926-27	South Melbourne (VFL): 99 games, 128 goals. Top goalscorer in 1921 (19) and 1922 (28). Captain-coach 1922 (part). Coaches South Warrnambool (WDL) in 1921 finals. Wins *The Herald* award for the League's best follower in 1921; *The Sporting Globe* award for the League's best follower in 1922 and League's best all-round player in 1922, 1923 and 1924. Club best and fairest 1927. Plays for Waterside Workers (Wednesday Football League) in 1927.
1925	Captain-coach of Minyip (Wimmera League). Also plays for Litchfield-Carron (NWDFL) in mid-week competition.
1921-26	Plays 13 Victorian representative games, including at 1921 and 1924 Australian National Football Carnivals; kicks 8 goals.
1928-30	Captain-coach of City (NTFA). Local and state premiers 1928 and 1930.
1930	Tasmanian vice-captain, Australian National Football Carnival (Adelaide).
1931	Captain-coach of Preston (VFA) and Waterside Workers (Wednesday Football League).
1932-33	Captain-coach of North Hobart (TFL). Premiers in 1932.
1934-36	Captain-coach of New Town (TFL). Premiers in 1935.
1937-39	Coach of South Melbourne (VFL) Seniors (1937-38), Seconds (1939).
1941	Coach of Camberwell (VFA). Plays two games aged 48.

LIFE AND CAREER HIGHLIGHTS

1942 - 43	Coach of Hawthorn (VFL).
1944	Coach of Hobart Police (United Services Association). Southern and state premiers.
Post war	Physiotherapist in Hobart.
1948-51	Coach of New Town (TFL). Premiers in 1948, 1949 and 1951. State premiers in 1948.
1950	Liberal candidate for Denison (Hobart).
1954	TFL coach and state coach, Tasmania vs Australian Amateurs.
1956	Winning trainer, Tasmanian Pacing Championship, with Master Barry.
1963	Dies in Hobart aged 70.

Appendix 2

Contemporary Honours

National

Named in the AFL Australia Post Multicultural Team of Champions, 2013

Inducted into Sport Australia Hall of Fame (Athlete Member), 1987

Victoria

Inducted into South Melbourne Districts Football Club Hall of Fame, 2012

Named an inaugural Legend, Sydney Swans/South Melbourne Hall of Fame, 2009

Inducted into AFL Hall of Fame and named one of 12 inaugural Legends, 1996

Tasmania

Medal for coach of winning Tasmanian statewide league team named in his honour, 2009

Elevated to Icon status, Tasmanian Football Hall of Fame, 2007

One of four Legend coaches inducted into Tasmanian Football Hall of Fame, 2005

Named coach of Tasmanian Football Team of the Century, 2004

Inducted into Tasmanian Sporting Hall of Fame, 1987

Roy Cazaly Stand opened at North Hobart Oval, 1961

Tasmanian clubs

North Hobart and South Launceston compete for the Roy Cazaly Perpetual Trophy, 2011-13

Inducted into Glenorchy Hall of Fame, 2002

Named at half-forward in City/City-South's Team of the Century, 2002

Named coach of New Town Team of the Century, 2000

Named assistant coach of North Hobart Team of the Century, 2000

Glenorchy's best-and-fairest award named after him, 1980

Other

Cazaly Stadium in Cairns

'Cazalys' Sports Club opens in Palmerston, Northern Territory, 1999

Cazaly ward named in Darebin Council (Preston, Melbourne), 1994

Mike Brady writes Up There Cazaly, 1979

Truth Cazaly football awards, 1973-81

Appendix 3

Roy Cazaly's advice to players

Fitness

"Keep moving, so that the blood you have forced into circulation does not become cold again. A cold body is subject to cramp, takes the knocks and feels them, thus losing energy, and a slow muscle does not respond as quickly as a warm one. A warm man is 50 per cent more efficient than a cold man."

"Condition is a dominating factor in any game. Spare no effort to be fit. Be intelligent in this regard. Hard work without regard to strength and energy used up can make a man stale more quickly than anything else."

"Most young players who come into the game are callow. They become the butt of the old-timer, the wily old dogs who know every short-cut in the game. But the young fellow has one big advantage, the strength of his youth. He should be jumping out of his skin, while the veteran, after a few hot tussles, is back on his heels. So don't throw away your greatest asset: youth and perfect elastic fitness."

"My advice to any young footballer is to get himself in condition and retain that condition in summer and winter. If he is 100 per cent fit he will be able to use his ability to the full."

Health and diet

"Care for your health. A good point is to do your training and to have your shower and rub down without delay. Hanging about in a training room invites cold and body chills. Each prevent a man being at his top."

"Remember your feet have to carry you. Preserve them as much as possible. At times I have fortified the soles of my feet by rubbing them with methylated spirit. If your feet are tired after a game do not hesitate to bathe them in soda and water."

"For my part, I have always 'dried out', as a boxer would. I avoid as many liquids as possible from Thursday evening to Saturday evening."

"I neither drink alcohol nor smoke, and would pass on the same advice to the young player. Your wind must be clean and neither practice helps you achieve it."

"Those who lacked the guts to cut out beer and cigarettes and late nights had no business in a football team."

Training

"In regard to training, every man must know himself and what he requires. What is food for one is poison for another. Train as you hope to play. Do not be content to jog around the ground. Ten minutes of quick flashing work is worth two hours of slow, dragging work. The game is played in five-yard dashes, not in marathons."

"Do not let your football finish with the last game of the season. I am never out of training. I therefore do not have to undergo the grind of those first few training nights. My muscles are always fit, not flabby."

Treating injuries

"The player who attends to an injury without delay keeps in the game. Never neglect the slightest knock."

"I always worked to the idea that a footballer taking the field with even a bruised toe was a sick man. So I fussed over my injuries between matches, sparing no effort to be 100 per cent fit as a game started."

Equipment

"Care of your boots is vital … Be properly shod in a well-fitting pair of boots, properly laced, and light to the feet. A bad boot might mean the poor kick that loses the game."

Leadership

"There can be only one leader. If you don't agree with your captain's decisions obey him first and argue, if you must, afterwards."

Teamwork

"For a club to be successful it must also be necessary to sink individuality, and think only in a club spirit."

"Combination is not born into teams, it is ground into them by intelligent footballers. You have to work for everything you get."

"The secret of success in a team is balance … Teams might have their stars, but if there is not combination, balance, determination, and a willingness to give of their best they must expect to lose …"

"At all times be ready to back up a teammate. This is a forgotten art in a generation of individualists. A clever piece of shepherding that allows a teammate a way through the ranks is better than some spectacular effort that gets the team nowhere in particular."

"A player should remember that loyalty to his club counts for a lot more than selfishness. Football matches are won through sacrifice. If you are beaten, be beaten as a team, with every man in the last ditch and still full of fight."

Strategy and tactics

"I always impress on players to 'think football'. It is not sufficient that they should remain idle when the ball is at the other end. They must think all the time of what might happen, and look for weaknesses in the opposing side that can be played on, and the best way to overcome the strength of opposing teams."

"If you are clever enough, go round, never 'come through'. Leave that for the bullocks of the game, but have the courage to keep on your feet when the world is spinning round you, to keep on leading out when you hardly have the strength to reach the ball, to have the sense to throw yourself in the road of an opponent that a teammate may take advantage of the opening, even if it is the last thing you do that day."

"You have to go four quarters if called upon. No matter how fit you are, there is only one way to do this. Use your grey matter. Do not hesitate to walk if the opportunity presents itself. Stand still, if need be. Cultivate that anticipation and ball sense that sends you to the right place without traversing unnecessary ground."

"Don't run with the ball. You can kick it farther and faster and with less effort … Don't mark with a teammate. Remember only one pair of hands can hold the ball. Talk to him, and if he is nominated for the mark, scout in case he misses it."

"More kicks come a player's way on the ground than in the air. A player will therefore get more kicks if he applies himself to learning to dash, to bend, to turn or dodge to get the ball on the ground, and to break clear …"

Natural ability

"It seems to me that a champion footballer is both born *and* made."

Persistence

"[South Melbourne's masseur Jack Marshall] always impressed upon me that, when I might feel like giving in, to fight back the hardest, as it was then that the other fellow was most likely to be feeling the same. That advice I consider should be followed in all walks of life. A man might be feeling down and out, but then is the time he needs to assert himself, and fight back for his place in society, and maybe his self-respect."

"If you want to know whether a man is washed up, look at his feet. If he can't lift his feet he can't lift his game—his heart may still be willing, but his best will be second-rate."

"If a match is going against your side, if you are fighting hard and your best isn't good enough, remember one thing, your opponent is human like yourself. Just keep pegging away at him. Maybe he is nearer to cracking than you think. Never give up."

"In conclusion, it is the little things that make for success in football. Watch out for the details."

Appendix 4

'UP THERE CAZALY' OVER TIME

"[Fred Fleiter] usually stood down when I was going for the ball, and every time he was near me would exclaim 'Up there, Cazza'. Well, the saying spread among my teammates, and then to the crowd, until it came to the time that whenever I jumped for a mark South's supporters would roar in unison, 'Up, Cazaly.' I heard the cry in Perth, again in the country centres in which I have played, and the cry seems to be general in Tasmania."
'BRAINS AND FOOTBALL: ROY CAZALY'S CAREER AND LESSONS LEARNED', *THE MERCURY*, 19 OCTOBER, 1935

"Everywhere in Australia where the national code of football is played, the saying 'Up there, Cazaly' is as well known as any other sporting term in any game."
PERCY TAYLOR IN *THE ARGUS*, 3 APRIL, 1937

"People who know nothing of the cry's origins, even in the remotest parts of Australia, when the occasion suits the sense, yell 'Up there, Cazaly!' No war cry has travelled so far as that started by the South Melbourne ruck, and taken up by the Southern followers."
THE SPORTING GLOBE, 28 APRIL, 1937

"There's a lot of danger in these auctions, when you come to notice … 'Two shillings', says a woman in the front row. 'Up a shilling', says the one next to

her. 'Up sixpence', comes a voice from the fringes. 'Up there, Cazaly', says I, catching the infection ..."
GORDON WILLIAMS, 'GOING, GOING, GONE' IN *THE ARGUS*, 14 JANUARY, 1939

"Everyone on board is in fine fettle, the South boys especially. The old cry 'Up there, Cazaly' is quite common."
AUSTRALIAN SOLDIER JOHN O'MULLANE'S LETTER HOME FROM A TROOP SHIP, THE *SOUTH MELBOURNE RECORD*, 3 AUGUST, 1940

"*Up there Cazaly!* Used as a cry of encouragement."
SIDNEY BAKER, *A POPULAR DICTIONARY OF AUSTRALIAN SLANG* (3RD ED), 1943

"Cheers of 'Up there, Cazaly!' greeted the Townies' non-playing coach, Roy Cazaly, as he stood on a table to address players."
THE EXAMINER, 3 OCTOBER, 1949

"[BARNEY reading the telegram, gives an "Ah" of fond relief]
BARNEY: Whaddya know—it's from Nancy.
OLIVE [tightly]: I guessed it would be.
BARNEY [reading]: Up there Cazaly, lots of love—Nance."
RAY LAWLER, *SUMMER OF THE SEVENTEENTH DOLL*, ACT ONE, SCENE ONE, 1957

"[The expression] is still heard on its 'home' ground. A cockatoo which lives at the clubrooms sometimes even shatters the sedate atmosphere of a district cricket match on a Saturday afternoon with a shrill shriek across the ground, 'Up there Cazaly—Oh you beaut!'"
THE AGE, 22 JANUARY, 1958

"While coolly robbing a jeweller's or sticking up a bank, one or other of them is usually heard to utter some give-away locution like 'Stone the crows' or 'Up there, Cazaly'."
THE BULLETIN, 26 FEBRUARY, 1972

"Today, another pest (sometimes described as a fever and sometimes as a religion) threatens New South Wales, the curious Victorian aberration known as 'Australian Rules'. It crossed the Murray years ago, but now it has crossed the Murrumbidgee and before long, unless vigorous methods are invoked, the cry of 'Up there Cazaly!' will resound throughout Sydney ..."
CYRIL PEARL, LETTER TO *THE AGE*, 13 SEPTEMBER, 1972

"To many Australians the words 'Up there Cazaly' have a special meaning as a form of greeting and a sign of recognition between fellow countrymen."
THE *DAILY MIRROR*, 9 JUNE, 1978

"It was 1979, when Carlton beat Collingwood in the Grand Final and it was the first time 'Up there Cazaly' had come out … When they played it before the game, I had tears in my eyes—I thought to myself, 'you silly, old bugger'."
ST KILDA PREMIERSHIP PLAYER KEVIN 'COWBOY' NEALE, THE *CANBERRA TIMES*, 26 MAY, 1995

"If the current obsession with statistical mumbo-jumbo had been around 20 years ago, the song *Up There Cazaly* would have been titled *Contested Mark Cazaly*."
ANTHONY SHARWOOD, 'STATISTICAL JARGON KILLING FOOTY', ONLINE BLOG, 2005

"Nothing is more uplifting than a rousing 'Up there Cazaly', no matter what time of the year. I will never get sick of hearing it."
ANN O'NEILL, *THE HERALD SUN* LETTERS ONLINE, 2 OCTOBER, 2007

"I can remember being in Mildura at half-time and *Up There Cazaly* would come on. Since then that little boy just wanted to play football."
AFL PLAYER JASON AKERMANIS IN *THE AGE*, 22 JULY, 2010

"Up there Cazaly."
EDWARD 'WEARY' DUNLOP'S FINAL NOTE TO AUTHOR MARTIN *FLANAGAN, WRITTEN SHORTLY* BEFORE HIS DEATH IN 1993. *IN SUNSHINE OR IN SHADOW*, 2002, P. 206.

Appendix 5

Roy Cazaly
Playing career summary

Season	Team and League	Games	Goals
1910	Nelson Rovers (J K Smith's Competition)	1	
1911	Middle Park Wesleys (Protestant Churches Association)	7	1
1911–15 AND 1918–20	St Kilda (Victorian Football League)	99	39
1912	Carlton District (Metropolitan Amateur Football Association)	9	7
1915	St Kilda vs Ballarat League patriotic fundraising match	1	
	St Kilda vs North Melbourne patriotic fundraising match	1	
1916	Camberwell (Victorian Junior Football Association)	2	
1917	South Melbourne District (Victorian Junior Football Association)	17	4
1920	Elmore vs Colbinabbin (Elmore and District Association)	1	
	St Kilda vs North Gippsland Association charity match	1	
1921–24 AND 1926–27	South Melbourne (Victorian Football League)	99	128
1921	South Melbourne vs Ballarat League benefit game	1	3
1922	South Melbourne vs Ballarat League charities match	1	1
1921–24 AND 1926	Victoria	13	8
1925	Minyip (Wimmera District Football League)	13	14
	Litchfield-Carron (North West District Football Association)	6	4

Year	Match	Games	Goals
1927	VFL representative side vs Wimmera League	1	
	Waterside Workers (Wednesday Football League)	6	5
1928–30	City (Northern Tasmanian Football Association)	53	62
	Northern Tasmanian Football Association representative games	15	22
1928	City (state premiers) vs Fingal	1	2
1929	Combined City/North Launceston/Longford vs Collingwood	1	2
1930	City (state premiers) vs Campbell Town	1	2
	Tasmania	5	
1931	Preston (Victorian Football Association)	19	25
	Preston vs South Warrnambool	1	
	Waterside Workers (Wednesday Football League)	2	3
1932	Tasmanian Football League vs VFL (inter-league game)	1	2
1932–33	North Hobart (Tasmanian Football League)	26	35
1934–36	New Town (Tasmanian Football League)	47	42
1935	South Melbourne Past vs Present Players fundraising match	1	4
	Tasmanian Football League vs Northern Tasmanian Football Associationn	1	
	Tasmanian Football League vs St Kilda	1	
1936	New Town vs Tasman Peninsula	1	4
1937	South Melbourne Past vs Present Players charity match	1	2
1939	South Melbourne Seconds (Victorian Football League)	14	4
	St Kilda Veterans vs Fitzroy Veterans (RACV charity carnival)	1	1
1941	Camberwell (Victorian Football Association)	2	1
1949	Novelty football match, Hobart Football Club Gala Night Carnival	1	
1950	Clarence vs Sandy Bay 'Past Players' charity match	1	
1951	New Town vs Glenorchy 'Old Buffers' charity match	1	1
	The Sporting Globe-3DB Children's Hospital Appeal match	1	
1952	Past Champions charity match at Latrobe (Tas)	1	
1959	City Old Players vs North Launceston Old Players	1	
	St Kilda Veterans vs Richmond Veterans	1	
Total		**480**	**428**

NB. These totals are conservative as the exact number of games played and goals scored in some junior and minor-league games cannot be verified with certainty, including the Nelson Rovers (J K Smith's Competition) in 1910, Camberwell (Victorian Junior Football Association) in 1916 and South Warrnambool (Western District League) in 1919 and 1921.

VFL Playing Career

Season summary

Season[1]	Team	Jumper Number[2]	Games[3]	Goals	Brownlow votes[4]
1911	St Kilda	N.A.	4	1	N.A.
1912	St Kilda	13	4	0	N.A.
1913	St Kilda	22	19	6	N.A.
1914	St Kilda	22	15	4	N.A.
1915	St Kilda	10	16	7	N.A.
1918	St Kilda	14	15	10	N.A.
1919	St Kilda	14	10	4	N.A.
1920	St Kilda	14	16	7	N.A.
1921	South Melbourne	1	16	19	N.A.
1922	South Melbourne	1	16	28	N.A.
1923	South Melbourne	11	17	16	N.A.
1924	South Melbourne	11	19	32	2
1926	South Melbourne	11	18	23	2
1927	South Melbourne	11	13	10	-
Total			198	167	4

[1] St Kilda went into recess during 1916 and 1917. Cazaly played for Minyip in 1925.
[2] Jumper numbers were introduced from the start of the 1912 season.
[3] Includes three finals in 1913, one in 1918, two in 1923 and three in 1924.
[4] The Brownlow Medal for the 'Fairest and Best' player in the VFL was introduced in 1924. Until 1930 only one vote was awarded each match by the central umpire.

Games played and goals scored, by opponent

Opposition [1]	Games	Goals	Average
Essendon	25	23	.92
Fitzroy	25	19	.76
Collingwood	25	14	.56
Richmond	24	28	1.17
Carlton	23	21	.91
Geelong	22	11	.50
Melbourne	19	19	1.00
South Melbourne	12	6	.50
St Kilda	11	13	1.18
Footscray	4	6	1.50
North Melbourne	4	5	1.25
Hawthorn	2	2	1.00
University	2	0	0
Total	198	167	.84

[1] Footscray, North Melbourne and Hawthorn joined the VFL from the VFA in 1925. University was only in the VFL from 1908 to 1914.

Games played and goals scored, by tenant and venue

Tenant [1]	Venue [2]	Games	Goals	Average
South Melbourne	Lake Oval	53	65	1.23
St Kilda	Junction Oval	52	21	.4
Melbourne/University	Melbourne Cricket Ground	20	14	.70
Richmond	Punt Road Oval	12	17	1.42
Essendon	East Melbourne/ Windy Hill	12	14	1.16
Carlton	Princes Park	12	12	1.00
Collingwood	Victoria Park	11	8	.73
Geelong	Corio Oval	11	2	.18
Fitzroy	Brunswick Street	10	5	.50
Footscray	Western Oval	2	4	2.00
North Melbourne	Arden Street	2	4	2.00
Hawthorn	Glenferrie Oval	1	1	1.00
Total		198	167	.84

[1] University was only in the VFL from 1908 to 1914. Footscray, North Melbourne and Hawthorn joined the VFL from the VFA in 1925.
[2] University played at the East Melbourne Cricket Ground from 1908 to 1910, then at the MCG (as co-tenant with Melbourne) from 1911 to 1914. Essendon played at the East Melbourne Cricket Ground until 1921 and then at the Essendon Recreation Reserve (Windy Hill) from 1922.

VFL SEASON-BY-SEASON SUMMARY

1911 – St Kilda

10 teams, 18 rounds

Game	Jumper	Opponent	Round	Result	Position	Goals	Remarks
1	N.A.	Carlton	15	L 114	Forward		VFL debut aged 18 years, 197 days
2	N.A.	Essendon	16	L 125	Forward		Conspicuous
3	N.A.	Richmond	17	L 87	Ruck	1	Consistent in ruck, kicks first VFL goal
4	N.A.	Collingwood	18	L 57	Forward		Improving

1912 – St Kilda

10 teams, 18 rounds

Game	Jumper	Opponent	Round	Result	Position	Goals	Remarks
5	13	Richmond	1	L 7	HFF		Among best
6	13	Geelong	2	L 46	HFF		
7	13	Collingwood	3	W 57	CHF		First VFL win
8	13	South Melbourne	5	L 15	HFF		

1913 – St Kilda

10 TEAMS, 18 ROUNDS

Game	Jumper	Opponent	Round	Result	Position	Goals	Remarks
9	22	South Melbourne	1	L 9	HBF		Good work in defence
10	22	Fitzroy	2	W 33	HFF		High marking noted
11	22	University	3	W 8	Forward		Did good work
12	22	Richmond	4	L 14	Ruck	1	
13	22	Melbourne	5	W 5	Ruck		Fast and clever
14	22	Carlton	6	L 13	Ruck		Solid play
15	22	Collingwood	7	L 35	HFF		Among best
16	22	Essendon	8	W 10	BP		
17	22	Geelong	9	W 7	BP		Clever runs downfield
18	22	Fitzroy	11	L 14	Ruck		Returned after injury
19	22	Richmond	13	W 26	HFF	1	Sterling game
20	22	Melbourne	14	W 36	HFF		Among best
21	22	Carlton	15	W 1	FP		Prominent
22	22	Collingwood	16	W 38	HFF		
23	22	Essendon	17	W 12	HFF	1	Among best
24	22	Geelong	18	L 68	HFF		
25	22	South Melbourne	SF	W 33	HFF		Very handy
26	22	Fitzroy	Final	W 35	HFF	3	Excelled up forward
27	22	Fitzroy	GF	L 13	HFF		St Kilda finish runners up

1914 – St Kilda

10 TEAMS, 18 ROUNDS

Game	Jumper	Opponent	Round	Result	Position	Goals	Remarks
28	22	Carlton	2	W 13	FP	1	
29	22	Essendon	3	L 17	HFF		Solid work
30	22	Melbourne	4	W 60	HBF		
31	22	South Melbourne	5	L 11	FP	2	First-rate game
32	22	Collingwood	6	W 38	FP		
33	22	Fitzroy	7	L 25	Centre		Good early
34	22	Geelong	8	W 24	Centre		Solid
35	22	Richmond	10	L 2	Defence		Prominent
36	22	Carlton	11	L 3	HFF		Injured wrist
37	22	Essendon	12	Draw	BP		
38	22	South Melbourne	14	W 22	BP		Useful work in defence

Game	Jumper	Opponent	Round	Result	Position	Goals	Remarks
39	22	Collingwood	15	L 39	HFF		Occasionally prominent
40	22	Fitzroy	16	L 2	HFF		
41	22	Geelong	17	L 16	HFF	1	Among best, cautioned after charge
42	22	University	18	W 41	HFF		Performed well

1915 – St Kilda

9 teams, 18 rounds. St Kilda had byes in rounds 8 and 17

Game	Jumper	Opponent	Round	Result	Position	Goals	Remarks
43	10	South Melbourne	1	W 27	BP		
44	10	Geelong	2	L 2	BP	1	Rendered good service
45	10	Collingwood	3	L 20	BP		
46	10	Fitzroy	4	L 31	Centre		Consistent
47	10	Essendon	5	L 12	FP		Among best
48	10	Melbourne	6	L 24	Forward	4	Prominent. 4 goals in third quarter.
49	10	Richmond	7	W 2	HBF		
50	10	Carlton	9	L 38	HBF		Prominent in defence
51	10	South Melbourne	10	L 18	HFF	1	Among best
52	10	Geelong	11	W 34	HFF	1	Always prominent
53	10	Collingwood	12	L 98	Ruck		Cumberland and James absent
54	10	Fitzroy	13	L 49	CHF		Held his own
55	10	Essendon	14	W 39	Ruck		Showed good form
56	10	Melbourne	15	L 25	Ruck		
57	10	Richmond	16	W 24	Centre		Among best
58	10	Carlton	18	L 56	Ruck		Notable effort

1918 – St Kilda

8 teams, 14 rounds

Game	Jumper	Opponent	Round	Result	Position	Goals	Remarks
59	14	Fitzroy	1	W 6	Ruck		Carried ruck
60	14	Essendon	2	L 7	Ruck	1	Below form
61	14	Carlton	3	L 26	Ruck	2	Among best
62	14	South Melbourne	4	W 5	Ruck	1	Great worker in the ruck

Game	Jumper	Opponent	Round	Result	Position	Goals	Remarks
63	14	Collingwood	5	L 60	Ruck	2	Rucked well until injured in third quarter
64	14	Richmond	6	W 17	Ruck	1	Among best
65	14	Geelong	7	W 64	Ruck		Solid effort
66	14	Fitzroy	8	L 25	Ruck		Battled hard
67	14	Essendon	9	W 8	Ruck		Customary usefulness
68	14	Carlton	10	W 27	Ruck	1	Conspicuous
69	14	South Melbourne	11	L 50	Ruck	1	Hard slogging ruck work
70	14	Collingwood	12	W 13	Ruck		Among best
71	14	Richmond	13	W 10	Ruck	1	Prominent
72	14	Geelong	14	L 45	HFF		Among best
73	14	Collingwood	SF	L 9	Ruck		Followed well

1919 – St Kilda

9 teams, 18 rounds. St Kilda had byes in rounds 9 and 18

Game	Jumper	Opponent	Round	Result	Position	Goals	Remarks
74	14	Melbourne	1	W 28	Ruck	1	Played well then hurt leg. Misses six games due to injury then flu
75	14	Fitzroy	8	L 45	CHF		Brother Ernest plays in back pocket
76	14	Melbourne	10	W 10	CHF	1	
77	14	Collingwood	11	L 52	CHF		Best in side
78	14	South Melbourne	12	L 171	Ruck		
79	14	Essendon	13	W 12	Ruck	1	Among best
80	14	Geelong	14	W 13	Ruck		Played well
81	14	Carlton	15	L 16	Ruck		Conspicuous
82	14	Richmond	16	L 59	Ruck	1	Rucked well
83	14	Fitzroy	17	L 20	CHF		Among best

1920 – St Kilda

9 teams, 18 rounds. St Kilda had byes in rounds 2 and 11

Game	Jumper	Opponent	Round	Result	Position	Goals	Remarks
84	14	Carlton	1	L 29	Centre		First game as captain
85	14	Geelong	3	W 22	HFF	2	Conspicuous
86	14	Melbourne	4	L 40	Ruck		Among best

Game	Jumper	Opponent	Round	Result	Position	Goals	Remarks
87	14	Essendon	5	L 9	Ruck	1	Played well
88	14	Collingwood	6	L 31	HFF		Made key half-time changes
89	14	South Melbourne	7	L 35	CHF		Among best
90	14	Richmond	8	L 75	HFF		
91	14	Fitzroy	9	L 74	Ruck	1	Worked hard
92	14	Carlton	10	L 24	Ruck		Among best
93	14	Geelong	12	L 51	Ruck		Among best
94	14	Essendon	13	W 19	Ruck	1	Valuable work in ruck
95	14	Melbourne	14	L 62	Ruck		Useful in ruck
96	14	Collingwood	15	L 58	Ruck		Followed well
97	14	South Melbourne	16	L 51	HFF	1	Improving
98	14	Richmond	17	L 35	CHF		Among best
99	14	Fitzroy	18	L 80	HFF	1	Marked and kicked well

1921 – South Melbourne

9 teams, 18 rounds. South Melbourne had byes in rounds 7 and 16

Game	Jumper	Opponent	Round	Result	Position	Goals	Remarks
100	1	St Kilda	1	W 1	CHF	2	100th VFL game, kicks winning goal
101	1	Richmond	2	L 31	CHF	1	Among best
102	1	Essendon	3	L 43	CHF		Did well
103	1	Melbourne	4	L 1	Ruck	2	First game teamed with Fleiter in ruck
104	1	Carlton	5	Draw	Ruck	2	First game with Tandy as rover
105	1	Collingwood	6	L 23	Ruck	1	
106	1	Geelong	8	W 21	Ruck	1	Best on ground
107	1	Fitzroy	9	W 18	Ruck	2	Among best
108	1	St Kilda	10	W 13	Ruck	2	Injured knee but splendid game
109	1	Richmond	11	L 5	Ruck	1	Sturdy player
110	1	Essendon	12	L 18	Ruck	1	Best in side
111	1	Melbourne	13	W 16	Ruck	1	Among best
112	1	Carlton	14	L 25	Ruck	2	Among best, minor injury to side
113	1	Collingwood	15	L 15	Ruck	1	Rucked and marked well
114	1	Geelong	17	L 39	Ruck		Among best
115	1	Fitzroy	18	L 34	Ruck		Did well in ruck

1922 – South Melbourne

9 teams, 18 rounds. South Melbourne had byes in rounds 6 and 15

Game	Jumper	Opponent	Round	Result	Position	Goals	Remarks
116	1	Melbourne	1	L 13	Ruck	1	Solid first game as captain
117	1	Collingwood	2	W 6	Ruck	3	Played with injured elbow. Kicked three in last term
118	1	Essendon	3	L 23	Ruck	1	Strong game
119	1	St Kilda	4	L 16	Ruck	1	Best on ground
120	1	Carlton	5	W 28	Ruck	3	Dominated the ruck
121	1	Richmond	7	L 5	Ruck	1	Among best in losing side
122	1	Fitzroy	8	L 11	CHF	2	Excellent when in ruck
123	1	Geelong	9	L 84	Ruck		Good service
124	1	Melbourne	10	L 28	Ruck	1	Best for South
125	1	Collingwood	11	L 8	Ruck	1	Best on ground. Resigns as captain-coach
126	1	Essendon	12	W 25	Ruck	4	Brilliant following and fine kicking
127	1	St Kilda	13	Draw	Ruck	1	Effective
128	1	Carlton	14	L 28	Ruck	4	Best on ground
129	1	Richmond	16	L 22	Ruck	1	Some good marks but a poor game
130	1	Fitzroy	17	L 15	Ruck	2	Followed well, sprained a thumb
131	1	Geelong	18	W 78	Ruck	2	Marked well, thumb still troublesome

1923 – South Melbourne

9 teams, 18 rounds. South Melbourne had byes in rounds 7 and 16

Game	Jumper	Opponent	Round	Result	Position	Goals	Remarks
132	11	Collingwood	1	L 22	Ruck	1	Among best
133	11	Fitzroy	2	L 2	Ruck		Played with poisoned arm, out of form
134	11	Essendon	3	L 10	Ruck	1	Followed well
135	11	Melbourne	4	L 35	Ruck	2	Injured thigh, misses round-five win over Geelong
136	11	Carlton	6	W 2	CHF		Among best
137	11	Richmond	8	W 51	Ruck		Returning to form
138	11	St Kilda	9	L 11	Ruck		Among best, breaks a toe
139	11	Collingwood	10	W 21	Ruck	2	Splendid ruck work
140	11	Fitzroy	11	W 4	Ruck	1	Busy in ruck

VFL SEASON-BY-SEASON SUMMARY

141	11	Essendon	12	L 17	Ruck		Not as reliable as usual
142	11	Melbourne	13	W 26	Ruck	1	Among best
143	11	Geelong	14	W 7	Ruck		One of best
144	11	Carlton	15	L 21	Ruck	1	Splendid in ruck
145	11	Richmond	17	W 45	Ruck	5	In best form. Cut above eye, reported
146	11	St Kilda	18	W 20	Ruck		Conspicuous and near best
147	11	Essendon	SF	W 17	Ruck		Played well, despite strained tendon
148	11	Fitzroy	PF	L 12	Ruck	2	Injured cheek and ribs early, only fair

1924 - South Melbourne

9 teams, 18 rounds. South Melbourne had byes in rounds 8 and 17

Game	Jumper	Opponent	Round	Result	Position	Goals	Remarks
149	11	Richmond	1	W 27	Ruck	2	Among best
150	11	Fitzroy	2	L 29	Ruck	1	Useful in 150th VFL game.
151	11	Essendon	3	L 26	HFF	1	Strong in ruck
152	11	St Kilda	4	W 28	HFF	4	Showed old brilliance at half-forward
153	11	Melbourne	5	L 7	HFF		Fair game
154	11	Collingwood	6	W 13	HFF	2	Good work
155	11	Carlton	7	W 6	HFF	2	Most effective half-forward
156	11	Geelong	9	W 3	HFF	1	Played well
157	11	Richmond	10	W 18	CHF	3	Skilled effort
158	11	Fitzroy	11	W 23	CHF	2	Back to old form
159	11	Essendon	12	W 13	CHF	1	Excellent marking and passing, injured chest
160	11	St Kilda	13	L 4	CHF	3	Among best
161	11	Melbourne	14	W 47	CHF	4	Brilliant display
162	11	Collingwood	15	L 19	CHF		South's best
163	11	Carlton	16	W 66	CHF	2	Played first-class football
164	11	Geelong	18	W 1	CHF		Among best
165	11	Richmond	SF[1]	L 28	CHF	2	Well held
166	11	Essendon	SF	L 33	CHF	1	Battled hard
167	11	Fitzroy	SF	W 13	CHF	1	Among best

[1] The 1924 finals were a round-robin series between four clubs—Essendon won.

1926 – South Melbourne

12 teams, 18 rounds

Game	Jumper	Opponent	Round	Result	Position	Goals	Remarks
168	11	Richmond	1	L 8	CHF	1	Out of form
169	11	Footscray	2	W 33	CHF	2	Good forward
170	11	St Kilda	3	L 3	Ruck		Showing old form
171	11	Carlton	4	L 5	Ruck	1	Prominent
172	11	North Melbourne	5	W 2	FP		Among best
173	11	Collingwood	6	L 29	CHF		One of South's best
174	11	Melbourne	7	L 23	CHF	1	
175	11	Fitzroy	8	W 34	Ruck	1	Among best
176	11	Essendon	9	W 12	Ruck	2	Best game of season
177	11	Hawthorn	10	W 24	Ruck	1	Among best
178	11	Geelong	11	W 11	Ruck	1	Great form
179	11	Richmond	12	W 33	Ruck	4	Brilliant
180	11	Footscray	13	W 59	Ruck	2	Among best
181	11	St Kilda	14	W 28	Ruck		Played well. Injured elbow and knee
182	11	Carlton	15	W 23	Ruck		Fine form
183	11	North Melbourne	16	W 36	Ruck	3	Among best
184	11	Collingwood	17	L 6	Ruck	1	Tireless in ruck
185	11	Essendon	18	W 3	Ruck	3	Outstanding. South miss finals on percentage.

1927 – South Melbourne

12 teams, 18 rounds

Game	Jumper	Opponent	Round	Result	Position	Goals	Remarks
186	11	Footscray	5	L 6	Ruck	2	Misses first four rounds through illness
187	11	North Melbourne	6	W 34	Ruck	1	Showing better form
188	11	Richmond	7	L 36	Ruck	1	Misses next game through influenza
189	11	Essendon	9	W 15	HFF	3	In fine form
190	11	Hawthorn	10	W 56	HFF	1	Prominent forward
191	11	Geelong	11	L 6	HFF		
192	11	Carlton	12	W 11	HFF		Among best
193	11	Melbourne	13	L 69	Ruck		
194	11	St Kilda	14	W 41	Ruck		Did well
195	11	Collingwood	15	L 79	Ruck		Among best
196	11	Footscray	16	W 4	Ruck		

| 197 | 11 | North Melbourne | 17 | W 18 | Ruck | 1 | One of best |
| 198 | 11 | Geelong | 18 | L 10 | Ruck | 1 | Marked grandly. Last VFL game and goal. |

Victorian Football Association (VFA)

Season	Team	Games	Goals
1931	Preston	19	25
1941	Camberwell	2	1
Total		21	26

Interstate Representation

Victoria

Game	Date	Opponent	Venue	Result	Scores	Position	Goals
1	6/8/1921	SA [1]	Fremantle	W 35	11.12.78 / 6.7.43	HFF	1
2	10/8/1921	WA [1]	Subiaco	L 5	6.11.47 / 6.16.52	HFF	
3	8/7/1922	SA [2]	MCG	W 22	9.10.64 / 5.12.42	HFF	
4	12/8/1922	SA [2]	Adelaide Oval	L 6	6.14.50 / 7.14.56	HFF	
5	18/8/1923	SA [2]	MCG	W 40	9.15.69 / 4.5.29	HFF	1
6	7/8/1924	Tas [3]	North Hobart	W 39	13.16.94 / 7.13.55	HFF	2
7	9/8/1924	WA [3]	North Hobart	W 8	15.13.103 / 14.11.95	HFF	2
8	12/8/1924	NSW [3]	North Hobart	W 80	14.26.110 / 4.6.30	HFF	
9	14/8/1924	Qld [3,4]	North Hobart	W 95	31.23.209 / 17.12.114	HFF	1
10	16/8/1924	SA [3]	North Hobart	W 53	17.16.118 / 9.11.65	HFF	
11	12/6/1926	SA [2]	MCG	L 11	10.17.77 / 13.10.88	HFF	1
12	24/7/1926	WA [2]	Perth	L 3	7.14.56 / 9.5.59	CHF	
13	27/7/1926	WA [2]	Perth	L 8	10.8.68 / 11.10.76	HFF	

[1] 1921 Australian National Football Carnival, Perth. Only Victoria, Western Australia and South Australia competed.
[2] Interstate games.
[3] 1924 Australian National Football Carnival, Hobart. Six states competed.
[4] Cazaly captained Victoria for the 1924 carnival game against Queensland; Paddy O'Brien was captain for the other four carnival matches.

Tasmania

CAZALY WAS VICE-CAPTAIN OF THE TASMANIAN TEAM FOR THE 1930 AUSTRALIAN NATIONAL FOOTBALL CARNIVAL HELD IN ADELAIDE. SIX STATES COMPETED.

Game	Date	Opponent	Venue	Result	Scores	Position	Goals
1	31/7/1930	Victoria	Adelaide Oval	L 102	7.8.50 22.20.152	Ruck	-
2	2/8/1930	NSW	Adelaide Oval	L 75	6.12.48 18.15.123	Ruck	-
3	4/8/1930	Qld	Adelaide Oval	W 45	18.13.121 10.16.76	CHF	-
4	6/8/1930	SA	Adelaide Oval	L 71	5.11.41 15.22.112	CHF	-
5	9/8/1930	WA	Adelaide Oval	L 59	10.7.67 20.6.126	HFF	-

STATISTICAL SOURCES:
AFL Record Season Guides; AFL tables at *http://stats.rleague.com/afl/afl_index.html, australianfootball.com;* Australian Football League records including 'Victorian Football League Team Lists 1908-29'; 'Interstate selections' and 'Victorian teams', Australian National Football Carnival programs, 1921, 1924 and 1930; Col Hutchinson, AFL statistician; newspaper match reports; sporting newspapers; Stephen Rodgers; *Every Game Ever Played: VFL Results 1897-1982;* Tasmanian statistics compiled with the assistance of Adrian Collins and Ross Smith; VFA statistics compiled with the assistance of Andrew Robinson and Wal Williams; *VFA Recorder,* VFL *Record.*

Appendix 6

Roy Cazaly

Coaching Career Summary

Season	Team and League	Games	Win	Loss	Draw	Winning Percentage
1917	South Melbourne District (VJFA)	17	10	6	1	58.8
1922	South Melbourne (VFL)	10	2	8	-	20.0
1925	Minyip (WDFL)	14	7	7	-	50.0
	Litchfield-Carron (NWDFA)	7	3	4	-	42.9
1928	City (NTFA)	19	12	6	1	63.2
	Northern Tasmanian Football Association	5	3	2	-	60.0
1929	City (NTFA)	17	1	16	-	5.8
	Northern Tasmanian Football Association	6	4	2	-	66.6
1930	City (NTFA)	17	11	5	1	64.7
	Northern Tasmanian Football Association	4	2	2	-	50.0
1931	Preston (VFA)	19	13	5	1	68.4
	Waterside Workers (Wednesday League)	14	7	7	-	50.0
1932	North Hobart (TFL)	19	16	3	-	84.2
1933	North Hobart (TFL)	18	9	9	-	50.0
1934	New Town (TFL)	18	5	13	-	27.7
1935	New Town (TFL)	20	13	7	-	65.0
1936	New Town (TFL)	15	2	12	1	13.3
1937	South Melbourne (VFL)	18	6	11	1	33.3
1938	South Melbourne (VFL)	18	2	16	-	11.1
1941	Camberwell (VFA)	20	12	8	-	60.0
1942	Hawthorn (VFL)	15	1	14	-	6.7
1943	Hawthorn (VFL)	15	9	6	-	60.0
1944	Southern Tasmania Police (United Services)	18	13	5	-	72.2
1948	New Town (TFL)	18	13	4	1	72.2
1949	New Town (TFL)	18	13	5	-	72.2
1950	New Town (TFL)	23	15	8	-	65.2

1951	New Town (TFL)	17	11	6	-	64.7
1954	Tasmanian Football League	4	2	2	-	50.0
	Tasmania	1	1	-	-	100.0
Total		424	218	199	7	51.4

NB: These totals are conservative, as the exact number of games Cazaly coached in some junior and minor leagues cannot be verified with certainty, including Camberwell (Victorian Junior Football Association) in 1916 and South Warrnambool (Western District League) in 1919 and 1921.

Victorian Football League (VFL)

Season Summary

Season	Team	Games	Win	Loss	Draw	Winning Percentage
1922	South Melbourne	10	2	8	-	20.0
1937	South Melbourne	18	6	11	1	33.3
1938	South Melbourne	18	2	16	-	11.1
1942	Hawthorn	15	1	14	-	6.7
1943	Hawthorn	15	9	6	-	60.0
Total		76	20	55	1	26.3

1922 – South Melbourne

9 TEAMS, 18 HOME AND AWAY ROUNDS.
EACH TEAM HAD TWO BYES.
CAZALY RESIGNED AS COACH AND CAPTAIN AFTER ROUND 11.

Game	Opponent	Round	Venue	Result and Margin	Ladder Position
1	Melbourne	1	Junction Oval	L 13	5
2	Collingwood	2	Victoria Park	W 6	5
3	Essendon	3	Windy Hill	L 23	8
4	St Kilda	4	Lake Oval	L 16	9
5	Carlton	5	Lake Oval	W 28	6
6	Richmond	7	Lake Oval	L 5	7
7	Fitzroy	8	Brunswick St	L 11	7
8	Geelong	9	Corio Oval	L 84	9
9	Melbourne	10	MCG	L 28	9
10	Collingwood	11	Lake Oval	L 8	9

COACHING CAREER SUMMARY

1937 – SOUTH MELBOURNE

12 TEAMS, 18 HOME AND AWAY ROUNDS

GAME	OPPONENT	ROUND	VENUE	RESULT AND MARGIN	LADDER POSITION
11	Carlton	1	Princes Park	L 70	12
12	Collingwood	2	Lake Oval	L 55	12
13	Richmond	3	Lake Oval	Draw	12
14	Geelong	4	Corio Oval	L 39	12
15	Fitzroy	5	Brunswick St	L 22	12
16	Hawthorn	6	Lake Oval	W 3	9
17	Essendon	7	Windy Hill	L 32	12
18	North Melbourne	8	Lake Oval	W 44	9
19	Footscray	9	Western Oval	W 51	8
20	St Kilda	10	Lake Oval	W 42	7
21	Melbourne	11	MCG	L 6	7
22	Carlton	12	Lake Oval	W 31	7
23	Collingwood	13	Victoria Park	L 23	8
24	Richmond	14	Punt Rd	L 30	8
25	Geelong	15	Lake Oval	L 19	9
26	Fitzroy	16	Lake Oval	L 22	9
27	Hawthorn	17	Glenferrie Oval	L 27	9
28	Essendon	18	Lake Oval	W 3	9

1938 – SOUTH MELBOURNE

12 TEAMS, 18 HOME AND AWAY ROUNDS

GAME	OPPONENT	ROUND	VENUE	RESULT AND MARGIN	LADDER POSITION
29	Footscray	1	Lake Oval	W 29	2
30	North Melbourne	2	Arden St	L 20	4
31	St Kilda	3	Lake Oval	L 23	10
32	Melbourne	4	MCG	L 52	10
33	Essendon	5	Windy Hill	L 20	10
34	Hawthorn	6	Lake Oval	L 26	10
35	Geelong	7	Corio Oval	L 76	10
36	Richmond	8	Lake Oval	L 73	11
37	Fitzroy	9	Brunswick St	L 52	11
38	Carlton	10	Lake Oval	L 36	11
39	Collingwood	11	Victoria Park	L 12	12

Game	Opponent	Round	Venue	Result and Margin	Ladder Position
40	Footscray	12	Western Oval	L 63	12
41	North Melbourne	13	Lake Oval	L 1	12
42	St Kilda	14	Junction Oval	L 18	12
43	Melbourne	15	Lake Oval	L 29	12
44	Essendon	16	Lake Oval	W 5	12
45	Hawthorn	17	Glenferrie Oval	L 43	12
46	Geelong	18	Lake Oval	L 22	12

1942 – Hawthorn

11 TEAMS, 16 HOME AND AWAY ROUNDS.
FIVE TEAMS (INCLUDING HAWTHORN) HAD ONE BYE
AND SIX HAD TWO.

Game	Opponent	Round	Venue	Result and Margin	Ladder Position
47	North Melbourne	1	Glenferrie Oval	L 34	8
48	St Kilda	2	Toorak Park	L 38	10
49	Footscray	3	Glenferrie Oval	L 76	11
50	Melbourne	4	Punt Rd	L 46	11
51	Collingwood	5	Glenferrie Oval	W 8	10
52	Fitzroy	7	Brunswick St	L 16	10
53	Essendon	8	Windy Hill	L 106	10
54	Carlton	9	Glenferrie Oval	L 28	11
55	South Melbourne	10	Punt Rd	L 3	11
56	Richmond	11	Glenferrie Oval	L 32	11
57	North Melbourne	12	Arden St	L 12	11
58	St Kilda	13	Glenferrie Oval	L 18	11
59	Footscray	14	Yarraville Oval	L 79	11
60	Melbourne	15	Glenferrie Oval	L 61	11
61	Collingwood	16	Victoria Park	L 14	11

1943 – Hawthorn

11 TEAMS, 16 HOME AND AWAY ROUNDS.
EACH TEAM HAD ONE BYE. THE LAST CLUB (ST KILDA) WAS ELIMINATED
AFTER ROUND 11.

Game	Opponent	Round	Venue	Result and Margin	Ladder Position
62	St Kilda	1	Toorak Park	W 2	5
63	Essendon	2	Glenferrie Oval	L 31	7
64	Melbourne	3	Punt Rd	W 45	5
65	Fitzroy	4	Glenferrie Oval	W 11	4
66	South Melbourne	5	Princes Park	W 10	4
67	North Melbourne	7	Glenferrie Oval	W 41	3
68	Richmond	8	Punt Rd	L 44	4
69	Footscray	9	Glenferrie Oval	W 10	3
70	Carlton	10	Princes Park	L 25	4
71	Collingwood	11	Glenferrie Oval	W 25	4
72	Essendon	12	Glenferrie Oval	L 11	4
73	Carlton	13	Princes Park	L 22	5
74	Richmond	14	Punt Rd	W 5	4
75	South Melbourne	15	Glenferrie Oval	W 32	5
76	North Melbourne	16	Arden St	L 1	5

Victorian Football Association (VFA)

Season Summary

Season	Team	Games	Win	Loss	Draw	Winning Percentage
1931	Preston	19	13	5	1	68.4
1941	Camberwell	20	12	8	-	60.0
Total		39	25	13	1	64.1

1931 – Preston

12 teams, 18 home and away rounds

VFA Games Played	Opponent	Round	Result	Goals	Position	Remarks
-	Northcote	1	L 3	-	-	Awaiting clearance
1	Coburg	2	W 3	2	Ruck	Sixth best
2	Prahran	3	L 28	1	Ruck	Best
3	Brunswick	4	W 32	2	Ruck	Second best
4	Port Melbourne	5	L 69	1	HFF	Third best
5	Williamstown	6	W 19	-	HFF	Seventh best
6	Oakleigh	7	L 60	1	Ruck	Second best
7	Yarraville	8	L 4	1	Ruck	Best
8	Sandringham	9	W 26	5	Ruck	Broke toe but stayed on field
9	Camberwell	10	W 38	1	Forward	Played with broken toe
10	Brighton	11	W 27	1	Forward	
11	Yarraville	12	Draw	-	HFF	
12	Prahran	13	W 15	1	Ruck	
13	Sandringham	14	W 72	3	Forward	Second best
14	Northcote	15	W 6	2	Forward	Fourth best
15	Brighton	16	W 48	3	HFF	Third best
16	Brunswick	17	W 8	1	Forward	Third best
17	Coburg	18	W 6	-	Ruck	Second best
18	Oakleigh	SecondSemi	W 23	-	Ruck	Best
19	Northcote	Final	L 37	-	Ruck	Injured leg but stayed on

COACHING CAREER SUMMARY

1941 – Camberwell

12 TEAMS, 20 HOME AND AWAY ROUNDS.
CAZALY PLAYED THE LAST TWO ROUNDS AT HALF-FORWARD

VFA GAMES PLAYED	Opponent	Round	Venue	Result and Margin	Ladder position
-	Oakleigh	1	Oakleigh	L 45	8
-	Prahran	2	Camberwell	L 87	10
-	Port Melbourne	3	Port Melbourne	L 10	10
-	Williamstown	4	Camberwell	L 1	11
-	Brighton	5	Camberwell	W 12	9
-	Preston	6	Preston	L 35	10
-	Brunswick	7	Camberwell	W 21	10
-	Yarraville	8	Yarraville	W 9	8
-	Coburg	9	Camberwell	W 11	8
-	Northcote	10	Northcote	W 30	7
-	Sandringham	11	Camberwell	W 101	7
-	Oakleigh	12	Camberwell	W 23	6
-	Prahran	13	Toorak Park	W 5	6
-	Port Melbourne	14	Camberwell	L 10	7
-	Williamstown	15	Williamstown	W 2	7
-	Brighton	16	Elsternwick Park	L 2	7
-	Preston	17	Camberwell	W 34	7
-	Coburg	18	Coburg	L 91	7
20	Northcote	19	Camberwell	W 33	7
21	Sandringham	20	Beach Road	W 42	6

Tasmanian Playing Coach

Season Summary

Season	Team	Games	Goals	Remarks
1928	City	19	20	Defeated North Launceston for NTFA premiership. Defeated North Hobart for state premiership.
	Northern Tasmanian Football Association	5	5	Defeated TFL once and NWFU twice. Lost to TFL and East Fremantle.
1929	City	17	21	City won one game for the season.
	Northern Tasmanian Football Association	6	10	Defeated TFL once and NWFU twice. Lost to TFL once. Defeated North Broken Hill. Lost to Collingwood.
1930	City	17	21	Defeated Launceston for NTFA premiership. Defeated Lefroy for state premiership.
	Northern Tasmanian Football Association	4	7	Defeated TFL and NWFU once. Lost to TFL and NWFU once.
	Tasmania	5	-	Vice-captain of Tasmanian carnival team in Adelaide.
1932	North Hobart [1]	14	22	Defeated Cananore for TFL premiership. Lost state premiership to City.
	Tasmanian Football League	1	2	Vice-captain of TFL team in loss to VFL.
1933	North Hobart [2]	12	13	Defeated by Cananore for TFL premiership.
1934	New Town [3]	14	12	New Town didn't make the finals.
1935	New Town	20	19	Defeated North Hobart for TFL premiership. Lost state premiership to Launceston.
	Tasmanian Football League	2	-	Captained TFL in defeat of NTFA. Captained TFL in loss to St Kilda.
1936	New Town	13	11	New Town didn't make the finals.
	New Town v Tasman Peninsula	1	4	Captained New Town in defeat of Tasman Peninsula during mid-season bye.
Total		150	167	

[1] Suspended after round 14 for remainder of 1932 season and first six games of the 1933 season.
[2] Didn't play until round seven due to suspension.
[3] Missed four games after breaking several ribs. Hilton Buckney was acting coach during his absence.

Northern Tasmanian Football Association

SEASON SUMMARY

Season	Team	Games	Win	Loss	Draw	Winning Percentage
1928	City	19	12	6	1	63.2
1929	City	17	1	16	-	5.8
1930	City	17	11	5	1	64.7
Total		53	24	27	2	45.3

Tasmanian Football League

SEASON SUMMARY

Season	Team	Games	Win	Loss	Draw	Winning Percentage
1932	North Hobart	19	16	3	-	84.2
1933	North Hobart	18	9	9	-	50.0
1934	New Town	18	5	13	-	27.7
1935	New Town	20	13	7	-	65.0
1936	New Town	15	2	12	1	13.3
1948	New Town	18	13	4	1	72.2
1949	New Town	18	13	5	-	72.2
1950	New Town	23	15	8	-	65.2
1951	New Town	17	11	6	-	64.7
Total		166	97	67	2	58.4

1932 – North Hobart

4 TEAMS, 17 HOME AND AWAY ROUNDS

TFL Games	Opponent	Round	Result	Goals	Position	Remarks
1	Lefroy	1	W 40	4	CHF	
2	Cananore	2	W 2	1	CHF	Tenth best
3	New Town	3	W 33	3	CHF	Best
4	Lefroy	4	W 28	4	CHF	Fifth best

5	Cananore	5	W 36	2	CHF	Eighth best
6	New Town	6	W 74	1	CHF	Best
7	Lefroy	7	W 36	1	CHF	Third best
8	Cananore	8	W 74	1	CHF	Sixth best
9	New Town	9	W 57	1	FF	Eighth best
10	Lefroy	10	W 6	-	CHF	Thirteenth best
11	Cananore	11	L 4	1	CHF	Eighth best
12	New Town	12	W 46	1	Ruck	Fifth best
13	Lefroy	13	W 3	1	Ruck	Eighth best
14	Cananore	14	W 9	1	Ruck	Reported for charging and striking, found guilty
-	New Town	15	W 100	-	DNP	Suspended
-	Lefroy	16	W 45	-	DNP	Suspended
-	Cananore	17	L 12	-	DNP	Suspended
-	Cananore	Grand Final	W 52	-	DNP	TFL premiers
-	City	State Final	L 6	-	DNP	Lost state final against City

1933 – North Hobart

4 teams, 16 home and away rounds

TFL Games	Opponent	Round	Result	Goals	Position	Remarks
-	New Town	1	W 8	-	DNP	Suspended
-	Cananore	2	L 19	-	DNP	Suspended
-	Lefroy	3	L 17	-	DNP	Suspended
-	New Town	4	W 9	-	DNP	Suspended
-	Cananore	5	L 7	-	DNP	Suspended
-	Lefroy	6	W 16	-	DNP	Suspended
15	New Town	7	L 18	-	FF	Resumed
16	Cananore	8	L 5	-	Ruck	Second best
17	Lefroy	9	W 12	1	Ruck	Fifth best
18	New Town	10	L 17	-	Ruck	Fourth best
19	Cananore	11	L 37	2	Ruck	Played despite having flu
20	Lefroy	12	W 26	2	Ruck	Third best
21	New Town	13	W 28	1	Centre	Eleventh best
22	Cananore	14	L 17	-	Centre	
23	Lefroy	15	W 39	1	Ruck	Best

COACHING CAREER SUMMARY

24	New Town	16	W 22	-	Centre	Sixth best
25	New Town	Semi	W 46	3	Centre	Best
26	Cananore	Final	L 56	3	Ruck	Sixth best

1934 – New Town

4 TEAMS, 18 HOME AND AWAY ROUNDS

TFL Games	Opponent	Round	Result	Goals	Position	Remarks
27	Lefroy	1	L 22	3	Ruck	Seventh best
28	Cananore	2	L 13	-	Ruck	Seventh best
29	North Hobart	3	L 33	-	CHF	Broke ribs
-	Lefroy	4	L 37	-	DNP	Injured
-	Cananore	5	W 16	-	DNP	Injured
-	North Hobart	6	L 61	-	DNP	Injured
-	Lefroy	7	L 39	-	DNP	Injured
30	Cananore	8	W 42	1	Ruck	Resumed
31	North Hobart	9	L 29	2	Ruck	Third best
32	Lefroy	10	L 33	-	CHF	Eighth best
33	Cananore	11	L 3	-	CHF	Fifth best
34	North Hobart	12	L 29	-	Ruck	Fourth best
35	Lefroy	13	W 25	-	Ruck	Eighth best
36	Cananore	14	L 32	1	Ruck	Fifth best
37	North Hobart	15	L 13	2	Ruck	Second best
38	Lefroy	16	W 6	1	Ruck	Second best
39	Cananore	17	L 16	1	Ruck	Third best
40	North Hobart	18	W 24	1	Ruck	Fourth best

1935 – New Town

4 TEAMS, 18 HOME AND AWAY ROUNDS

TFL Games	Opponent	Round	Result	Goals	Position	Remarks
41	Cananore	1	W 33	2	Ruck	Fourth best
42	North Hobart	2	W 8	1	Ruck	Best
43	Lefroy	3	L 2	-	Ruck	Tenth best
44	Cananore	4	W 26	4	Ruck	Second best
45	North Hobart	5	W 17	1	Ruck	

TFL Games	Opponent	Round	Result	Goals	Position	Remarks
46	Lefroy	6	W 18	3	Ruck	Second best
47	Cananore	7	L 34	-	Ruck	Re-injured ribs
48	North Hobart	8	W 9	-	Ruck	Fifth best
49	Lefroy	9	W 17	1	Ruck	Second best
50	Cananore	10	W 20	1	Ruck	
51	North Hobart	11	L 3	1	Ruck	Third best
52	Lefroy	12	L 11	-	Ruck	Fourth best
53	Cananore	13	W 8	-	FF	Injured shoulder
54	North Hobart	14	L 32	-	Ruck	Played with injury until third quarter
55	Lefroy	15	L 43	1	Ruck	Recovered, played
56	Cananore	16	W 67	-	Ruck	Best
57	North Hobart	17	W 18	2	Ruck	Reported for attempted striking. Charge dismissed.
58	Lefroy	18	W 18	-	Ruck	Seventh best
59	North Hobart	Final	W 14	1	Ruck	TFL Premiers
60	Launceston	State Final	L 65	1	Ruck	Lost state final to Launceston

1936 – New Town

4 Teams, 15 Home and Away Rounds

TFL Games	Opponent	Round	Result	Goals	Position	Remarks
-	Lefroy	1	L 84	-	DNP	
61	North Hobart	2	W 6	1	Ruck	Eighth best
-	Cananore	3	L 64	-	DNP	
62	Lefroy	4	L 31	-	Ruck	Sixth best
63	North Hobart	5	L 35	2	Ruck	Fifth best
64	Cananore	6	L 4	2	Ruck	Best
65	Lefroy	7	L 23	1	CHF	Third best
66	North Hobart	8	L 58	1	CHF	Fourth best
67	Cananore	9	W 40	2	Ruck	Sixth best
68	Lefroy	10	L 33	-	Ruck	Eighth best
69	North Hobart	11	L 59	1	Ruck	Seventh best
70	Cananore	12	Draw	-	Ruck	Second best
71	Lefroy	13	L 33	1	Ruck	Eighth best
72	North Hobart	14	L 13	-	Ruck	
73	Cananore	15	L 20	-	Ruck	Third best

COACHING CAREER SUMMARY

Non-Playing Coach

Season Summary

Season	Team	Games	Comments
1948	New Town	18	Seniors defeated North Hobart for TFL premiership and North Launceston for state premiership. Seconds won TFL premiership but lost state title.
1949	New Town	18	Seniors defeated North Hobart for TFL premiership, lost state title to North Launceston. Seconds lost TFL premiership.
1950	New Town	23	Seniors lost TFL premiership to Hobart. Seconds won TFL premiership and state title.
1951	New Town	17	Seniors defeated North Hobart for TFL premiership. Seconds won TFL premiership. No state premiership matches played.
1954	Tasmanian Football League	4	Coached TFL to two wins and two losses against the NTFA and NWFU
	Tasmania	1	Coached Tasmania to victory over Australian Amateurs
Total		81	

1948 – New Town

Six teams, 15 home and away rounds

Round	Opponent	Venue	Result
1	Clarence	Bellerive	W 26
2	New Norfolk	Boyer	L 11
3	Hobart	North Hobart	L 6
4	Sandy Bay	New Town	W 1
5	North Hobart	North Hobart	W 22
6	Clarence	North Hobart	W 96
7	New Norfolk	New Town	W 30
8	Hobart	TCA	W 11
9	Sandy Bay	North Hobart	Draw
10	North Hobart	New Town	W 28
11	Clarence	New Town	W 84
12	New Norfolk	North Hobart	W 60
13	Hobart	New Town	L 23
14	Sandy Bay	Queenborough	L 20
15	North Hobart	North Hobart	W 32
Second Semi	Sandy Bay	North Hobart	W 16
Grand Final	North Hobart	North Hobart	W 16
State Final	North Launceston	North Hobart	W 2

1949 – New Town

Six teams, 15 home and away rounds

Round	Opponent	Venue	Result
1	Hobart	North Hobart	L 3
2	North Hobart	New Town	L 78
3	Sandy Bay	Queenborough	W 23
4	New Norfolk	New Town	W 45
5	Clarence	North Hobart	W 40
6	Hobart	North Hobart	L 26
7	North Hobart	North Hobart	W 56
8	Sandy Bay	Sandy Bay	W 55
9	New Norfolk	North Hobart	W 50
10	Clarence	Bellerive	W 63
11	Hobart	TCA	L 26
12	North Hobart	New Town	W 32
13	Sandy Bay	North Hobart	W 47
14	New Norfolk	Boyer	W 7
15	Clarence	New Town	W 62
Second Semi	Hobart	North Hobart	W 12
Grand Final	Hobart	North Hobart	W 32
State Final	North Launceston	York Park	L 40

1950 – New Town

Six teams, 20 home and away rounds

Round	Opponent	Venue	Result
1	Hobart	New Town	W 5
2	Sandy Bay	New Town	L 26
3	Clarence	New Town	W 72
4	North Hobart	North Hobart	L 40
5	New Norfolk	Boyer	L 40
6	Hobart	TCA	L 69
7	Sandy Bay	North Hobart	W 12
8	Clarence	Bellerive	W 64
9	North Hobart	New Town	L 17
10	New Norfolk	North Hobart	W 6
11	Hobart	New Town	W 33

12	Sandy Bay	Queenborough	W 4
13	Clarence	North Hobart	W 33
14	North Hobart	North Hobart	W 17
15	New Norfolk	New Town	L 7
16	Hobart	North Hobart	L 23
17	Sandy Bay	New Town	W 24
18	Clarence	Bellerive	W 99
19	North Hobart	New Town	W 36
20	New Norfolk	Boyer	W 12
First Semi	Sandy Bay	North Hobart	W 86
Prelim Final	North Hobart	North Hobart	W 25
Grand Final	Hobart	North Hobart	L 2

1951 – New Town

Six teams, 15 home and away rounds

Round	Opponent	Venue	Result
1	Clarence	North Hobart	L 3
2	Hobart	New Town	L 12
3	New Norfolk	Boyer	L 19
4	Sandy Bay	Queenborough	W 48
5	North Hobart	North Hobart	L 8
6	Clarence	Bellerive	W 50
7	Hobart	North Hobart	L 11
8	New Norfolk	New Town	W 39
9	Sandy Bay	North Hobart	W 6
10	North Hobart	New Town	W 2
11	Clarence	New Town	W 43
12	Hobart	TCA	L 9
13	New Norfolk	North Hobart	W 29
14	Sandy Bay	New Town	W 67
15	North Hobart	North Hobart	W 22
Second Semi	Hobart	North Hobart	W 50
Grand Final	North Hobart	North Hobart	W 71

TFL and Tasmania

Year	Team	Games	Win	Loss	Draw	Winning Percentage
1954	TFL	4	2	2	-	50
1954	Tasmania	1	1	-	-	100

STATISTICAL SOURCES :
AFL Library records; *AFL Record Season Guides;* AFL tables at *http://stats.rleague.com/afl/afl_index.html; australianfootball.com;* club histories; newspaper match reports; sporting newspapers; Stephen Rodgers; *Every Game Ever Played: VFL Results 1897-1982;* Tasmanian statistics compiled with the assistance of Adrian Collins and Ross Smith; VFA statistics compiled with the assistance of Andrew Robinson and Wal Williams; VFA *Recorder;* VFL *Record.*

Appendix 7

Truth Cazaly award winners

1973-81

Year	Gold Cazaly winner	Brownlow Medallist
1973	Kevin Bartlett (Richmond)	Keith Greig (Nth Melbourne)
1974	Kevin Bartlett (Richmond)	Keith Greig (Nth Melbourne)
1975	Leigh Matthews (Hawthorn) and John Newman (Geelong)	Gary Dempsey (Footscray)
1976	Graham Moss (Essendon)	Graham Moss (Essendon)
1977	Leigh Matthews (Hawthorn)	Graham Teasdale (Sth Melbourne)
1978	Garry Wilson (Fitzroy)	Malcolm Blight (Nth Melbourne)
1979	Gary Dempsey (Nth Melbourne)	Peter Moore (Collingwood)
1980	Gary Dempsey (Nth Melbourne) and Kelvin Templeton (Footscray)	Kelvin Templeton (Footscray)
1981	Rod Ashman (Carlton)	Bernie Quinlan (Fitzroy)

Appendix 8

A NOTE ON OBJECTIVES, METHODS AND SOURCES

When I embarked on this project, I likened the task to starting a large jigsaw puzzle without knowing how many pieces it contained or what the final picture should look like. It seemed an apt analogy: keep adding the pieces, I told myself, and a picture will eventually emerge.

After some time spent gathering material, I began to think that I *must* have completed the edges of the puzzle, and was starting to "fill in" the middle. I had convinced myself that writing a biography was a straightforward, linear exercise, with a clear beginning, middle and end.

I eventually realised the folly of my analogy. Whereas a jigsaw has a finite number of pieces that can only be fitted together to form a single picture, every biography is unique. There is no pre-determined number of words, no designated starting point and no clear finish line. There is no standard template or blueprint to follow, which means that a thousand biographers working on the same subject will produce a thousand different stories.

Having realised this, I decided to simply focus on telling Cazaly's story as comprehensively, accurately and honestly as I could. Mindful of the near-mythical status of my subject, and wary of biographies in which the protagonist always influences events but is seemingly never influenced *by* them, I knew that background, circumstance and context were crucial in telling his story. Cazaly sought to shape his own destiny but he was also the product of powerful historical forces, including the persecution of the French Huguenots during the 17th century, the rise and decline of the English silk-weaving industry, the Victorian gold rushes of the 1850s and Melbourne's boom and bust economy of the late 19th century. These key events influenced his forebears, who, in turn, influenced him.

This need for context guided my search for source material. If I was going to write about the young Roy taking up rowing, for instance, I needed to know something about rowers' training techniques and dietary habits, as well as the contemporary schisms between amateur and professional rowers. Likewise, an examination of his marking ability and ruck skills needed to be informed by a discussion of his training techniques and the rule changes which helped pave the way for his emergence as a champion footballer. Similarly, any conversation about the divisive issue of organised football during World War I would be incomplete without exploring enlistment rates, the conscription debate and the possible reasons why Cazaly didn't join up while others around him did.

The same applies to any number of apparently random yet inter-connected events that shaped Cazaly or were shaped by him: the internecine squabbles that regularly gripped St Kilda; the game's increasing professionalism and the debate over player payments prior to World War I; the huge increase in football's popularity during the 1920s; the ongoing feud between the VFL and VFA; the growth of physiotherapy treatments during the 1930s and '40s; and the vagaries of Tasmania's Hare-Clark electoral system in the 1950s.

The amount of information written about Cazaly grew exponentially as his career progressed, but one of the key challenges was finding clues to his early life. Historian Su Leslie has written about the challenge of "working class invisibility", noting that "ordinary working folk don't leave long paper trails behind them".[1] The branch of the Cazaly family which emigrated to Victoria in the 1850s may have come from the English middle class, but by the time Roy was born in 1893 their story was no different from hundreds of thousands of others scrabbling to survive in the economically depressed colony.

Coincidentally, both Cazaly and his father worked for large, established businesses, making their progress easier to trace than if they had worked for more obscure firms. In the case of Roy it is also fortuitous that he went to a school with a distinguished sporting history and worked at several places—including Dunlop Rubber, Johns and Waygood and on the Melbourne wharves—for which histories were available.[2] Where employment records no longer existed, his involvement in various workplace-sponsored sporting teams helped to pinpoint where he was working at a particular time.

Newspaper accounts helped me trace Cazaly's sporting career. Metropolitan papers consulted included *The Age*, *The Argus*, *The Australasian*, *The Examiner*, *The Herald*, *The Mercury* and *Punch*. Important regional and suburban papers included *The Ballarat Star*, the *Preston Leader*, *The Weekly Times* and South Melbourne's local paper *The Record*.[3] The *Minyip Guardian* for the period covering Cazaly's time in the Wimmera in 1925-26 proved extremely useful: a research highlight was being able to read the original yellowing copies in the old *Guardian* office.

Depending on the period and league, sporting papers that yielded important information included the *Monotone Sporting Record*, the *Northern Football Record*, *The Referee*, *The Sporting Judge*, the VFA *Recorder*, the VFL *Record* and *Winner*. *The Sporting Globe* proved especially useful: the paper's birth in 1922 coincided with Cazaly's rise to prominence at South Melbourne, and his friendship with its chief football writer Hec de Lacy led to a series of reminiscences published between 1931 and 1938. Written after Cazaly had all but finished playing (but not yet coaching) they provide valuable insights into his career, his fitness and coaching theories, and his recollections of those he played with and against across a quarter of a century. Cazaly and de Lacy's friendship also resulted in an important retrospective *Sporting Globe* article published in 1953.

Libraries are digitising many newspapers, and I particularly acknowledge the National Library of Australia's excellent 'Trove' project. A fantastic cooperative venture between the AFL and the State Library of Victoria also means the VFL *Record* is now available online. Many other important sources can now be read electronically, including post office, street and trade directories; electoral rolls; birth, death and marriage records; year books and government gazettes. These provided a myriad of small but important details, such as where the Cazaly family were living in Ballarat in 1863, the number of inner-city Melbourne residents per acre of parkland in 1903 and how much an unskilled labourer earned in 1924.

Despite increasing digitisation, some primary sources are still only available in their original paper form. The fragile copies of *Sport* held by the State Library of Victoria, for instance, were extremely useful for charting the labyrinthine world of junior football in Melbourne prior to World War I. Researching in this way can be painstakingly slow but is always rewarding whenever a new piece of information is uncovered.

Original minute books were another important primary source, especially those of St Kilda, South Melbourne and Hawthorn. Minutes provide important details about committee deliberations, revenues, player payments and a wealth of other minutiae in the life of a club, allowing the reader to build up a comprehensive picture of a club's relationship with its players and the local community. In this respect, the re-discovery of the original *1920-24 South Melbourne Football Club Minutes Book* during the research process was particularly exciting.

The archives of retired journalists proved useful. The AFL Library has a collection of clipping books collated by former *Herald* chief football writer Alf Brown, and Launceston's Queen Victoria Museum and Art Gallery holds an extensive collection of working papers compiled by *The Examiner*'s long-time sports editor Jack Donnelly.

Most of the clubs Cazaly played for or coached have their own historians. All were willing to help in my search for information and several shared their painstakingly compiled team lists and player statistics. Many other academics, researchers and statisticians provided valuable assistance and advice; I have listed them in the acknowledgments.

Other source material cropped up in unexpected places. I was delighted to find, for example, that the Ballarat Gold Museum has a pocket watch presented to James Cazaly after he won a rowing contest in 1866 and that the Sound Preservation Association of Tasmania has a recording of a radio broadcast by his son in 1962.

Given he died more than 50 years ago, finding people still alive who knew Cazaly was not easy. In the course of my research I was fortunate to get to know his last surviving child Pat Whitecross and many of his grandchildren. All had important memories to share, and provided valuable insights into Cazaly the man, father and grandfather. I also interviewed a number of descendants of Cazaly's friends, teammates and opponents. Many generously shared their family stories and precious photos and newspaper clippings, and all helped to place his life and achievements in further context.

A few surviving eyewitnesses were able to provide first-hand accounts of Cazaly the player and coach. I interviewed Joffre Hewitt, who watched him train at Minyip in 1925; Harold Dilger, who played both with and against him in Launceston in 1928; Arch Flanagan, who knew him in Launceston and later saw him play in Hobart during the 1930s; and several players he coached at Camberwell and Hawthorn during the war or at New Town in the late 1940s and early '50s. I spoke to retired journalists Keith Welsh and Larry Noye, who knew Cazaly in Hobart after the war, a number of patients who went to him for physiotherapy or polio treatment during the 1950s, and several players he coached in the 1954 Tasmanian team.

I consulted many football references during my research but the ones I kept closest to hand were Russell Holmesby and Jim Main's *Encyclopedia of AFL Footballers*, Stephen Rodgers' epic three-volume *100 Years of AFL Players* and the annual *AFL Record Season Guide*, which is rapidly approaching the famous *Wisden Cricketers' Almanack* in both its scope and detail.

Noel Counihan's working papers from his 1978 Australian Dictionary of Biography (ADB) entry on Cazaly proved extremely useful, especially his correspondence with Roy jnr and ADB editor Geoffrey Serle. Counihan's work aside, much of the material written after Cazaly's death proved less useful. His story has always been open to exaggeration and it was disconcerting how many writers simply repeated—and thereby perpetuated—inaccuracies about his life and career. While I didn't set out to produce an academic tome, I still felt it important for a serious biography to be credible and accurate. Where source material was occasionally contradictory I noted the ambiguities and footnoted accordingly.

The most enigmatic contributor was Roy Cazaly himself. He did not keep a diary, unless you count the shipboard account he and Aggie kept during

A NOTE ON OBJECTIVES, METHODS AND SOURCES

their only trip abroad in 1958. There are no surviving letters and just a few telegrams. Instead, I relied on his own thoughts as recalled by his family and friends and as set out in contemporary newspaper articles and interviews. While most of his observations naturally concern football, they also reveal much, much more about his remarkable personality, temperament and approach to life.

ENDNOTES

1. Correspondence with Su Leslie. Her blog site, *Shaking the tree*, is at *https://suzysu.wordpress.com/*.
2. As an interesting aside, eminent historian Geoffrey Blainey has authored several books of direct relevance to Cazaly's story, including one on the origins of Australian Football, a history of Australian mining, a history of Victoria, company histories of Johns and Waygood and Dunlop Rubber and a history of Camberwell.
3. *The Record* is referenced as *The South Melbourne Record* to avoid confusion with the VFL match-day program of the same name.

Appendix 9

ACKNOWLEDGEMENTS

Many people helped make this book possible. First and foremost I wish to thank the descendants of Roy Cazaly for entrusting me with their cherished memories of a much-loved father and grandfather.

Russell Fogarty and Nathan McMahon provided crucial early support, and Hobart social historian Peter MacFie conducted several important interviews on my behalf during the project's formative stages.

Libby and Fred Shade very kindly shared their extensive research on the Cazaly family's ancestry, and Australian Huguenot Society secretary Rob Nash provided expert advice on French and British Huguenot history.

Michael Conaty's important 1996 PhD thesis on Cazaly alerted me to many potential sources and themes to explore. Football historians, museum curators and administrators who provided valuable expertise included Georgie Day, Russell Holmesby and Rory Sackville (St Kilda), Barb Cullen, Jim Main and Tony Morwood (Sydney Swans), Peter Haby (Hawthorn), Brian Membrey (Preston), David Barker (Camberwell), Brett and John Gillow (City/South Launceston), Adrian Collins (North Hobart and TFL), Graham Kelly (New Town), Ross Smith (NTFA), Fred Hughson (South Warrnambool), Peter Burke (Wednesday Football League), Ross Oakley (AFL), Trevor Ruddell (Melbourne Cricket Club Library) and Jed Smith (National Sports Museum).

ACKNOWLEDGEMENTS

Many other academics, historians, researchers and writers also assisted, including David Allen, Steve Alomes, Rhett Bartlett, Geoffrey Blainey, Dale Blair, Mark Branagan, Anthea Bundock, Lynda Carroll, Mick Counihan, Greg de Moore, John Devaney, Phil Dimitriadis, John Ficarra, Martin Flanagan, Lionel Frost, Nicolá Goc, Harry Gordon, Rob Hess, Tim Hogan, Simon Huggard, Terry Keenan, Anne Killalea, Ken Mansell, Gregor McCaskie, Robert Pascoe, Mark Pennings, Ken Piesse, Nick Richardson, Michael Riley, Michael Roberts, Ian Shaw, Mike Sheahan, Simon Smith, John Stoward, Ned Wallish, Greg Wardell-Johnson and Bart Ziino.

Several eminent football statisticians generously provided data and expertise, especially Ted Hopkins, Col Hutchinson and Cameron Sinclair (VFL), Andrew Robinson and Wal Williams (VFA), and Paul Jeffs, Stephen Rodgers and Kevin Taylor (VFL/AFL). Memorabilia experts who assisted included Damien Green, Rick Milne and Eric Panther.

A number of historians kindly provided specialist advice regarding Cazaly's involvement in other sports, including Peter Burke, Robert Grogan and Rick Smith (cricket), Grace Blake, Kath Elliott and Andrew Guerin (rowing), Peter Cooley and Richard Stamford (harness racing) and Greg Fahey (greyhound racing).

Footballers coached by Cazaly who shared their memories included Harold Dilger (Northern Tasmania), Reg Horkings and Laurie Peters (Camberwell and Hawthorn), Jack Brain, Ken Feltscheer and Peter O'Donohue (Hawthorn), Charlie Aiken, Rex Garwood, Maurie Oborne, Kev Orpwood, Doug Scott and Doug Smith (New Town) and Noel Atkins, Gordon Bowman, Mike Clennett, Geoff Long, Laurie Moir, Sam Purdon, Ray Stokes and Athol Webb (1954 Tasmanian team). Retired umpire Harry Beitzel, former New Town president Keith Dickenson and retired Hobart journalists Larry Noye and Keith Welsh also provided valuable insights into Cazaly the coach.

Many relatives of teammates, opponents, administrators and journalists connected with Cazaly provided important information and recollections, including Alec Albiston's son Ian; Jack Barker's son John; Jim Bohan's son Michael; Norm Beckton's daughter Jill Widmer; Dr Joseph Milton D'Amer Drew's descendants Ian and Don Hewson; Hec de Lacy's daughter

Mavis Burgess and son Dennis; Fred 'Skeeter' Fleiter's nephews Brendan, Brian, Ian, Roy and Tony; Alby Goggins' daughter Helen Baker; Gordon Goldsmith's son Ken; Bernard 'Mannie' Grenda's son Ron; Arthur Hando's son Boyd; Frank Huggard's grandson Simon; Laurie Nash's daughter Noelene Dean; Jack O'Keefe's son Gary; Alan Saker's widow Thelma; Joe Scanlan's sons Brian and Jack, and daughter Helen Laing; Mark 'Napper' Tandy's grandson Rod; Laurie Taylor's son Wayne; Ron Tyson's son Des; Danny Wheelahan's son Denis and Eric Zschech's daughter Diane Gordon.

Several patients with direct experience of the Cazalys' post-war physiotherapy techniques and poliomyelitis treatments kindly shared their stories, including Margie Bryce, Mary Guy, Shane Johnson, Rosemary Nichols, Graeme Salmon, John Thompson and Gordon Triffett. Family friends and neighbours who recalled their years at Brushy Creek Road included Don Bratt, Paul Howard, Muriel Lawry, David Ponsonby and Marjory Woolford.

Several artists generously discussed their shared link with Cazaly's story, including singer/songwriter Mike Brady, NIDA's former director John Clark, cartoonist Paul Harvey and playwright Ray Lawler. Brian Hansen and Brian Morris provided the background to the Truth Cazaly Awards and Lindsay McCarthy and Norm Stone from the Sound Preservation Association of Tasmania shared their precious recording of Cazaly's 1962 Hobart radio interview.

A heartfelt thank you to the collections staff of the National Library of Australia, the State Library of Tasmania, the State Library of Queensland, the University of Queensland's Fryer Library, the State Library of Victoria and the Australian National University's National Centre of Biography and Noel Butlin Archives Centre. Thank you also to Gary Edge from Darebin Libraries, Trevor Hart from the Camberwell Historical Society, Monica Simpson from *The Age*'s Research Library, Donna Bishop from *The Herald Sun*'s library, Kevin Bracken and Pat Grainger from the Port Melbourne Historical Society, Port Phillip Local History Librarian Kay Rowan, Elizabeth O'Callaghan from the Warrnambool and District Historical Society and Ballarat historians Anne Doggett, Ken James, Bill Loader and Claire Muir.

Many people helped to flesh out the history of Australian Football in

ACKNOWLEDGEMENTS

Minyip during the mid-1920s, especially Joy King and Shirley Smith from the local historical society, Minyip-Murtoa Football Club secretary Peter Haney, Noël Barber, Gillian Heintze, Ken 'Dasher' Milgate, Tom Wood and descendants of Minyip players from the Arnel, Boschen, Drum, Krelle, Penny, Petering and Power families. Historians from other Wimmera towns who provided contemporary newspaper reports included Lilian Kirk and Ron Falla (Donald), Jim Melbourne (Stawell), Kay Scott (Nhill), Marie Scott (Rupanyup) and Lindsay Smith (Horsham).

I will always be grateful to Warren Boyles, former editor of *40 Degrees South*, for publishing my first piece on Cazaly, and to John Harms and Paul Daffey of *footyalmanac.com.au*, Peter di Sisto and Michael Lovett of the AFL *Record* and Adam Cardosi and Adam Gigacz from *australianfootball.com* for providing publishing opportunities and advice. A special thank you to my publisher Geoff Slattery, for taking a punt, and to my editor Simone Egger for her thoroughness, patience and expertise.

Elizabeth and Alan Ruthven, Judith and David Jones and Geoff Paterson very kindly accommodated me during my many research forays to Tasmania and Victoria. My great friends Conor Fogarty and Damian Power provided encouragement throughout, as did my loved and loving family, to whom I can now say, 'Yes, it's finished'. This book is for them.

Appendix 10

CHAPTER ENDNOTES

PREFACE

1 *The Australasian*, 6 June, 1914.
2 Maurice Guillaux had set several speed and endurance records in Europe before visiting Australia in 1914. A few weeks after arriving in Melbourne he made aviation history by becoming the first to carry official airmail between Melbourne and Sydney.
3 *The Argus*, 29 June, 1914. Guillaux must have caused quite a distraction because neither side scored a goal for the quarter. Carlton went on to win the game by three points.
4 George Challis enlisted in July 1915 and was killed a year later at Fromelles. Stan McKenzie was posted overseas in early 1915, served at Gallipoli and died of appendicitis in Alexandria that December. Of the other players in this match who later enlisted, Vic Cumberland was wounded three times but played a final season with St Kilda in 1920, Percy Jory played in a famous wartime exhibition match in London in 1916 while on active service, Bill Lowrie won a military medal, Herb Burleigh injured an arm in France but managed to play a few games on his return, Alf Baud received a fractured skull and never played again and Frank Triplett was mentioned in despatches for outstanding conduct. Ross McMullin, 'True love, war and football', *The Sydney Morning Herald*, 27 September, 2012, Jim Main and David Allen, *Fallen - The Ultimate Heroes: Footballers Who Never Returned from War*, pp. 33-36 and 125-28, Russell Holmesby and Jim Main, *The Encyclopedia of AFL Footballers: Every AFL/VFL Player since 1897*, 7th Ed, and the Carlton Blueseum at *http://www.blueseum.org/tiki-index.php?page=homepage*.
5 When World War I broke out Guillaux returned to Europe on an Australian troop ship, accompanying the 1st Australian Imperial Force to Egypt and then on to France. He left his Blériot in Australia when he returned to France and it passed through a succession of owners before eventually being acquired by Sydney's Powerhouse Museum. The plane remains on display there today, an unlikely link between a pioneering French aviator and Australia's most famous football aerialist. See *http://www.powerhousemuseum.com/collection/database/?irn=288461*.

Chapter 1. BEGINNINGS: FRANCE AND ENGLAND, 1700-1854

6 Robin Gwynn, 'England's First Refugees', *History Today*, Vol. 35 Number 5, May 1985 and Robert Nash, 'Some Huguenot Families in Nineteenth Century New South Wales', *Descent*, 2000, pp. 193-96.
7 Christopher Clay, *Economic Expansion and Social Change: England 1500–1700*, Vol. 2, p. 161, quoted in Linda Levy Peck, 'Creating a Silk Industry in Seventeenth-Century England', *Shakespeare Studies* Number 28, 2000, p. 225.
8 Robin Gwynn, *op cit*. The success of many Huguenot emigrants aroused local fears and jealousies: an anonymous pamphlet, circulated in London around 1730, warned that "… considering their Sobriety and Diet, and the Fruitfulness of their Women, the City, in time, will probably be called a French colony." Quoted in Tessa Murdoch, 'The Quiet Conquest', *History Today*, Vol. 35 Number 5, May 1985, p. 32.

CHAPTER ENDNOTES

9   Excerpt from R Campbell, *The London Tradesman*, 1747, pp. 260-1, reprinted in *Huguenot Families* Number 7, September 2002, pp. 28-31.
10   Writing later about this bloody period, French author Alexandre Dumas graphically described the region as "the scene of action and reaction, revenge and retaliation, till the religious annals of the South resemble an account-book kept by double entry, in which fanaticism enters the profits of death, one side being written with the blood of Catholics, the other with that of Protestants."
Alexandre Dumas, *Celebrated Crimes Series, Book Three: Massacres of the South, 1551–1815*, page 1.
11   Sir Frank Warner, *The Silk Industry of the United Kingdom: Its Origin and Development*, pp. 35-36.
12   Based on the naming pattern in subsequent generations, Monsieur Cazaly's first name may have been Guillaume. Information kindly provided by Cazaly family historian Elizabeth Shade.
13   Louisa Nettlefold (née Cazaly) successfully applied for admission to the French Hospital in 1846, stating that "her father's grandparents were natives of France, and Protestants, and his grandmother, when a widow, had considerable property, which was confiscated at the [Revocation of the] Edict of Nantes, and she became a refugee to England." In fact, more than 50 years had elapsed between the Revocation and the family's emigration, but their departure may have been prompted by fear of a new wave of persecutions. *http://www.frenchhospital.org.uk/french-hospital-history/*. Huguenot Society Quarto vol 53 and Daniel Röthlisberger, *http://www.bfhg.de/die-hugenotten/hugenotten-und-ihre-nachkommen/cazaly-guilhaume/*.
14   *The Times*, 3 October, 1803.
15   Robert Nash, '"Up There, Cazaly!" Some Famous Huguenot Descendants in Australia', *Huguenot Families* Number Three, Huguenot Society of Great Britain and Ireland, Huguenot Library, August 2000, pp. 15-17 and information provided by Elizabeth Shade.
16   William Cazaly paid 95,000 francs for the property. In his will, he bequeathed equal amounts to the Protestant and Catholic poor of Sommieres. Daniel Röthlisberger, *op cit* and F. Obert, 'Le Domaine De Pie Bouquet', *SSH Bulletin* no. 11, 2003.
17   The Poulains were Huguenots from Normandy who settled in Kent before moving to the Threadneedle Street district of Spitalfields. Information provided by Elizabeth Shade.
18   Information provided by Elizabeth Shade.
19   'House of Lords Journal Volume 39: March 1792 11-20', pp. 305-18. See *http://www.british-history. ac.uk/report.aspx?compid=116913&strquery=Doxat*.
20   John Doxat raised money for Huguenots in Switzerland and plague sufferers in Spain, helped establish a religious college in London and donated to the Spitalfields Soup Society. *The Times*, 3 February 1794, the *Morning Chronicle*, 7 December, 1821, the *Standard*, 8 July, 1828 and the *Morning Post*, 24 January, 1832.
21   The *Morning Post*, 28 September, 1821. By this time the company principals included two of John's sons and his nephew Alexis, who married John's daughter Louisa and eventually took over the firm. Alexis Doxat continued his uncle's philanthropic work. When he died in 1867, he bequeathed £8000 to hospitals and charities in the United Kingdom and Switzerland. The *Bury Times*, 6 April, 1867 and *British Medical Journal*, 13 April, 1867.
22   *Old Bailey Proceedings Online* at *http://www.oldbaileyonline.org/browse.jsp?path=sessionsPapers%2F18380820.xml* and the *Morning Chronicle*, 1 August 1838.
23   Doxat understood the plight of local silk weavers. In a letter to the President of the Board of Trade in 1829 he had expressed his "deep conviction that there does not exist in these realms, or in any part of the world, a class of people more industrious, more moral, and in every sense more deserving the protecting hand of a government, than the Spitalfields weavers." From a letter Doxat tabled during his evidence to the House of Commons Select Committee on the Silk Trade, p. 230.
24   Tellingly, Doxat told the Select Committee that falling prices for plain woven cloth meant the average Spitalfields weaver earned just three shillings and sixpence per week after costs, compared with seven shillings several years earlier. *Report from Select Committee on the Silk Trade, with Minutes of Evidence, an Appendix and Index*, House of Commons, 2 August, 1832. See pp. 973-74 for a summary of Doxat's evidence to the Committee.
25   Information provided by Elizabeth Shade based on English census and family baptism records.
26   The mistake probably arose because James was not baptised until 4 February, 1846. His younger sister Elisabeth ('Bessy') had been born in October 1845 and their parents took the opportunity to have them both baptised on the same day.
27   National Archives 1851 UK Census.
28   Photos of Charles, Charlotte and Kate Cazaly held by Elizabeth Shade.

29   Anne Doggett, 'Beyond Gentility: Women and music in early Ballarat', *History Australia*, Vol. 6. No. 2, 2009, p. 37.4.
30   See Neil Wigglesworth's *A Social History of English Rowing* for an account of the development of professional and amateur rowing in England during the nineteenth century.
31   The Lea, London's "second great river" after the Thames, was the aquatic playground for many professional, amateur and pleasure boatmen living in East London during the 19th century. Churches, factories, political clubs and inns all formed rowing clubs based on the Lea. Information kindly provided by Lea rowing historian Dick Anderson, author of *Springhill: Two Centuries of River Lea Rowing*, 2014.
32   The *Era*, 12 August, 1855, the *Morning Post*, 16 August, 1855 and 20 and 21 August, 1856 and the *Daily News*, 21 August, 1856.
33   *The Times*, 13 June, and the *Morning Chronicle*, 14 June, 1854.
34   The *Morning Chronicle* and the *Daily News*, September 4 and *The Times*, 5 September, 1854.
35   Quoted in Michael Cannon, *Melbourne After the Gold Rush*, p. 23.

Chapter 2. MIGRATION ON A MASSIVE SCALE: BALLARAT 1855-70

36   The exact date of Peter and Henry's arrival in Victoria is unclear, but a letter was awaiting Henry at the Melbourne General Post Office in April 1855 and in July a notice in *The Argus* asked him to write to Barratt Grove, Stoke Newington. It is thought that Owen and John emigrated in early 1856. It is not known exactly when Elizabeth, Kate, James and Bessy arrived, but there were unclaimed letters awaiting Elizabeth and Bessy at the Ballarat Post Office in September 1857. *The Argus*, 18 April and 31 July, 1855 and 25 February, 1856 and the *Star*, 1 September, 1857.
37   Charles and Charlotte never left England. Charlotte was married and widowed twice and died in 1907, aged 77. Charles, a merchant clerk, remained involved with rowing. In 1872 it was reported that "Mr Cazaly is captain of the Albion Rowing Club, and is one of the staunchest supporters of rowing on the Lea." He died in 1913, aged 84. *The Australasian*, 18 May, 1872 and information provided by Elizabeth Shade.
38   *The Argus*, 17 October, 1851, quoted in Henry James Stacpoole, *Gold at Ballarat: The Ballarat East Goldfield. Its Discovery and Development*, p. 63.
39   A W Strange, *Ballarat: A Brief History*, p. 19, Weston Bate, *Lucky City: The first generation at Ballarat*, p. 114 and Geoffrey Serle, *The Golden Age*, p. 369.
40   Geoffrey Serle, *Ibid*, p. 369.
41   Don Garden, *Victoria: A History*, pp. 79-80.
42   Weston Bate, *op cit* p. 146.
43   Ken James and Learmonth and District Historical Society, *A History of Weatherboard*, pp. 41-42 and the *Star*, 28 September, 1860.
44   The *Star*, 25 February, 1857.
45   Ken James, *op cit* pp. 198-99 and information kindly provided by Bill Loader from the Learmonth and District Historical Society.
46   As Ballarat historian Weston Bate noted, "[East Ballarat] was more Australian because it was less subjected to imported urban forms and institutions and had a restless larrikin quality. Yet the West was probably more typical of what British migrants hoped for in Australia—material success—and it contained large numbers of pioneers who had had the best of both worlds". Weston Bate, *op cit* p.184.
47   Ballarat's town hall was a case in point: the original wooden building was built in 1856, burned down in 1859, rebuilt in stone in 1861 and further expanded in 1872.
48   By 1865, Ballarat was home to 230 mining companies, 186 hotels, 11 banks, eight brewers and three daily newspapers. A W Strange, *op cit* p. 51 and F M Dicker (compiler), *Ballarat and Ballarat District Directory for 1865-66*.
49   *Ballarat Petitions 1860-66*, transcribed and published by the Ballarat and District Genealogical Society, 2007.
50   Elizabeth Cazaly's death notice, the *Star*, 4 August, 1863. 'Phthisis' is a Latin term taken from the Greek, meaning "to waste away".
51   Decades later, a district pioneer recalling Ballarat's early days drew a pen portrait of the family: "Peter Cazaly, an amateur vocalist; was a great worker for charity; medium height, solidly built, breezing life, slightly dark, his own walk; a secretary to the Benevolent Asylum … he and his brothers— James, John

CHAPTER ENDNOTES

and Owen—were a formidable quartette in rowing contests; their sister, Mrs. Wm. Little, was the first lady organist on Ballaarat officiating at the Lydiard Street Wesleyan Church …" Robert Gay, *Some Ballaarat Pioneers*, 1935, p. 57.

52 The *Star* remarked on Kate's "superior talents" as an organist, noting that: "As ladies frequently preside at the organ in our home churches, and the custom is now introduced here, it is to be hoped the present organist will be permanently retained". The *Star*, 25 December, 1860, quoted in Anne Doggett, 'Beyond Gentility: Women and music in early Ballarat', *History Australia*, Vol. 6. No. 2, 2009 and Kate's death notice, *The Ballarat Star*, 26 October, 1903.

53 Fred Shade, *William Little of Ballarat. Some writings*, p. 75.

54 Information provided by Elizabeth Shade.

55 Nathan Spielvogel, *A History of Ballarat*, p. 27.

56 A "sleeping" shareholder plays no active role in the company's affairs but is still entitled to a share of the profits. The Koh-i-Noor mine was one of the first in the district to employ miners on regular wages. Its shaft reached an eventual depth of 465 feet, its largest nugget weighed 69 lbs and its highest paid dividend was £146. Robert Gay, *op cit*, p. 22-23.

57 Nathan Spielvogel, *op cit*, p. 32.

58 *The Ballarat Star*, 30 May, 1865 and *The Argus*, 4 August, 1865.

59 *The Ballarat Star*, 19 March, 1866. Henry was also an auditor for several mining companies and the collector and secretary of the Victoria Temperance Hall.

60 The *Star*, 2 and 21 January, 1861.

61 *Ibid*, 5 February and 2 April, 1861.

62 *Ibid*, 3 March, 1862.

63 *Ibid*, 7 March, 1862, *The Argus*, 10 March, 1862 and http://cricketarchive.com/Archive/Scorecards/134/134509.html.

64 Edward and William Gilbert Grace were both doctors; Edward's nickname was 'the Coroner'. The *Star*, 14 January, 1864 and *The Sydney Morning Herald*, 22 May, 1911.

65 *The Ballarat Star*, 1 February, 1867.

66 Rowing had begun in the region in 1862, when local enthusiasts formed a committee to conduct races, first on Lake Burrumbeet, then on Lake Learmonth and finally on Lake Wendouree. Lake Wendouree had originally been a swamp and acres of weeds had to be removed before rowing could become a regular fixture. Even then, frequent droughts sometimes had to be moved or postponed. John Lang, *The Victorian Oarsman with a rowing register 1857-1919*, p. 190 and Kathryn Elliott, *The Boys from the Rush Beds: The history of the Ballarat City Rowing Club 1870-2004*, pp. 6-15.

67 Elliott, *Ibid*, pp. 17-18. Ned Williams was later described by district pioneer Robert Gay as "a very able oarsman; in the first flight, a large, actively built man, florid [and] clean faced …", Robert Gay, *op cit*, p. 53.

68 *The Argus*, 4 July, 1864.

69 The *Star*, 10 October, 1864.

70 *Ibid*, 24 December, 1864.

71 Kathryn Elliott, *op cit*, p. 23.

72 An article by 'Punt' from *The Ballarat Star* dated 24 January, 1884, reproduced by Kathryn Elliott, *Ibid*, p. 80.

73 Kathryn Elliott, *Ibid*, and John Lang, *op cit*, appendices.

74 *The Ballarat Star*, 22 and 27 December, 1866. James Cazaly's chief backers were George Lovitt and the hotel publican Alex Crow. The watch they gave James is now in the collection of Ballarat's Gold Museum.

75 *The Ballarat Star*, 9 October, 1884, quoted by Kathryn Elliott, *op cit*, p. 75.

76 The committee's fundraising efforts were desultory until Peter Cazaly suggested the bells be named in honour of Prince Alfred, the second son of Queen Victoria, who had visited Ballarat in December 1867 and narrowly escaped an assassination attempt in Sydney three months later. The Royal Alfred Bells, as they became known, were cast in England and installed in West Ballarat's Town Hall, where they first rang out on Christmas morning 1871. Petition dated 20 July 1866, *Ballarat Petitions 1860-1866*; an advertisement in *The Ballarat Star* 30 July, 1866; *The Ballarat Star*, 20 March, 1868; Anne Doggett, 'Harmony on the Goldfields: Music and identity in multicultural Ballarat'; *Victorian Historical Journal* Vol. 75, No. 1, April 2004, p 61; and Anne Doggett, *"And for harmony most ardently we long": Musical life in Ballarat, 1851-1871* Vol. 2, p. 251 and p. 398.

77 By the end of 1869 the Benevolent Asylum was caring for 200 residents and providing "out-door relief"

78 to a further 816. F M Dicker (compiler), *op cit*, p. 155 and Supplement to *The Ballarat Star*, 18 January, 1870.
78 News of the financial scandal spread as far as Sydney, where one newspaper wondered how a man so well known in rowing circles could have found himself in such a predicament. Peter eventually left Ballarat and became a music teacher in Melbourne. Ballarat Benevolent Asylum, *Twenty-Ninth Annual Report*, June 1886, p 6 quoted in Helen Kinloch, *Ballarat and its Benevolent Asylum: A Nineteenth-Century Model of Christian Duty, Civic Progress and Social Reform*, pp. 202-06; the *Globe*, 30 June, 1886; and *The Age*, 27 April, 1896.
79 The *Star*, 24 August, 1863.
80 *Ballarat Rate Assessments 1856-64* and F M Dicker (compiler), *Ballarat and Ballarat District Directory for 1865-66*, pp. 12-13. This directory lists a "James Colenay, miner" living in Ascot Street. This could have been a typographical error, and it was actually James Cazaly.
81 Information provided by Elizabeth Shade.
82 The *Queenslander*, 25 July, 1868.
83 Letter from Alex Mackenzie dated 10 July, 1868, reprinted in *The Ballarat Star*, 20 July, 1868.
84 Letter from Owen Cazaly dated 6 August, 1868, reprinted in *The Australasian*, 29 August, 1868.
85 A W Strange, *op cit*, p. 29 and Henry James Stacpoole, *op cit*, p. 71.
86 Stacpoole, *Ibid*, p. 71 and Spielvogel, *op cit*, p. 32.

Chapter 3. BOOM AND BUST: MELBOURNE, 1871-93

87 John Lang, *The Victorian Oarsman with a rowing register 1857-1919*, pp. 33-34. Melbourne's rowing regattas relocated to the lower Yarra from 1874.
88 *The Argus*, 4, 7 and 9 January, 1871. Despite his move to Melbourne the Ballarat Rowing Club was still claiming James as a member as late as May 1873, long after he had left Ballarat.
89 See Andrew Guerin (ed), History of Australian Rowing website at http://www.rowinghistory-aus.info/club-histories/melbourne/01-1.php.
90 *The Age*, 17 April, 1871.
91 *The Australasian*, 25 March, 1871. Writing in 1898, English rowing coach Rudy Lehmann said an ideal stroke should be a "long-backed, supple-jointed" man. "As to temperament, I would select a good fighter, a man, that is, who would rather die than abandon the struggle, and whose fiery determined nature does not exclude perfect coolness and mastery over himself when a crisis calls for response." R C Lehmann, *Rowing*, pp. 74-75.
92 *The Argus*, 17 April, 1871.
93 *Ibid*, 21 April, 1871.
94 *The Australasian*, 28 October, 1871.
95 *Ibid*, 8 February, 1873.
96 *The Illustrated Australian News*, 22 April, 1873.
97 John Lang, *op cit*, p. 70, Kathryn Elliott, *The Boys from the Rush Beds: The History of the Ballarat City Rowing Club 1870–2004*, pp. 47-49 and Andrew Guerin, History of Australian Rowing website at http://www.rowinghistory-aus.info/interstate-championships/1873-1879.php
98 *The Age*, 7 April and *The Argus*, 9 April, 1873.
99 *The Australasian*'s reporter counselled that: "a *gentleman* amateur who has come to another colony to row under that colony's terms (terms which he knew perfectly well before he started) should manage to control his feelings a little more, and not find fault with those terms *after* the race. We doubt very much if, had the Sydney men won, we would have heard a word on the subject of amateur." *The Australasian*, 12 April, 1873.
100 *Ibid*, 13 December, 1873 and John Lang, *op cit*, p. 46.
101 Watson and Sons were unusually progressive in encouraging their workers' sporting activities: most employer-sponsored recreation in Australia did not begin until much later in the century. *The Argus*, 8 December, 1873 and 23 February, 1874, the *Official Program, Melbourne Annual Regatta*, Saltwater River, 21 March, 1874 in the State Library of Victoria's Rare Books Collection and Nikola Balnave, 'Company-Sponsored Recreation in Australia: 1890-1965' in *Labour History* No. 85, November 2003, pp. 129-51.
102 *Melbourne Directory 1854*, quoted in Philip and Jan Gregory, *The Business of Empire: William Watson and Sons*, p. 18 and advertisements in *The Argus*, 10 March and 16 May, 1854.

CHAPTER ENDNOTES

103   *Tanner's Melbourne Directory 1859*, p. 56.
104   The amount of money turned over by Watson and Sons can be gleaned from an 1863 court case which heard that one of its clerks had embezzled £1000 over six months before being detected. *The Argus*, 12 September, 1863.
105   *Sands and McDougall's Melbourne and Suburban Directory 1865*, p. 433. That year, Robert Watson joined other members of Melbourne's commercial establishment to protest what they saw as the inequities of a new import tariff regime. In a letter to the colonial press, he candidly described himself as "one of the soft-goods clique—neither a shoddy aristocrat, nor an aristocrat of any kind, but a plain business man, and a free trader". Quoted in a supplement to *The Ballarat Star*, 13 December, 1865.
106   For example see *The Argus*, 19 August, 1870.
107   The Watsons' political influence was shown by the fact that Melbourne's mayor and a number of other politicians attended the warehouse's formal opening. *The Argus*, 6 February, 1874.
108   'Australian Assisted and Unassisted Passenger Lists 1839–1923' VPRS 7666 and Elizabeth Cazaly's 1927 death certificate No. 2685.
109   1841 United Kingdom Census and Noel Counihan, Roy Cazaly (1893–1963) in *Australian Dictionary of Biography*, National Centre of Biography, Australian National University, http://adb.anu.edu.au/biography/cazaly-roy-5541/text9441.
110   James' and Elizabeth's marriage record No. 4460 and James William's birth registration No. 3590. Their marriage record lists James' age as 31, but as indicated earlier he was most likely born in November 1840, making him 33 in December 1873.
111   Andrew Brown-May, *Melbourne Street Life: The Itinerary of our Days*, pp. 8-9 and Weston Bate, *Essential but Unplanned: The Story of Melbourne's Lanes*, pp. 11-12.
112   *Sands and McDougall Melbourne and Suburban Directory 1874*, pp. 21-24.
113   James William's birth registration No. 3590. Elizabeth and James' wedding day was backdated by four months on his birth registration and by up to two years on subsequent family birth records.
114   As James' name did not appear on the electoral rolls until 1903 his occupations for this period are taken from his children's birth records. Elizabeth first appeared on the Federal roll in 1906 and the Victorian roll in 1914.
115   Noel Counihan, 'Roy Cazaly' in *Australian Dictionary of Biography*, *op cit*.
116   *The North Melbourne Advertiser*, 21 January, 1876.
117   John Cazaly performed best in a crew but also fancied himself as a sculler. After several years of losing races, *The Australasian* felt obliged to point out that "[John] Cazaly ought to have discovered, after all these years, that sculling is not his forté; but that is evidently a point on which he has not been able to satisfy himself yet." *The Australasian*, 22 March 1879.
118   *The Argus*, 23 December 1874. Crews from Watson and Sons won a further four Challenge Cups between 1881 and 1889.
119   The Warehousemen Rowing Club crew wore a white cap with a red Maltese cross. Their 1875 Melbourne Regatta prizes included a silver cup for each rower and a medal for the coxswain. John Lang, *op cit*, p. 132 and p. 324 and *The Age*, 27 April, 1875.
120   *The Argus*, 30 November and 20 December, 1875. Christie, who was at various times a police detective, customs inspector, boxer and bodyguard for visiting English royalty, was something of a rowing *bête noire* to the Cazaly brothers. In 1876 he defeated John Cazaly to win the Challenge Sculls at the Melbourne Regatta to retain the title of Amateur Champion Sculler of Victoria and in 1877 defeated James in the same event. J B Castieau, *The Reminiscences of Detective Inspector Christie*, pp. 105-09 and Hugh Anderson, 'John Mitchell Christie', *Australian Dictionary of Biography*, http://adb.anu.edu.au/biography/christie-john-mitchell-5589/text9541.
121   *The Australasian*, 10 May, 1879 and 18 June, 1881.
122   Jill Roe, *Marvellous Melbourne: The emergence of an Australian city*, pp. 11-12 and 69.
123   Information taken from Edgar Cazaly's birth record no. 13262 and an auction notice in *The Argus*, 18 March, 1914. The original home appears to be one of three co-joined brick terraces.
124   Bessy's son Charles played full-forward for Essendon and later died of wounds in 1901 while fighting in South Africa during the Anglo-Boer War. The previous year his uncle Peter Cazaly had penned a patriotic song, *The Soldiers of Australia*. The Charles Moore Drinking Fountain built in his memory still stands in St Vincent Gardens. Jim Main and David Allen, *Fallen - the Ultimate Heroes: Footballers Who Never Returned from War*, pp. 3-6 and the *Geelong Advertiser*, 8 June, 1900.
125   South St Kilda played in a local junior competition that also included sides from South Yarra, Leopold (Albert Park) and Pembroke (Middle Park). *South Melbourne Record*, 8 June, 22 June and 29 June, 1895

and 16 June, 1906 and *The Australasian*, 9 September, 1905.
126 Geoffrey Blainey, *A History of Victoria*, p. 148.
127 *Ibid*, p. 149 and Don Garden, *Victoria: A History*, p. 207.
128 See chapter four 'Speculators, Bankrupts and Nationalists: Boom and Bust' of Don Garden's *Victoria: A History* for a detailed examination of Melbourne's economic fortunes between the 1870s and 1890s.
129 One of the local financial institutions that collapsed was the South Melbourne Permanent Building and Investment Society, which had been founded by 14 prominent South Melbourne citizens in 1875. Its secretary Matthias Larkin was convicted of company fraud and served six years in prison. Susan Priestley, *South Melbourne: A History*, p. 137 and pp. 169-73.
130 *Ibid*, p. 220.
131 Charles Daley, *The History of South Melbourne*, pp. 195-96 and Susan Priestley, *op cit*, p. 239.
132 Watson and Sons' insolvency was attributed to its accumulation of bad debts. *The Argus* reported that during the boom "the company was doing fairly well but since then suburban dealers who were customers of the firm have failed in every direction, and the heavy losses entailed on the wholesale house have crippled it". *The Argus*, 20 February and 10 March, 1891 and Philip and Jan Gregory, *op cit*, pp. 107-08.
133 John was reported as rowing bow for the R Reid and Sons crew in the 1892 Warehousemen's Challenge Cup. *The Age*, 5 December, 1892.
134 ANU *Australian Dictionary of Biography* project memorandum from Margaret Glover to Sally O'Neill, based on information provided to Glover by Roy Cazaly jnr, 1 September, 1978.
135 Information obtained from *South Melbourne Rates Books*. I thank South Melbourne historian Brian Membrey and City of Port Phillip Local History Librarian Kay Rowan for their assistance in researching various properties rented by the Cazalys around South Melbourne during this period.

Chapter 4. A CHILDHOOD BY THE LAKE: ALBERT PARK, 1893-1911

136 Interview with Roy Cazaly's daughter Pat Whitecross.
137 Keith Welsh, 'Up there Cazaly! The famous cry still lingers on', *The Saturday Evening Mercury*, 2 May, 1964.
138 Letter from Roy Cazaly jnr to Noel Counihan, 20 September, 1976 and Australian Dictionary of Biography memorandum from Margaret Glover to Sally O'Neill, based on information provided to Glover by Roy Cazaly jnr, 1 September, 1978.
139 Adam Smith, 'They still talk about Roy Cazaly', *Sport*, May 1958.
140 'Up There, Cazaly' in *People*, 11 March, 1953.
141 Interview with Pat Whitecross.
142 *The Argus*, 12 January, 1897.
143 South Melbourne's abundance of parklands meant its population density in 1903 was just 17 people for every acre, compared with 27 per acre in Richmond and 35 in Fitzroy. *1903 Victorian Year Book*, p. 86 and p. 131.
144 Charles Daley, *The History of South Melbourne*, p. 36 and pp. 204-05.
145 Deborah Towns, 'May Cox: Leading Swimming and Lifesaving Advocate and Patriotic Fundraiser, 1910-1938' in *Seizing the Initiative: Australian Women Leaders in Politics, Workplaces and Communities*, p. 199.
146 Numerous junior and minor clubs also came and went during this time, including Alberts, Albion, Britannia, Defiance, Rising Sun and Young Victorians. See Mark Pennings, *Origins of Australian Football: Victoria's Early History*, Volumes 1 (1858 to 1876) and 2 (1877 to 1885) for a comprehensive description of clubs, results and the evolution of Australian Football during this period.
147 Other clubs affiliated with the VFA waxed and waned during this period: three teams from Ballarat competed between 1886 and 1888, for example, but their presence in a Melbourne-based competition eventually proved impractical. Marc Fiddian, *The VFA: A History of the Victorian Football Association 1877-1995*, p. 22 and p. 214.
148 *Ibid*, p. 205 and Jim Main, *In the Blood: Celebrating the Red and White 1874-2009*, pp. 12-13.
149 *The South Melbourne Football Club's Guide*, 1890 and *South Melbourne Football Guide*, 1892.
150 Stewart Bale (compiler), *The ABC Football Guide, Register and Directory for 1893*. The roster was rectified the following season, when each team played 18 matches.
151 Sometimes the team that drew or even lost a game would have won if their behinds had been counted.

CHAPTER ENDNOTES

Two of Essendon's three draws during the 1892 VFA season would have been wins if behinds had been included and in 1893 a Victorian side drew two games with Tasmania in which they were technically outscored. The VFA and VFL both began to count behinds in match scores from 1897. Stewart Bale (compiler), *ABC Football Guide, Register and Directory* for 1893 and 1894, and Geoffrey Blainey, *A Game of Our Own*, pp. 169-71.

152 Stewart Bale, 1893, *op cit.*
153 Joseph Johnson, *For the Love of the Game, the Centenary History of the Victorian Amateur Football Association, 1892-1992*, p. 16.
154 Stewart Bale, 1893, *op cit.*
155 *1904 Victorian Year Book*, p. 6 and pp. 116-17.
156 Butcher Phil Skehan was a ruckman in South Melbourne's 1918 premiership side. He was seriously injured while playing for Williamstown in the VFA in 1921 and died several days later without regaining consciousness. *The South Melbourne Record*, 25 June, 1921, South Melbourne electoral rolls and information provided by William Cazaly's granddaughter June Thornton.
157 The South Melbourne Council approved a business registration for the Cazaly brothers at 113 Hambleton Street, Middle Park in late 1908. James jnr must have joined his brothers there soon after because he was described as a butcher in Middle Park's annual 'north versus south' football match in June 1909. Participants were limited to married men over 30, and the north-south demarcation line was Armstrong Street. James played for the northern side and scored two goals; his team defeated the south by eight points. William and Sydney's business partnership was dissolved in 1910 but each continued to trade from different premises: William at the Hambleton Street address and Sydney at 54 Herbert Street Albert Park. The *South Melbourne Record*, 28 November, 1908, *The Age* and *The Argus*, 8 June, 1909, *The Age*, 8 March, 1910 and Susan Priestley, *South Melbourne: A History*, p. 301.
158 The Dunlop Rubber Company of Australasia was originally established as the local branch of the English firm Dunlop Pneumatic Tyre Company, before being bought out by investors and floated on the Australian stock exchange in 1899. The new factory was established in 1902 at Montague, an industrial suburb between South Melbourne and the Yarra River. Geoffrey Blainey, *Jumping Over the Wheel*, pp. 38-48.
159 *The Argus*, 16 February, 1906 and Geoffrey Blainey, *Ibid*, pp 54-55.
160 *The Age*, 29 October, 1907.
161 Susan Priestley, *op cit*, p. 78 and Janet Walsh and Ian Spalding, *Albert Park Primary School 1181 Centenary 1873–1973*, p. 11.
162 Albert Park Primary School website at *http://www.albertparkps.vic.edu.au/about-apps/history* and *South Melbourne Record*, 3 February, 1900.
163 L J Blake (ed), *Vision and Realisation: A Centenary History of State Education in Victoria*, Volume 1, p. 992.
164 In 1901 Albert Park was the only school affiliated with the Victorian Amateur Swimming Association. *Sportsman*, 10 December 1901, *South Melbourne Record*, 20 October, 1900 and Deborah Towns, *op cit*, p. 199.
165 W S Sharland, 'Footballer, cricketer: Roy Cazaly an all rounder', *Sporting Globe*, 12 March, 1927.
166 Deborah Towns, *op cit*, pp. 198-99.
167 A photo of the school's 1905/06 swimming team shows 14-year-old Frank Beaurepaire to be a strong, powerfully built athlete. 'Albert Park State School Swimming Club, Boys' Championship Team, 1905-06', Picture Collection, State Library of Victoria.
168 Beaurepaire won three state school championships in 1906. He became a champion distance and Olympic swimmer and later joined May Cox in organising Victoria's statewide swimming and lifesaving programs. 'The Beaurepaire Story', The *Sun Herald*, 2 May, 1954, Graham Lomas, *The Will to Win: The Story of Sir Frank Beaurepaire*, p. 5, the *Daily Mirror*, 9 June, 1978, Roy Smith, 'They still talk about Roy Cazaly', *Sport*, May 1958, *Referee*, 21 February, 1906 and Deborah Towns, *op cit*, p. 200.
169 The state school competition was district-based: neighbouring schools played each other with the winner progressing through a series of finals against the winners from other districts.
170 *The Argus* reported that, despite Albert Park's size disadvantage, "in language some of them weighed ten stone", leading the school's head teacher to write an indignant letter to the editor denying his students had used objectionable language. *Referee*, 21 September and *The Argus*, 19 and 20 September, 1904.
171 Albert Park lost their 1906 semi-final match to North Fitzroy but the match had to be replayed after North Fitzroy's headmaster discovered to his chagrin that he had inadvertently included a boy in its team who was over 16. Albert Park won the replay. They went on to defeat St Kilda to win the championship but were defeated for the interstate title by the Fort Street schoolboys from Sydney. Albert Park were

runners up in 1907 but won further school championships in 1908 and 1909. *The Age*, 6, 14 and 17 August, 1906, *Prahran Telegraph*, 8 September, 1906, *Referee*, 19 September 1906 and *South Melbourne Record*, 17 October and 26 December, 1908 and 9 October, 1909.

172 Stan Veale's letter to the editor, *The Bulletin*, 18 September, 1979.

173 *Ibid*. Veale later recalled that the "great thrill in the life of the school occurred on the day the late Mr H.C.A. Harrison, the founder of our Australian football game, came to the school and presented to all the boys of the team—including Roy Cazaly and me—uniforms generously provided by the Victorian Football League". Stan Veale's letter to the editor, *Southern Cross* (Prahran edition), 10 October, 1979.

174 *The Age*, 21 March and 4 and 5 April, 1906. Albert Park had been undefeated during the 1906 cricket season prior to this loss.

175 Stan Veale joined the naval cadets at 15, served with the Royal Australian Navy in both World Wars and retired as a commander in 1952. Emil Fleiter joined the Australian Imperial Force's 39th Infantry Battalion in 1916, was promoted to lieutenant and was awarded a Military Cross for conspicuous gallantry. John Treloar joined the AIF in 1914, served at Gallipoli and on the western front and later became an influential war archivist and director of the Australian War Memorial. The *South Melbourne Record*, 3 November, 1900 and Australian military records.

176 Howard Kushner, 'Retraining the King's left hand' in *The Lancet*, Vol. 377, Issue 9782, 11 June, 2011 and 'Retraining left-handers and the aetiology of stuttering: the rise and fall of an intriguing theory', *Laterality*, 17(6) 2012, pp. 673-93.

177 Interview with Pat Whitecross and Stephen Park by Peter MacFie. A causal link between "enforced right handedness" and the onset of stuttering was accepted for many years. The theory fell from favour in the mid-20th century but there are still many anecdotal accounts of left-handed children developing a stutter after being made to switch writing-hands. A current middle-ground hypothesis suggests that enforcing right handedness *may* bring on a stutter, depending on how the corrective action is taken and the child's age at the time. The United States' National Stuttering Association suggests that stress caused when a child is forced to switch hands may exacerbate an *existing* stutter; this might have occurred in Cazaly's case. See http://www.anythinglefthanded.co.uk/stuttering-and-changed-lefthanders.html#sthash.t7vWqIxR.dpbs and http://www.westutter.org/who-we-help/common-myths-about-stuttering/.

178 While Victorian school children were supposed to attend at least 75 per cent of classes the average attendance in 1906 was only 67 per cent. A new *Truancy Act* passed in 1907 increased the minimum attendance to 80 per cent but a subsequent review found many parents continued to ignore this requirement. *1903 Victorian Year Book*, pp. 61-62, *1905 Victorian Year Book*, p. 177 and *The Age*, 18 May, 1907.

179 Charles Daley, *op cit*, pp. 248-49 and 254.

180 *The Argus*, 24 October, 1940.

181 Noel Counihan, 'Roy Cazaly (1893–1963)', Australian Dictionary of Biography, National Centre of Biography, Australian National University, http://adb.anu.edu.au/biography/cazaly-roy-5541/text9441 and information provided by Cazaly's grandson Stephen Park.

182 Susan Priestley, *op cit*, pp. 240-41.

183 J M Rohan, 'Whenever he crouched for a spring the crowd yelled Up There Cazaly!', *The Sporting Globe*, 8 May, 1935.

184 The *South Melbourne Record*, 7 and 28 November, 1908.

185 *Sport*, 5 May, 1911. As well as sponsoring football and cricket competitions, the Boyle and Scott's sporting goods store regularly published a penny guide containing the latest rules, senior club fixtures and equipment prices.

186 J K Smith had been a manager with Boyle and Scott's before opening his own Sports Emporium in Elizabeth Street in 1896.

187 Others to play well in the same match included an "H Cazaly"; this may have been Roy's brother William, better known as Harry. *Sport*, 22 July, 1910.

188 *The Argus*, 29 August and *The Australasian*, 3 September, 1910 and John Lang, *The Victorian Oarsman*, p. 167.

189 Rudolph Chambers Lehmann, *The Complete Oarsman*, pp. 2-3.

190 *Sport*, 19 May, 1911. The Middle Park Wesleys (also known as the Methodists) were one of nine teams in the open age division of the Protestant Churches' Association.

191 Thomas Power (compiler), *The Footballer: An annual record of football in Victoria*, 1876, p. 10.

192 'Up There, Cazaly' in *People*, 11 March, 1953.

193 Historian Geoffrey Blainey refers to three followers in each team during the mid-1870s while South

CHAPTER ENDNOTES

Melbourne champion Peter Burns later recalled that each team during the 1880s had four followers and two rovers. In 1897, the VFA reduced the number of players from 20 to 18 by abolishing two of the ruck positions. The VFL copied their move two years later. Geoffrey Blainey, *A Game of Our Own*, pp. 121-22 and 169, Peter Burns quoted in *The Sporting Globe Football Book 1948*, p. 35 and Rob Hess and Bob Stewart (eds), *More than a Game*, p. 90.
194   *Sport*, 7 and 14 July, 1911.

Chapter 5. A RAW COLT FROM THE PADDOCK: ST KILDA, 1911-12

195   Joseph Johnson, *For the Love of the Game*, p. 42.
196   The *South Melbourne Record*, 13 July, 1907.
197   Despite his suspension Ernest received a club trophy for his on-field efforts. Bill Woodcock, who was also reported, joined St Kilda's VFL side the following year. *South Melbourne Wednesday Football Club Minutes 1907–1909*, p. 95 in the La Trobe Australian Manuscripts Collection, State Library of Victoria, *The Age*, 16 July, 1907 and Russell Holmesby and Jim Main, *The Encyclopedia of AFL Footballers*, Seventh Edition, pp. 864-5.
198   *South Melbourne Wednesday Football Club Minutes 1907–1909*, p. 167 and additional information provided by Peter Burke.
199   *Sport*, 21 May, 1909 and the *South Melbourne Record*, 3 July, 1909.
200   *St Kilda Football Club Minutes Book 12 March, 1908–6 May, 1909*. Football historian Stephen Rodgers discovered the error when reviewing player registration records. A *VFL Player Registration Book* held by the AFL Library confirms that Ernest was first registered on 4 May, 1910 and Roy on 1 May, 1911.
201   *Victorian Football Follower*, 7 May, 1910. Ernest's surname was misspelled as 'Cazall' in some reports.
202   *St Kilda Football Club Minutes Book 17 May, 1909 – 9 February, 1911*.
203   *Victorian Football Follower*, 28 May and 23 July, 1910, *The Argus*, 18 and 23 May, 1911 and *Sport*, 20 May, 1910 and 19 May, 1911. Gower Ross (his full name was Adam Gower Sutherland De Ross) played half-back with Brunswick for several years before joining the Royal Flying Corps in Britain during World War I. He was shot down and killed over the French town of Gueudecourt on Valentine's Day 1917 while on an observation patrol. *Brunswick and Coburg Leader*, 30 March, 1917 and British military records.
204   *The Argus*, 2 July, 1910.
205   Jules Feldman and Russell Holmesby, *The Point of It All: The Story of the St Kilda Football Club*, p. 48 and Stephen Rodgers, *100 Years of AFL Players*, Volume 3, p. 1567.
206   *St Kilda Football Club Minutes Book 15 March, 1911–28 August, 1911* and *The Argus*, 22 July, 1911.
207   *The Argus*, 22 July, 1911.
208   *Ibid*, 24 July, 1911.
209   *Sport*, 28 July, 1911.
210   *The Argus*, 24 July, 1911.
211   *Ibid*.
212   *The Argus*, 26 July and *Sport*, 28 July, 1911.
213   *The Argus*, 28 July, 1911.
214   Roy Cazaly, 'Club ruck that won interstate fame', *The Sporting Globe*, 12 June 1937.
215   *The Age*, 31 July 1911.
216   *The Argus*, 31 July, 1911.
217   They were Bill Woodcock (who was named as captain), Bert Pierce and Harry Hattam.
218   Kevin's Taylor's AFL Footystats at http://footystats.freeservers.com/Daily/Diary.html#Footystats.
219   Fred Elliott had played in two of Carlton's trifecta of premierships between 1906 and 1908 and been both captain and coach since mid-way through the 1908 season. He ended up playing 209 VFL games.
220   J M Rohan, 'Whenever he crouched for a spring the crowd yelled Up There Cazaly!', *The Sporting Globe*, 11 May, 1935.
221   Vin Gardiner scored 10 of Carlton's goals. St Kilda's second goal came in comical fashion during a severe downpour when Sellars neatly sidestepped Carlton's fullback Jamieson, who was sheltering under an umbrella being held over the boundary line by a supporter. *The Argus*, 31 July, 1911.
222   *The Argus* and *The Age*, 31 July and *Sport*, 29 July, 1911.
223   One St Kilda teammate that day was Claude Crowl, who later died during the Anzac landings at

	Gallipoli on 25 April, 1915. Stephen Rodgers, *100 Years of AFL Players* Volume 1, pp. 165-6 and Jim Main and David Allen, *The Fallen*, pp. 47-8.
224	*The Argus*, 18 August, 1911.
225	*The Age*, 21 August, 1911.
226	*Sport*, 1 September, 1911.
227	By comparison, the average number of players used by each VFL club in 1911 was just 37. Stephen Rodgers, *100 Years of AFL Players* Volume 3, p. 1540 and p. 1574.
228	John Lang, *The Victorian Oarsman*, pp. 167 and the *South Melbourne Record*, 4 November, 1911.
229	*The Argus*, 17 October, 1911.
230	John Lang, *op cit*, p. 183 and the *South Melbourne Record* and *The Australasian*, 4 November, 1911.
231	Edgar Cazaly had absconded from the Kew Asylum 10 months earlier and somehow made his way aboard the naval cruiser *HMS Psyche* moored off Port Melbourne before being discovered. The *Port Melbourne Standard*, 25 February, 1911, *The Age*, 28 December, 1911, *The Argus*, 29 December, 1911 and 12 January, 1912 and Coronial certificate No. 2425 dated 15 January, 1912.
232	Rule 29 stated that 'Any player receiving payment directly or indirectly for his services as a footballer shall be disqualified for any period the League may think fit, and any Club paying a player either directly or indirectly for his services as a footballer, shall be dealt with as the League may think fit.' *Victorian Football League Constitution, Rules, Permits and Laws of the Game 1910*, p. 15.
233	The 'shamateurism' allegation was not a new one: in 1896 a journalist used it to deride the VFA after a player named Len Webb candidly claimed he had been a "professional footballer" while playing with Essendon during 1891. Essendon denied the claim and an investigation by the VFA subsequently cleared the club and disqualified Webb for life. The *Sportsman*, 16 June, 11 August, 1 and 5 September, 1896 and information kindly provided by VFA historian Mark Pennings.
234	Dave McNamara, *Football*, 1914, p. 62 and pp. 66-67.
235	Melbourne's delegate Dr Bill McClelland argued player payments would force weaker clubs to the wall and introduce "professional parasites" into the game. The *Weekly Times*, 29 April, 1911.
236	*Sport*, 26 May, 1911.
237	*Ibid*, 9 June, 1911 and Jules Feldman and Russell Holmesby, *op cit*, p. 48.
238	League delegates had discussed introducing player numbers as early as 1905 after a letter writer to *The Age* suggested the idea. Collingwood secretary Ernest Copeland supported the proposal and Melbourne delegate Amos Norcott said his club intended trialling it but other delegates argued that numbers would interfere with club colour schemes. The rival VFA introduced player numbers in 1907. *The Age*, 10 June, 1905, *Sport*, 26 April, 1912 and Marc Fiddian, *The VFA: A History of the Victorian Football Association 1877-1995*, p. 25.
239	Russell Holmesby, *Heroes with Haloes: St Kilda's One Hundred Greatest*, pp. 241-42.
240	*Ibid* and Roy Cazaly with H A de Lacy, 'Roy Cazaly's cavalcade of great footballers', *The Sporting Globe*, 5 June, 1937.
241	*Sport*, 7 July, 1912.
242	*The Argus* and *The Age*, 22 June and *Sport*, 28 June, 1912.
243	*Sport*, 2 August, 1912.
244	*Ibid*, 9 and 16 August, 1912.
245	*The Australasian*, 7 September, 1912.
246	Beverley went on to defeat South Yarra to win the 1912 MAFA premiership. *Sport*, 30 August and 6, 13 and 20 September, 1912.

Chapter 6. A PREMIERSHIP THROWN IN THE AIR: ST KILDA, 1913-14

247	*Sport*, 18 April, 1913. Several writers later claimed that Cazaly left Carlton Districts disappointed after failing to receive proper medical treatment following a shoulder injury but I have been unable to find any contemporary or subsequent reports to confirm this account.
248	*Football Record*, No. 1 and No. 7, 1913.
249	*Sport*, 2 and 9 May, 1913.
250	*Ibid*, 23 May, 1913.
251	H A de Lacy, 'Up there Cazzer', *The Sporting Globe*, 9 August, 1941.
252	*Sport*, 6 June, 1913.

253 St Kilda's officials had the game ball mounted and presented to Billy Schmidt. Jules Feldman and Russell Holmesby, *The Point of It All: The Story of the St Kilda Football Club*, p. 54 and *Football Record* No. 17, 1913.
254 *Sport*, 29 August, 1913.
255 For his sterling effort, Park won a suit of clothes from a Melbourne tailor worth four guineas. Stephen Rodgers, *Every Game Ever Played*, p. 97 and *Football Record* No. 21, 6 September, 1913.
256 *Football Record* No. 24, 27 September, 1913.
257 *Ibid*.
258 *St Kilda Football Club Minutes*, 25 September, 1913 and Joe St John, *AFL Premiers: The fascinating history of every AFL / VFL Grand Final*, p. 63.
259 Roy Cazaly with H A de Lacy, 'Thrills in fights for football honors', *The Sporting Globe*, 29 May, 1937.
260 Robert Cornish, a stockbroker, must have had strong links with local businesses as he undertook to try to find ruckman Bill Woodcock employment at the Dunlop Rubber Company the following year. *St Kilda Football Club Minutes*, 28 August and 29 September, 1913 and 2 April, 1914.
261 Patrick Murtha had previously lived at Violet Town near Benalla in central Victoria, which certainly places him in the proximity of the Kelly family. In later life Aggie revealed she had known one of Ned Kelly's sisters and his mother, Ellen, who she described as a handsome but aggressive woman. Information based on a surviving written account Aggie gave her grandson Carl Cazaly around 1979.
262 Delia divorced Patrick sometime around 1900. He moved to Western Australia and she later remarried John Harrison. Delia Pettis' birth certificate no. 1641; Delia and Patrick's marriage certificate no. 3484; Aggie Murtha's birth certificate no. 14937; an interview with Pat Whitecross conducted by Peter MacFie and information provided by Sue Hardstaff.
263 J M Rohan, 'Whenever he crouched for a spring the crowd yelled Up There Cazaly!', *The Sporting Globe*, 8 May, 1935.
264 The *City of Brunswick Rates Book* for 1914 lists Cazaly's mother, Elizabeth, as the nominated De Carle Street tenant. The house's owner, Frank Drew, lived in the same street.
265 Roy and Aggie's marriage certificate no. 10229. Aggie's maiden surname is given as Murtha while her mother's surname is listed as Harrison. In 1920, Aggie's older sister Blanche, a widow, married Roy's widowed older brother Ernest. Information provided by Elizabeth Shade.
266 *The Argus*, 17 February, the *Brunswick and Coburg Star*, 20 February, the *South Melbourne Record*, 21 February and *The Herald*, 24 February, 1914 and Coronial reference 1914/146.
267 *Sport*, 24 April, 1914.
268 *Ibid*, 26 June, 1914.
269 *The Argus*, 24 August and *Sport*, 28 August, 1914 and Jim Main, *Football's Black Book*, p. 161.
270 *St Kilda Football Club Minutes*, 13 August, 1914.
271 *Football Pantomime Programme*, South Melbourne Cricket Ground, 15 August, 1914, AFL Library.
272 The Challenge Fours crew were George Barrell (stroke), Roy Cazaly, Freddy Loud and Arthur Crook. The *South Melbourne Record*, 26 September, 1914 and information from the *South Melbourne Rowing Club Annual Report 1913-14* provided by rowing historian Grace Blake.
273 *Winner*, 9 September and the *South Melbourne Record*, 26 September, 1914. The 5km *Albert parkrun* is regularly conducted around the same course and Cazaly's time would still be competitive.
274 The South Melbourne Rowing Club photo was published in *Punch*, 3 December, 1914. My thanks to Grace Blake for providing a copy of the original.
275 'Up there, Cazaly' in *People*, 11 March, 1953 and *St Kilda Football Club Minutes*, 14 and 28 August, 1913.
276 Letter from Roy Cazaly jnr to Noel Counihan, 20 September, 1976 and interview with Pat Whitecross conducted by Peter MacFie.
277 A jury later found the accused, Butchun Singh, not guilty on grounds of insanity and he was committed to an asylum. The *Shepparton News*, 17 and 31 December-1914, *The Argus*, 19 December, 1914 and 17 February, 1915 and an interview with Pat Whitecross conducted by Peter MacFie.

Chapter 7. FOOTBALL DURING WAR: ST KILDA, 1915

278 Victorian electoral records and *Victoria Birth Index, 1836-1920*. https://archive.org/details/AustraliaVictoriaBmdHistoricalIndex_104. Registration Number 01323.
279 The *Punch* newspaper described the colours as "so obnoxious, that no-one outside Germany cares to wear

280 them." It also quoted one unnamed St Kilda player as saying he'd rather "give up the game and take to dominoes" than face their barrackers wearing German colours. *Punch*, 8 April, 1915.
280 St Kilda registered their new colours with the VFL in April 1915. The club did not revert to its traditional colour scheme until 1923. *St Kilda Football Club Minutes*, 26 February, 4 March and 22 April, 1915 and Dale Blair, 'War and Peace' in Hess and Stewart (eds) *More Than a Game*, p. 117.
281 Nineteen former University players died on active service during the war, including one-time captain George Elliott. Daniel Cherny, 'Remembering football's forgotten club: 100 years since University', *The Age*, 23 August, 2014.
282 Dale Blair, *op cit*, p. 118.
283 *South Melbourne Record*, 6 February and 7 August, 1915 and *The Argus*, 15 July, 1915.
284 Levi Tate was a South Melbourne councilor for the Canterbury ward from 1911 until 1923. Charles Daley, *History of South Melbourne*, pp. 263-65 and Susan Priestley, *South Melbourne: A History*, p. 284.
285 South Africa was the only other Allied combatant that did not have military conscription during World War I.
286 Dale Blair, *op cit*, p. 117 and Ernest Scott, *Official History of Australia in the Great War of 1914-18: Volume XI. Australia During the War*, Appendix 5, p. 874.
287 By mid-1915, for example, 19 players from the South Melbourne District Football Club and 18 from South Yarra had enlisted. During one Dookie District Association game in July, both captains and 12 other players volunteered at half-time. The same month, the Ballarat League decided to end its season early due to the large number of player enlistments. Robert Grogan, *Blood, Sweat and Cheers: South Melbourne District Sports Club from footy beginnings to sporting diversity*, p. 4, *The Argus*, 26 April and 13 July, 1915 and the *Winner*, 14 July, 1915.
288 A total of 262 Victorian rowers died during the war including Freddy Loud, Cazaly's former rowing partner and treasurer of the South Melbourne Rowing Club. Loud enlisted with the AIF's 7th Battalion in July 1915 and died of wounds in France a year later. John Lang, *The Victorian Oarsman with a rowing register 1857-1919*, p. 33 and *The Argus*, 6 September, 1916.
289 Ernest Scott, *op cit*, p. 405 and Susan Priestley, *op cit*, p. 284.
290 Tradesmen and labourers represented 64 per cent of all AIF enlistments while clerical workers comprised a further 7 per cent. Ernest Scott, *op cit*, Appendix 6, p. 874.
291 A 1915 Dunlop's advertisement boasted that their 5¾-acre site made it the largest mill in the southern hemisphere. Susan Priestley, *op cit*, p. 261 and a Dunlop Rubber Company advertisement in the *Bulletin*, 11 February, 1915 in the collection of the Noel Butlin Archives Centre, ANU Archives Program.
292 Dale Blair, *op cit*, p. 272 and Geoffrey Blainey, *op cit*, pp. 93 – 98.
293 Dale Blair, *Ibid*, p. 271.
294 Australia's monthly enlistments reached 10,000 only once after May 1916, and were often fewer than half this number. Ernest Scott, *op cit*, Appendix 3, pp. 871-2.
295 See Bart Ziino, 'Enlistment and Non-enlistment in Wartime Australia: Responses to the 1916 Call to Arms Appeal', *Australian Historical Studies*, 41, 2010, pp. 217-32 for a detailed examination of the Australian Government's Call to Arms Appeal and the responses to it.
296 Private Albert 'George' Cazaly, service record no. 5359, enlisted in the AIF's 7th Battalion on 12 February, 1916. National Archives of Australia war records and Arthur Dean and Eric W Gutteridge, *The Seventh Battalion, AIF: Resume of the activities of the Seventh Battalion in the Great War, 1914-1918*, p. 146.
297 *The Argus*, 8 May, 1915.
298 A famous recruiting poster featured Lieutenant Albert Jacka urging athletes to "Enlist in the Sportsmen's Thousand". Born three days before Cazaly in 1893, Jacka was awarded Australia's first Victoria Cross of World War I. State Library of Victoria image collection, H2001.34/1.
299 *Sport*, 9 July, 1915.
300 *The Argus*, 22 April, 1915.
301 Marc Fiddian, *The VFA: A History of the Victorian Football Association 1877-1995*, p. 28.
302 By 25 June 1917, the *Sport*'s roll call included the names of 1514 footballers who had volunteered. The *Winner*, which profiled enlisted athletes from all sporting codes, itself became a casualty of the war, suspending publication in June 1918 due to the cost and shortage of newsprint.
303 Quoted in Leonie Sandercock and Ian Turner, *Up Where Cazaly?*, p. 72 and *The Argus*, 21 December, 1918.
304 *Punch*, 3 June and *Sport*, 11 June, 1915.
305 *The Argus*, 12 June, 1915.

CHAPTER ENDNOTES

306 *The Australasian*, 21 August and *The Argus*, 16 August, 1915. The lasting animosity between the League and Association stemming from this match meant it was another nine years before teams from the two competitions played each other again.
307 *The Argus*, 23 December and *South Melbourne Record*, 18 December, 1915.

Chapter 8. RECESS AND RESUMPTION: ST KILDA, 1916-18

308 'Up there, Cazaly', *People*, 11 March, 1953.
309 'The Labour of Sport: Football preparation, training and coaching', *The Argus*, 19 June, 1909.
310 *Sport*, 23 June, 1911.
311 *Ibid*, 27 June, 1913.
312 'Up there, Cazaly', *People*, 11 March, 1953.
313 Best also taught Swedish gymnastics and was secretary of the German Gymnasts' Association. The *Prahran Telegraph*, 20 April and 7 December, 1895, Phillip Bentley with David Dunstan, *The Path to Professionalism: Physiotherapy in Australia to the 1980s*, p. 26, the Museum Victoria website entry at *http://museumvictoria.com.au/collections/themes/1998/german-club-melbourne-victoria* and the German-Australian Aliens of Militarism website at *http://germanaustralianalienstomilitarism.blogspot.com.au/2011/09/b-surnames-germanic-emigrants-1870-1920.html#comment-form*.
314 *The Argus*, 24 July, 1914. In 1935 Best was included in a topical St Kilda team song of the day. In 1938 he became the Melbourne club's masseur and was still there five years later, aged 80. Laurie Melrose and John Robertson, *Give 'em a cheer Saints*, Allan and Co, Melbourne 1935 and *The Herald*, 29 October, 1943.
315 *St Kilda Football Club Minutes*, 18 November, 1915.
316 Mineral water treatments were offered at the Bath House, which had opened at Hepburn Springs in 1895, and the Pavilion, which opened in 1908. By the mid-1920s, the Bath House was offering hydrotherapy, massage, electric baths and a variety of mineral water treatments. Edward and Maura Wishart et al, *Spa Country: Victoria's mineral springs*, p. 149 and p. 155.
317 *St Kilda Football Club Minutes*, 13 January, 1916.
318 Despite being in recess St Kilda still sold season tickets, which provided voting rights at the club's annual meeting, and donated the proceeds to patriotic funds. Stephen Rodgers, *Tooheys Guide to Every Game Ever Played: VFL Results 1897-1982*, p. 117.
319 The VJFA's rules at this time allowed only one senior player to play for each club, and this player was also usually the coach. Camberwell named Hawthorn (VFA) vice-captain Joe Antonie as their captain and coach at the beginning of the 1916 season but his name disappeared from their list mid-season and Cazaly may have taken his place. Cazaly's transfer to Camberwell was granted in early May. The *Winner*, 3 and 17 May and 9 August, *The Age*, 11 May, *Sporting Judge*, 20 May, the *South Melbourne Record*, 5 August and *The Argus*, 14 August, 1916; *The Sporting Globe Football Book*, 1930, p. 65; and information kindly provided by Hawthorn historian Peter Haby.
320 Ross McMullin, 'The 1915 Grand Final: love, war and football', *AFL 2013 Grand Final Record*, pp 147-151 and Jim Main and David Allen, *Fallen - the Ultimate Heroes: Footballers Who Never Returned from War*, pp. 34-36.
321 The Infectious Diseases Hospital had opened at Yarra Bend, Fairfield in 1904 and was funded by subscriptions from neighbouring local councils. Bessie Cazaly was one of 148 patients who died at the Hospital during 1916. *Victorian Year Book 1916-17*, pp. 343, 352, 356 and 362-64, death registration no. 9589 dated 17 August 1916 and Bessie's funeral notice in *The Age*, 18 August, 1916.
322 *The Argus*, 9 November, 1916.
323 The *South Melbourne Record*, 14 July, 1917.
324 *The Argus*, 3 March, 1917.
325 National Archives of Australia military records for Walter Thomas Laidlaw and the *Winner*, 6 June, 1917.
326 The *South Melbourne Record*, 11 August, 1917. Wally Laidlaw survived the war and played one further game for South Melbourne after he returned home in 1919.
327 Former club president Joe Hannan, quoted in Robert Grogan, *Blood, Sweat and Cheers: South Melbourne District Sports Club from footy beginnings to sporting diversity*, p. 1.
328 The *South Melbourne Record*, 31 March, 1917.

329 Several other St Kilda players coached local junior sides while their team was in recess, including winger Edward Collins (Havelock) and forward Les Boyd (Australian Jam Company). Robert Grogan, *op cit*, pp 1-4, *South Melbourne Record*, 19 May and the *Prahran Telegraph*, 26 May, 1917.
330 The *South Melbourne Record*, 14 April and 9 June, 1917.
331 Of the Dunlop strikers, 1000 were men and 250 were women. Robert Bollard PhD thesis, *'The Active Chorus': The Mass Strike of 1917 in Eastern Australia*, School of Social Sciences, Faculty of Arts, Education and Human Development, Victoria University, 2007, p 77, available online at *http://vuir.vu.edu.au/1472/1/bollard.pdf*.
332 *The Argus*, 19 September, 1917.
333 The *Prahran Telegraph*, 20 October, 1917.
334 *The Age*, 17 October 1917, the *South Melbourne Record* and *Prahran Telegraph*, 20 October 1917, *Richmond Guardian*, 12 January, 1918 and Peter Burke, *By the Lake: A History of the Middle Park Cricket Club*, p. 15.
335 The *Malvern Standard*, 9 November, 1918 and *The Argus*, 21 December, 1918.
336 The *Prahran Telegraph*, 4 May, 1918.
337 *The Argus*, 13 May, 1918, *Sporting Judge*, 18 May, 1918 and *Football Record* Round 2, 1918.
338 *The Argus*, 21 December, 1918.
339 *The Age*, 19 August, 1918.
340 National Archives of Australia military records and Arthur Dean and Eric W Gutteridge, *The Seventh Battalion, AIF: Resume of the activities of the 7th Battalion in the Great War, 1914-1918*, p. 146.
341 Australian War Memorial records and War Casualty List no. 434, as published in *The Age* on 15 October, 1918.
342 Australian enlistment and casualty figures provided by the Australian War Memorial at *http://www.awm.gov.au/atwar/ww1/*. South Melbourne's enlistment and casualty figures are taken from Susan Priestley, *South Melbourne: A History*, p. 284, *The Argus*, 25 May, 1921 and the *Albert Park State School Great War Honour Book*.
343 The *South Melbourne Record*, 21 September, 1918.
344 The A M Taylor Memorial Shield to acknowledge St Kilda's best player was instituted by club supporters in 1914. The *Prahran Telegraph* and *The Argus*, 21 December, 1918.
345 Roy had been born on a Friday the 13th; his father died on another. James Cazaly's funeral notice in *The Age*, 14 December, 1918, his bereavement notice in *The Age*, 10 January, 1919 and *The Sporting Globe*, 29 May, 1935.
346 James' death registration no. 3148, 21 December, 1918.

Chapter 9. PEACE AND INSTABILITY: ST KILDA, 1919-20

347 *South Melbourne Rates Books* and information kindly provided by historian Brian Membrey.
348 Cazaly's occupations for this period are taken from the Victorian state electoral rolls for 1919, 1924 and 1925.
349 *Referee*, 19 February and 9 April, *The Age*, 14 April and the *Port Melbourne Standard*, 22 February, 15 March, 13 September and 11 October, 1919.
350 *The Argus*, 23 June 1919. Profiles of Claude Crowl and Hugh Plowman are included in Jim Main and David Allen's *Fallen - the Ultimate Heroes: Footballers Who Never Returned from War*.
351 Susan Priestley, *South Melbourne: A History*, p. 310.
352 The Spanish Influenza pandemic caused up to 40 million deaths worldwide in the years immediately after World War I. Around 11,500 Australians died. See Graham Whitehead, 'Spanish influenza strikes Melbourne suburbs' available online at *http://localhistory.kingston.vic.gov.au/htm/article/214.htm* and *A framework for an Australian Influenza Pandemic Plan*, Technical Report Series No. 4, the Influenza Pandemic Planning Committee of the Communicable Diseases Network Australia New Zealand, Version 1, June 1999, pp. 6-9, available online at *https://www.health.gov.au/internet/main/publishing.nsf/Content/cda-cditech-influenza.htm/$FILE/influenza.pdf*.
353 The cross-bar idea was revived during the lead-up to the 1923 Australian Football Council meeting, when NSW delegates proposed a bar be added across the goalposts 10 feet above the ground. Goals would only count if the ball went over the bar; one point would be given if it went under. Several VFL club delegates supported the idea, including South Melbourne's former VFA premiership captain Henry 'Sonny' Elms, who believed it would reduce congestion in front of goal and encourage longer kicking.

CHAPTER ENDNOTES

Cazaly's old school friend Frank Beaurepaire, now living in Sydney, also thought the cross bar idea had merit and that goals should only count for three points instead of six. Beaurepaire took a pragmatic approach, believing Australian Football should adopt the best features of other codes in order to improve and strengthen the national game. Despite such high profile support, a majority of Council delegates rejected the cross-bar proposal. 'Rover', 'Career of St Kilda's Champion', *The Weekly Times*, 26 July, 1919, Rob Hess et al, *A National Game: The History of Australian Rules Football*, p. 72, Geoffrey Blainey, *A Game of Our Own*, pp. 167-68 and *The Sporting Globe*, 20 and 27 September, 1923.

354   Roy Cazaly, 'My toughest league game', *Sporting Globe*, 8 May, 1937.
355   Only six other players had a longer interruption to their careers in the first hundred years of VFL / AFL football. Stephen Rodgers, *100 Years of AFL Players* Volume 3, 'Appendix 9 – Long Breaks in League Careers', pp. 1610-11.
356   It remains the only time a team has kicked more than 100 points in any quarter of VFL or AFL football. *AFL 2014 Season Guide*, p. 313 and p. 1015.
357   *Football Record*, Round 18, 1919, p. 21.
358   Curiously, and perhaps because of the local league's residency requirements, Roy and Aggie are listed as living at a Warrnambool address on the 1919 Federal electoral roll. Ron Cole et al, *Birth of the Blues: Warrnambool Football Netball Club* 1861-2007, p. 50, 1919 Federal roll for Corangamite, *The Sporting Globe*, 7 May and 5 July, 1924 and Roy Cazaly, 'Some strange bush happenings', *The Sporting Globe*, 12 June, 1935.
359   Roy Cazaly, 'A famous game that drew a crowd of 49,000', *The Sporting Globe*, 22 May, 1937 and *The Sporting Globe*, 5 July, 1924.
360   *The Argus*, 10 March, 1920.
361   *Ibid*, 8 and 14 June, 1920.
362   *Football Record*, Round 7, 1920.
363   Vic Cumberland played 10 matches for St Kilda during 1920, more than two decades after his first VFL season with Melbourne in 1898. He retired at the end of the season aged 43, the oldest to have ever played VFL football. Stephen Rodgers, *op cit*, 'Appendix 8 Part 1 – Longest Year-Spans in League Football', pp. 1606-07.
364   *The Argus*, 8 June, 1920.
365   *The Australasian*, 19 June, 1920.
366   Roy Cazaly, 'Football ring-in with £500 at stake', *Sporting Globe*, 1 May, 1937, Arthur Fehring, 'Original "Ring-In" tells of famous match', *Sporting Globe*, 15 May, 1937 and Graeme Atkinson, *Everything you ever wanted to know about Australian Rules Football*, pp. 4-5.
367   Stephen Rodgers, *op cit*, 'Appendix 3 – Composition of Clubs' Player Lists, Year-By-Year', p. 1567.
368   The *Gippsland Times*, 13 September, 1920.
369   'Leander', 'The luck of a change: R Cazaly improves South', *The Herald*, 9 July, 1921.

Chapter 10. 'UP THERE CAZALY!': SOUTH MELBOURNE AND VICTORIA, 1921

370   Roy Cazaly, 'My toughest league game', *Sporting Globe*, 8 May, 1937.
371   J M Rohan, 'Whenever he crouched for a spring the crowd yelled Up There Cazaly!', *Sporting Globe*, 11 May, 1935.
372   The *Prahran Telegraph*, 21 December, 1918. See Ross Booth, 'History of Player Recruitment, Transfer and Payment Rules in the Victorian and Australian Football League', *Australian Society of Sports History Bulletin* No. 26, June 1997, pp. 13-33 for a discussion of the VFL's zonal scheme.
373   *South Melbourne Football Club Minutes*, 17 March 1921, p. 75. Reg Seedsman was probably asked to handle discussions with Cazaly because he knew him.
374   *Ibid*, 17 March, 1921, p. 73.
375   Two weeks later, Vice President Frank Killingsworth, who had seconded Caldwell's nomination for coach, claimed 16 votes had been cast in the ballot despite only 14 members being at the meeting. A new vote was held and Wood was again declared elected. Caldwell later resigned from the match committee and became coach of Williamstown in the VFA. *South Melbourne Football Club Minutes*, 31 March, p. 78 and 14 April, 1921, p. 87 and *Football Record*, Round 1, 1921.

376 *VFL Players' Registration Book* and *South Melbourne Football Club Minutes*, 5 May, 1921, p. 102. Carl Willis had played 46 games for University before the war and played the 1915 season for South Melbourne before enlisting in the AIF. He resumed playing for South in 1920. Marc Fiddian, *Days by the Lake*, p. 48.
377 *Daily Herald*, 20 May, 1921. The Commonwealth Serum Laboratories had developed an influenza vaccine during the 1919 epidemic.
378 *The Age*, 27 June, 1921.
379 *South Melbourne Football Club Minutes*, 14 July, 1921, p. 147.
380 *The Age*, 11 July, *The Herald*, 29 July, *The Argus*, 22 August and *The Australasian*, 3 September, 1921.
381 Thomas Power (compiler), *The Footballer: An annual record of football in Victoria*, 1875, pp. 26-33.
382 Trevor Ruddell, 'The evolution of the rules of football from 1872 to 1877' in *The Yorker*, Issue 41, Autumn 2010, p. 20.
383 Peter Burns writing in 1940, as quoted in *The Sporting Globe Football Book* 1948, p. 35.
384 Thomas Power (compiler), *The Footballer: An annual record of football in Victoria*, 1876, p. 12.
385 Geoffrey Blainey, *A Game of our Own: The Origins of Australian Football*, pp. 116-17.
386 'Commotion' Pearson's nickname came not from his style of play, but from the fact his uncle William owned a famous racehorse of the same name. The horse was, appropriately, the son of 'Panic' and grandson of 'Alarm'. *The Australasian*, 14 March 1925 and *The Argus*, 14 October, 1885.
387 'Laws of The Australasian Game of Football', adopted by a conference of intercolonial delegates in Melbourne on 5 November, 1890, as printed in *Boyle and Scott's Footballers' Pamphlet for 1891*, p. 26. Revised rules adopted in 1906 went even further in protecting the player during and after the act of marking. See the '1906 Australasian Rules of Football', as reprinted in Geoffrey Blainey, *A Game of our Own: The Origins of Australian Football*, pp. 237-38.
388 C C Mullen, *History of Australian Rules Football 1858 to 1958*, p. 146.
389 Richard Stremski, *Kill for Collingwood*, p. 68. Dick Lee played 17 consecutive seasons for Collingwood from 1906 to 1922, led the VFL goalkicking list eight times and scored more than 700 goals for an average of more than three goals per game.
390 Hec de Lacy, 'Dick! Dick! – Dick-e-e-e!', *The Sporting Globe*, 21 June, 1941. After watching a semi-final match in 1919, one journalist wrote: "In the language of the moving pictures, Saturday's game might have been advertised as Collingwood v. Carlton – featuring 'Dick' Lee. Lee was the magnetic personality that held the crowd's interest from first to last." *The Argus*, 29 September, 1919.
391 Examples of crowd chants quoted in Michael Conaty's Honours thesis *"Up there, Cazaly" – the legend of Roy Cazaly*, Department of History at the University of Sydney, 1996. Available online at *http://hdl.handle.net/2123/2318*.
392 Roy Cazaly jnr quoted in Sam Simpson, 'Cazaly, the myth, the magic' in *The Saturday Evening Mercury*, 29 September, 1979.
393 'Up there, Cazaly', *People*, 11 March, 1953 and Cazaly's interview with Bill Barwick, broadcast on radio station 7HT on 19 April, 1962.
394 *Football Record*, Round 13, 1921.
395 Roy Cazaly with H A de Lacy, 'Right road for juniors', *The Sporting Globe*, 3 July, 1937.
396 'Up there, Cazaly', *People*, 11 March, 1953.
397 'Leander', 'The luck of a change: R Cazaly improves South', *The Herald*, 9 July, 1921.
398 Percy Bentley, 'Ruck drives team' in Hec de Lacy (compiler), *The 1946 Sporting Globe Football Book*, pp. 41-42.
399 The South Melbourne Open Sea Bathing Club was formed in 1914 to promote lifesaving classes and soon had more than 300 members. When Fred Fleiter saved a Mr Meeks from drowning at South Melbourne beach in January 1918 the Bathing Club presented him with a gold medal and Mr Meeks' parents gave him a "handsome wallet" in appreciation. Fleiter's birth certificate, no. 9695/97, *South Melbourne Record*, 21 February, 1914, 15 December, 1917 and 9 February, 1918 and *The Argus*, 7 February, 1923.
400 'Leander', 'South's vigorous follower', *The Sporting Globe*, 22 July, 1922.
401 Roy Cazaly, 'My toughest league game', *The Sporting Globe*, 8 May, 1937.
402 'Mark Tandy has great record', *The Sporting Globe*, 23 June, 1923 and the *South Melbourne Record*, 19 October, 1918.
403 Roy Cazaly, 'My toughest league game', *The Sporting Globe*, 8 May, 1937.
404 *Ibid*.
405 *Football Record*, Round 16, 1921.

406 *The Australasian*, 30 July, 1921.
407 Cigarette cards originated during the late 19th century when tobacco manufacturers placed a piece of cardboard in packets to prevent them being crushed in the pockets of smokers. These 'stiffeners' evolved into picture cards featuring popular themes such as athletes, military leaders and music hall singers. From around 1900 Australian manufacturers began using images of local footballers, cricketers and race horses to differentiate their product from the overseas makers. The best known Melbourne manufacturers were Gershon Sniders and Louis Abrahams, who issued several series of local footballers between 1904 and 1914 under the 'Standard' and 'Peter Pan' brands. The other major local manufacturer was Johan Schuh, who emigrated from Germany in the mid-1870s and became a cigar importer and tobacconist in Bourke Street. The J J Schuh Tobacco Company issued several series of cards featuring footballers between 1920 and 1925 under the 'Magpie' brand. *Argus*, 12 April, 1875, *Advertiser*, 16 January, 1920, *Evening News*, 13 October, 1922, *Adelaide News*, 24 February, 1926, Dion Skinner, *Cigarette Cards: Australian Issues and Values*, 1983 and information kindly provided by Australian Cartophilic Society President Eric Panther.
408 In 1909, the *Sport* newspaper had noted that "the followers of the Yarra may be easily recognised by their cry, 'Up there!'" Football correspondent 'Rover' in *Sport*, 10 September, 1909.
409 'Up there, Cazaly', *People*, 11 March, 1953.
410 In 1996, Michael Conaty tried to pinpoint the first crowd usage of 'Up there Cazaly' to a specific match. He scoured numerous match reports from 1921 and 1922 but found no documented reference to the crowd's first use of the expression. Neither could the author.
411 *The Argus*, 11 July, 1921.
412 *South Melbourne Football Club Minutes*, 3 September, 1921, p. 169.
413 Fred Ion, from East Fremantle, went on to finish second in the Sandover Medal for the West Australian Football League's Fairest and Best player for 1922. John Devaney, *Full Points Footy's WA Football Companion*, p. 160, *Football Record*, Round 18, 1923 and additional information kindly provided by football historian Greg Wardell-Johnson.
414 Cazaly himself later wrote that "South at one stage thought of dumping Fleiter" early in his career. Roy Cazaly, 'My toughest league game', *The Sporting Globe*, 8 May, 1937.
415 *South Melbourne Football Club Minutes*, Annual Meeting, 27 February, 1922, p. 270. The club does not recognise their first Best and Fairest as having been awarded until 1926 but Cazaly's 1921 Best All-Round award suggests a revision is necessary.
416 J M Rohan, 'Whenever he crouched for a spring the crowd yelled Up There Cazaly!', *The Sporting Globe*, 11 May, 1935.
417 Ron Cole et al, *Birth of the Blues: Warrnambool Football Netball Club 1861–2007*, p. 51, *The Sporting Globe*, 17 May and 5 July, 1924 and a photo of South Warrnambool's 1921 premiership team kindly provided by Fred Hughson.
418 Cazaly received 3753 votes. Newspapers and sporting periodicals had been conducting readers' polls to determine the season's best footballers for some years. As early as 1910, the *Victorian Footballer Follower* had run a competition sponsored by whiskey maker Johnnie Walker to find the season's best League and Association players.

Chapter 11. AN UNHAPPY COACHING STINT: SOUTH MELBOURNE, 1922

419 *South Melbourne Cricket Club Annual Report and Balance Sheet* for season 1921-22.
420 The selection panel chose 'Likely' McBrien to replace the retiring Herb Howson, a former champion winger and premiership coach who had been secretary for 17 years. *South Melbourne Football Club Minutes*, 14 February, p. 180, 20 February, p. 184 and 6 March, 1922, p. 187.
421 *Ibid*, 14 March, pp. 190-91 and 23 March, 1922, p. 194.
422 *Ibid*, 23 March, p. 195, Special General Meeting, 27 February, p. 196 and Special General Meeting, 30 March 1922, p. 200.
423 *Ibid*, Players' Meeting, 4 May, p. 212 and Match Committee, 4 May, 1922, p. 215.
424 VFL attendance figures quoted in Nick Richardson, 'Melbourne's Sporting Globe and Football in the 1920s', *Sporting Traditions* vol. 29, no. 1, May 2012. On 25 April, 1924 *The Age* reported that League

attendances for the previous season had totalled nearly 2 million; this figure presumably included finals crowds.

425 *Football Record*, Round 13, 1923.
426 Stephen Rodgers, *Tooheys Guide to Every Game Ever Played: VFL Results 1897-1982*, p. 158.
427 See Nick Richardson, *op cit*, for a discussion of the correlation between increased football reporting and growing football attendances.
428 *The Sporting Globe*, 22 July, 1922.
429 Player information gathered from team lists, private research and Russell Holmesby and Jim Main's *Encyclopedia of AFL Footballers*.
430 Susan Priestley, *South Melbourne: A History*, p. 291 and http://www.parliament.vic.gov.au/re-member/bioregfull.cfm?mid=1004.
431 'Likely' McBrien (he was named after a distant English ancestor, Sir John Likely) served as VFL secretary for 27 years, was an independent member of the Legislative Council for six years and was awarded an Order of the British Empire for his services to sport. Journalist Percy Taylor described him as "a big man in every respect: a big frame, a deep booming voice, a big heart and big ideas for the advancement of sport". *South Melbourne Record*, 17 June, 1917, *Table Talk*, 1 May, 1930, *The Argus*, 12 January and 28 April, 1950 and 24 December, 1956 and http://www.parliament.vic.gov.au/re-member/bioregfull.cfm?mid=1255.
432 Born in 1858, 'Twister' Marshall gained his nickname not because of his profession but because he was a prominent spin bowler in his youth. *The Australasian*, 20 July, 1935.
433 Austin 'Ocker' Robertson first heard the story of Murphy's dog while having his ankle strapped before his first League game in 1927. He thought no more about it until later that season, when South Melbourne kicked a goal late in a game to lead Richmond by a point. As they ran back to the centre, Joe Scanlan said to him: "For Christ's sake Ocker, hang on like Murphy's dog!" Marshall died in 1935 aged 77, having been a trainer at South Melbourne for 50 years, and head trainer for 25. Austin Robertson, *Ocker: The Fastest Man Alive!*, p. 30 and the *Referee*, 25 July, 1935.
434 '47 Years with South: Great record of Jack "Twister" Marshall', *The Sporting Globe*, 29 June, 1932.
435 'Brains and Football: Roy Cazaly's career and lessons learned', *Mercury*, 19 October, 1935.
436 Billy Meeske was a sergeant with the AIF in Belgium during World War I, wrestled throughout the 1920s and '30s and was an army physical instructor during World War II.
437 *Australian Medical Journal*, January 15, 1891, p. 52, *The Argus*, 23 January, 1935 and 15 April, 1939 and further biographical information kindly provided by Dr Joseph Milton D'Amer Drew's descendants Ian and Don Hewson.
438 Russell Holmesby and Jim Main, *Encyclopedia of AFL Footballers*, p. 860.
439 Susan Priestley, *op cit*, p. 268 and Killingworth's obituary in *The Argus*, 14 November, 1944.
440 Susan Priestley, *op cit*, pp. 294-95.
441 These examples are all taken from the original *South Melbourne Football Club Minutes Book* for the period 1920–24, which was rediscovered during the research for this book.
442 Bernard Smith, *Noel Counihan: Artist and Revolutionary*, pp. 18-19.
443 *The Age*, 15 May and *Football Record*, Round 3, 1922.
444 *Football Record*, Round 4, 1922.
445 *Ibid*, Round 6, 1922.
446 *Referee*, 17 May, 1922.
447 *Football Record*, Round 5, 1922.
448 *The Age*, 19 June and *Football Record*, Round 8, 1922.
449 *Football Record*, Round 11, 1922.
450 The *South Melbourne Record*, 8 July, 1922.
451 *Ibid*, 22 July, 1922.
452 The club minutes and local papers all recorded Cazaly's resignation, contradicting some later accounts that he had been sacked. The *Football Record* reported that "Roy relinquished the offices of captain and coach voluntarily [and] on the motion of Harry Brereton, the players passed a vote of thanks to him for his services in those positions." *South Melbourne Football Club Minutes*, 27 July, p. 247, the *South Melbourne Record*, 29 July, *The Age*, 31 July and *Football Record*, Round 13, 1922.
453 *South Melbourne Football Club Minutes*, General Meeting 27 July, p. 247 and Special Players' Meeting 27 July, 1922, p. 249.
454 *Football Record*, Round 13 and *The Age*, 31 July, 1922.
455 'The art of forward play: by Carlton's own Clover', *The Sporting Globe*, 30 August, 1922. Clover topped

CHAPTER ENDNOTES

the VFL's goalkicking list that season.
456 The Herald and Weekly Times had transferred the competition from *The Herald* to *The Sporting Globe* to help boost the new paper's circulation. Nick Richardson, *op cit.*
457 The public nominated 91 different League players for the Best All-Round award. Mark Tandy was runner up to Melbourne's George Haines in the vote for Best Rover and polled seventh in the Best All-Round Player category. *The Sporting Globe*, 16 and 19 August and 2, 6, 9 and 20 September, 1922.

Chapter 12. TRIALS AND TRIBUNALS: SOUTH MELBOURNE, 1923

458 St Patrick's was a predominantly Catholic club but its officials were obviously prepared to overlook Cazaly's Protestantism in their search for a coach. *Football Record*, Week 2 Finals, 1922, *The Age*, 13 April, 1923, *The Herald*'s 'Football Souvenir', 1923 and *Referee*, 25 April and 2 May, 1923.
459 *The Sporting Globe*, 25 April, 1923.
460 *South Melbourne Football Club Minutes*, Finance Committee, 8 March, 1923, p. 284.
461 Collingwood's intransigence meant Pannam had to stand out of the game for three years. He coached South Melbourne from 1923 until 1926, and was then captain-coach until 1928. Russell Holmesby and Jim Main, *The Encyclopedia of AFL Footballers: Every AFL/VFL Player since 1897*, 7th Ed., p. 614.
462 Gus de Brito, 'Why they loved Cazaly' in *Everybody's*, June 24, 1964.
463 Roy Cazaly, 'Football ring-in with £500 at stake', *The Sporting Globe*, 1 May, 1937.
464 Table showing 'Movements in Average Home and Away Attendances for VFL: Selected Years 1923–1984' in R K Stewart, 'The Economic Development of the Victorian Football League 1960–84' *Sporting Traditions*, Vol. 1 no. 2, May 1985, p. 11, quoted in Michael Conaty's Honours Thesis *"Up there, Cazaly" – the legend of Roy Cazaly*, University of Sydney Department of History, 1996. Available online at *http://hdl.handle.net/2123/2318.*
465 *Football Record*, Round 5, 1923.
466 *The Age*, 25 April, 1924.
467 *Ibid*, 30 April, 1923.
468 Ted Johnson went on to kick 385 goals during a 136-game career with South Melbourne. Russell Holmesby and Jim Main, *op cit,* p. 400.
469 The *South Melbourne Record*, 21 April and 14 July and *The Age*, 30 April, 14 May and 9 July, 1923.
470 *The Age*, 6 August, 1923.
471 *The Sporting Globe*, 18 August, 1923.
472 *The Age*, 13 August and *The Sporting Globe*, 15 August, 1923.
473 Roy Cazaly, 'How a cut eye cost Richmond a game', *The Sporting Globe*, 15 May, 1937 and *The Age* and *The Argus*, 10 September, 1923.
474 *The Sporting Globe*, 12 September, 1923.
475 *The Age*, 10 September, 1923. During this period umpires recorded their reports after the game, not at the time of the alleged incident.
476 *The Argus* and *The Age*, 14 September and the *South Melbourne Record*, 15 September, 1923. Of the 17 players reported during the 1923 season only four, including Cazaly, were acquitted. South Melbourne's committee were so pleased with the outcome they sent a letter of thanks to Mr Les Naylor, who had defended Cazaly at the hearing. Jim Main, *Football's Black Book*, pp. 162-63 and *South Melbourne Football Club Minutes*, 20 September 1923, p. 332.
477 Simon Huggard, *Frank Huggard: The Untamed Tiger*, pp. 44-47.
478 Roy Cazaly, 'How we stopped the WA rough-house', *The Sporting Globe*, 28 April and 'How a cut eye cost Richmond a game', *The Sporting Globe*, 15 May, 1937.
479 Joe Scanlan, quoted in Gus de Brito, 'Why they loved Cazaly' in *Everybody's*, June 24 1964.
480 Roy Cazaly, 'How a cut eye cost Richmond a game', *The Sporting Globe*, 15 May, 1937.
481 *The Age*, 17 September, 1923.
482 *Ibid*, and *Football Record*, Round 22, 1923.
483 South Melbourne's roll-call of injuries from the game included Cazaly (cheek bone and ribs), Boyd Hando (both knees), Syd James (dislocated ankle), Ted Johnson (crushed shin), Frank Laird (twisted elbow), and Artie Wood (head injury and cut elbow). *The Age*, 8 October, *The Sporting Globe*, 10 October and *Football Record*, Round 25, 1923.
484 Cazaly received 3305 votes. He also polled third in the Best Follower category, behind Fitzroy's Les

Bryant and Carlton's Maurie Beasy. *The Sporting Globe*, 17 October, 1923.

Chapter 13. CARNIVAL CAPERS: SOUTH MELBOURNE AND VICTORIA, 1924

485   *South Melbourne Rates Books* and information kindly provided by Brian Membrey.

486   The loan repayments were deducted from Cazaly's weekly match fees. *South Melbourne Football Club Minutes*, Finance Committee 10 April, p. 361 and 29 May, 1924, p. 369.

487   'Up there, Cazaly' in *People*, 11 March, 1953.

488   By comparison, members of the Melbourne Wharf Labourers Union who worked the smaller vessels on the Yarra wharves were known as the 'top enders' or 'river rats'. Because the Port Phillip Stevedores only worked on foreign vessels they did not have to deal with Australian ship owners and were more autonomous than other wharf unions, a fact which led to occasional tensions with their parent body, the Waterside Workers' Federation, whenever industrial action was contemplated. The Stevedores owned their own building in Bay Street, Port Melbourne, which they extended in 1924 to include a billiard room, reading room and bar. Wendy Lowenstein and Tom Hills, *Under the Hook. Melbourne waterside workers remember working lives and class war: 1900-1980*, p. 7, the *South Melbourne Record*, 13 September and *The Argus*, 1 December, 1924.

489   Wendy Lowenstein and Tom Hills, *op cit*, pp. 35-36; 'Tippo' Hayes interviewed by Wendy Lowenstein for the Melbourne Waterside Workers collection, available online at *http://nla.gov.au/nla.oh-vn6295026*; and a table of average weekly wages by trade, *Victorian Year Book 1924-25*, p. 377.

490   William Bridgeman interviewed by Alistair Thomson, *Australian Veterans of the Great War Oral History Project*, Australian War Memorial, 1 May, 1983. Available online at *https://www.awm.gov.au/collection/S01307/*.

491   *South Melbourne Football Club Minutes*, 24 April, 1924, pp. 365-66 and Jim Main, *In the Blood: Celebrating the Red and White 1874–2009*, p. 86.

492   *The Sporting Globe*, 22 and 29 March and 9 April, 1924.

493   *South Melbourne Football Club Minutes*, 12 June, 1924, p. 376.

494   *The Sporting Globe*, 31 May, 1924.

495   'Jumbo' Sharland, 'Great Player: R Cazaly, Footballer' in *The Sporting Globe*, 25 June, 1924.

496   *The Australasian*, 10 May, 1924, p. 34.

497   *The Sporting Globe*, 25 June, 1924.

498   Arthur Hando, born and raised in the tiny township of Buckrabanyule in north-central Victoria, had already led an eventful life. Enlisting soon after the outbreak of World War I, he served at Gallipoli and was shot in both knees during the Battle of Lone Pine. Following his evacuation he was operated on in Egypt and sent back to Gallipoli where he was blinded in his left eye by a bullet fragment and finally repatriated home. After the war Hando played for Port Melbourne and Brunswick in the VFA before being recruited by South Melbourne as a defender in 1922, playing his first VFL game three days before his 31st birthday. He also played for the Watersiders in the Wednesday Football League. Hando had a long reach and a great leap despite his wartime injuries, and Cazaly said later he was amazed he could play football at all. Hando left South Melbourne at the end of 1924 and captain-coached South Bendigo in the Bendigo Football League and Mimosa in New South Wales. W S Sharland, 'South Melbourne's defender' in *The Sporting Globe*, 31 May, 1924, Roy Cazaly, 'A famous game that drew a crowd of 49,000' in *The Sporting Globe*, 22 May, 1937 and biographical information kindly provided by Hando's son Boyd and Port Melbourne historian Terry Keenan.

499   Several Geelong players told the hearing they had seen Hando shake the goalpost during the second quarter, resulting in the ball hitting the post. A similar event occurred in the third quarter, but did not prevent a goal being scored. Goal umpire Fox was more circumspect in his evidence, stating that in the third quarter he saw the goalpost shaking and then saw Hando with both his hands on the post. In his defence of Hando, South captain Pat Scanlan said he had seen him bump the post, but that he did not shake it. Hando said he had no recollection of the second quarter incident, but that in the third quarter he had been bumped just as the ball had been kicked, and had grabbed hold of the goalpost to steady himself. *The Argus*, 4 July, 1924.

500   In an interesting sequel, Richmond's Jim Spain was reported a week after the Hando incident for

CHAPTER ENDNOTES

shaking a goalpost while South's full-forward Ted Johnson was lining up a place kick. The Hando and Spain charges were both dealt with on the same night. Spain claimed he shook the post as a joke after spectators in the crowd egged him on. As in Hando's case, the investigation committee found the charge proven, but ruled his actions had been foolish rather than a desire to be unsportsmanlike. In a clear message to any future copycats the committee warned that further incidents would be severely dealt with. *The Sporting Globe*, 2 July and *The Argus*, 4 July, 1924 and Jim Main, *Football's Black Book*, p. 163.

501   *The Argus*, 14 July, 1924.
502   Norm Beckton was an aerialist noted for his "rocket-like ascents". He served in the AIF in France during World War I before playing 173 games and kicking 157 goals for Essendon between 1921 and 1930. A tall man for his day at 6 feet 2½ inches, he played in their 1923 and 1924 premiership teams and captained the side in 1929 and 1930. He represented Victoria nine times during his VFL career and went on to captain-coach Sandringham in the VFA. *Football Record*, Round 4, 1922 and biographical information kindly provided by Beckton's daughter Jill Widmer.
503   A report of the match in the same edition made particular mention of Cazaly's "hitting out from the ruck". *The Sporting Globe*, 16 July, 1924 and Roy Cazaly, 'An eye for an eye with WA', *The Sporting Globe*, 26 June, 1937.
504   I am indebted to the detective work of Michael Conaty, who examined the 'mark versus ruck tap' issue as part of his Honours thesis on Cazaly published in 1996.
505   *The Advocate*, 6 August and *Mercury*, 8 August, 1924.
506   *The Advocate* and the *Daily Telegraph*, 11 August and the *Western Argus*, 12 August, 1924.
507   Cazaly learned much later that a practical joker had told McDiarmid before the game that Cazaly was out to "get" him: "That was enough for McDiarmid. He decided to get in first. As soon as the ball was bounced he came at me, and, naturally, I had to look after myself." Roy Cazaly with H A de Lacy, 'An eye for an eye with WA', *The Sporting Globe*, 26 June, 1937 and Alf Brown, 'Why the 1924 game was so hard', *The Herald*, 1 August, 1947.
508   *The Advertiser*, 11 August, 1924.
509   'Brains and Football: Roy Cazaly's career and lessons learned', *The Mercury*, 19 October, 1935.
510   Roy Cazaly, 'How we stopped the WA rough-house', *The Sporting Globe*, 28 April, 1937.
511   *The Advocate*, 13 August, 1924.
512   *The Age*, 15 August, 1924.
513   Victoria's full list of goalscorers against Queensland were Hagger (6), Sharland, Duncan, Cockram, Thorp, O'Connell, Taylor, Brew, Tandy (2 each), Greeves, Fitzmaurice, Cazaly, Elliott, Macintosh, Shelton, Pringle, Pink and Wilson (1 each).
514   *The Age* and *The Mercury*, 15 August, 1924.
515   The VFL presented the Victorian players with specially commissioned gold medals for winning the carnival. *The Sporting Globe*, 27 August, 1924.
516   Ibid, 13 August, the *Westralian Worker*, 29 August and the *Football Record*, Round 16, 1924.
517   In 1924 there was a slight difference to the finals formula used in 1897: if the minor premiers at the end of the regular season did not then finish atop the ladder following the finals they had the right to challenge the winner of the finals in a Grand Final. As it transpired this provision was not needed. Stephen Rodgers, *Tooheys Guide to Every Game Ever Played: VFL Results 1897-1982*, p. 158.
518   South Melbourne's other Brownlow Medal vote getters in 1924 were Jack O'Connell (2) and Arthur Hando (1). A total of 37 players shared in the 72 votes awarded for the inaugural Medal. *The Argus*, 18 September, 1924 and Peter Blair, *History of the Brownlow Medal*, p. 138.
519   *Football Record*, Round 1, 1925.
520   The *Sporting Globe* proprietors presented Cazaly with a silver trophy for his Best All-Round win. *The Sporting Globe*, 15 September and 15 October, 1924 and 28 March, 1925.
521   *South Melbourne Football Club Minutes*, 10 April, 1924, p. 364.
522   Other clubs considered for admission by the League prior to the 1925 season included VFA sides Brighton, Brunswick, Camberwell, Caulfield and Prahran and a new team which would have represented the public service.

Chapter 14. A SPELL IN THE COUNTRY: MINYIP, 1925-26

523   Minyip and District Historical Society, *That's My Block: Minyip's Pioneers*, p. 1.

524 Graeme Turnbull, 'A History of the Wimmera Football League', in the *Wimmera Grand Final Footballer*, September 1992.
525 Incentives were not always strictly monetary: in 1922 Les Arnel, a returned serviceman and useful forward from Donald, was lured to Minyip after the club offered to build him a four-room house. The move paid dividends as Arnel was part of Minyip's premiership team that year. Conversation with Les' son John.
526 Billy Schmidt had returned to Richmond in 1921 following his falling out with St Kilda. The Wimmera League was then a mid-week competition so he played for Warracknabeal on Wednesdays and Richmond on Saturdays. Schmidt led Warracknabeal to premierships in 1921 and 1923. John Brennan (editor), *Warracknabeal Football Club Centenary 1886-1986*, p. 26.
527 *Minyip Guardian*, 27 October and 10 November, 1925.
528 *The Argus*, 14 February, 1925.
529 *Minyip Guardian*, 3 March, 1925.
530 Several other VFL players were signed as Wimmera coaches for the 1925 season, including Hawthorn's former captain Bill Walton (Stawell), Geelong's Bert Rankin (Dimboola), South Melbourne's Percy Wilson (Murtoa), Collingwood's Ted Baker (Horsham) and Richmond's Norm McIntosh (Rupanyup). Warracknabeal retained the services of Richmond's Billy Schmidt. *The Age*, 12 March, 1925, *Minyip Guardian*, 10, 17 and 31 March and 7, 17 and 21 April, 1925 and Graeme Turnbull, *op cit*.
531 *Football Record*, Round 10, 1924.
532 *The Argus* and *The Age*, 2 April and *Minyip Guardian*, 7 April, 1925.
533 'Minyip Primary School Register' held by the Minyip and District Historical Society and Joffre Hewitt, *The life and times of Joffre Hewitt*, p. 4.
534 *Minyip Guardian*, 12 May, 1925.
535 Strawbridge had also played for Preston in the VFA and later coached Longford (Tas) in 1929.
536 Author's conversations with Joffre Hewitt.
537 Zschech later said "I played under him as a kid, and I'll say now if ever I succeeded in the game I owe it to 'Cazzer'. Night after night he took me aside and taught me how to do things and what not to do." *The Sporting Globe*, 17 April, 1943. Zschech played in Minyip's Seniors in 1927 and the following year won the Cameron Cup, the Wimmera League's Best and Fairest award. After Cazaly tipped off several VFL scouts to Zschech's abilities Richmond secured his signature in 1930. He became a star centre man for the Tigers, playing in four Grand Finals between 1931 and 1934, for premierships in 1932 and 1934.
538 *Minyip Guardian*, 12 May, 1925.
539 *Ibid*, 19 May, 1925.
540 *Ibid*, 26 May, 1925.
541 *Ibid*, 2 June, 1925.
542 *Horsham Times*, 2 June, 1925.
543 *Minyip Guardian*, 9 June, 1925.
544 *The Argus*, 20 July and *Minyip Guardian*, 21 July, 1925.
545 *Minyip Guardian*, 16 June, 1925.
546 *Ibid*, 23 June, 1925.
547 *Nhill Free Press*, 29 June, 1925.
548 *Minyip Guardian*, 30 June, 1925.
549 *Ibid*, 7 July, 1925.
550 One of the NWDFA's more notable players was Billy Gambetta, who had played four games for South Melbourne in 1922. Billy's brother Cyril 'Jazz Legs' Gambetta played 129 games with Fitzroy.
551 Cliff Glen's father Hector played during this era, and he recalls hearing stories of teams "playing their guts out" to lead handsomely at three-quarter time.Their connections then bet money on the opposition at which point the winning team "ran dead" in the last term and duly lost the game. Conversation with Cliff Glen.
552 *Donald Times*, July 10, 1925.
553 J M Rohan, 'Whenever he crouched for a spring the crowd yelled Up There Cazaly!', *The Sporting Globe*, 11 May, 1935 and 'Roy Cazaly tells of football ring-in with £500 at stake', *The Sporting Globe*, 1 May, 1937.
554 *Minyip Guardian*, 21 July, 1925.
555 *The Argus* and the *Donald Times*, 7 August, 1925.
556 *Minyip Guardian*, 11 August and 8 September, 1925. 'Codger' Perrett would later join Cazaly in Launceston in 1928 and play one season alongside him with the City club.

557 Several descendants of players spoke candidly about the two 'rival camps' in the Minyip football club in 1925. I have chosen to respect their anonymity.
558 Phil McCumisky played nine games for Carlton from 1917-19, studied Medicine at Melbourne University, was a GP at Minyip for several years, trained as a surgeon in England in the early 1930s, became Carlton's medical officer in 1937 and later served as vice-president and chairman of selectors. W S Sharland, 'Greatest all-round footballer: "Up there, Cazaly!"', *The Sporting Globe* 26 July, 1930, *The Argus*, 19 February, 1937 and 6 August, 1956 and Tony De Bolfo, 'A personal tribute to the Carlton doctor', at *http://www.carltonfc.com.au/news/2015-10-07/a-personal-tribute-to-the-carlton-doctor*.
559 The *South Melbourne Record*, 22 August and 12 September, 1925.
560 *Minyip Guardian*, 6 October, 1925.
561 *Ibid*, 3 November, 1925.
562 *Ibid*, 19 January and 26 January, 1926.
563 *The Argus*, 4 March, *Minyip Guardian* 9 March and *Camperdown Chronicle*, 9 March, 1926.
564 *Minyip Guardian*, 9 March, 1926.
565 'Minyip Primary School Register' held by the Minyip and District Historical Society.
566 *Minyip Guardian, 20 April, 1926.*
567 *Victoria Government Gazette No. 47,* April 14, 1926, p. 1103.
568 *The Argus*, 22 March, 1926, Minyip Guardian, 4 May,1926 and Graeme Turnbull, op cit.

Chapter 15. BACK TO THE LAKE: SOUTH MELBOURNE AND VICTORIA, 1926-27

569 'South Melbourne Football Club Season 1926' players' booklet, AFL Library.
570 The club's 1927 annual report noted of the two doctors: "Ability, combined with personality endeared them both to players and officials, who are deeply grateful for their magnificent services." Tom Sealey was the club's honorary dentist for 45 years and was made a life member in 1950. He was later described as being "as big in generosity, in good-fellowship, in humor, kindness and in selflessness as he was in build." The *South Melbourne Record*, 12 March, 1949, 21 January and 5 August, 1950.
571 Roy Cazaly, 'As game as you're fit', *The Sporting Globe Football Book*, 1948.
572 The *West Australian*, 14 July, 1926.
573 The transcontinental railway line connecting Western Australia with the eastern states was completed in 1917, fulfilling a political commitment made prior to Australia's Federation in 1901. A holidaying Tasmanian locomotive foreman who made the journey from Melbourne to Perth two months before the Victorians remarked that the train's average speed of 25 miles per hour, delays caused by taking on coal and water and the need to change trains because of different rail gauges made the whole trip "very trying". The *Daily News*, 26 May, 1926.
574 *Ibid*, 23 July, 1926.
575 The *Bunbury Herald and Blackwood Express*, 30 July, 1926.
576 *The Sporting Globe*, 4 August, 1926.
577 The *West Australian*, 26 July, 1926.
578 *The Sporting Globe*, 4 August, 1926.
579 Quoted in the *Daily News*, 13 August, 1926.
580 *The Sporting Globe* and the *Referee*, 8 September, 1926.
581 Essendon's percentage at the end of the home and away rounds was 124.3; South Melbourne's was 118.9.
582 Paddy Scanlan, who had turned 30 five days earlier, bowed out after playing exactly 100 games for South Melbourne. He went on to captain-coach Footscray for the next two seasons, returned to coach South Melbourne in 1930 and 1931 and later coached North Melbourne in 1936/37.
583 Jim Main, *Honour the Names*, p. 255.
584 C H Gardner, 'The best eight footballers in the league and why', *The Sporting Globe*, 18 August, 1926.
585 Charlie Pannam also received two Brownlow votes while Syd Hogg, Peter Reville and Les Woodfield received one each. The players' vote for Best All Round footballer was conducted by secret ballots cast after each game. Cazaly won with 68 votes from Hogg (51) and Reville (28). Peter Blair, *History of the Brownlow Medal*, p. 132, the *South Melbourne Football Club 1926 Annual Report*, the *South Melbourne Record*, 9 October 1926 and *The Argus*, 14 February, 1927.

586 'Complimentary Dinner and Smoke Concert Program, 13 October, 1926', in private hands and the *South Melbourne Record*, 9 and 16 October 1926. A contemporary advertisement for the Café Francais in Little Collins Street listed an extensive set menu for six shillings per head, including wine. *The Argus*, 10 July, 1926.
587 *AFL Record Season Guide* 2014, p. 622. South Melbourne also presented Cazaly with an elaborate, hand-illustrated certificate to mark five years of service to the club.
588 The *South Melbourne Record*, 20 and 27 November 1926 and WS Sharland, 'Footballer, Cricketer: Roy Cazaly an all rounder', *The Sporting Globe*, 12 March, 1927.
589 Elizabeth Cazaly's death certificate no. 4636, *The Argus*, 1 February and the *South Melbourne Record*, 5 February, 1927.
590 *South Melbourne Football Club Annual Report and Balance Sheet* for 1927.
591 The *South Melbourne Record*, 19 and 26 February, 1927.
592 *The Sporting Globe*, 30 March and the *Football Record*, Round 1, 1927.
593 The *South Melbourne Record*, 7 May, 1927.
594 *The Age*, 6 and 13 May, 1927.
595 Jim Main, *In the Blood: Celebrating the Red and White 1874-2009*, p. 94.
596 Only four members from Victoria's 1924 carnival side were selected for the 1927 carnival: Bert Chadwick, Alex Duncan, Jack Moriarty and Dick Taylor. Other high-profile players from previous state sides to miss selection included Carlton's Maurie Beasy, Footscray's Paddy O'Brien, Richmond's Vic Thorp, Fitzroy's Len Wigcraft and Geelong's Tom Fitzmaurice and Lloyd Hagger. *The Age*, 30 July, and *The Mercury*, 5 August, 1927.
597 The others were Harry Clarke, Hec McKay, Charlie Nicholls and Charlie Stanbridge.
598 The *Horsham Times*, 16 August, 1927.
599 'Jumbo' Sharland, 'Father Time does not deal too leniently with footballers', *Sporting Globe*, 17 September, 1927. Sharland had played in Geelong's ruck between 1920 and 1925 and would have known Cazaly well.
600 Cazaly was later quoted as saying "I always 'dried out', as a boxer would. I avoided as many liquids as possible from Thursday evening to Saturday evening." *The Sporting Globe Football Book*, 1948, p. 27.
601 Rudy Lehmann believed rowers "generally find that if they exercise a little self-control during the first few days of training their desire to drink will gradually diminish, until at last they are quite content with their limited allowance." He cited as an authority the *British Medical Journal*, which stated that "thirst is the want of fluid in the blood, not want of fluid in the stomach, and that a pint or more may be drunk before a single ounce is absorbed. Any attempt, then, to assuage thirst by rapid drinking must of necessity lead to far more being taken than is wanted." Rudolph Chambers Lehmann, *Rowing*, 1898, pp. 118-19.
602 Christopher Dodd, *Henley Royal Regatta*, pp. 75-76.
603 The *Referee*, 14 September and the *South Melbourne Record*, 17 September, 1927.
604 The unionised nature of the WFL came to the fore in 1925, when delegates from the Watersiders and Railways blocked an application from the Police Football Club to join the competition. Resentment lingered because the State Government had sacked striking police officers in 1923, hired special constables to replace them and later refused to re-employ the strikers. Trades Hall officials argued that anyone who played for the Police team had either not participated in the strike or been hired as "scab" labour to replace those who had. When several teams again objected to the Police being admitted for the 1926 season the WFL was effectively abandoned and replaced with a scaled down mid-week competition. The competition resumed in 1927 with nine teams including the Police, despite continuing opposition to their involvement from Trades Hall. *The Argus*, 22 April, 1925 and 28 March, 1927, *The Sporting Globe*, 24 April, 1926 and *The Age*, 30 April, 1927.
605 The WFL was the brainchild of Ross Pearl, the secretary of the Fire Brigade Football Club, and delegates met at the Metropolitan Brigade Headquarters in Eastern Hill. For more information on the history of the WFL, see Peter Burke's PhD thesis, 'A Social History of Workplace Australian Football 1860-1939', available online at *http://researchbank.rmit.edu.au/eserv/rmit:6624/Burke.pdf* and the Charles Boyles website at *http://www.boylesfootballphotos.net.au/tiki-index.php?page=Wednesday+League*.
606 *The Argus*, 23 August, 1923 and 20 August, 1925.
607 *Ibid*, 13 December, 1926 and information provided by Port Melbourne historian Terry Keenan.
608 Jack Dyer and Brian Hansen, *Captain Blood*, p. 25.
609 *The Argus*, 23 June, 2 August and 1 September and *The Sporting Globe*, 2 July, 1927.
610 *South Melbourne Football Club Finance Committee Minutes* 27 April, 1922, p. 207. Peter Reville did in fact

injure an ankle during one WFL game in June 1927, causing him to miss South Melbourne's next match. The local paper asked whether VFL footballers should be allowed to play mid-week football and risk injury before answering its own question: "We say not. It is unfair to the club and to the supporters." *The Argus*, 16 June, *The Age*, 17 June and the *South Melbourne Record*, 18 June, 1927.

611   Background information and WFL match summaries kindly provided by Peter Burke.

612   The Watersiders' captain Lowry was suspended for six matches and vice-captain Woods for 10. *The Argus*, 22 and 27 September, 1927.

613   *Ibid*, 26 and 29 September and *The Age*, 29 September, 1927.

Chapter 16. ROAST CHICKEN EVERY SUNDAY: CITY, TASMANIA, 1928-30

614   *The Argus*, 19 December, 1927 and 13 February, 1928.

615   *The Sunday Examiner-Express*, 10 May, 1980. Ron Tyson was City's secretary from 1912 until 1932. He may have been pointed in Cazaly's direction by Hugh Cameron, a City committee member who was a life member of the South Melbourne Football Club.

616   Judging by 'to let' advertisements in the Launceston papers around this time, the address in Stone Street was a boarding house with a number of self-contained furnished flats.

617   A former rubbish dump, York Park was redeveloped and used for senior football matches from 1923. Now formally known as UTAS Stadium, it hosts several AFL games each season.

618   Conversation with Ailsa Bain.

619   The *Daily Telegraph*, 13 March and *The Examiner*, 12 and 29 March, 1928.

620   Interview with Des Tyson and subsequent correspondence.

621   *The Examiner*, 22 February, 1928.

622   Bernard 'Mannie' Grenda came from a Scottsdale family of athletes which included several champion cyclists. He played in the NWFU for Burnie in 1925, Latrobe's premiership side in 1926 and then for City in 1927/28. Also known as 'Inky' because he was a newspaper typesetter, Grenda developed lead poisoning from his trade and died in 1943, aged just 40. *The Examiner*, 22 February, 1943, notes from the Jack Donnelly Collection, Queen Victoria Museum and Art Gallery (QVMAG) and information kindly provided by Bernard's son Ron.

623   *The Mercury*, 13 April, 1928.

624   *The Mercury*, 20 June, 1928 and Susan Priestley, *South Melbourne: A History*, p. 245.

625   Senior Melbourne teams began to visit the state from the early 1880s, usually on end-of-year tours. Visiting teams would sometimes use such visits to experiment with new techniques: Dick Condon, for example, is said to have perfected the 'stab kick' pass in Launceston during a Collingwood tour in 1902. *The Examiner* later described the stab kick as "really a drop kick, in which the foot strikes the underside of the ball at the nearest possible point to the ground, and practically at the instant of contact. In fact, the ground, ball and feet meet at the same time. The foot is kept perfectly rigid, and meets the ball with more of a stab than a kick." Michael Roberts and Glen McFarlane, *The Official Collingwood Illustrated Encyclopedia*, pp. 114-5 and *The Examiner*, 5 July, 1910.

626   The southern-based league underwent a number of name changes over the years. It was known as the Tasmanian Football Association from 1879, the Southern Tasmanian Football Association from 1887 to 1905, the Tasmanian Football League from 1906 to 1927 and the Tasmanian Australian National Football League from 1928 to 1985 and the TFL again from 1986 to 2000. Because the league is commonly referred to as the 'TFL' regardless of playing era this title is used throughout this book. Ken Pinchin and Allan Leeson, *A Century of Tasmanian Football, 1879-1979* and John Devaney, *Full Points Footy's Tasmanian Football Companion*, pp. 123-24 and 161.

627   Judith Hollingsworth, 'North-South Relations' in Alison Alexander (editor), *The Companion to Tasmanian History*, pp. 253-54. Tasmania's north-south divide continues today. As Martin Flanagan has noted, "In Tasmania, a clear majority of people do not live in the capital city. This simple fact distinguishes it from every other Australian state and affects all aspects of Tasmanian life." Martin Flanagan, 'Footy Divided, That's Tassie to a T', *The Age*, 30 August, 2003.

628   By 1928, the two sides had played 68 matches, of which the North had won just 16. Ken Pinchin and Allan Leeson, *op cit*, p. 32 and notes from the Jack Donnelly Collection, QVMAG.

629   The reference to Bert Hinkler was topical: the aviator, fresh from completing the first ever solo flight from England to Australia, had visited Tasmania in May.

630 *The Examiner*, 18 June, 1928.
631 *Ibid*, 16 July, 1928.
632 Raymond Ferrall, *90 Years On: A Tasmanian Story*, pp. 43-44.
633 Raymond Ferrall writing in *100 Years of the South Launceston Cricket Club: 1907-2007*, p. 12.
634 Martin Flanagan, *1970 and Other Stories of the Australian Game*, p. 102 and an interview with Arch Flanagan.
635 It was simple advice but it must have resonated because Arch could still recall it more than 75 years later. Interview with Arch Flanagan.
636 *The Mercury* and *The Advocate*, 29 September, 1928.
637 *The Examiner*, 8 October, 1928 and an interview with Des Tyson.
638 Even Launceston mayor Charles Barber wrote to the club expressing his delight at the result. Letter dated 8 October 1928 in the Jack Donnelly Collection, QVMAG.
639 Cazaly was also presented with a gold medal and a wallet of notes at another end-of-season function. *The Examiner*, 19 October, 1928.
640 *Ibid*, 23 October, 1928.
641 *Ibid*, 12 February, 1929.
642 Harold Dilger was born in 1907 and grew up on Tasmania's east coast before his parents sent him to board in Launceston. He left high school at 14 to work in a warehouse and was signed up with North Launceston at 16. He moved to Melbourne in the 1930s, joined Warner Brothers as a dispatch clerk and worked his way up the company ladder to become general manager by the time he retired in 1975. Correspondence with Harold Dilger and information kindly provided by his daughter Nanette Lord.
643 Correspondence with Noel Atkins.
644 Interview with Pat Whitecross.
645 Many City players lived in the worst affected areas and some of their names are recorded in the Council's relief payment records. Footballing families who received flood relief included Best, Connell, Cox, Dalton and Lewis. The payment of £62/1/6 to J B Emms of Bernard Street, Invermay to replace furniture, clothing and bedding and undertake house repairs was typical of many claims. 'Tasmanian Flood Relief Fund – Town Claims' book, held at the QVMAG.
646 It has been estimated that Launceston did not fully recover economically from the flood until 1940. Phil and Matt Stephens, 'The Flood of 1929', Launceston Historical Society, available online at http://launcestonhistory.org.au/history-of-launceston/notable-events-in-launceston/the-flood-of-1929/.
647 The 20 players who left the club at the end of 1928 had 730 games worth of experience between them; the 17 that remained had played just 531 games between them. 'List of City-South Players' held in the Jack Donnelly Collection, QVMAG.
648 John Devaney, *Full Points Footy's Tasmanian Football Companion*, pp. 17-18. 'Codger' Perrett would go on to play 123 games for Port Melbourne in the VFA in the late 1920s and early 1930s.
649 This compared with 37 players used in 1928. 'List of City-South Players' held in the Jack Donnelly Collection, QVMAG.
650 Born in 1903, Stan 'Snowy' Joolen (his father Henry's surname was actually 'Van Joolen') was a wharfie from Port Melbourne who had played alongside Cazaly in the 1927 Waterside Workers' premiership team. After two seasons with City he reunited with Cazaly at Preston in 1931 and then at New Town in 1936, where he also joined the staff of Cazaly's Hobart physiotherapy business. Information kindly provided by QVMAG researcher Ross Smith, Preston historian Brian Membrey and Port Melbourne historian Terry Keenan.
651 Of City's 31 new players in 1929, only six played 10 games or more and only 11 played again in 1930. 'List of City-South Players' held in the Jack Donnelly Collection, QVMAG.
652 Cazaly kicked two goals against Collingwood. *The Examiner*, 14 October, 1929.
653 City's Secretary Ron Tyson played for the 'Buffs' team in the same competition. *The Examiner*, 18 September and 19 and 26 November, 1929 and interview with Des Tyson.
654 The four senior teams in the NTCA at this time were Launceston, South Launceston, Esk and Tamar. The NTCA's secretary was the redoubtable Ron Tyson. Ron Williams (ed), *A Century of Northern Tasmanian Cricket*, pp. 11 and 19.
655 Raymond Ferrall, *90 Years On: A Tasmanian Story*, p. 35.
656 The NTCA did not introduce finals matches until the 1952/53 season.
657 Cazaly played five innings for South Launceston in 1929/30, for an average of 21.5. *The Examiner*, 11 April and 8 September 1930, Raymond Ferrall, 'Played in the dark' in *100 Years of the South Launceston Cricket Club: 1907-2007*, pp. 11-12 and information kindly provided by cricket historian Rick Smith.

658   Of the 33 players used during 1930, 16 played 13 games or more. 'List of City-South Players' held in the Jack Donnelly Collection, QVMAG.

659   Laurie Nash would go on to play 45 games for City (including their 1930 and 1932 premierships) and win the Tasman Shields Trophy as the NTFA's Best and Fairest player in 1931 and 1932. In 1933 he joined South Melbourne and was part of its famed 'foreign legion' premiership side that year. Ned Wallish, *The Great Laurie Nash*, p. 359.

660   Interview with Des Tyson.

661   'Brains and football: Roy Cazaly's career and lessons learned', *Mercury*, 19 October, 1935.

662   Ken Pichin and Allan Leeson, *op cit*, p. 183.

663   *Carnival Football Budget* Vol 11, No. 2, Australian National Football Council, Adelaide, 31 July, 1930.

664   Laurie Nash was named Tasmania's Best and Fairest player of the Carnival. Ken Pinchin and Allan Leeson, *op cit*, p. 182.

665   *Monotone Sporting Record*, 9 August, 1930.

666   *The Examiner*, 1 September, 1930.

667   *Ibid*, 20 October, 1930 and Ken Pinchin, *The Redlegs 1880-1980: A History of the City-South Football Club*, p. 27.

Chapter 17. DEPRESSION FOOTBALL: PRESTON, 1931

668   *The Examiner* had reported on 10 November, 1930 that "Cazaly will take up a coaching appointment on the mainland next season".

669   The *South Melbourne Record*, 11 April, 1931.

670   *South Melbourne Rates Books* and information provided by Brian Membrey.

671   The *South Melbourne Record*, 11 April, 1931 and information kindly provided by Preston Football Club historian Brian Membrey.

672   The *South Melbourne Record*, 18 April, 1931. Avery transferred to Melbourne as planned. A follower and defender, he had played 25 games with South Melbourne and went on to play 39 for Melbourne.

673   H W Forster, *Preston: Lands and People 1838-1967*, pp. 86-90.

674   Marc Fiddian, *The VFA: A history of the Victorian Football Association 1877-1995*, p. 90.

675   Henry Zwar was president of Preston for 26 years and also served a two-year term as VFA president. 'White footballs: boon to late practice' and Zwar Pty Ltd advertisement showing Preston players using the ball during night training, *The Sporting Globe*, 28 June, 1939, H W Forster, *Preston: Lands and People 1838-1967*, p. 95 and Marc Fiddian, *The Bullants: A history of the Preston Football Club*, pp. 100-01 and 107.

676   Three-quarters of those who played for the nearby Reservoir Football Club were unemployed in 1930. H W Forster, *op cit*, p. 101.

677   *Ibid*, p. 99.

678   The club's modest assets included a piano valued at £95 and goalposts valued at £8. *Preston Football Club Annual Report and Balance Sheet 1930*.

679   Payments to the coach, players, trainers and the boot studder had totalled more than £1400 in 1930; this fell to £715/16 during 1931. *Preston Football Club Annual Report and Balance Sheets* for 1930 and 1931.

680   Rob Hess *et al* (eds) *A National Game: The History of Australian Rules Football*, p. 182. Cazaly's reputed £8 a week salary has often been mentioned but not confirmed as it was not a separate line item in the club's *Annual Report and Balance Sheet* for 1931.

681   Brian Membrey and Northern Bullants Football Club, *Where We Come From: 1903 to 2002*, p. 96.

682   *Preston Football Club Annual Report and Balance Sheet 1931*, *The Argus*, 5 April, 1931 and information provided by Brian Membrey.

683   The VFA *Recorder*, 9 May, 1931 and information provided by Brian Membrey.

684   A number of Cazaly's former VFL opponents were playing for Association teams in 1931, including Norm Beckton (Sandringham), Alex Duncan (Coburg), George Rudolph (Oakleigh), Percy Rowe (Northcote) and Tom Fitzmaurice (Yarraville).

685   The VFA *Recorder*, 16 May, 1931.

686   Brian Membrey and Northern Bullants Football Club, *op cit* p. 96, the *Preston Football Club Annual Report and Balance Sheet 1931* and the VFA *Recorder* for 1931, copies kindly provided by John Ficarra.

687   Roy Cazaly, 'Think about the game', *The Sporting Globe*, 5 September, 1931.

688 H A de Lacy, 'Up there Cazzer!', *The Sporting Globe*, 9 August, 1941. Despite de Lacy's later assertion that Cazaly had "sacked half the team" and replaced them with juniors, research by Preston's historian Brian Membrey suggests Cazaly's restructuring of the side was more of a "natural evolution".
689 Cazaly kicked two of his five goals *after* breaking his toe. *The Sporting Globe*, 20 June and *The Australasian*, 27 June, 1931.
690 *The Sporting Globe*, 5 August, 1931.
691 H A de Lacy, 'Up there Cazzer!', *The Sporting Globe*, 9 August, 1941.
692 Summaries of Preston's social events are taken from the VFA *Recorder* for the 1931 season.
693 The *Northcote Leader*, 11 September and *The Sporting Globe*, 9 September, 1931.
694 *The Sporting Globe*, 16 September, 1931.
695 Marc Fiddian, *The Bullants: A history of Preston Football Club*, p. 29, the *Preston Football Club Annual Report and Balance Sheet 1931* and the *Northcote Leader*, 18 and 25 September, 1931.
696 *The Sporting Globe*, 23 September, 1931.
697 Marc Fiddian, *The Bullants: A history of Preston Football Club*, p. 29 and best player information kindly provided by VFA historians Andrew Robinson and Wal Williams.
698 *The Age*, 7 March, 1931.
699 *The Argus*, 19 May, 1931.
700 This estimate is conservative: Cazaly was often named by the press in the weekly list of available players but subsequent match reports were usually brief, making it impossible to state categorically that he had played unless he was named among the goalkickers or best players.
701 When Melbourne and country league figures were aggregated, McBrien estimated that 1452 clubs, 43,680 players, 24,640 officials and 457,800 spectators were involved in football matches across Victoria each week. These figures were included in 'Football's amazing grip on Victoria', *The Age*, 12 June, 1931. They were updated in L H McBrien, 'A Great Industry: How Code Fights Depression', *The Sporting Globe*, 27 April, 1932 and were noted by Leonie Sandercock and Ian Turner in *Up Where Cazaly? The Great Australian Game*, pp. 108-09.
702 In April 1931 Port Melbourne's town clerk took exception to a WFL delegate's reference to the "howling Dervishes of Port Melbourne", noting in a terse letter that media reports from other grounds showed "disturbances are inseparable from the class of football played by your league." *The Age*, 11 April, 1931.
703 Eligibility rules were also a bone of contention. The Watersiders were stripped of one win against the Markets after it was revealed one of their players had not worked on the wharves for more than six months. A retaliatory counter-claim against the Markets team the next time they played was dismissed. *The Age*, 10 June and *The Argus*, 4 and 13 June and 11 and 29 July, 1931.
704 Umpire George Macauley, who failed to report any of the players, was later stood down from umpiring duties for his failure to control the game. *The Age*, 16 July and *The Argus*, 25 July, 1931.
705 Palmer, another Waterside player, was disqualified for the remainder of 1931 and the entire 1932 season after he kicked a Railways opponent the following week. *The Argus* and *The Age*, 11 August, 1931.
706 Club delegates passed a motion deploring the incidents of rough play during the season and seeking to assure the sporting public that "all efforts will be made to prevent a repetition." *The Argus*, 15 August, 1931.
707 *The Examiner*, 5 June and *The Argus*, 9 July and 29 September, 1931.
708 *The Age*, 6 August, 1931.
709 Post and Telegraph easily defeated Yellow Cabs at the Motordrome to win the WFL premiership in front of several thousand spectators. Cazaly's former protégé from Minyip Eric Zschech played for Post and Telegraph while Jack Dyer played for Yellow Cabs. *The Age* and *The Argus*, 1 October, 1931.
710 Cazaly's better bowling performances over the summer included 6 for 85 against Garden City and 5 for 48 against Victoria Brewery. The *South Melbourne Record*, 13 February and 19 March, 1932.
711 At the end of Preston's 1931 season his re-appointment had been reported as "practically certain". *The Age*, 23 September, 1931.
712 The *Preston Leader*, 12, 19 and 26 February, 1932 and information provided by Brian Membrey.
713 The *Preston Leader*, 12 February, 1932 and information kindly provided by former Melbourne Football Club historian Lynda Carroll.
714 The *Preston Leader*, 12 February, 1932.
715 The other applicant North Hobart considered for the post was Doug Ringrose, a rover who had played for Brighton in the VFA and was captain-coach of Fitzroy in 1929. *The Argus*, 5 March and *The Mercury*, 18 March, 1932.

Chapter 18. FIGHTS AND A FLAG: NORTH HOBART, 1932-33

716 Cazaly later described Alby Goggins as the best back-pocket player he had seen. According to his daughter Helen, Goggins "never went round anything, he always went through." Goggins rode a motorbike to training and games, a round trip from Bothwell of almost 100 miles twice a week. He played 10 seasons with North Hobart from 1932 and featured in seven premierships. *The Sporting Globe*, 14 June 1933 and information kindly provided by Helen Baker.
717 *The Mercury*, 8 April, 1932.
718 *Ibid*, 30 March and 5 and 7 April, 1932.
719 *Ibid*, 18 and 25 April, 1932. Collier was troubled with boils on his neck throughout his career.
720 The *Monotone Sporting Record*, 21 May, 1932.
721 Other prominent VFL players included Collingwood's Harry Collier and Richmond's Jack Dyer.
722 *The Mercury*, 13 June and 1 July, 1932. Despite the fact the TFL side wore state guernseys, it was an inter-league rather than an interstate game.
723 *The Mercury*, 22 August, 1932.
724 *Ibid* and the *Monotone Sporting Record*, 27 August, 1932.
725 *The Mercury*, 26 August, 1932.
726 The *Monotone Sporting Record*, 3 September, 1932.
727 Arnie Walters, quoted in Nicolá Goc, *Tasmanians Remember 1900-1969*, p. 159.
728 *The Mercury*, 5 October, 1932. Albert Ogilvie was the Opposition Leader at the time he defended Cazaly. He later served as Labor Premier from mid-1934 until his death in June 1939, aged 49.
729 *Ibid*, 3 October, 1932.
730 The *Monotone Sporting Record*, 8 October, 1932. The state final was Laurie Nash's last game in Tasmania, having announced five days earlier that he had signed to play for South Melbourne.
731 Rait would top the league's goalkicking list again in 1935, 1936 and 1937. Including club games, TFL representative games and one season with Footscray in 1933, he kicked 847 goals between 1927 and 1937. Ken Pinchin and Allan Leeson, *A Century of Tasmanian Football*, p. 152 and p. 180.
732 *The Mercury*, 18 and 19 April, 1933.
733 Known originally as the Lewis Building, at different times during the 20th century Hobart residents knew it as the Barnet Glass Building and then Red Cross House after its principal tenant. Other occupants during the mid-1930s included the Boomerang Tea Rooms, the Royal Agricultural Society and Miss Lily Allport, an artist still actively painting at 75. *Wise's 1935 Post Office Directory* and Katheryn Bennett, *Central Area Heritage Review* prepared for the Hobart City Council, 2003.
734 Interview with Pat Whitecross.
735 *The Sporting Globe*, 3 May, 1933.
736 Information from Rick Cazaly and letter from Roy Cazaly jnr to Noel Counihan, 21 September, 1976.
737 Phillip Bentley with David Dunstan, *The Path to Professionalism: Physiotherapy in Australia to the 1980s*, p.68.
738 *Wise's 1934/35 Post Office Directory*. The Hobart telephone directory also listed him as a 'masseur' during this period.
739 The use of electrical current in medicine was first trialled in London hospitals during the 18th century. Phillip Bentley with David Dunstan, *op cit*, p. 11.
740 *The Mercury*, 7 February, 1933.
741 Information from North Hobart's 1932 and 1933 *Annual Reports*, kindly provided by football historian Adrian Collins.
742 *The Mercury*, 2 May and *The Sporting Globe*, 17 May, 1933.
743 *The Mercury*, 12 January, 1933. Alan Rait went on to play 19 games and kick 62 goals for Footscray during 1933-34 before he returned to Tasmania. Len 'Apples' Pye's transfer to Fitzroy fell through and he returned to North Hobart but he later played 16 games and kicked 39 goals for Fitzroy during 1934-35.
744 Moreover, Cazaly argued, discussions to secure a player's clearance—and the negotiation of any transfer fee—should be conducted by the relevant clubs and not left up to the player. *The Sporting Globe*, 12 April, 1933.
745 *The Examiner*, 29 September, 1933.

Chapter 19. FROM UGLY DUCKLINGS TO PREMIERS: NEW TOWN, 1934-36

746 *The Mercury*, 30 October, 5 November and 21 and 30 December, 1933 and 15 and 17 January, 1934 and *The Advocate*, 2 April, 1934.
747 *The Mercury*, 18 January and the *South Melbourne Record*, 27 January, 1934. Footscray retained Bill Cubbins as non-playing coach.
748 *The Mercury*, 8 March and *The Sporting Globe*, 14 March, 1934.
749 For example, in mid-1934 North Hobart paid Cazaly £3 for Max Felmingham's massage treatment and 15 shillings for Alfred 'Oxy' Pratt's electrical treatment. Information from North Hobart Football Club minutes, 21 and 28 June, 1934, kindly provided by Adrian Collins.
750 Ken Pinchin and Allan Leeson, *A Century of Tasmanian Football 1879-1979*, p. 60 and p. 178.
751 The *Monotone Sporting Record*, 28 April, 1934 and *The Mercury*, 5 April, 1934.
752 Buckney had unsuccessfully applied to transfer from Lefroy to New Town at the start of the 1934 season, and had been playing district football before his call-up. *The Examiner*, 14 May and *The Mercury*, 15 May, 1934.
753 The *Monotone Sporting Record*, 7 July, 1934.
754 *Ibid*, 4 August, 1934.
755 *The Mercury*, 22 May, 1934 and photo kindly supplied by Marie Hanley.
756 Letter from Roy Cazaly jnr to Noel Counihan, 20 September, 1976 and Tom Prior, 'Up there with bounce for Cazaly jnr', *The Sun*, 28 February, 1984.
757 Pat Whitecross interviewed by Peter MacFie.
758 *The Mercury*, 7 and 22 February, 1935.
759 *The Herald*, 2 October and *The Advocate*, 3 October, 1935.
760 *The Advocate*, 7 May, 1935.
761 *The Age*, 7 May, 1935. Others who turned out for the past players included Fred 'Skeeter' Fleiter, Joe Scanlan, Ted Johnson, Syd Hogg and Artie Wood.
762 The *South Melbourne Record*, 11 May, 1935.
763 *Ibid*, *The Mercury*, 13 May and *The Sporting Globe*, 25 May, 1935.
764 Despite the TFL's success under his captaincy, Cazaly was omitted for the return match against the NTFA at York Park at the end of August, which the southerners won by a goal.
765 *The Mercury*, 26 June, 1935.
766 *Ibid*, 4 July, 1935.
767 The *Monotone Sporting Record*, 27 July, 1935. St Kilda led comfortably throughout, despite Cazaly's ongoing attempts to reshuffle his side, and eventually won by 45 points.
768 *The Mercury* and *The Examiner*, 29 July, 1935 and official smoke social program held by the Cazaly family.
769 The *Monotone Sporting Record*, 31 August, 1935.
770 *The Mercury*, 21, 23 and 26 August and 27 September and the *Monotone Sporting Record*, 28 September, 1935. Fitzroy's secretary Harry Trevena was a spectator at the match where Cazaly was reported. Asked his opinion of the incident, he replied that: "Cazaly was reported for allegedly 'attempting' to do what many others 'succeeded' in doing".
771 Ted Freeman, 'Debt days of New Town', *Tasmanian Football Record*, 14 June, 1958.
772 The *Monotone Sporting Record*, 19 October, 1935.
773 'Brains and football: Roy Cazaly's career and lessons learned', *The Mercury*, 19 October, 1935.
774 *The Mercury*, 14 October, 1935 and 'Brains and football: Roy Cazaly's career and lessons learned', *The Mercury*, 19 October, 1935.
775 Interviews with Arch Flanagan.
776 The NTFA season had finished a number of weeks before the TFL's and in his annual report to members New Town's secretary Ted Freeman suggested that "Southern teams would perform more successfully [against the north] if the season were curtailed" several weeks earlier. *New Town Football Club's Annual Report and Financial Statement for the 1935 Season*.
777 The *Monotone Sporting Record*, 19 October, 1935.
778 The *South Melbourne Record*, 8 February, 1936.
779 *The Mercury*, 28 February 1936.
780 Player statistics kindly provided by Adrian Collins.
781 *The Mercury*, 29 January and 9 April, 1936.
782 *Ibid*, 11 May, 1936.

783 The *Monotone Sporting Record*, 18 July, 1936 and information from the Jack Donnelly Collection held by the Queen Victoria Museum and Art Gallery, Launceston.
784 North Hobart won the 1936 Grand Final against Lefroy by four points, then defeated Launceston for the state title.
785 Quoted in *The Mercury*, 27 November, 1936. New Town used 41 players during the season, North Hobart 33 and Lefroy and Cananore 30 each. From player statistics kindly provided by Adrian Collins.
786 *The Mercury*, 8 September, 1936.
787 David Young, *Sporting Island, A history of sport and recreation in Tasmania*, pp. 196-97 and Damian Morgan and Greg Fahey, *Go Greyhound: 50 years of the Hobart Greyhound Racing Club*, pp. 2 and 5.
788 Antique, a brindle bitch, had been whelped in November 1934 by Heritage out of Queenie Box. Information kindly provided by Tasmanian greyhound historian Greg Fahey.
789 *The Mercury*, 30 July and 5 and 14 December, 1936 and 21 January, 1937.

Chapter 20. LAKESIDE LAMENT: SOUTH MELBOURNE, 1937

790 South's preferred candidate was their former captain-coach John Leonard but Cazaly became their next choice after Leonard decided to stay in Western Australia. Chris Donald, *Haydn Bunton: Best and Fairest*, pp. 136-37 and Mark Branagan and Mike Lefebvre, *Bloodstained Angels: The Rise and Fall of the Foreign Legion*, pp. 110-11.
791 *The Age* and *The Argus*, 10 and 11 February, 1937. Fitzroy eventually appointed its former star player and captain Gordon Rattray as non-playing coach. Jack Bisset briefly coached Port Melbourne in the VFA while Richmond's vice captain Basil McCormack was appointed to fill the coaching vacancy at New Town.
792 *The Mercury*, 20 and 27 February and 3 March and *The Herald*, 9 March, 1937.
793 The earliest newspaper cartoon suggesting the Swan emblem was drawn by Alex Gurney and appeared in *The Herald* on 15 September, 1933. Jim Main, 'Excellence from afar' in Ashley Browne (ed) *Grand Finals: The stories behind the premier teams of the Victorian Football League*, Vol. 1, p. 373 and Michael Riley, 'Alex Gurney – Cartoonist', *http://boylesfootballphotos.net.au/article65-Alex-Gurney-Cartoonist*.
794 Jack Rohan agreed to stay on as vice president. In 1934, he replaced Wallace 'Jumbo' Sharland as a football writer with *The Sporting Globe*.
795 Archie Crofts had started his grocery store empire with a single shop in Park Street, South Melbourne in 1905. He was a local councillor between 1931 and 1942, South Melbourne Mayor in 1934–35, president of the football club from 1933 to 1937 and a Member of the Victorian Legislative Council from 1935 until his death in 1942. Susan Priestley, *South Melbourne: A History*, pp. 267-8 and *http://www.parliament.vic.gov.au/re-member/bioregfull.cfm?mid=995*.
796 The *Mirror*, 9 April, 1932 and Jim Main and Russell Holmesby, *Encyclopedia of AFL Footballers*, p. 244.
797 Jim Main, 'Excellence from afar', *op cit*, pp. 370-72.
798 When South Melbourne inaugurated its Life Membership badge in 1934, it was fitting that the design featured a swan and that the first one was awarded to Jack Rohan. The *Daily News*, 2 October 1933 and the *Sunday Times*, 21 January, 1934.
799 During the four seasons between 1933 and 1936 South Melbourne won 65 out of 82 games, for a winning percentage of 79.3 per cent but just one premiership. By comparison, Richmond also played 82 games between 1931 and 1934, appeared in four consecutive Grand Finals and won two with a winning ratio of 80.5 per cent. Collingwood played the same number of games between 1927 and 1930 and won four consecutive flags with a slightly higher winning ratio of 85.4 per cent.
800 The *South Melbourne Record*, 13 February and Bert Barclay, 'Cazaly hopes to make South football machine', *The Herald*, 9 March, 1937.
801 By round one of 1937, the seven survivors of the 1933 premiership side were Jacky Austin, Terry Brain, Billy Faul, Herbie Matthews, Laurie Nash, Bob Pratt and Len Thomas. Graeme Atkinson, *The Complete Book of AFL Finals*, p. 126 and Stephen Rodgers, *100 Years of AFL Players*, Volume 2, p. 527.
802 See Mark Branagan and Mike Lefebvre's *Bloodstained Angels: The Rise and Fall of the Foreign Legion* for an excellent account of the club's fortunes during the 1930s.
803 *The Age*, 7 April, 1937.
804 The *South Melbourne Record*, 13 March, 1937.
805 'Brighton Diggins' in Lionel Frost, *Immortals: Football people and the evolution of Australian Rules*, p. 99.

806 Mark Branagan and Mike Lefebvre, *op cit*, pp. 113-14. After considering coaching offers from numerous VFL, VFA, country and Western Australian clubs, Diggins coached briefly in Perth and was eventually cleared to Carlton.
807 Cartoonist McRae in *The Sporting Globe*, 5 May, 1937.
808 Bert Barclay, 'Cazaly hopes to make South football machine', *The Herald*, 9 March, 1937.
809 H A de Lacy, 'Cazaly to play? Willing to help South', *The Sporting Globe*, 28 April, 1937.
810 *The Sporting Globe*, 8 May, 1937.
811 *Ibid*, 5 June and 14 August, *The Argus*, 9 and 10 June, *The Herald*, 14 August and the *South Melbourne Record*, 21 August, 1937.
812 *The Sporting Globe*, 28 April to 3 July, 1937. Cazaly wrote four follow-up articles on coaching techniques for the *Globe* the following season.
813 'Cazaly shows the right road for junior footballers', *The Sporting Globe*, 3 July, 1937 and 'Coaching talks by Roy Cazaly on building up a formidable ruck', *The Sporting Globe*, 23 May, 1938.
814 An auction listing for the Page Street home four years earlier had described it as "a superior double fronted brick villa, on choice corner position, with entrance porch and verandas, six large bright rooms and scullery, well-fitted bathroom, tiled cooking recess, built-in presses, most expensive tiled hearths and mantels, side entrance and easy motor entrance." Interview with Pat Whitecross by the author, *South Melbourne Rates Books* and an auctioneer's advertisement in *The Argus*, 17 May, 1933.
815 Interview with Pat Whitecross by Peter MacFie.
816 Interview with Pat Whitecross by the author.
817 Interview with Pat Whitecross and Edie Cameron by Peter MacFie.
818 George Cazaly's name appears in a surviving Johns and Waygood wages book from April 1936, where he was earning £3/3/7 for a 40 hour week. He was described as an ironworker when he died intestate in 1952. Information kindly provided by Helen Hopper from the Noel Butlin Archives Centre at the Australian National University and the *Victorian Government Gazette* No. 781, 3 September, 1952, p. 5162.
819 The company had been founded in the 1850s by steel fabricator Peter Johns in Flinders Lane, where he turned out girders and bridge beams before expanding into hydraulic engineering from the late 1870s. The business became a public company in 1888, bought out rival Richard Waygood four years later and moved to a larger site in South Melbourne in 1908. Here the company fabricated steel framework and enjoyed a near monopoly building and installing elevators for Melbourne's increasing number of high rise buildings. *The Argus*, 5 August, 1937, Geoffrey Blainey, *One Hundred Years: Johns and Waygood Limited, 1856-1956* and Susan Priestley, *South Melbourne: A History*, p. 258.
820 Mark Branagan and Mike Lefebvre, *op cit*, pp. 118-20, Jim Main, *In the Blood*, pp. 121-22 and Austin Robertson, *Ocker: The Fastest Man Alive!*, pp. 47-50.
821 *The Age*, 11 June, 1937.
822 Stephen Rodgers, *100 Years of AFL Players*, Volume 2 p. 527 and a list of South Melbourne's 1937 players held by the AFL Library.
823 *The Sporting Globe*, 11 August, 1937 and Mark Branagan and Mike Lefebvre, *op cit*, p.122.
824 The *South Melbourne Record*, 4 September, 1937.
825 South Melbourne's *Annual Report* for 1937 told a sobering story: the club lost a staggering £512/19/4 once gate takings were offset against players' wages, staff costs, general expenses, umpires, police, gate keepers and tax. The club's profit of £252/15/9 would have been wiped out were it not for the social club's efforts in raising £206 and the cricket club's waiving of the football club's £106/0/9 share of the principal and interest owing on the Grandstand Account. Mark Branagan and Mike Lefebvre, *op cit* p. 125, *The Herald*, 7 December, 1937 and the *South Melbourne Football Club Sixty-Third Annual Report and Balance Sheet*, AFL Library.
826 *The Age*, 15 November and 6 December, 1937. Other teams in the Mercantile Association included Sands and McDougall, Dimmey's, Kitchen and Sons, Myers, Buckley and Nunn and the Jolimont Rail Workshops.

Chapter 21. THE LEGION OF THE LOST: SOUTH MELBOURNE, 1938-39

827 *The Argus*, 30 March, 1938 and *The Sporting Globe*, 3 May, 1939. Other current and former League players and coaches who supported the introduction of the throw pass included Gordon Rattray, Len

CHAPTER ENDNOTES

Wigcraft, Jack Titus, Percy Bentley and Barney Herbert.
828 *The Sporting Globe*, 6 April, 1938.
829 *The Sporting Globe* estimated that 30,000 of those at the 1938 VFA Grand Final were VFL fans who attended out of curiosity. In late 1938 the Australian National Football Council held its line and reaffirmed its opposition to the throw pass. The VFA retained the rule for the next 10 years, finally abandoning it in 1949 as one of the pre-conditions for rejoining the Council. *The Sporting Globe*, 2 November, 1938 and 11 October, 1939 and Marc Fiddian, *The VFA: A history of the Victorian Football Association 1877-1995*, p. 35.
830 Russell Holmesby, 'In a new league, 1925-1945' in Rob Hess and Bob Stewart (eds), *More than a Game*, p. 155.
831 Jim Main, *In the Blood*, p. 123 and E A Wallish, *The Great Laurie Nash*, pp. 189-90.
832 The *South Melbourne Record*, 2 April, 1938.
833 *The Argus*, 28 March and 8 April and the *South Melbourne Record*, 9 April, 1938. Moore had a consistent season, top scoring for South Melbourne with 34 goals in 17 games.
834 The *South Melbourne Record*, 14 May, 1938.
835 Letters to the editor, the *South Melbourne Record*, 4 and 11 June, 1938.
836 The *South Melbourne Record*, 11 June, 1938.
837 *Ibid*, 18 June, 1938.
838 Accepting Camberwell's offer would have seen Graham earn as much in three seasons as he could in seven at South Melbourne. The *South Melbourne Record*, 11 June, 1938.
839 *Ibid*, 18 June, 1938.
840 *The Herald* and *The Argus*, 10 August, 1938.
841 The losses ranged from £1/17/9 against Footscray in round 12 to £93/4/4 against North Melbourne the following week. The net loss for the season was more than £663. The *South Melbourne Record*, 3 December, 1938 and the *South Melbourne Football Club Annual Report and Balance Sheet* for 1938.
842 Roy Cazaly, 'A forward's brains must be in his feet', *The Sporting Globe*, 15 June, 1938.
843 Jim Blake, 'Camberwell rise due to Cazaly', *The Sporting Globe*, 11 June, 1941.
844 *The Age* and *The Argus*, 25 February and the *South Melbourne Record*, 4 March, 1939.
845 'Roy Cazaly back in South's colours', the *South Melbourne Record*, 13 May and Hec de Lacy, 'Cazzer plays again', *The Sporting Globe*, 17 May, 1939.
846 Prior to this he had played for the Wayside Rovers, kicking four goals on debut against the Collingwood Juniors in 1937. The *South Melbourne Record*, 12 June and *The Age*, 20 June, 1937.
847 Aggie wanted Roy jnr to continue the family name 'Roy' when his own son was born but he refused, saying "He can have the initial but I'm not putting him through that." Conversation with Roy jnr's son Rick.
848 Tom Prior, 'Up there with bounce for Cazaly junior', *The Sun*, 28 February, 1984.
849 Emily, one of seven daughters of a Port Melbourne wharfie, also played competitive netball with Kath. Conversation with Emily Davies.
850 *The Argus*, 23 June and the *South Melbourne Record*, 24 June, 1939.
851 *The Argus*, 1 July, 1939.
852 *The Sporting Globe*, 29 July and *The Examiner*, 31 July, 1939.
853 *The Age*, 14 August and the *South Melbourne Record*, 19 August, 1939.
854 Jim Blake, 'Roy Cazaly marks time', *The Sporting Globe*, 13 March, 1940.

Chapter 22. AMONG THE WOWSERS: CAMBERWELL, 1941

855 VFA historian Marc Fiddian wrote that "As with any other club, Camberwell had its share of downs, except that when Camberwell went into a decline it lasted longer than most and a bad year for the Wells could be horrendous." Marc Fiddian, *The VFA: A history of the Victorian Football Association 1877-1995*, p. 138.
856 Victorians were asked at the state election in October 1920 whether hotels in their district should continue trading, have their hours reduced or be closed altogether. Camberwell was one of only two of Victoria's 214 licensing divisions which voted for prohibition. Ten local liquor retailers were subsequently closed, including the historic Camberwell Hotel which had given the suburb its name. Geoffrey Blainey, *A History of Camberwell*, pp. 78-81.

857   Despite slower growth during the Depression, the population of Camberwell and surrounding suburbs reached 69,000 by 1941. A H Stevens (editor), *Souvenir of Camberwell, Melbourne's most beautiful garden suburb*, 1933 and Geoffrey Blainey, *op cit* p. 88.
858   Barry Humphries hated organised sport. He would later recall being at home on Saturday afternoons and hearing "borne with terrible clarity across the housetops, the spasmodic applause of the cricket fans and, worse, in winter, the frighteningly mindless roar of the football rabble." Barry Humphries, *More Please*, 1992, p. 57.
859   Barry Humphries, Excerpt from 'An Ode to the City of Camberwell', *Neglected Poems and Other Creatures*, 1991, pp. 13-15.
860   Robert Menzies' 'Forgotten People' speech, in which he spoke of "the great and sober and dynamic middle-class" was delivered on 22 May, 1942, one of a series of radio addresses he made during 1941/42. See *http://menziesvirtualmuseum.org.au/transcripts/the-forgotten-people*.
861   Interestingly, Nash's playing contract was with Hartnett himself rather than with the Camberwell club. In 1939, Hartnett was unsuccessful in trying to lure an even bigger football star, triple Brownlow medallist Haydn Bunton, back to Melbourne from Western Australia. Geoff Wilkinson, 'Thanks for the memory', *The Herald Sun*, 6 December, 2003, Marc Fiddian, *op cit*, pp. 139-40 and *East Side Story: History of the Camberwell Football Club*, 2003 reprint, no pagination.
862   Information kindly provided by Reg Horkings' son Laurie.
863   *The Sporting Globe*, 29 March, 1941. Local sportsmen were among the many to enlist, including more than 60 players from the Camberwell Cricket Club.
864   Geoffrey Blainey, *op cit*, pp. 88-89.
865   Hec de Lacy, 'The blast of the whistle once more', *The Sporting Globe*, 23 April, 1941.
866   A few years later, the house was described as a modern brick and tile villa with built-in cupboards, wall-to-wall carpets, gas stove and copper, garage and garden. *The Argus* classifieds, 29 October, 1949.
867   Kooyong and Camberwell electoral rolls for 1941 and 1943 and information provided by Pat Whitecross.
868   Interview with Edie Cameron (née Harrison) by Peter MacFie. Edie's father Robert was Aggie's brother.
869   The Art Deco Regal Cinema on the corner of Camberwell and Toorak Roads had opened in May 1937. Edie became a dancer at the Tivoli Theatre during her teens. *The Argus*, 8 May, 1937 and an interview with Edie Cameron by Peter MacFie.
870   Many of the player and match statistics in this chapter are taken from copies of the VFA *Recorder* kindly provided by John Ficarra and best player information held by VFA historians Andrew Robinson and Wal Williams.
871   *The Sporting Globe*, 11 and 18 June, 1941.
872   Information provided by Reg Horkings' son Laurie.
873   Interview with Laurie Peters, 22 August, 2010.
874   Seelenmeyer, who was also a handy district cricketer, had played 10 games for the season. He managed to play several games for South Australian club Norwood during the war and returned to Camberwell in 1945. Marc Fiddian, *op cit* p. 140, *The Sporting Globe*, 27 August, 1941 and 1941 Camberwell player statistics kindly provided by David Barker.
875   Jim Blake, 'Camberwell rise due to Cazaly', *The Sporting Globe*, 11 June, 1941.
876   *The Sporting Globe*, 13 August, 1941.
877   Other VFA players who played in their forties include Dick Condon (44), Dick Harris (42), Harry Vallence (41) and Billy Findlay (41). There are no reports of any others playing at 48, although it should be noted that the birthdates of some early VFA players are unknown. *The Argus*, 29 August, 1941, Graeme Atkinson, *Everything you ever wanted to know about Australian Rules Football*, pp. 61-65 and information kindly provided by Col Hutchinson, Andrew Robinson, Stephen Rodgers and Wal Williams.
878   *The Sporting Globe*, 3 September, 1941.
879   Cazaly kicked one goal against Sandringham, his 26th and last in the VFA.
880   Recorder Cup votes were awarded by central and goal umpires after each match. In 1941 Des Fothergill (Williamstown) won easily with 62 votes. Of Camberwell's players, Laurie Nash polled 29 votes, Reg Horkings 19 and Reg Henderson 8. The VFA *Recorder*, 20 September, 1941 and Marc Fiddian, *op cit*, p. 248.
881   *The Age* speculated on Cazaly's possible appointment to Hawthorn on 10 October and it was confirmed in both *The Age* and *The Argus* on 22 October, 1941.

Chapter 23. MODEST EXPECTATIONS: HAWTHORN, 1942

882 Marc Fiddian, *A History of the VFA*, p. 211.
883 *Hawthorn Football Club Annual Report and Financial Statement 1941*. Jacob Jona, a popular local GP, was Hawthorn's president from 1932 until 1949.
884 Interestingly, Hawthorn did not seek formal applications for the coaching position. *Hawthorn Football Club Minutes*, 14 October, 1941, *The Herald*, 21 October, 1941 and *Hawthorn Football Club Annual Report and Financial Statement 1941*.
885 *Hawthorn Football Club Minutes*, 21 October, 1941.
886 *Ibid*, 11 November, 1941.
887 Cazaly and Secretary Vic Hocking worked well together because both were of a similar temperament. Player Laurie Peters later described them as "two real gentlemen. It's unusual to get two guys like that who don't touch alcohol, and they don't swear. You couldn't say a hard word against either of those guys." Interview with Laurie Peters.
888 Some long-established sporting events were suspended due to the war: in 1942 the famous Stawell Gift was cancelled for the first time in its history due to travel restrictions and "the uncertain war position". It resumed in 1946. *The Argus*, 4 March and *The Sporting Globe*, 11 March, 1942.
889 Quoted in *The Sporting Globe*, 18 March, 1942.
890 *The Argus* and *The Sun*, 9 December, 1941.
891 *Hawthorn Football Club Minutes*, 22 January, 1942.
892 Geelong returned to the League in 1944.
893 Melbourne and Collingwood also discussed a possible amalgamation but decided to continue as separate clubs after encouraging numbers attended training. *Hawthorn Football Club Minutes*, 7 April, 1942 and *The Argus*, 1, 2, 21 and 24 April, 1942.
894 *The Sporting Globe*, 7 March, 1942.
895 *The Argus*, 15 April and *The Sporting Globe*, 18 April, 1942. Owned by the local council and officially called the Hawthorn Sports Ground, the narrow Glenferrie Oval was colloquially known to supporters as the 'sardine tin' because it was jammed up against the Belgrave/Lilydale railway line.
896 *Hawthorn Football Club Minutes*, 27 April and 5 May, 1942.
897 *The Argus*, 20, 22, 27 and 29 April, 1942.
898 Harry Gordon, *The Hard Way: The Story of the Hawthorn Football Club*, p. 77.
899 Hawthorn's request was denied despite President Jona being one of the organisers of the local Air Raid Precaution Movement. *Hawthorn Football Club Minutes*, 2 May, 1942 and a photo of the leaders of the Air Raid Precaution Movement in Hawthorn held by the City of Boroondara Library.
900 Roy Lionel Cazaly's naval service records and information provided by his son Rick.
901 Marriage certificate no. 9268 dated 11 April, 1942, *The Age*, 13 April and the *South Melbourne Record*, 2 May, 1942.
902 Marc Fiddian, *History of the VFA*, p. 33 and *The Argus*, 21 April, 1942.
903 *The Argus*, 24 April, 6 May and 9 May, 1942.
904 Tommy Lahiff had previously played for Port Melbourne in the VFA and then for Essendon for three seasons, before returning to Port Melbourne as captain-coach in 1938. Ken Linnett, *Game for Anything: The Tommy Lahiff Story*, pp. 152-53 and the VFA *Recorder*, Vol. XVII, no. 24, 20 September, 1941.
905 Stephen Rodgers, *100 Years of AFL Players* Volume 2, pp. 599-600 and *AFL Record Season Guide 2014*, pp. 201-02.
906 Jim Bohan, a fireman at the Ivanhoe Fire Station, had been recruited from Camberwell at the start of 1938 as a 17-year-old and played virtually every position during his 131-game VFL career. He had a phenomenal drop kick and regularly kicked goals from the centre of Glenferrie Oval. His marking improved under Cazaly, a fact attributed to the coach making him leap repeatedly for a football tied to a stick. *The Argus*, 5 June 1942, Harry Gordon, *op cit* p. 78, information kindly provided by Jim's son Michael and a profile at *http://www.hawkheadquarters.com/player.aspx?playerid=237*.
907 Interview with Laurie Peters.
908 Interview with Peter O'Donohue.
909 *Hawthorn Football Club Minutes*, 5 May, 1942.
910 Alec Albiston was the team's highest goalscorer for the 1942 season, with 32, followed by Jim Bohan with 16. *Hawthorn Football Club Annual Report and Financial Statement 1942* and information provided by Alec's son Ian.

911 One local paper had reported during the previous season that: "football writers for the daily papers have been instructed to cut their reports down to very small proportions. The public is clamouring for more war news." The *Richmond, Hawthorn and Camberwell Chronicle*, 4 April, 1941.
912 Geoffrey Blainey, *One Hundred Years: Johns and Waygood Limited, 1856-1956*, pp. 38-9.
913 Noel Counihan included this assertion in his 1978 *Australian Dictionary of Biography* entry on Cazaly and mentioned it in a letter to ADB editor Geoffrey Serle but didn't cite a source. Cazaly's involvement in the campaign is plausible, although it should be noted that there is nothing in Bertha Walker's papers at the State Library of Victoria to support the contention. Cazaly's ADB online entry at *http://adb.anu.edu.au/biography/cazaly-roy-5541/text9441* and the *Bertha Walker papers*, SLV MS 10772, La Trobe Australian Manuscripts Collection, State Library of Victoria.
914 Melanie Oppenheimer, *Volunteering: Why we can't live without it*, pp. 41-42. Political activist Jessie Street was another leading figure in the 'Sheepskins for Russia' campaign.
915 *Hawthorn Football Club Minutes*, 5 June, 1942.
916 *The Sporting Globe*, 24 June, 1942.
917 Quoted in *The Mercury*, 27 July, 1942.
918 Collingwood's 29 consecutive victories over Hawthorn between 1925 and 1941 remains the longest winning streak by one club over another in VFL/AFL history. Harry Gordon, *op cit*, p. 77 and p. 326, the *Hawthorn Football Club Minutes*, 9 June, 1942 and Glenn McFarlane, 'A streak we may never break', Collingwood website, 1 July, 2015.
919 Jim Main and David Allen, *Fallen - the Ultimate Heroes: Footballers Who Never Returned from War*, pp. 299-303.
920 *Hawthorn Football Club Minutes*, 1 September and 22 December, 1942.
921 *Ibid*, 19 January, 1943.
922 *Ibid*, 16 February, 1943.

Chapter 24. FROM MAYBLOOMS TO HAWKS: HAWTHORN, 1943

923 It proved to be St Kilda, which won just one game for the season and drew another.
924 Information provided by Jack O'Keefe's son Gary.
925 Interview with Ken Feltscheer. Feltscheer had played four games for Melbourne in 1935-36 before joining Hawthorn midway through 1937.
926 Interview with Alan Saker's widow Thelma.
927 *Ibid*.
928 Interview with Peter O'Donohue.
929 Interview with Laurie Peters.
930 Harry Gordon, *The Hard Way: The story of the Hawthorn Football Club*, p. 79 and interview with Jack Brain.
931 Lahiff later claimed that Cazaly had used a megaphone on such occasions, but this conflicts with an opinion piece written by Cazaly in 1953, who mused about "what would happen [in Melbourne] if a coach used a big megaphone and instructed his men from over the fence, as I did in Hobart a few years back". Tom Lahiff, 'The Turk Tells', *Footy Week*, 7 August, 1967 and Roy Cazaly, 'Football is living on hand-outs!', *The Sporting Globe*, 1 August, 1953.
932 Information provided by Laurie Taylor's son Wayne.
933 Andy Angwin quoted in Harry Gordon, *op cit*, p. 78.
934 Interview with Pat Whitecross. Her version of events was supported by her sister Joan, who recalled the conversation "plain as day" in 1979. Sam Simpson, 'Cazaly! The myth, the magic', *Saturday Evening Mercury*, 29 September, 1979.
935 Peter Haby, 'The Hocking Collection', Hawthorn Football Club website, 12 August, 2012, available online at *http://www.hawthornfc.com.au/news/2012-08-10/the-hocking-collection*.
936 Peter Haby, 'Hawthorn's oldest Maybloom visits the Hawk Museum', Hawthorn Football Club website, 30 April, 2010 and author's interview with Laurie Peters.
937 *Hawthorn Football Club Minutes*, 25 May, 1943. Two stuffed hawks were subsequently acquired by the club: one was displayed in the boardroom and the other in the Social Club until the early 1990s. Both are now on display in the Hawks' Museum at Waverley. A hawk logo was soon formally adopted on the club's letterhead. It featured on the front of the 1943 annual report, on membership cards from 1948 and

CHAPTER ENDNOTES

on club badges from 1949. Peter Haby, 'The Hawk turns 70 in 2013', Hawthorn Football Club website, 15 December, 2012, available online at *http://www.hawthornfc.com.au/news/2012-12-15/the-hawk-turns-70-in-2013*.
938   'Mayblooms now Hawks' and 'Lightning hawks must strike hard', *The Sporting Globe*, 15 and 19 May, 1943.
939   Peter Haby, 'Jack King, a Maybloom and Hawk forever', *Hawktalk*, August 2005.
940   Harry Gordon, *op cit*, p. 78. Wally Culpitt finished the season as Hawthorn's leading goalscorer with 43.
941   Marc Fiddian, *Boilovers, Thrillers and Grand Eras*, p. 43.
942   Harry Gordon, *op cit*, p. 77.
943   Tommy Lahiff quoted in Harry Gordon, *Ibid*, p. 78.
944   Correspondence from Jack Barker's son John.
945   Russell Holmesby and Jim Main, *The Encyclopedia of AFL Footballers*, Seventh Ed., p. 71.
946   Interview with Laurie Peters. Peters' assessment may well have been correct, as Bobby Williams played only one game in 1944 before retiring.
947   Hec de Lacy, 'Chagrin must not ruin bright future of Hawks', *The Sporting Globe*, 1 September, 1943.
948   'R. Cazaly's 40 Years in Football', *The Mercury*, 27 September, 1949. In fact, while Hawthorn *had* beaten Richmond and Fitzroy during the season they had not defeated the other two finalists Carlton and Essendon.

Chapter 25. HOMEFRONT: BUSH LIFE IN LENAH VALLEY

949   Pat Whitecross interviewed by Peter MacFie.
950   Kangaroo Valley was officially renamed Lenah Valley in 1922. Trevor Owen Wilks, *A History of Kangaroo Valley – Lenah Valley 1847-1995*, p. 1 and p. 81.
951   *Wise's Tasmanian Post Office Directory for 1947*.
952   *The Mercury*, 25 June, 1947. Aggie later embarked on another challenge, when she took up a suggestion by a member of the Lenah Valley Progress Association that Brushy Creek Road be renamed 'Cazaly Lane'. Despite Aggie's best efforts, the push failed when a majority of Association members voted to retain the existing name. It was one of the rare occasions Aggie didn't get her own way. Conversation with Marjory Woolford, and subsequent correspondence.
953   Cliff Hurburgh, for example, was a dentist who had played for Lefroy before the war. Knocked back by the Air Force because he was colour blind, he enlisted in the Navy and played as a rover for their team. Hurburgh went on to play for North Hobart after the war. Conversation with Cliff Hurburgh.
954   *The Mercury*, 6 October, 1944 and John Stoward (ed), *Australian Rules Football in Tasmania*, p. 37.
955   *The Mercury*, 2 June, 13 October and 25 October, 1944.
956   *Ibid*, 22 December, 1944.
957   *Ibid*, 28 March, 4 April and 9 October, 1945.
958   *Ibid*, 3 and 18 March and 13 November, 1944.
959   Both horses were usually driven by leading reinsman Jack Mogford. Various newspaper reports and information kindly provided by pacing historian Peter Cooley.
960   The new association replaced the defunct Owners and Breeders' Association. *Mercury*, 15 November, 1945.
961   *The Mercury*, 13 December, 1945.
962   The 9th Division AIF was formed in 1940 and served in North Africa and the South West Pacific.
963   John Hetherington, writing in *The Age*, 22 January, 1958.
964   Chester Wilmot, 'Tobruk Ack-Ack Post', radio broadcast recorded by the Australian Broadcasting Commission's Field Unit, 21 October, 1941. Transcript kindly provided by Greg Colgan of Electric Pictures.
965   'His name became the soldiers' battle cry', *Sydney Morning Herald*, 13 January, 1963, Gus de Brito, 'Why they loved Cazaly', *Everybody's*, 24 June, 1964 and 'The man who made a battle cry!', *Football Life*, July 1969. The author Peter FitzSimons has written that Australian soldiers sometimes yelled 'Up there Cazaly' in battle during the New Guinea campaign. See FitzSimons', *Kokoda*, 2006, p. 297.
966   Colin Pura, 'Up there Cazaly!', *Parade*, April 1973. Pura edited the serviceman's journal *Guinea Gold* and later wrote a history of the 9th Division's Cavalry Regiment.
967   The use of 'Hoh! Hoh! Hoh!' was frowned upon by the Division's senior officers, which only encouraged

the soldiers to continue using it. John Glen, *Tobruk to Tarakan*, p. 66.
968 Conversation with Keith Rossi, retired brigadier and Victorian RSL historian.
969 *The Herald*, 10 January and *The Argus*, 11 January, 1944.
970 Interview with Pat Whitecross.
971 Engagement notice in *The Mercury*, 31 May, 1947 and wedding notice in *The Mercury*, 22 March, 1948.
972 Engagement notice in *The Mercury*, 15 August, 1947 and wedding notice in *The Mercury*, 26 February, 1948.
973 Allan 'Nedda' Park was a champion schoolboy footballer, played for Hobart before and after the war and transferred to New Town in 1948. He acquired his nickname because of his resemblance to American movie actor Ned Sparks. 'Personality - Nedda Park' in *Waterfront*, 23 February, 1963 and interview with Pat Whitecross and Stephen Park by Peter MacFie.
974 Information provided by Ted Trappett, a leading cook who was part of the early draft sent to refit the *Shropshire* at Chatham Dockyards.
975 See Stan Nicholls' *HMAS Shropshire* for a detailed military history of the ship and those who served in her.
976 Interviews and correspondence with Eric 'Slim' Curtis, Sam Hasell, Stan Nicholls and Ted Trappett. I am deeply indebted to them and Cazaly's other shipmates Bob Boyd, Len Burgess, 'Jock' Epstein, Mackenzie 'Mac' Gregory and Ron Russell for providing details and stories about life aboard the *Shropshire*.
977 United States' sailors called the 'pom-poms', "Chicago pianos" because their ammunition magazines looked like piano keys when viewed from above. Stan Nicholls, *HMAS Shropshire*, p. 162.
978 Discussions and correspondence with 'Slim' Curtis and 'Mac' Gregory.
979 Parts of the plane landed so close that the concussion shook the ship. Bob Boyd suffered a perforated eardrum while Len Burgess, who was below decks at the time, "thought we had copped a packet". Correspondence with Bob Boyd and extract from Len Burgess's wartime diary, 'A brief description of a trip around the world'.
980 *The Advocate*, 25 February, 1994.
981 Roy Cazaly jnr was presented with his Distinguished Service Medal by the Governor General in late 1946. Distinguished Service Medal Citation Registration no. PM 2228, *The Argus*, 2 May, 1945 and *The Mercury*, 19 November, 1946.
982 Interview with Wayne Park.
983 Interview with Pat Whitecross and Stephen Park by Peter MacFie.
984 *Ibid*.
985 Interviews with Barry Robins, Wayne Park, Teresa Parsey and Gail Lawrence.
986 Don Bratt was a friend of 'Nedda' Park. They had met at Flinders Naval Depot during entry service but then served on different ships. They renewed their friendship after the war, both played for Hobart and both met their future wives at the Belvedere dance studios.
987 *The Mercury*, 17 September, 1953.
988 Information provided by Anthony Whitecross.
989 Interview with Pat Whitecross and Stephen Park by Peter MacFie, and author's interview with Pat Whitecross.
990 Interview with Pat Whitecross and Stephen Park by Peter MacFie.
991 Roy Ransley still has the shooting trophy he won as a nine year old.
992 Conversations with Marjory, Ian and Tony Woolford and subsequent correspondence from Marjory.
993 Cazaly was initiated into Hobart's Lodge Loyalty on 3 April, 1937. Information kindly provided by Ron Neve. A family bible records that 'Bro. R. Cazaly' later joined the Acacia Lodge no. 276 after he returned to Melbourne in 1937. He was a member of Hobart's Masonic Temple in 1945.
994 Interview with Pat Whitecross and Stephen Park by Peter MacFie.
995 Lawry's wife Muriel ran a Friday night youth club for teenagers and Cazaly once gave a talk in which he invoked Abraham Lincoln's appeal to "the better angels of our nature" to always do the right thing. Conversation with Muriel Lawry.
996 Interview with Pat Whitecross.
997 *Ibid*. One of Cazaly's favourite tunes was George Botsford's *Black and White Rag*, later made famous as the theme for the BBC snooker program *Pot Black*.
998 Conversation with Marjory Woolford and subsequent correspondence.
999 Keith Welsh quoted in Sam Simpson, 'Cazaly! The myth, the magic', *Saturday Evening Mercury*, 29 September, 1979.

CHAPTER ENDNOTES

1000 Interview with Pat Whitecross.
1001 Conversation with Stephen Park.

Chapter 26. HEALING HANDS: POST-WAR PHYSIOTHERAPY

1002 Patients during this period usually paid either five or seven shillings for their consultation. *1943 Patient Book*, courtesy of Stephen Park.
1003 Reflecting these changes in the profession, the Australian Massage Association was renamed the Australian Physiotherapy Association during World War II. Pat McRae, 'Physiotherapy' in Alison Alexander (editor), *The Companion to Tasmanian History*, p. 275 and Lucy Chipchase et al, 'Looking back at 100 years of physiotherapy education in Australia', *Australian Journal of Physiotherapy* 2006 Vol. 52, pp. 3-7.
1004 'Up there, Cazaly' in *People*, 11 March, 1953.
1005 *Wise's Tasmanian Post Office Directory for 1947*.
1006 *The Mercury*, 29 July, 1947, p. 15.
1007 'Cazaly Aids King's Cup Men', *The Herald*, 21 April, 1948.
1008 Roy jnr maintained this index card system into the 1990s. Interview with Barry Robins.
1009 Interview with Pat Whitecross and Stephen Park by Peter MacFie. The practice of rendering and straining pig fat to make ointments and plasters is a centuries-old traditional remedy.
1010 Phillip Bentley with David Dunstan, *The Path to Professionalism: Physiotherapy in Australia to the 1980s*, p.11 and information provided by Carl Cazaly.
1011 Information provided by Rick Cazaly.
1012 *The Mercury*, 29 July, 1947 and Jack Donnelly, *Tasmanian Football Guide 1947*, p. 174. The advertisement in the *Football Guide* included a rare photo of Cazaly positioning a ball for a place kick while he was playing with City in Launceston.
1013 Other sportsmen on the program included the wrestler Chief Little Wolf and champion cyclist Hubert Opperman. Advertisement in *The Mercury*, 30 July, 1947.
1014 Interview with Gordon Triffett.
1015 Information provided by John Thompson.
1016 Conversation with Rosemary Nichols.
1017 Tasmania's polio infection rate during 1937-38 was 421 people in every 100,000. Only Iceland in 1924 is believed to have had a higher per capita outbreak. See Anne Killalea's *The Great Scourge: The Tasmanian Infantile Paralysis Epidemic 1937-1938* for a detailed study of Tasmania's polio epidemic and treatments during this period.
1018 Fear of the polio epidemic spreading among school children had led to classes, picnics and other large gatherings being cancelled across Melbourne during much of 1937. The *South Melbourne Record*, 15 January, 1938.
1019 Philip Bentley with David Dunstan, *op cit*, pp. 93-95.
1020 *Ibid*, p. 101 and Anne Killalea, *op cit*, pp. 9-10.
1021 Tasmania recorded 367 cases of polio and 24 deaths during the 1948-52 epidemic. Anne Killalea, *op cit*, p. 128.
1022 Interview with Mary Guy. Although Mary retained her paralysis for the rest of her life she became a long-serving Glenorchy City Councillor and a prominent disability services advocate. She died in February 2010, aged 67.
1023 Poor appetite and weight loss are other symptoms of Still's Disease, and Cazaly's strict dietary instructions to Margie Bryce included lemons, blackcurrants, full-cream milk, cod liver oil capsules and waterglass, an "awful tasting" sodium solution traditionally used to preserve eggs. Correspondence from Margie Bryce and subsequent conversations.
1024 Interview with Cheryl Kaimatsoglu.
1025 Interviews with Gail Lawrence and Barry Robins.
1026 Cazaly was formally registered as a certified physiotherapist from 1 January, 1953. Certificate of Registration no. 17, dated 15 May, 1953.
1027 The Board's responsibilities were wide-ranging, and included the power to approve physiotherapy providers and to fine or deregister anyone who breached the Physiotherapists' Registration Act or its regulations.

1028   Information provided by Stephen Park.
1029   Interview with Barry Robins.
1030   Interview with Don Bratt.

Chapter 27. **RETURN OF THE PRODIGAL SON: NEW TOWN, 1948-50**

1031   *The Mercury*, 2 October, 1947.
1032   Ken Pinchin and Allan Leeson, *A Century of Tasmanian Football*, p. 87.
1033   *The Mercury*, 20 November, 1947.
1034   Dickenson later recalled that Cazaly had been attracted back to his old club by the prospect of coaching a team of "good young blokes", and that the money on offer was immaterial. *The Mercury*, 5 December, 1947 and interviews with Keith Dickenson and Maurie Oborne.
1035   *New Town District Football Club Annual Report for 1948*.
1036   Parsons played for Lefroy before the war but someone "pulled some strings" to enable him to play for New Town in 1945 while home on leave from the Army and he had stayed on after the war ended. Keith Dickenson later recalled Parsons arriving at the team bus without any luggage for an end-of-season trip to Port Arthur. When he asked Parsons where his bag was, he replied: "Keith, you know we do not go to bed on football trips and I've got all I need in my pocket". His toothbrush was sticking out of his top pocket. Keith Dickenson, *To Take a Chance*, p. 48 and John Briggs, 'Little man with a big heart', *The Sunday Tasmanian*, 23 June, 1985.
1037   Of the total players used, 21 played 10 or more games for the Seniors and 23 played 10 or more for the Seconds. *The Mercury*, 5 May, 1948, *New Town District Football Club Annual Report for 1948* and statistics provided by Adrian Collins.
1038   John Briggs, 'Little man with a big heart', *The Sunday Tasmanian*, 23 June, 1985.
1039   Interview with Kev Orpwood and subsequent correspondence.
1040   Conversation with Keith Welsh. Welsh was *The Mercury*'s chief football writer from 1947 until his retirement in 1970, writing under the pen name 'Drop Kick'. He was among the first to be inducted into the Tasmanian Football Hall of Fame in 2005 and died in July 2009, aged 103. Tasmania's annual award for outstanding contribution to journalism is named in his honour.
1041   Interview with Keith Welsh by Peter MacFie and *The Mercury*, 9 April, 1948.
1042   Information provided by Adrian Collins.
1043   Correspondence from Kev Orpwood.
1044   Correspondence from Doug Scott.
1045   Interview with Rex Garwood, correspondence from Doug Scott and match summaries provided by Adrian Collins.
1046   *The Mercury* 27 July, 1948, John Briggs, 'Little man with a big heart', *The Sunday Tasmanian*, 23 June, 1985 and information provided by Adrian Collins.
1047   Fittingly, New Town's first premiership in 13 years was against North Hobart, the same opponent they had vanquished in 1935. *The Mercury*, 27 September 1948 and David Costelloe, *Magpie Memories: A History of the New Town – Glenorchy Football Club 1948-1990*, pp. 90-91.
1048   *The Voice*, 25 September, 1948.
1049   *The Mercury*, 27 September, 1948 and David Costelloe, *op cit*, p. 91.
1050   Buckingham played in the State School Old Boys' Association and a number of its players graduated to New Town's ranks. *New Town District Football Club Annual Report for 1948*.
1051   *Ibid*.
1052   'New Town brilliantly wins state premiership', *The Mercury*, 4 October, 1948.
1053   'Townies' exciting state title victory', *The Examiner*, 4 October, 1948.
1054   *New Town District Football Club Annual Report for 1948* and interview with Doug Scott.
1055   *The Mercury*, 22 April, 1949 and interview with Doug Smith.
1056   Interview with Kev Orpwood and subsequent correspondence.
1057   Interview with Keith Welsh by Peter MacFie.
1058   Maurie Oborne later became a school teacher, umpire and close friend of the Cazaly family. Interview with Maurie Oborne.
1059   Match information provided by Adrian Collins.
1060   *The Mercury*, 25 August, 1949.

1061 *Ibid*, 22 September, 1949.
1062 *Ibid*, 24 September, 1949.
1063 While Brian Kelly had played in the ruck several times during 1948 he had only played four Senior games in 1949 on the backline prior to the finals. Player information provided by Adrian Collins.
1064 David Costelloe, *op cit*, p. 92.
1065 Ken Pinchin and Allan Leeson, *op cit*, p. 88.
1066 *The Mercury*, 26 September, 1949.
1067 *The Advocate*, 8 April, 1950.
1068 Letter from Noel Counihan to Geoff Serle, 10 October, 1976, held in the Australian Dictionary of Biography files at the Australian National University. It may be naive to assume that Cazaly would be a Labor supporter just because he had worked on the wharves. As Wendy Lowenstein and Tom Hills noted after interviewing former Melbourne dock workers, "It is hard to tell [their political affiliations] from their stories because on the waterfront a conservative may be more radical on industrial matters than many a militant in another industry". Wendy Lowenstein and Tom Hills, *Under the Hook: Melbourne waterside workers remember working lives and the class war 1900-1980*, p. 4.
1069 *The Mercury*, 18 April, 1950 and 'Up there, Cazaly', *People*, 11 March, 1953.
1070 *The Mercury*, 5 May, 1950.
1071 Counting votes cast under the Hare-Clark system is a complex process. Once all first preferences are counted, any candidate with a quota is declared elected and their surplus votes are distributed according to the voters' next preference. If there are still candidates to be elected, the one with the least number of primaries is eliminated and the ballots distributed to the remaining candidates according to the voters' next preference. This process is repeated until six candidates have obtained a quota. *The Mercury*, 13 May, 1950 and Scott Bennett and Barbara Bennett, *Tasmanian Electoral Handbook 1851-1982*, p. 208.
1072 Despite a slight statewide increase in the Liberal Party vote the status quo held in Denison, with the ALP retaining three seats, the Liberals two and independent Bill Wedd the sixth. Wedd resigned three years later and another independent, Leo McPartlan, was elected in a recount to fill the vacancy, despite having polled fewer primary votes than Cazaly in 1950. *The Mercury*, 26 October, 1953.
1073 'Up there, Cazaly', *People*, 11 March, 1953 and interview with Barry Robins.
1074 Garwood was a champion athlete who would go on to represent Tasmania at football, cricket and lawn bowls. Ken Pinchin and Allan Leeson, *op cit*, p. 155 and interview with Rex Garwood.
1075 During one match Garwood was rotated through four different positions including full-back. *New Town District Football Cub Annual Report for 1951* and interview with Rex Garwood.
1076 Interview with Rex Garwood.
1077 Correspondence from Doug Scott.
1078 Interview with Rex Garwood.
1079 The Seconds lost just two games during the season. *New Town District Football Club Annual Report for 1950*.
1080 David Costelloe, *op cit*, p. 14.

Chapter 28. ONE LAST HURRAH: NEW TOWN AND TASMANIA, 1951-54

1081 Match statistics provided by Adrian Collins.
1082 Interview with Rex Garwood.
1083 '"Cazza" strips again', *The Mercury*, 9 August, 1951 and information provided by Adrian Collins.
1084 *The Age*, 3 September and *The Sporting Globe*, 5 September, 1951.
1085 'Cazaly may retire after this season', *The Mercury*, 12 September, 1951.
1086 'Players petition Cazaly', *Ibid*, 24 September, 1951.
1087 New Town's score of 19.9.123 was the highest Grand Final total since the war and remained a record until 1974. One immediate beneficiary of the win was centre John Chick, who was snapped up by Carlton after a visiting scout noted his eye-catching performance. Chick debuted for Carlton in round one of 1952 and played 119 games for the Blues over nine seasons. David Costelloe, *Magpie Memories: A History of the New Town – Glenorchy Football Club 1948-1990*, p. 15 and Tony De Bolfo, 'Champion wingman John Chick dies', http://www.carltonfc.com.au/news/2013-03-19/champion-wingman-john-chick-dies.
1088 Garwood also won *The Mercury*'s trophy for the best league footballer and tied for the Wander Medal as

| 1089 | *The Mercury*, 9 October, 1951.
| 1090 | 'No better footballers, says Roy Cazaly', *Ibid*, 18 October, 1951.
| 1091 | 'Veteran Cazaly retires', *Ibid*, 30 November, 1951.
| 1092 | New Town's 1951 captain Roy Witzerman had been appointed playing coach of Devonport. *The Mercury*, 30 and 31 January, 19 March, 31 July, 28 August and 12 September and *The Advocate*, 13 August, 1952.
| 1093 | 'Up there, Cazaly', *People*, 11 March, 1953.
| 1094 | The boy was Graeme Salmon, a 13-year-old Hutchins School boarder from Tasmania's midlands who had been injured by a truck and was undergoing physiotherapy. Conversation with Graeme Salmon.
| 1095 | *The Sporting Globe*, 20 May, 1953.
| 1096 | Under Cazaly, the TFL defeated the NWFU on 12 June and the NTFA on 14 June but lost to the NTFA on 3 July and the NWFU on 31 July, 1954.
| 1097 | *The Mercury*, 4 May, 1954.
| 1098 | Dickenson's motion to appoint Cazaly non-playing coach for the 1950 carnival was defeated on the casting vote of TFL chairman Mervyn McNeair. Somewhat bizarrely, officials appointed a team manager and a head trainer but no coach. North Hobart's Len McCankie was appointed Tasmania's captain and coach in 1953 but the pitfalls of this part solution were highlighted when the side lost a pre-carnival practice match to a combined Midlands side. The loss was an ominous—and accurate—portent for Tasmania's carnival prospects. *The Mercury*, 18 April, 1950 and *The Examiner*, 8 June, 1953.
| 1099 | *The Mercury*, 3 June, 1954.
| 1100 | A champion centre half-forward, Geoff Long is one of only a handful of Tasmanians to have played at three national carnivals. He was awarded an All Australian blazer in Perth in 1956 and was one of the inaugural Legends inducted into the Tasmanian Football Hall of Fame in 2005. Ken Pinchin and Allan Leeson, *A Century of Tasmanian Football*, p. 182 and interview with Geoff Long.
| 1101 | VFL player records and interviews and correspondence with Gordon Bowman, Ray Stokes and Athol Webb.
| 1102 | *The Sporting Globe*, 23 June, 1954 and an *ANFC Sectional Championship Final Challenge Program* kindly provided by Andrew Hay, a member of the Australian Amateur team.
| 1103 | Interview with Laurie Moir. Moir's father Les had played under Cazaly at City in 1928-30 and Laurie was named after the great Laurie Nash.
| 1104 | *The Advocate*, 7 July, 1954, Ken Pinchin and Allan Leeson, *op cit*, p. 187 and interview with Geoff Long.
| 1105 | *The Mercury*, 9 July, 1954.
| 1106 | *Ibid*, 8 July, 1954.
| 1107 | Interview with Geoff Long and subsequent correspondence.
| 1108 | Interview with Noel Atkins and subsequent correspondence.
| 1109 | *Ibid*.
| 1110 | *The Mercury*, 9 July, 1954 and interview with Mike Clennett and subsequence correspondence.
| 1111 | Interview with Geoff Long and subsequent correspondence.
| 1112 | *Saturday Evening Mercury*, 10 July, 1954.
| 1113 | Interview with Keith Welsh by Peter MacFie.

Chapter 29. TIME ON: 1955-60

| 1114 | Stephen Park and Pat Whitecross interviewed by Peter MacFie.
| 1115 | Details of Master Barry's career kindly provided by pacing historian Peter Cooley.
| 1116 | Stephen Park and Pat Whitecross interviewed by Peter MacFie and 'Up there Cazaly: the man behind the legend', *The Weekender*, 6 October, 1979.
| 1117 | Peter Ford, *Tasmanian Trotting 1917–1980*, p. 74.
| 1118 | The trophy was a silver tea and coffee service worth £100. Master Barry's victory took his total wins to 14 and his total earnings to £4260. 'Blue Peter, Master Barry to run in Inter Dominion', undated newspaper clipping from January 1956 kindly provided by Jack Stamford's son Richard.
| 1119 | *The Argus*, 31 January, 1956 and Peter Ford, *op cit*, p. 99.
| 1120 | *The Argus*, 10 March, 1956.
| 1121 | Another of Cazaly's pacers was Miss Stephanie, who the veteran reinsman Jack Mogford drove to victory

at Richmond on 13 January, 1962, Cazaly's 69th birthday. In 1965, the Southern Tasmanian Trotting Club named the Cazaly Free-For-All race at the Elwick Showgrounds in honour of one of Tasmania's "trotting stalwarts". *The Mercury*, 29 June, 1965 and information provided by Peter Cooley.

1122 *Herald* cartoonist Samuel Wells used the phrase to signal the start of the 1945 football season and *The Argus*' cartoonist Mick Armstrong borrowed it as an allegory for rising commodity prices the following year. 'Camera ready' cartoons by Samuel Wells in the State Library of Victoria's Picture Collection Accession no H2009.110/91-128 and 'Today's Armstrong' in *The Argus*, 1 June, 1946.

1123 Lawler included the phrase in the play and in two subsequent plays ('Kid Stakes' and 'Other Times'), which together became known as the 'Doll trilogy'.

1124 Letter from Ray Lawler. Joe Ryan played 74 game for Footscray between 1935 and 1939, and a further nine for North Melbourne in 1940-41.

1125 Conversation with Ray Lawler and subsequent correspondence.

1126 Encouraged by the *Doll*'s West End success, the producers took the play to Broadway in 1958 but it proved a box-office failure. Ray Lawler resisted strong pressure to edit the script and American audiences were baffled by the Australian slang. "No one in America understood it", Lawler said later. The play was later heavily adapted—including a change of location from Melbourne to Sydney—and made into a movie starring English actor John Mills and American actors Ernest Borgnine and Angela Lansbury. Steve Meacham, 'A lucky play', *Sydney Morning Herald*, 3 September, 2011.

1127 Fran Voss, 'Showbiz a life role for Clark', *The Examiner*, 9 November, 2003.

1128 Conversation with John Clark.

1129 Fran Voss, op cit.

1130 Interview with Larry Noye and Noye's letter to *The Mercury*, 30 March, 2002.

1131 Lena died while Roy and Aggie were overseas, leaving Roy as James and Elizabeth's last surviving child.

1132 Peter Plowman, *Australian Migrant Ships*, 2006, pp 21-22.

1133 Aerogramme from Roy to his son, dated 31 March, 1958. Roy and Kath's divorce was finalised later that year.

1134 Roy and Aggie Cazaly's *Trip Book*.

1135 *Herald*, 17 October, 1958. *Abide With Me* has been sung at every FA Cup Final since 1927. The Final that Cazaly attended on 3 May, 1958 between Manchester United and Bolton Wanderers was particularly poignant as 11 Manchester United players and officials had died in the Munich air disaster three months earlier. Given Cazaly's enthusiasm for the hymn it was fitting that, 21 years later, Mike Brady would write Up There Cazaly, Australian Football's own, albeit secular, sporting hymn.

1136 Correspondence from Geraldine Cazaly.

1137 Their son Brett was born in 1960, followed by Teyana (1961), Zena (1963), Zane (1965) and Carl (1969).

1138 Keith Welsh, 'The famous cry still lingers on', *Saturday Evening Mercury*, 2 May, 1964.

1139 *Herald*, 25 April, 1959.

1140 Correspondence from Geraldine Cazaly.

1141 Information provided by Rick Cazaly.

Chapter 30. SIREN: 1961-63

1142 Larry Noye, 'Champions are made not born!', *Sports Novels*, April 1961, p 35.

1143 Interview with Keith Welsh by Peter MacFie.

1144 Tony Thiessen went on to play several games for Melbourne, Carlton and North Melbourne between 1963 and 1965. His son James played three seasons for Adelaide and was a member of their 1998 premiership team. Keith Welsh, 'A master helps out', *The Mercury*, 20 September, 1961 and conversation with Tony Thiessen.

1145 7HT interview broadcast on 19 April, 1962. Copy of recording and details of the broadcast kindly provided by Lindsay McCarthy and Norm Stone from the Sound Preservation Association of Tasmania.

1146 Sam Simpson, 'Cazaly! The myth, the magic', *Saturday Evening Mercury*, 29 September, 1979.

1147 Interview with Pat Whitecross.

1148 Interviews with Larry Noye and subsequent correspondence.

1149 *The Herald* and *The Sporting Globe*, 5 January, *The Sun* and *The Age*, 7 January and 'His name became the soldier's battle cry', *Sydney Morning Herald*, 13 January, 1963.

1150 Interview with Pat Whitecross.

1151 Interviews and correspondence with Larry Noye, *op cit*, and Larry Noye, 'Role of the nursing nun' *Queanbeyan Age*, 15 December, 1982 and 'Up there Cazaly!', *Heritage*, Vol. 25, no. 109, 2004.
1152 'SMFC was represented at Roy Cazaly's funeral', undated newspaper clipping in a Cazaly family scrapbook and 'Great names again', *The Mercury*, 17 July, 1979.
1153 Copy of Roy Cazaly's will dated March 1962 held in the Archives Office of Tasmania, reference AD960/1/96 431 44469.
1154 Roy Cazaly's death certificate no. 2645, copy on his Australian Dictionary of Biography file, Australian National University.
1155 Quoted in Sam Simpson, 'Cazaly! The myth, the magic', *Saturday Evening Mercury*, 29 September, 1979 and 'Cazaly – truth more outstanding than the legend', *The Sun*, 26 September, 1981. Longevity was not a strong point for Roy and his siblings; their father's generation lived, on average, much longer than they did. With the exception of Catherine, who died of illness at 64, James Cazaly and three of his siblings lived to at least 74 and the remaining four lived into their 80s or 90s. Of Roy's generation, Edgar died on a railway line aged 21, Sydney committed suicide at 35, Florence died aged 47, Ernest aged 53, James jnr aged 58, Lena and Daniel aged 66, Roy aged 70 and George aged 71. Only William reached 75.

Chapter 31. POST 1963

1156 Glenorchy full-forward and former Hawthorn champion Peter Hudson kicked his 200th goal of the season during the game but Clarence won an epic encounter by three points.
1157 Ward McNally, 'Roy Cazaly, Australia's "Mr Football"', *Sports Novels*, February 1952 and 'Up there, Cazaly' in *People*, 11 March, 1953.
1158 Conversations and correspondence with Geraldine Cazaly.
1159 Information provided by Geraldine and Rick Cazaly.
1160 Cazaly Fitness Centre proposal, July 1980.
1161 Interview with Rick Cazaly.
1162 'Cazaly fitness centre comes to D'port', *The Advocate*, 29 May, 1984.
1163 'Centre creates new phase in Cazaly family's history', the *Southern Star*, 6 April, 1988.
1164 Tom Prior, 'Up there with bounce for Cazaly junior', *The Sun*, 28 February, 1984.
1165 Various conversations with Rick Cazaly.
1166 Correspondence with Carl Cazaly.
1167 Discussion with Cazaly's son Brett and 'Footy hero's son saved cruiser in kamikaze raid', *Herald Sun*, 19 September, 1994.
1168 Marriage certificate no. 8584, interview with Pat Whitecross and information kindly provided by Rod Tandy.
1169 Jim Main, *Honour the Names*, p. 251 and Mark Tandy's death certificate no. 12392/65.
1170 Marriage certificate no. 1691/37 and the *Record*, 23 January, 1937.
1171 Bill Lockwood played football for Geelong and then football and cricket in Perth during the 1890s. After being Collingwood's curator for 17 years he was South Melbourne's ground supervisor from 1921 until 1945. He died in 1953, aged 81. *The Argus*, 7 November, 1921 and 6 April, 1937, the *South Melbourne Record*, 7 November, 1921 and 4 July, 1953 and *The Age*, 22 January, 1958.
1172 Fred Fleiter's death certificate no. 1312/73 and information kindly provided by Brian, Roy and Tony Fleiter.
1173 'Laurie Nash loses coaching job', the *South Melbourne Record*, 21 November, 1953. His successor as coach, Herbie Matthews, managed no better than ninth over the next four seasons.
1174 'Great names again', *The Mercury*, 17 July, 1979.
1175 Information kindly provided by Mavis Burgess and Dennis de Lacy.
1176 *Herald Sun*, 30 November, 2014.
1177 Cazaly's silver nameplate from 1918 was missing, souvenired by someone who recognised his name. The club arranged a replacement. Article by Russell Holmesby in the *Saint* magazine, December 2005.
1178 http://en.wikipedia.org/wiki/Lakeside_Stadium and http://www.watpac.com.au/project/state-sports-facilities-project/.
1179 As one journalist wrote, "Among the 68 nominees, one has to look no further than inaugural best-and-fairest Roy Cazaly ..." James MacSmith, 'Legends are all up there with Cazaly', *Sun Herald*, 3 August, 2003.
1180 Football commentator Mike Sheahan wrote: "No Cazaly! He's an original AFL Legend, yet doesn't

make the best team at the club where he reportedly played his best football." Mike Sheahan, 'No sense in holding a grudge at omission', *Herald Sun*, 9 August, 2003. As with St Kilda's Team of the Century, there were only a handful of players selected from the era prior to World War II, but the inclusion of seven interchange players in the side suggests the selection panel found the culling process a difficult task.

1181   The Swans' inaugural Hall of Fame included inductees from across five playing eras. Cazaly was selected from the 1919-45 era, alongside Bob Pratt, Mark Tandy, Laurie Nash, Herbie Matthews and Jack Bisset. *Sunday Age* and *Sunday Herald Sun*, 19 July, 2009.
1182   Cazaly was 33 years and 260 days old when he won it. *AFL Record Season Guide* 2014, p. 622.
1183   *http://en.wikipedia.org/wiki/Northern_Blues*.
1184   Information kindly provided by Preston historian Brian Membrey.
1185   *http://en.wikipedia.org/wiki/Camberwell_Football_Club* and *http://oldscotchfc.com.au/*
1186   *http://en.wikipedia.org/wiki/Wimmera_Football_League*.
1187   Robert Allen, 'Looking for Roy' in Paul Daffey and John Harms (editors), *Footy Town*, 2013 and 'Under Wimmera Skies', the Footy Almanac at *http://www.footyalmanac.com.au/under-wimmera-skies/*.
1188   Ken Pinchin and Allan Leeson, *A Century of Tasmanian Football*.
1189   The Western Storm subsequently replaced South Launceston in the TSL and signed many of their former players.
1190   Information kindly provided by Brett Gillow; John Stoward, *Football in Tasmania*; p. 95, John Devaney, *Full Points Footy's Tasmanian Football Companion*, pp. 28-30 and 154-55; *http://ntfa.org.au/*, *http://en.wikipedia.org/wiki/South_Launceston_Football_Club*; and *http://en.wikipedia.org/wiki/Western_Storm_Football_Club*.
1191   Warren Brewer (editor), *Never Say Die: The North Hobart Football Club*, p. 143.
1192   *Ibid*, p. 115.
1193   *http://en.wikipedia.org/wiki/Hobart_City_Football_Club*.
1194   John Stoward, *op cit*, p. 94, John Devaney, *Full Points Footy's Tasmanian Football Companion*, pp. 61-65, *http://www.glenorchymagpies.org.au/* and *http://en.wikipedia.org/wiki/Glenorchy_Football_Club*.

Chapter 32. THE LEGEND GROWS

1195   Sidney J Baker, *The Australian Language*, 1966, pp. 203-04.
1196   Brian Hansen, *The Awful Truth*, 2004, p. 462.
1197   Conversations with Brian Hansen and Brian Morris and subsequent correspondence.
1198   The *Truth*, 24 March, 1973.
1199   Existing footballer awards in 1973 were run by *All Sport – 3KZ* (the John Coleman Memorial Trophy), *3UZ*, the *ABC*, *The Age*, Channel Seven's *Football Inquest* and *World of Sport*, *The Herald*, *Inside Football*, *The Sporting Globe* (Bunton Medal) and the *Sunday Telegraph*. The *Football Record*, 23 June and 1 September, 1973.
1200   Conversation with Brian Morris.
1201   The *Truth*, 29 September, 1973. In 1976, the *Truth* gave Aggie a replica Cazaly Award statuette.
1202   Newman and Matthews tied for the 1975 Gold Cazaly and Dempsey and Templeton tied for the 1980 Gold Cazaly.
1203   Ironically, the ship which brought Brady's family to Australia in 1959 was the *Strathnaver*, the same one which had taken Roy Cazaly jnr to England during the war and Roy and Aggie on their trip to England the previous year.
1204   Interview with Mike Brady.
1205   Noel Delbridge, *Up There Mike Brady*, 2004, p. 169.
1206   Brady has met several of the Cazaly family in the years since and learned more about him: "I stumbled into their life by using their names but in hindsight I couldn't have chosen a better person. I'm so impressed with the values that he espoused … part of the pride I feel having written the song is that it helped to immortalise a person that deserved recognition." Interview with Mike Brady.
1207   Noel Delbridge, *op cit*, p. 170 and interview with Mike Brady.
1208   Noel Delbridge, *op cit*, p. 172.
1209   Sullivan, a classically trained musician, did the arrangement, particularly the clever key changes. Sullivan and Brady played all the instruments and sang the choruses together and the song was released

1210   as a single under the pseudonym 'The Two Man Band', which didn't actually exist. Interview and correspondence with Mike Brady.
1210   Noel Delbridge, *op cit*, p. 180. The song went to number one in all Australian markets except Sydney, where it reached number two.
1211   The*Herald Sun*, 10 June, 2013.
1212   Brady didn't know about the Clayderman version until he heard it being played as background music while dining in a Chinese restaurant. Interview with Mike Brady.
1213   The Sydney Swans' version begins: "Up there for Sydney, in there and fight. The Spirit of Cazaly, the red and the white ..."
1214   *The Herald Sun*, 27 October, 2001.
1215   *Ibid*, 2 October, 2007.
1216   Melbourne's *Herald Sun*, for example, included it in its list of top 10 iconic football images. *Herald Sun*, 13 May, 2014.
1217   *The Sporting Globe Football Book*, 1946, p. 40.
1218   *The Sun 50th Anniversary Souvenir*, 5 September 1972 and Scott Palmer and Greg Hobbs, *100 Great Marks*, p. 9.
1219   The 100 cards featured photographs of past and current players taking spectacular marks, including a version of Cazaly's 1924 'mark'.
1220   Dubbed 'Victoria's Bayeux Tapestry', the artwork features the woven images of 230 footballers, cricketers, athletes and others who have played a part in the ground's history. *The Herald Sun's 100 Years of Footy*, pp. 3-4, Keith Dunstan, 'Banner from heaven', the *Bulletin*, 22 July, 2003 and Kyle Hansen, 'Dream weavers', *The Herald Sun*, 20 September, 2003.
1221   Martin Flanagan, 'History goes to the wall', *The Age*, 7 June, 2004. The store closed in 2012 but the mural was preserved as part of the residential development which took its place.
1222   The confusion probably arose because of a 1975 version of the famous event by artist Brian Clinton showing Carlton as South Melbourne's opponent. Adding to the confusion was the fact that both Beckton and McSwain wore the number 3 jersey. The publication date of the original photo and match report, however, confirms it was a South Melbourne-Essendon game and Norm Beckton was Cazaly's opponent. *The Herald Sun*, 15, 22 and 29 June, 2008.
1223   I am indebted to Michael Conaty for pointing out this enigma.

Chapter 33. REAPPRAISING THE LEGEND

1224   Laurie Nash said Cazaly was the best player and coach he'd known. Vic Thorp rated Cazaly ahead of Ivor Warne-Smith, Syd Coventry and Colin Watson. Alex Eason said Cazaly "stood alone" as the best all-rounder he ever saw, and Syd Coventry named him as the most consistent follower. Gordon Coventry named the Cazaly-Fleiter-Tandy ruck trio as "the most brilliant working combination" he saw in 18 years playing League football. *The Mercury*, 17 July, 1979, *The Sporting Globe*, 29 September 1934, 3 September, 1938 and 8 April and 6 and 25 May, 1939.
1225   Reg Wilmot, 'The Champion Player', *The Argus*, 29 June, 1923.
1226   Thurgood played for Essendon in the VFA and then the VFL between 1892 and 1902 and again in 1906. W S Sharland, 'Greatest All-Round Footballer', *Sporting Globe*, 26 July, 1930.
1227   Harold Prider, 'Great stalwarts of the Australian game', the *Referee*, 24 September, 1930.
1228   Hec de Lacy, 'Best footballers for 20 years', *The Sporting Globe*, 3 October, 1942.
1229   The others were Albert Thurgood, Dave McNamara, Harry 'Vic' Cumberland, David Christy, Peter Burns, Dick Reynolds, Haydn Bunton, Jack Dyer, Dick Lee, Syd Coventry, Ivor Warne-Smith and Laurie Nash. C C Mullen, *History of Australian Rules Football 1858 to 1958*, pp. 186-94.
1230   Trevor Ruddell, 'Introducing Cec Mullen, pioneer sports historian', *The Yorker* Issue 42, Spring 2010.
1231   Jim Main, *Australian Rules 100 Greatest Players*, K G Murray Publishing, Sydney, 1977.
1232   Greg Hobbs and Mike Sheahan, *The VFL Hall of Fame: The Greats of Victorian Football*, Herald and Weekly Times, Melbourne, 1981. Alf Brown was *The Herald*'s chief football writer from 1945 to 1979.
1233   See http://www.sahof.org.au/hall-of-fame/athlete-members/ for a list of all Sport Australia Hall of Fame members.
1234   Ross Oakley, *The Phoenix Rises*, p. 174.
1235   Conversation with Ross Oakley. The inaugural committee comprised Richmond great Kevin Bartlett,

South Australian football administrator Max Basheer, former Melbourne premiership player and *Age* journalist Percy Beames, respected football journalists Geoff Christian, Harry Gordon, Mike Sheahan and Caroline Wilson, former Victorian Premier Joan Kirner, former Hawthorn player and AFL Players' Association president Michael Moncrieff, former Federal Minister and AFL Commissioner Peter Nixon, Victorian Sports Minister Tom Reynolds and former Collingwood player Lou Richards. John Kennedy snr chaired the meetings and the League's Col Hutchinson provided statistical advice.

1236 Conversation with Ross Oakley and *AFL Record Season Guide 2014*, p. 624.
1237 Initially only players could be considered for Legend status; the eligibility criteria was later changed to also include coaches.
1238 Ted Whitten died a few weeks later in August 1995.
1239 Several members of the inaugural Australian Football Hall of Fame Committee kindly agreed to speak to me about their deliberations. I have chosen to respect their anonymity in relation to specific views expressed.
1240 The first Hall of Fame inductees were announced in February 1996. Up to eight new members have been inducted each year since, with the number of Legends restricted to no more than 10 per cent of the total. As of 2016 there were more than 260 Hall of Fame members, including 26 Legends. 'AFL names Hall of Fame', AFL media release, 8 February, 1996 and http://www.afl.com.au/news/event-news/hall-of-fame.
1241 Lou Richards, a former Collingwood captain better known for his post-football media career, was already a Hall of Fame member, but under the selection criteria Legend status could only be awarded for playing or coaching achievements, not off-field contributions. Many supporters of the push to elevate Richards didn't understand or disagreed with this distinction and the resulting debate even drew in the Victorian Premier and the Prime Minister. Mark Stevens, 'Lou Richards rejects AFL Hall of Fame offer', *Daily Telegraph*, 19 May, 2009.
1242 At the height of the 2009 public debate the AFL asked the selection committee to relax their criteria and consider elevating Richards. The committee refused to revisit the issue and several members subsequently resigned in protest at the League's intervention. A compromise offer from the AFL to honour Richards with a special lifetime achievement award was rejected by his family but in April 2014 the League presented him with the inaugural John Kennedy Lifetime Achievement Award to acknowledge his contribution to the game. The Hall of Fame processes were reviewed in the aftermath of the Richards episode and the AFL later reaffirmed that Legend selection criteria would only relate to significant playing or coaching careers. It also confirmed the selection committee's independence and amended its charter so that its future recommendations are submitted for the League's "endorsement" rather than "approval". Jon Ralph, 'Ross Oakley says Lou Richards not eligible for Legend status', *The Herald Sun*, 11 March, 2009, Mark Stevens, 'Lou Richards rejects AFL Hall of Fame offer', *Daily Telegraph*, 19 May, 2009, Julie Tullberg, 'AFL legend status even more exclusive', *Herald Sun*, 22 February, 2010, Michael Warner and Evonne Barry, 'AFL closes door on legend Lou Richards', *The Herald Sun* 23 February, 2010 and 'Lou Richards granted AFL achievement award', the *Australian*, 17 April, 2014.
1243 *The Herald* published the committee's list of the Top 200 players and Top 20 coaches in July 1999.
1244 Mike Sheahan, 'Cream of the crop' in Geoff Slattery (ed), *The Australian Game of Football since 1858*, pp. 114-159.
1245 *Ibid*, p. 117.
1246 Trevor Grant, 'Noises at night are restless ghosts of footy past', *The Herald Sun*, 12 March, 2008.
1247 See the *AFL Record Season Guide 2014*, p. 609 and http://www.afl.com.au/news/2013-07-09/jesaulenko-you-beauty for the full team.
1248 Main 'delisted' Bill Mohr, Dinny Ryan, Wilfred Smallhorn, Allan Ruthven, Les Foote, Jock Spencer, Allen Aylett, Lindsay White, Harold Bray, Colin Watson, Neil Mann, Peter Box, Des Tuddenham, John Murphy, Graham Moss, Kevin Sheedy, Francis Bourke, Graham Arthur, Don Scott and Geoff Southby. He added both Gary Abletts (snr and jnr), James Hird, Craig Bradley, Dermott Brereton, Wayne Carey, Tony Lockett, Adam Goodes, Robert Harvey, Simon Madden, Stephen Kernahan, Malcolm Blight, Bernie Quinlan, Michael Tuck, Nathan Buckley, Matthew Lloyd, Chris Judd, Michael Voss, Greg Williams and Jason Dunstall. Jim Main, 'Revisiting the 100 greatest players', available online at http://australianfootball.com/articles/view/Revisiting+the+100+greatest+players/320.
1249 Adam Cardosi, 'Neglected heroes: the sad case of the Australian Football Hall of Fame', at www.australianfootball.com.
1250 AFL statistician Col Hutchinson cited by Peter di Sisto, 'Numbers game', the *AFL Record*, June 5-8 1999, p. 4.
1251 Robert Allen, 'The Gospel according to Harry' at http://australianfootball.com/articles/view/The+gospel+acc

ording+to+Harry/507 and Ted Hopkins, *The Stats Revolution*, p. 96.
1252   Discussion with Ted Hopkins and subsequent correspondence.
1253   Larry Noye, 'Champions are made not born!', *Sports Novels*, April 1961, p 35.

34. AFTERWORD

1254   Noel Counihan's own son Mick later wrote that his father was the only person in history to have shaken hands with both Roy Cazaly and Pablo Picasso. Bernard Smith, *Noel Counihan: Artist and Revolutionary*, pp. 18-19 and Mick Counihan, 'Barracker Noel' in Ross Fitzgerald and Ken Spillman (editors) *The Greatest Game*, p. 10.
1255   Letters from Noel Counihan to Geoffrey Serle dated 23 September and 10 October, 1976 in ADB files, Australian National University.
1256   'Brains and football: Roy Cazaly's career and lessons learned', *The Mercury*, 19 October, 1935.
1257   *The Sporting Globe Football Book 1948*, p. 26.
1258   Stephen Rodgers, *100 Years of AFL Players* Volume 3, 'Appendix 8 Part 1 – Longest Year-Spans in League Football', pp. 1606-07.
1259   The first player to achieve the milestone of playing 100 games at two different VFL clubs was Ian Hampshire in 1981. Hampshire played 113 games for Geelong and 111 for Footscray. Leonard Colquhoun, 'V/AFL double centurions – 100 games at each of two clubs' originally published on *fullpointsfooty.com* and Russell Holmesby and Jim Main, *The Encyclopedia of AFL Footballers: Every AFL/VFL Player since 1897*, 7th Ed, p. 322.
1260   Letter from Roy Cazaly jnr to Noel Counihan, 20 September, 1976 in ADB files, Australian National University.
1261   Letter from Noel Counihan to Geoffrey Serle, 10 October, 1976 in ADB files, Australian National University.
1262   *The Mercury*, 24 September, 1951.

Appendix 11

REFERENCES

BOOKS

Alexander, Alison (ed), *The Companion to Tasmanian History*, Centre for Tasmanian Historical Studies, University of Tasmania, 2005
Allen, Beverley J, *We Are Hawthorn*, Playright Publishing, 2001
Anonymous, *Boyle and Scott's Footballers' Pamphlet for 1891*, Pater and Knapton, 1891
Anonymous, *Premier Football Guide*, S C Wilcox and Son, 1911
Anonymous, *South Melbourne Football Guide*, E Unger and Co, 1892
Anonymous, *The South Melbourne Football Club's Guide*, Reardon, Unger and Mitchel, 1890
Anonymous, *Victorian Football Guides* published by the Victorian Cricketing and Sports Company Ltd, 1891, 1892, 1893 and 1894
Anonymous, *Victorian Football League Constitution, Rules, Permits and Laws of the Game*, Saxton and Buckie, 1910 and 1911
Atkinson, Graeme, *Everything you ever wanted to know about Australian Rules Football*, Five Mile Press, 1982
Atkinson, Graeme and Brant Atkinson, *The Complete Book of AFL Finals*, Five Mile Press, 2009
Baker, Sidney J, *A Popular Dictionary of Australian Slang*, 1943
Baker, Sidney J, *The Australian Language*, Angus and Robertson, 1945
Bale, Stewart (compiler), *ABC Football Guide and Register and Directory*, Melbourne Sports Depot, 1893 and 1894
Barnard, Jill and Jenny Keating, *People's Playground: A History of the Albert Park*, Chandos Publishing, 1996
Bate, Weston, *Essential but Unplanned: The Story of Melbourne's Lanes*, State Library of Victoria, 1994
Bate, Weston, *Lucky City: the first generation at Ballarat, 1851-1901*, Melbourne University Press, 2003
Bentley, Philip with David Dunstan, *The Path to Professionalism: Physiotherapy in Australia to the 1980s*, Australian Physiotherapy Association, 2006
Blainey, Geoffrey, *A Game of Our Own: The Origins of Australian Football*, Black Inc, 2003
Blainey, Geoffrey, *A History of Victoria*, Second edition, Cambridge University Press, 2013.
Blainey, Geoffrey, *A History of Camberwell*, Jacaranda Press, 1964
Blainey, Geoffrey, *One Hundred Years: Johns and Waygood Limited 1856-1956*, Caulfield and Sons, 1956
Blainey, Geoffrey, *Jumping Over the Wheel*, Allen and Unwin, 1993
Blainey, Geoffrey, *The rush that never ended: a history of Australian mining*, Melbourne University Press, 1993
Blair, Peter R, *History of the Brownlow Medal: Fairest and Best*, Sabey and Associates, 1997
Blake, L J (editor), *Vision and Realisation: A Centenary History of State Education in Victoria* Volume 1, Education Department of Victoria, 1973
Branagan, Mark and Mike Lefebvre, *Bloodstained Angels: The Rise and Fall of the Foreign Legion 1932-1938*, Mark

Branagan, 1995
Brennan, John, *Centenary: Warracknabeal Football Club, 1886-1986*, The club, 1986
Brewer, Warren (editor), *Never Say Die: The North Hobart Football Club*, Rev Ed., North Hobart Football Club, 2006
Brown-May, Andrew, *Melbourne Street Life: The Itinerary of our days*, Australian Scholarly/Arcadia and Museum Victoria, 1998
Buggy, Hugh, *Let's Look at Football*, Argus, 1952
Bunton, Haydn, J F McHale and R Pratt (edited by E C H Taylor), *Our Australian Game*, C G Hartley and Co, 1936
Burke, Peter, *By the Lake: A History of the Middle Park Cricket Club*, The Author, 1997
Butler, John (compiler), *Birtchnell's Ballarat Directory 1862*, S L Birtchnell, 1862
Cannon, Michael, *Melbourne after the Gold Rush*, Loch Haven Books, 1993
Caruso, Santo with Jim Main and Marc Fiddian, *Football Grounds of Melbourne*, Pennon Publishing, 2002
Cashman, Richard, *Paradise of Sport: The rise of organised sport in Australia*, Oxford University Press, 1995
Cole, Ron et al, *Birth of the Blues: Warrnambool Football Netball Club 1861-2007*, Warrnambool Football Netball Club, 2008
Costelloe, David, *Magpie Memories: A History of the New Town - Glenorchy Football Club 1948-1990*, A and J Printers, 1991
Courier, *150 not out: A history of Ballarat cricket*, The Courier, 2007
Craven, John, *Football the Australian Way*, Lansdowne, 1972
Cromie, John A, *Minyip: 100 Years Strong*, Minyip Centenary Celebration Steering Committee, Wimmera Mail-Times, 1972
Daley, Charles, *The history of South Melbourne: from the foundation of settlement at Port Phillip to the year 1938*, Robertson and Mullens, 1940
Darian-Smith, Kate, *On the Home Front: Melbourne in wartime, 1939-45*, 1990
Davison, Graham *The rise and fall of Marvellous Melbourne*, Melbourne University Press, 1978
Dean, Arthur and Eric W Gutteridge, *The Seventh Battalion, AIF: Resume of the activities of the Seventh Battalion in the Great War, 1914-1918*, 1933
De Lacy, H A (compiler and editor), *The Sporting Globe Football Annual*, 1954
De Lacy, H A (compiler), *The Sporting Globe Football Book 1946*, Edgar H Baillie for The Herald and Weekly Times, 1946
De Lacy, H A (compiler and editor), *The Sporting Globe Football Book 1948*, Edgar H Baillie for The Herald and Weekly Times, 1948
Devaney, John, *Full Points Footy's Tasmanian Football Companion*, Full Points Publications, 2009
Devaney, John, *Full Points Footy Volume One: Encyclopedia of Australian Football Clubs*, Full Points Publications, 2008
Dickenson, Keith, *To Take a Chance*, K Dickenson, 2004
Dicker, F M (compiler), *Ballarat and Ballarat District Directory for 1865-66*, James Curtis, 1865
Dodd, Christopher, *Henley Royal Regatta*, S Paul, 1981
Donnelly, A J (Jack), *Tasmanian Football Guide 1947*, W R Rolph and Sons, 1947
Dutton, Geoffrey, *The Australian Heroes*, Angus and Robertson, 1981
Dyer, Jack and Brian Hansen, *Captain Blood*, Stanley Paul, 1965
Elliott, Kathryn, *The Boys from the Rush Beds: The History of the Ballarat City Rowing Club 1870-2004*, The club, 2004
Falla, Ron and Honor Falla (compilers), *Litchfield Carron: A Century of Settlement 1874-1974*, Time Print, 1974
Feldman, Jules and Russell Holmesby and the St Kilda Football Club, *The Point of It All: The Story of the St Kilda Football Club*, Playright for and on behalf of the St Kilda Football Club, 1992
Ferrall, Sir Raymond, *90 Years On: A Tasmanian Story*, Regal Publications, 1996
Fiddian, Marc and Preston Football Club, *The Bullants: A History of Preston Football Club*, Preston Football Club, 1983
Fiddian, Marc, *Days by the Lake: A History of the South Melbourne Football Club*, Racoon Tail Books, 2013
Fiddian, Marc, *East Side Story: A History of Camberwell Football Club*, Patrons of the Camberwell Football Club, 1980
Fiddian, Marc, *Team of the Century: Camberwell Cobras Souvenir Book*, Camberwell Football Club, 2003
Fiddian, Marc, *The Swan Lake Spectacular: How South Melbourne Won the 1933 VFL Premiership*, Galaxy Print and Design, Hastings, 2004
Fiddian, Marc, *The VFA: A History of the Victorian Football Association 1877-1995*, the Author, 2004

REFERENCES

Fitzgerald, Ross and Ken Spillman (editors), *The Greatest Game*, William Heinemann Australia, 1988
Flanagan, Martin, *1970 and Other Stories of the Australian Game*, Allen and Unwin, 2002
Forster, Harley, *Preston: Lands and People 1838-1967*, Cheshire, 1968
Garden, Don, *Victoria: A History*, Nelson, 1985
Gay, Robert, *Some Ballaarat Pioneers*, Mentone, 1935
Glen, John, *Tobruk to Tarakan*, Rigby, 2012
Gordon, Harry, *The Hard Way: The Story of the Hawthorn Football Club*, Lester-Townsend, 1990
Gregory, Philip and Jan Gregory, *The Business of Empire: William Watson and Sons*, 2003
Grogan, Robert, *Blood, Sweat and Cheers: South Melbourne District Sports Club from footy beginnings to sporting diversity*, Lothian Custom Publishing, 2012
Grogan, Robert, *Our Proud Heritage: A History of the South Melbourne Cricket Club from 1862*, South Melbourne Cricket Club, 2003
Gywnn, Robin, *Huguenot Heritage: The history and contribution of the Huguenots in Britain*, Sussex Academic Press, 2001
Hansen, Brian, *The Awful Truth*, Brian Hansen Publications, 2004
Herald Sun, *100 Years of Footy*, Herald and Weekly Times, Wilkinson Books, 1996
Hess, Robert, *A National Game: The History of Australian Rules Football*, Penguin, 2008
Hess, Rob and Bob Stewart, *More Than a Game: An Unauthorised History of Australian Rules Football*, Melbourne University Press, 1998
Hobbs, Greg and Alf Brown, *The Top 240*, Herald and Weekly Times, 1982
Hobbs, Greg and Scott Palmer, *Football's 50 Greatest*, Bradford Usher, 1976
Hobbs, Greg and Mike Sheahan, *The VFL Hall of Fame: The Greats of Victorian Football*, Herald and Weekly Times, 1981
Holmesby, Russell, *Heroes with Haloes: St Kilda's 100 Greatest*, Playright Publishing, Caringbah, 1995
Holmesby, Russell and Jim Main, *The Encyclopedia of AFL Footballers: Every AFL/VFL Player since 1897*, 7th Ed., Crown Content, 2007
Hopkins, Ted, *The Stats Revolution: The Life, Loves and Passion of Football's Futurist*, Slattery Media Group, 2011
Huggard, Simon, *Frank Huggard, the Untamed Tiger: The Story of a Football Career in Victoria in the 1920s*, S Huggard, 1992
Hutchinson, Garrie, *Great Australian Football Stories*, Viking O'Neil, 1989
Hutchinson, Garrie (editor), *The Australian Football Hall of Fame*, Harper Sports, 2000
Hutchinson, Garrie and Stephanie Holt, *Footy's Greatest Coaches: The Plays, the Tactics and the Characters Who Made Australian Football*, Coulomb Communications, 2002
Hutchinson, Garrie and Stephanie Holt, *Footy's Greatest Players*, Coulomb Communications, 2003
James, Ken and Learmonth and District Historical Society, *A History of Weatherboard*, Learmonth and District Historical Society, 2008
Johnson, Joseph, *For the Love of the Game: The Centenary History of the Victorian Amateur Football Association 1892-1992*, Hyland House, 1992
Killalea, Anne, *The Great Scourge: The Tasmanian Infantile Paralysis Epidemic 1937-1938*, Tasmanian Historical Research Association, 1995
Lang, John, *The Victorian Oarsman with a rowing register 1857-1919*, A H Massina, 1919
Laurence, L, *History of South Melbourne Football Club*, The Club, 1963
Lawler, Ray, *Summer of the Seventeenth Doll*, Angus and Robertson, 1957
Lehmann, Rudolph Chambers, *Rowing*, The Isthmian Library, 1898
Lehmann, Rudolph Chambers, *The Complete Oarsman*, Methuen and Co, 1908
Linnett, Ken, *Game for Anything: the Tommy Lahiff Story*, Allen and Unwin, 1999
Lomas, Graham, *The Will to Win: The Story of Sir Frank Beaurepaire*, Heinemann, 1960
Lovett, Michael, *AFL Record Season Guide 2011: The Official Statistical History of the AFL*, Slattery Media Group, 2011
Lovett, Michael, *AFL Record Season Guide 2012: The Official Statistical History of the AFL*, 2012
Lovett, Michael, *AFL Record Season Guide 2013: The Official Statistical History of the AFL*, 2013
Lovett, Michael, *AFL Record Season Guide 2014: The Official Statistical History of the AFL*, 2014
Lowenstein, Wendy and Tom Hills, *Under the Hook: Melbourne Waterside Workers Remember Working Lives and Class War: 1900-1980*, Melbourne Bookworkers, 1982
Main, Jim and David Allen, *Fallen - The Ultimate Heroes: Footballers Who Never Returned from War*, Crown Content, 2002
Main, Jim, *Australian Rules' 100 Greatest Players*, K G Murray Publishing, 2000

Main, Jim, *In the Blood: Celebrating the Red and White 1874-2009*, Bas Publishing, 2009
Main, Jim, *The Armchair Footy Record: For Planes, Trains and Favourite Rooms*, Geoff Slattery Publishing, 2005
Main, Jim, *Football's Black Book*, Five Mile Press, 1998
Main, Jim, *More Than a Century of AFL Grand Finals*, Pennon Publishing, 2001
Marmoy, Charles, *The French Protestant Hospital: Extracts from the archives of 'La Providence' relating to inmates and applicants for admission 1718-1957 and to recipients of and applicants for the Coqueau Charity 1745-1901* Volume I: Introduction; Entries A – K, Huguenot Society of London Quarto Series Vol LII, 1977
Marmoy, Charles (editor) *The Case Book of La Maison de Charite de Spittlefields 1739-41*, The Huguenot Society of London Quarto Series Vol. LV, 1981
McHale, Jock et al, *Our Australian Game of Football*, C G Hartley and Co, 1936
McKernan, Michael, *The Australian People and the Great War*, William Collins, 1984
McNamara, Dave, *Football*, Page and Bird, 1914
Melbourne Rates Book for 1870-1900, published by the Corporation of the City of Melbourne, 1989
Membrey, Brian and Northern Bullants Football Club, *Where We Come from 1903-2002*, 2 vols, Northern Bullants Football Club, 2002
Minyip and District Historical Society, *That's My Block – Minyip's Pioneers*, Minyip and District Historical Society, 1995
Mullen, C C, *History of Australian Rules Football 1858 to 1958*, Horticultural Press, 1958
Murray, John, *Our Great Game: The Photographic History of Australian Football*, Slattery Media Group, 2010
Nash, Robert (editor), *The Hidden Thread: Huguenot families in Australia*, The Huguenot Society of Australia, 2009
Nicholls, Stan, *HMAS Shropshire*, The Naval Historical Society of Australia, 1989
Palmer, Scot and Hobbs, Greg, *100 Great Marks*, Second Ed., Sun Books, 1975
Pascoe, Robert, *The Winter Game: The Complete History of Australian Football*, Text, 1995
Pennings, Mark, *Origins of Australian Football: Victoria's Early History, Volume I: Amateur heroes and the rise of clubs, 1858 to 1876*, Connor Court Publishing, 2012
Pennings, Mark, *Origins of Australian Football: Victoria's Early History, Volume 2: A golden era begins: Football in 'Marvellous Melbourne', 1877 to 1885*, Grumpy Monks Publishing, 2014
Pinchin, Ken and Allan Leeson, *A Century of Tasmanian Football 1879-1979*, Tasmanian Football League, 1979
Pinchin, Ken, *The Redlegs 1880-1980: A History of the City-South Football Club*, R K Pinchin, 1980
Plowman, Peter, *Australian Migrant Ships*, Rosenberg Publishing, 2006
Pollard, Jack, *High Mark: The Complete Book on Australian Football*, Second Edition, K G Murray, 1967
Power, Thomas P (compiler), *The Footballer: An annual record of football in Victoria,* Henriques and Co, 1875
Power, Thomas P (compiler), *The Footballer: An annual record of football in Victoria and the Australian colonies,* Henriques and Co, 1876
Power, Thomas P (compiler), *The Footballer: An annual record of football in Victoria and the Australian colonies,* R P Hurren, 1878
Power, Thomas P (compiler), *The Footballer: An annual record of football in Victoria,* R P Hurren, 1879
Priestley, Susan, *South Melbourne: A History*, Melbourne University Press, 1995
Robertson, Austin, *Ocker! The Fastest Man Alive*, Methuen, 1986
Rodgers, Stephen, *100 Years of AFL Players*, Three volumes, East-side Printing, 1996
Rodgers, Stephen, *Tooheys Guide to Every Game Ever Played: VFL Results 1897-1982*, Lloyd O'Neil, 1983
Roe, Jill, *Marvellous Melbourne: the emergence of an Australian city*, Hicks Smith and Sons, 1974
Sandercock, Leonie and Ian Turner, *Up Where, Cazaly? The Great Australian Game*, Granada, 1982
Sands and McDougall, *Melbourne and Suburban Directories*, 1865 and 1874
Serle, Geoffrey, *The Golden Age*, Melbourne University Press, 1963
Shade, Elizabeth, *The Cazaly Family in Australia and the family of William Little*, E Shade, 1993
Shade, Fred, *William Little of Ballarat: Some writings*, 2001
Sharland, 'Jumbo' (W S), *The Sporting Globe Football Book*, Herald and Weekly Times, 1930
Shaw, Robert, *Heart and Soul: A Tribute to the Game and its People*, Bas Publishing, 2004
Sheedy, Kevin and Warwick Hadfield, *The 500 Club: Footy's Greatest Coaches*, Herald Sun, News Custom Publishing, 2004
Slattery, Geoff (ed) and the Australian Football League, *The Australian Game of Football since 1858*, Geoff Slattery Publishing for the Australian Football League, 2008
Slattery, Geoff, *The Brownlow: A Tribute to the Greats of Australian Football*, Lothian, 2003
Smiles, Samuel, *Huguenots: their settlements, churches and industries in England and Ireland*, John Murray, 1889
Smith, Bernard, *Noel Counihan: Artist and Revolutionary*, Oxford University Press, 1993

REFERENCES

South Launceston Cricket Club, *100 Years of the South Launceston Cricket Club: 1909-2007*, Foot and Playstead, 1997

Spielvogel, Nathan, *A History of Ballarat, compiled for the Ballarat City Council*, Tulloch and King, 1935

Stacpoole, Henry James, *Gold at Ballarat: the Ballarat East goldfield; its discovery and development*, Lowden, 1971

Syme, Marten and Roebuck Society, *Shipping Arrivals and Departures, Victorian Ports vol 2 1846-1855*, Roebuck Society, 1987

St John, Joe, *AFL Premiers: The fascinating history of every AFL/VFL Grand Final*, New Holland, 2013

Stoward, John, *Australian Rules Football in Tasmania*, J Stoward, 2002

Stoward, John, *History of Football in the Western District*, J Stoward, 2008

Strange, AW, *Ballarat: A brief history*, Lowden, 1971

Stremski, Richard, *Kill for Collingwood*, Allen and Unwin, 1986

Tanner, John, *Tanner's Melbourne Directory for 1859*, 1859

Taylor, ECH, *100 Years of Football: The Story of the Melbourne Football Club 1858-1958*, Melbourne Football Club, 1957

Vlamplew, Wray and Brian Stoddart (eds), *Sport in Australia: A Social History*, Cambridge University Press, 1994

Wallish, Ned, *The Great Laurie Nash*, Ryan Publishing, 1998

Walsh, Janet and Ian Spalding, *Albert Park Primary School 1181 Centenary 1873-1973*, Ascot Press, 1973

Warner, Sir Frank, *The Silk Industry of the United Kingdom: Its Origin and Development*, Drane's, 1921

Wigglesworth, Neil, *A Social History of English Rowing*, Frank Cass and Co, 1992

Wilks, Trevor Owen, *A History of Kangaroo Valley - Lenah Valley 1847-1995*, T Wilks, 1995

Williams, Ron, Rick Smith and North Launceston Football Club, *The Robins, 1899-1990: A History of the North Launceston Football Club*, North Launceston Football Club, 1991

Wilmot, Chester, *Tobruk, 1941: Capture, Siege, Relief*, Angus and Robertson, 1944

Windle, John (compiler), *The Ballarat Directory 1869*, James Curtis, 1869

Wishart, Edward and Maura Wishart (contributors) et al, *Spa Country: Victoria's mineral springs*, Department of Sustainability and Environment in conjunction with the Victorian Mineral Water Committee, 2010

Withers, William Bramwell, *The History of Ballarat, from the First Pastoral Settlement to the Present Time*, Second ed., F W Niven and Co, 1887

Wise's Tasmanian Post Office Directories, H Wise and Co, 1933-1936 and 1947

Young, David, *Sporting Island: A History of Sport and Recreation in Tasmania*, Tasmanian Government, 2005

CHAPTERS, THESES, PAPERS AND JOURNAL ARTICLES

Balnave, Nikola, 'Company-Sponsored Recreation in Australia: 1890-1965' in *Labour History* No. 85, November 2003, pp. 129-51

Blair, Dale, 'The Greater Game: Australian Football and the Army in Melbourne and on the front during World War I', *Sporting Traditions*, Journal of the Australian Society for Sports History Vol. 11, no. 2, May 1995, pp. 91-102

Blair, Dale, 'War and Peace, 1915-1924' in Rob Hess and Bob Stewart, *More Than a Game: An Unauthorised History of Australian Rules Football*, Melbourne University Press, 1998, pp. 114-38

Bollard, Robert, PhD thesis, *'The Active Chorus': The Mass Strike of 1917 in Eastern Australia*, School of Social Sciences, Faculty of Arts, Education and Human Development, Victoria University, 2007. Available online at http://vuir.vu.edu.au/1472/1/bollard.pdf

Booth, Ross, 'History of Player Recruitment, Transfer and Payment Rules in the Victorian and Australian Football League', *Australian Society of Sports History Bulletin* no. 25, June 1997, pp. 13-23

Burke, Peter, PhD thesis, *'A Social History of Workplace Australian Football 1860-1939'*, School of Global Studies, Social Science and Planning Design and Social Context College, RMIT University, 2008. Available online at http://researchbank.rmit.edu.au/eserv/rmit:6624/Burke.pdf

Burke, Peter, 'Trades Football in Melbourne 1896-1909: From Middle Class Leisure to Working-Class Sport', *Sporting Traditions*, Journal of the Australian Society for Sports History vol. 19 no 1, November 2002, pp. 1-15

Conaty, Michael, Honours Thesis *"Up there, Cazaly" – the legend of Roy Cazaly'*, University of Sydney Department of History, 1996. Available online at http://hdl.handle.net/2123/2318

Counihan, Noel, 'Cazaly, Roy (1893-1963)', *Australian Dictionary of Biography*, National Centre of Biography, Australian National University. Available online at http://adb.anu.edu.au/biography/cazaly-roy-5541/text9441

Doggett, Anne, '"And for harmony most ardently we long": Musical life in Ballarat, 1851-1871' Volume Two, School of Behavioural and Social Sciences and Humanities, University of Ballarat, March 2006
Doggett, Anne, 'Beyond Gentility: Women and music in early Ballarat', *History Australia*, Vol. 6. No. 2, 2009, pp. 37.1-37.17
Doggett, Anne, 'Harmony on the Goldfields: Music and identity in multicultural Ballarat', *Victorian Historical Journal* Vol. 75 No. 1, April 2004, pp. 49-69
Fisher, Chay and Christopher Kent, 'Two depressions, one banking collapse', *Research Discussion Paper 1999-06*, System Stability Department, Reserve Bank of Australia, 1999
Gandy, Michael (editor), *Huguenot Families* Numbers 1-10, Huguenot Society of Great Britain and Ireland, Huguenot Library, September 1999–March 2004
Gwynn, Robert, 'England's First Refugees', *History Today*, Vol 35 Number 5, May 1985, pp. 22-28
Johnston, Robert, 'Roy Cazaly' in Ann Atkinson (general editor), *Footnote People in Australian History*, Fairfax Library, 1987
Kinloch, Helen W, 'Ballarat and its Benevolent Asylum: A Nineteenth-Century Model of Christian Duty, Civic Progress and Social Reform', University of Ballarat, 2004
McMullin, Ross, 'The 1915 Grand Final: Love, War and Football', *2013 AFL Grand Final Record*, pp. 147-151
Moore, Bruce, 'Military Slang' in Peter Dennis et al, *The Oxford Companion to Australian Military History*, Second edition, 2009. Available online at http://www.oxfordreference.com.ezproxy.slq.qld.gov.au/view/10.1093/acref/9780195517842.001.0001/acref-9780195517842-e-781
Morgan, David, PhD Thesis, *'Labour and Industrial Authority: Social and Industrial Relations in the Australian Stevedoring Industry 1800-1935'*, Department of Government, University of Queensland, 1997
Murdoch, Tessa, 'The Quiet Conquest', *History Today*, Vol 35 Number 5, May 1985, pp. 29-33
Nash, Robert, 'Some Huguenot Families in Nineteenth Century New South Wales', *Descent*, 2000, pp. 193-96
Nash, Robert, 'Up There, Cazaly!' Some Famous Huguenot Descendants in Australia', *Huguenot Families* Number Three, Huguenot Society of Great Britain and Ireland, Huguenot Library, August 2000, pp. 15-17
Pascoe, Robert and Mark Pennings, 'Watching Football in Marvellous Melbourne: Spectators, barrackers and working class rituals', *Sporting Traditions*, vol 28, no 1, Australian Society for Sports History, May 2011, pp. 1-20
Peck, Linda Levy, 'Creating a Silk Industry in Seventeenth-Century England', *Shakespeare Studies* Number 28, 2000, pp. 225-28
Richardson, Nick, 'Melbourne's Sporting Globe and Football in the 1920s', *Sporting Traditions* vol 29, no 1, Journal of the Australian Society for Sports History, May 2012
Ruddell, Trevor, 'The evolution of the rules of football from 1872 to 1877', *The Yorker*, Issue 41, Autumn 2010
Towns, Deborah, 'May Cox: Leading Swimming and Lifesaving Advocate and Patriotic Fundraiser, 1910-1938' in *Seizing the Initiative: Australian Women Leaders in Politics, Workplaces and Communities*, eScholarship Research Centre, University of Melbourne, 2012, pp. 198-210
Turnbull, Graeme, 'A History of the Wimmera Football League', in the *Wimmera Grand Final Footballer*, September 1992.
Ziino, Bart, 'Enlistment and Non-enlistment in Wartime Australia: Responses to the 1916 Call to Arms Appeal', *Australian Historical Studies*, 41, 2010, pp. 217-32

ARCHIVAL AND UNPUBLISHED SOURCES

Anonymous, *Albert Park State School Great War Honour Book*, Albert Park State School, 1919
Anonymous, *Football Pantomime Program, South Melbourne Cricket Ground, 15 August 1914*, Australian Football League Library
Anonymous, *Melbourne Annual Regatta Program, Saltwater River, 21 March 1873*, Rare Books Collection, State Library of Victoria
Anonymous, *Old Buffers Carnival, Souvenir program of Old Buffers season 1924, Middle Park*, State Library of Victoria
Ballarat Petitions 1860-1866, CD-ROM, transcribed and published by the Ballarat and District Genealogical Society, 2007
The Bertha Walker papers, SLV MS 10772, La Trobe Australian Manuscripts Collection, State Library of Victoria
Hawthorn Football Club Minutes 1941-43, Hawthorn Football Club, Waverley
Hewitt, Joffre, *The Life and Times of Joffre Hewitt*, Self published, Rupanyup, 1998

REFERENCES

The Jack Donnelly Collection, Queen Victoria Museum and Art Gallery, Launceston
The Johns and Waygood collection, AU NBAC 33, The Noel Butlin Archives Centre, Australian National University
Noel Counihan Papers, Australian Dictionary of Biography project, Australian National University
Papers of Noel Counihan (1913-1986) Series 2: Business correspondence and papers, 1940s-1987, Folder 7: Notes and correspondence relating to Counihan's entry on Roy Cazaly for the *Australian Dictionary of Biography*, MS 9107, National Library of Australia
South Melbourne Cricket Club Annual Reports and Balance Sheets for 1921-22, 1924-25 and 1925-26, Australian Football League Library
South Melbourne Football Club Annual Reports and Balance Sheets for 1922, 1923, 1925, 1926, 1927, 1928, 1937 and 1938, Australian Football League Library
South Melbourne Football Club Minutes Book 1921-24, in the possession of the Sydney Swans Football Club, Sydney
South Melbourne Wednesday Football Club Minutes 1907-09, La Trobe Australian Manuscripts Collection, State Library of Victoria
St Kilda Football Club Minute Books 1908-1916, in private hands
Victorian Football League Register of Players 1909-23, Australian Football League Library
Victorian Football League Team Lists 1908-19 and *1920-29*, Australian Football League Library
Wells, Samuel, *Camera Ready Caricatures*, Pictures Collection, State Library of Victoria

SPORTING NEWSPAPERS AND JOURNALS

Football Sporting Herald (Hobart), Footballer (Vic), Monotone Sporting Record (Hobart), Northern Football Record (Launceston), Record (VFL), Recorder (VFA), Referee (NSW), Sport (Vic), Sport and Playgoer (Vic), Sporting Globe (Vic), Sporting Judge (Vic), Sportsman (Vic), Tasmanian Football Record, Victorian Football Follower, Voice (Hobart), Winner (Vic).

NEWSPAPERS

MELBOURNE METROPOLITAN
Age, Argus, Australasian, Australasian Sketcher, Herald, Herald Sun, Illustrated Australian News, Punch, Sun, Sun News Pictorial, Table Talk, Truth.
MELBOURNE SUBURBAN
Brunswick and Coburg Leader, Brunswick and Coburg Star, Coburg Leader, Hawthorn Standard, Leader, Malvern Standard, Northcote Leader, North Melbourne Advertiser, Port Melbourne Standard, Prahran Chronicle, Prahran Telegraph, Preston Leader, Richmond, Hawthorn and Camberwell Chronicle, South Melbourne Record.
VICTORIAN REGIONAL
Ballarat Star, Birchip Advertiser, Dimboola Chronicle, Donald Times, Dunmunkle Standard, Geelong Advertiser, Horsham Times, Minyip Guardian, Nhill Free Press, Rupanyup Spectator, Star (Ballarat), Warracknabeal Herald, Weekly Times.
TASMANIA
Advocate, Daily Telegraph, Examiner, Illustrated Tasmanian Mail, Mercury, Saturday Evening Express, Saturday Evening Mercury, Weekly Courier.
SOUTH AUSTRALIA
Advertiser, News
WESTERN AUSTRALIA
Daily News, West Australian
UNITED KINGDOM
Daily News, Era, Morning Chronicle, Morning Post, Standard, Times.

WEBSITES

Albert Park Primary School [http://www.albertparkps.vic.edu.au/about-apps/history]
Ancestry [www.ancestry.com]
Australian Bureau of Statistics census figures [http://abs.gov.au/websitedbs/censushome.nsf/home/Census?opendocument#from-banner=GT]
Australian Dictionary of Biography [http://adb.anu.edu.au]
Australian Football [www.australianfootball.com]
Australian Football League [http://www.afl.com.au/]
Australian Rowing History [http://www.rowinghistory-aus.info/]
Australian Rules Football Cards [http://members.optusnet.com.au/~dgreen2/]
Australian War Memorial [http://www.awm.gov.au/]
Australians at War Film Archive [http://www.australiansatwarfilmarchive.gov.au/aawfa/search.aspx]
Ballarat and District Genealogical Society [www.ballaratgenealogy.org.au]
Ballarat Historical Society [www.ballarathistoricalsociety.com]
Cazaly family tree compiled by Libby Shade [http://www.shade.id.au/cazaly/Cazaly.htm]
Charles Boyles Photographs [http://www.boylesfootballphotos.net.au/tiki-index.php]
eMelbourne Encyclopedia [http://www.emelbourne.net.au/home.html]
Kevin Taylor's Footystats [http://footystats.freeservers.com/Daily/Diary.html#Footystats]
The French Hospital [http://www.frenchhospital.org.uk/]
The German Library of Huguenot history [http://www.bfhg.de/]
The Gold Museum, Ballarat [http://www.goldmuseum.com.au/]
The Huguenots of Spitalfields [http://www.huguenotsofspitalfields.org/]
The Huguenot Society of Australia [http://www.huguenotsaustralia.org.au/]
The Huguenot Society of Great Britain and Ireland [http://www.huguenotsociety.org.uk/]
National Archives, United Kingdom [http://www.nationalarchives.gov.uk]
Old Bailey Proceedings Online [www.oldbaileyonline.org]
Public Record Office of Victoria [www.prov.vic.gov.au]
River and Rowing Museum, Henley on Thames [http://rrm.co.uk/]
Sommieres history [http://www.sommieresetsonhistoire.org/SSH/]
Tasmanian Archive and Heritage Office [http://portal.archives.tas.gov.au/menu.aspx?search=9]
Victorian Government Gazette [http://gazette.slv.vic.gov.au/]
Victorian Year Books [http://www.abs.gov.au/AUSSTATS/abs.nsf/second+level+view?ReadForm&prodno=1301.2&viewtitle=Victorian%20Year%20Book%20%28Soft%20cover%29-1998~Previous~05/03/1998&&tabname=Past%20Future%20Issues&prodno=1301.2&issue=1998&num=&view=&]

INDEX

NUMBERS IN ITALICS REFER TO ILLUSTRATIONS

A

Adamson, Lawrence 'Dickie' 39, 62
Adelaide 96, 101, 125, 126, 142, 236
Aiken, Charlie 233
Air Force Football Club (WFL).................. 150
Albert Park 29, 33, 34, 49, 78
Albert Park Football Club (VFA) 34
Albert Park Lake 33, 34, 40, 47, 50, 57, 277
Albert Park State School...36-38, 40, 59, 63, 68, 69, 71
Albert Park (suburb)..29, 30, 33, 73, 86, 93, 100, 106, 144, 255
Albert Park Swimming and Lifesaving Club. 33
Albion Rowing Club 15-16
Albiston, Alec 198, 201
Albury 99
Alexander, Harry 108
Allison, Bobby 108, 110
Angwin, Andy 196, 203
Atkins, Les 139
Atkins, Noel 139, 238
Austen, Bob 197
Australian Football Hall of Fame 254, 255, 269-71, 272-73
Australian National Football Carnivals
    1921 (Perth)...............................89, 110, 125
    1924 (Hobart) 110-112, 125
    1927 (Melbourne)................................. 129
    1930 (Adelaide) 142
    1947 (Hobart) 218-19
    1950 (Brisbane) 236
    1953 (Adelaide) 236
    1956 (Perth) 239
Avery, Bert.. 144

B

Baird, Des.. 53
Ballarat 17-23, 25, 26, 54, 63, 327
Ballarat Football League............................... 63
Barassi, Ron.. 247
Baker, Sidney.. 260
Barker, Jack... 205
Barker, Syd.. 131
Barlow, Arthur.. 126
Bartlett, Kevin 262, 269
Barwick, Bill.. 248
Barwick, Stan 226, 229
Beard, Bert 'Blue' 170
Beasy, Maurie 113
Beaurepaire, Frank................................. 37, 37, 39
Beckton, Norm 109, 113, 264, 265
Beitzel, Harry 273
Bence, Roy.. 183
Bennett, Chris 153
Bennett, George 197
Bentley, Percy...................................... 85-86, 264
Berry, Reg..71, 74
Bertram, Hans 'Ossie'.................................. 170
Best, Heinrich 'Harry'................... 66, 157, 164
Beverley Football Club (MAFA).................. 50

| 391 |

Birchip Football Club (NWDFA)........118, 119
Bisset, Jack..............................166, 169, 172, 176
Bohan, Jim..197, 205
Boschen, Herb 'Choc'.................................. 116
Bowe, Johnny... 170
Bowman, Gordon 237
Boyle and Scott Association 40
Bradman, Don 249
Brady, Mike 262-4, 265, 270, 280
Brain, Roy...224, 227
Brain, Terry.. 186
Bratt, Don 214, 222
Brooks, Hec 135, 140
Brown, Alf 268, 327
Brownlow Medal..................112, 153, 166, 170, 178, 247, 260, 261, 262, 267, 268, 281
Brunswick..55, 58
Brunswick Football Club (VFA)........... 43, 107, 178, 194
Bryce, George 179, *179*
Bryce, Margie 221
Buckingham Football Club (SSOBA).........226, 229, 231, 234
Buckney, Hilton.. 161
Bunton, Haydn 166, 169, 247, 270, 271
Burgess, Mavis née De Lacy......................... 255
Burke, Jack... 196
Burns, Peter 34, *34*, 83, 271
Burrows, Lyall.......................135, 138, 141, 142

C

Caldwell, Jim 81
Calvary Hospital............................ 214, 248, 249
Camberwell .... 185 - 187
Camberwell Football Club (VFA)........ 178, 181, 185-190, 195, 196, 197, 257, 278, 328
Camberwell Football Club (VJFA) 67
Cameron, Ailsa... 135
Cameron, Bob 147
Cameron, Hugh.. 135
Cananore Football Club (TFL)... 153, 154, 155, 156, 159, 161, 162, 163, 166, 223
Carbarns, Les.. 189
Cardosi, Adam.......................................272-73
Carlton 27, 28, 86, 241
Carlton District Football Club (MAFA)....... 50
Carlton Football Club (VFA)......................... 34
Carlton Football Club (VFL) 9, 10, 37, 43, 44, 45-46, 50, 52, 56, 65, 67, 80, 81,
82, 83, 84, 95, 97, 101, 106, 113, 128, 146, 172, 175, 176, 182, 199, 204, 237, 247, 257, 265, 273
Carmody, Jack......................................196, 201
Cazaly Awards.......................251, 260-262, 281
Cazaly, Agnes 'Aggie' (wife)...........54-55, 57, 58, 67, 68, 106, 116, 119, 121, 123, 134, 135, 138, 162, 163, 187, 207, 208, 214, 215, 216, 218, 221, 222, 243, 244, 245, 249, 251, 254, 255, 262, 277, 279, 328
Cazaly, Agnes Dorien 'Dorrie' (daughter)......68, 116, 122, 161, 187, 196, 211, 221, 254
Cazaly, Albert 'George' (brother) 28, 35, 36, 39, 61, 71, 73, 175
Cazaly, Brett (grandson) 252, 253
Cazaly, Carl (grandson) 252, 253
Cazaly, Catherine 'Kate' (aunt) 15, 17, 19
Cazaly, Charles (uncle)........................ 15, 16, 17
Cazaly, Charlotte (aunt) 15, 17
Cazaly, Daniel (brother) 28, 35
Cazaly, Dorothy 'Dorrie' (daughter)..... 116, 122, 187, 196, 215, 216
Cazaly, Edgar (brother) 29, 47, 72
Cazaly, Eleanor 'Lena' Isabel (daughter)..........106, 116, 122, 161, 187, 196, 211, 254
Cazaly, Elizabeth née Eagles (grandmother) 14, 16, 17, 18, 19
Cazaly, Elizabeth Jemima née McNee (mother) 27, 28, 29, 30, 72, 73, 127-8, 272
Cazaly, Elizabeth 'Bessie' Florence (daughter)... 58, 67, 277
Cazaly, Elizabeth 'Bessy' (aunt) 17, 19-20, 29
Cazaly, Ernest (brother)28, 33, 42-43, 74-75, 91
Cazaly, Florence (sister)...................... 28, 32, 73
Cazaly, Foy 'John' (uncle) .. 15, 16, 17, 19, 21, 23, 25, 27, 28-29, 30
Cazaly, Geraldine née Belz (daughter-in-law) .. 245-6, 252
Cazaly, Henry (uncle)..............15, 17, 18, 19, 20
Cazaly, James Charles (father) 15, 16, 17, 19-30, 32, 35, 36, 40, 57, 71-72, 272, 327
Cazaly, James William (brother)...............28, 35
Cazaly, Jaques 'James' (grandfather) 13-16
Cazaly, Jean Pierre (great grandfather) 13
Cazaly, Joan Olive (daughter)...... 106, 161, 162, 187, 211, 216, 221, 240-1, 250, 254
Cazaly, Kathleen née Brady (daughter-in-law) 183, 184, 196, 213, 244
Cazaly, Lenore 'Lena' (sister) 28, 32, 36, 39, 243
Cazaly, Louis (cousin).................................... 29

INDEX

Cazaly, Marguerette
(great great grandmother) 12-13, 16
Cazaly, Owen (uncle) 15, 16, 17, 19, 20, 21, 22-23
Cazaly, Patricia Lilian 'Pat' (daughter)... 32, 106, 140, 157, 161, 162, 174, 187, 203, 207, 211, 214, 215, 216, 248, 254, 328
Cazaly, Peter (uncle) 15, 16, 17, 19, 20, 21, 22, 23, 25, 26, 29
Cazaly, Peter (grandson) 213, 214, 215
Cazaly, Rick (grandson) 213, 214, 244, 246, 248, 252, 253-4
Cazaly, Roy
   Birth 30
   Blackboard lectures 157, 179, 182, 198, 280
   Brownlow Medal votes 112, 127
   Captaincy methods 76, 96, 111
   Career longevity 129, 130, 189, 278
   Character 276-77
   Charity matches 63, 162, 173, 183, 233, 234, 235, 245, 278
   Club Best and Fairest awards 71-72, 90, 127, *127*, 278
   Coaching and training methods 96, 135, 137, 147, 148, 154, 161, 163, 167, 171, 174, 175, 179, 181-82, 183, 188, 189, 193, 195-96, 198-99, 202, 205, 224-25, 226-28, 231, 238-39, 248, 278-79
   Coaching salaries 99, 115, 122, 134, 139, 145-46, 151-52, 158, 193, 193, 223
   Cricket 32, 37-38, 39, 68, 70, 73, 75, 80. 91, 120, 121, 127, 134, 141, 144, 151, 156, 160, 176, 276
   Decline and death 248-50, 280
   Diet and fitness theories 41, 66, 84-85, 129-30, 180, 213-14, 221, 278
   Education 36-39
   Employment 39, 54, 60, 66, 73, 107, 115, 120-21, 122-23, 166, 175, 181, 198, 325-326
   Final VFA game 189
   Final VFL game 130
   First VFL game 45-46
   Goalkicking skills 46, 50, 53, 90, 95, 97, 102, 112, 127, 128, 129, 130, 138, 143, 147, 149, 154, 163, 173
   Greyhound training 167-68, 169, 187-88, 208-09
   Halls of Fame 256, 259, 268, 269-70
   Herald Best Follower award 90
   Homes 30, 35, 36, 55, 58, 73, 106, 116, 140, 144, 157, 174, 187, 207
   Horse training 10, 207, 209, 214, 215, 216, 235-36, 240-41, 275, 279, 280
   Injuries and illnesses ... 32, 50, 56, 65, 66, 74, 81-82, 94, 101, 102, 109, 118, 120, 125, 126, 128, 129, 130, 132, 148, 161, 163, 164, 199-200, 248
   Junior football 40-41, 80
   Kicking skills 32, 65, 95, 97, 108, 112, 116, 118, 128, 138, 164, 173, 174, 215, 224, 248, 277
   Left-handedness and stuttering ... 38, 276-77
   Love of animals 32-33, 209, 216, 236, 280
   Marking skills 46, 51, 82, 84-85, 87, 95, 97, 109, 110, 112, 118, 124, 130, 138, 154, 164, 173, 248, 277, 325
   Marriage to Aggie 55
   Massage and physiotherapy techniques ... 10, 66, 157, 160, 174, 188, 217-222, 235, 245-46, 255, 278
   Match payments 47-49, 78, 99-100
   Multicultural Team of Champions 272
   Pianist 139, 148, 215-16
   Poliomyelitis treatments 220-21
   Political candidate 229-30, 277, 279-80
   Religion and morality 215, 232, 243, 279
   Reports and cautions. 56, 101-104, 138, 155, 158, 165
   Rowing 40, 41, 47, 50, 57, 60, 100, 325
   Ruck and following skills 41, 46, 50, 51-52, 63, 70-71, 74, 77, 85, 86-88, 90, 94-95, 97-98, 107-08, 109, 110, 113, 119, 125, 127, 129, 138, 147, 148, 154, 159, 161, 163, 165, 167, 182, 183, 189, 233, 267, 272, 325
   Schoolboy football 37, 38, *38*
   Sporting Globe Best Footballer awards *97*, 97-98, 105, 113
   Support for rule changes .. 74, 177-78, 195-96
   Swimming 36, 86
   Tasmanian representative teams 142, 154, 163, 164, 236-39
   Teams of the Century 255-56, 258, 259
   Training methods 32, 49, 84, 125, 278
   United Kingdom cruise 243-44, 328-29
   Victorian representative teams 89, 95-96, 101, 110-112, 125-26, 254
Cazaly jnr, Roy Lionel (son) 73, 116, 122, 157, 161, 166, 183, 184, 187, 211-13, 215, 216, 217, 222, 223, 224, 226, 244, 245-46, 248, 252, 253, 328

Cazaly, Stephen (grandson) 213, 216, 222
Cazaly, Syd (nephew) 257
Cazaly, Sydney (brother)............... 28, 35, 55, 72
Cazaly, Teyana (grand daughter).................. 252
Cazaly, William 'Harry' (brother) 28, 35
Cazaly, Zena (grand daughter) 252
Chadwick, Bert.................................... 96, 112
Challis, George................................ 10, 52, 67
Chick, John.. 233
City Football Club (NTFA) ... 134-43, 146, 150, 155, 156, 158, 189, 257-58, 277
Clarence Football Club (TFL) 223
Clark, John 242-43
Cleary, Jim 174, *174*
Clennett, Mike 239
Clover, Horrie................... 84, 97, 113, 247, 271
Coburg Football Club (VFA) 146, 148, 178, 186, 190
Coleman, John..261, 270
Collier, Albert 'Leeter' 153, 154, 155, 271
Collier, Henry.. 271
Collingwood 33
Collingwood Football Club (VFA) 34
Collingwood Football Club (VFL) ... 46, 52, 53, 66, 67, 71, 75, 76, 82, 83, 87, 94, 96, 100, 107, 124, 126, 127, 140, 141, 146, 153, 172, 178, 195, 199, 204, 262, 263, 267, 270
Collins, Adrian 225
Collins, Goldsmith 'Goldie'.................... 104, 113
Condon, Bill 173
Connell, Jock 140, 141
Cooper, Jack 54
Cope Cope Football Club (NWDFA) 118
Cosgrove, Premier Robert 229, 230, 241
Counihan, John 94
Counihan, Noel 94, 230, 275-76, 279, 328
Coventry, Gordon................................267, 271
Coventry, Syd 127, 267, 268, 271
Cox, May 36
Crofts, Archie................ 170, 171, 172, 176, 179
Crowl, Claude... 73
Cubbins, Bill.......................... 73, 76, 95-96, 154
Cullen, Reg.. 140
Culpitt, Wally 196, 204, 205
Cumberland, Harry 'Vic' *51*, 51-2, 71, 76, 85, 268, 271
Curran, Frank 196
Curtin, Prime Minister John 194
Curtis, Eric 'Slim'... 212
Cuthbertson, Robert..................................... 93

D

Daly, Harold 196
Dangerfield, Gordon 74
Davie, Harry.................................. 146, *146*, 149
Davies, Emily 183
Daylesford 66
De Lacy, Dennis 255
De Lacy, Hector 'Hec'...........147, 148, 170, 173, 182-83, 187, 195, 206, 235, 236, 255, 267-68, 326
Dempsey, Gary 262, 271
Depression (1890s) 29-30, 34
Depression (1930s) 139, 145, 152, 170, 175, 220, 280
Dewar, Hayden 265
Dial, Billy 116
Dibbs, Charlie 146
Dickens, Charles.. 16
Dickenson, Keith 223, 236, 331
Diggins, Brighton.................170, 172, 176, 182
Dilger, Harold.....................................139, 328
Dimboola Football Club (WDFL) 114, 116, 118
Diphtheria 67, 277
Doherty, Jock.. 77
Donald Football Club (NWDFA) 118, 119
Donnelly, Jack... 327
Dooley, Pat 77
Dowling, Frank 'Dicky'................. 147, *147*, 149
Doxat, John... 14
Drew, Dr Joseph Harold D'Amer............93, 124
Drew, Dr Joseph Milton D'Amer.... 93, 94, 104, 124, 128
Duncan, Alex.. 113
Dunlop Rubber Company....... 36, 39, 60, 61, 68, 70, 73, 183, 326
Dunn, Charlie 153
Dunn, Jack.. 137, 138, 164
Dyer, Jack 131, 202, 234, 245, 262, 270, 271

E

Eason, Alex.. 267
Edwards, Burnell 'Sugar'......................153, 155
Eicke, Wellesley 'Wels'................. 63, 76, 82, 98
Elliott, Fred 'Pompey' *45*, *45*
Elmore vs Colbinabbin 'ring in' game 77
Elms, Henry 'Sonny'................................*34*, *34*
Emerald Hill (South Melbourne).............34, 92

Essendon Football Club (VFA).......... 34, 35, 51
Essendon Football Club (VFL)....46, 52, 56, 70, 82, 83, 84, 88, 95, 96, 104, 109, 112, 126, 129, 131, 204, 264, 265, 267, 268, 271
Eureka uprising 18, 19

F

Farmer, Graham 'Polly'................................. 270
Faul, Bill 170, *170*
Fehring, Arthur 77
Felmingham, Stan 153
Feltscheer, Ken 201, 202
Ferguson, Ted 165, 166
Ferrall, Raymond 137
Fire Brigade Football Club (WFL)..... 131, 150, 151
Fitzroy 28, 33, 37
Fitzroy Football Club (VFA) 34
Fitzroy Football Club (VFL)........37, 48, 51, 52, 53-54, 67, 70, 75, 84, 104, 109, 113, 116, 129, 146, 158, 166, 169, 183-84, 199
Flanagan, Arch 137-38, 166, 328
Fleiter, Emil.. 37
Fleiter, Fred 'Skeeter' ...86, 87, 88, *88*, 89, 90, 92, 94, 109, 173, 179, 245, 247, 254, 255, 267
Fleiter, Iola née Lockwood.......................... 254
Flint, Gerry 233
Footscray 24
Footscray Football Club (VFA) 34, 59, 113, 141
Footscray Football Club (VFL)... 113, 128, 145, 158, 160, 176, 179, 184, 194, 241, 248
Fothergill, Des.. 178
Fox, Bill 227, 228, 229, 232, 233, 234, 235
Freake, Jim.. 84
Freeman, Ted 165
Fyle, Les 223

G

Garwood, Rex........................231, 233, 234, 239
Geelong 21, 25, 108, 121
Geelong Football Club (VFA) 34
Geelong Football Club (VFL) 43, 52, 56, 68, 75, 82, 96, 101, 108, 112, 130, 181, 183, 194, 195, 201, 262, 267
Glenferrie Oval 196, 197, 201, 256
Glenorchy District Football Club........ 233, 235, 258-59

Goggins, Alby... 153
Goodluck, Len 164
Gorringe, Horrie 110, 164, 247
Graham, Jack................................ 179, 181, *181*
Grant, Trevor 271
Greeves, Edward 'Carji'......................112, 271
Gregory, Mackenzie 'Mac'....................212, 213
Grenda, Bernard 'Mannie'....................135, 138
Guillaux, Maurice *8*, 9-10
Guy, Mary 220-21
Gympie.. 22-23

H

Hacker, Jack..179, *179*
Haines, George... 95
Hammond, Joe 129
Hando, Arthur.............. 107, 108-09, 131, 132
Hansen, Brian................................... 260-61, 262
Harley, Harry... 186
Harris, Dick... 51
Harris, Ron 196
Harris, Wilbur 170, 174, *174*
Harrison, Arthur... 54
Harrison, Edie (Aggie's niece) 187-88
Hart, Aubrey... 56
Hartnett, Frank... 186
Hartnett, Pat.. 155
Hawkes, Bill 155
Hawthorn Football Club (MAFA)................ 50
Hawthorn Football Club (VFA) 77, 99, 113, 192
Hawthorn Football Club (VFL)   113, 145, 146, 175, 186, 189, 190, 191-206, 207, 248, 254, 256, 276
Healy, Gerard 271
Heifner, Fred 'Fritz'..................................... 166
Hemingway, Dick... 199
Henderson, Reg 'Hawk Eye'.................186, 189
Hendrie, Gil 186
Hetherington, John..................................... 210
Hewitt, Joffre 116, 328
Hillard, Norm 186
Hillis, Ron 176
Hird, James 271
Hiskins, Rupe 97
Hitchens, Herb.. 165
HMAS Shropshire............................. 211-13, 253

Hobart..... 25, 136, 139, 140, 153, 157, 163, 165, 166, 167, 170, 207, 211, 213, 217, 222, 235, 238, 243, 251, 252, 275
Hobart Football Club (TFL) 223, 224, 227, 228, 229, 232, 234
Hobbs, Greg 265, 268
Hocking, Vic 193, 197, 199, 203, 204
Hodgson, Arthur 237, *237*
Hogan, Joe 44
Hogarth, William 12
Holmes, Lou 73
Holmesby, Russell 328
Hopkins, Ted 273-74
Horkings, Reg 186, 197
Horsham 114, 117, 119, 119, 121, 129, 257
Hudson, Peter 269
Huggard, Frank *102*, 102-04, 138
Hughes, Prime Minister William 'Billy' 68
Hughson, Les 146, *146*, 151
Huguenots 11-14, 325
Humphries, Barry 185-86
Humphries, Reg 179, *179*
Hynes, 'Tammy' 96

I

Iles, Bert 135, 140
Influenza (see also Spanish Influenza)..... 54, 56, 75, 81, 129, 199
Ingpen, Robert 265
Inskip, George 62
Ion, Fred 'Fat' 89

J

James, Gerald 161
James, Jack 71, 74, 75, 85, 183
Jesaulenko, Alex 272
JK Smith Competition 40
Johns and Waygood 175, 176, 181, 198, 230, 326
Johnson, Robert 125
Johnson, Ted 101, 104, 108, 112, 113, 126
Johnson, Vic 153
Johnston, Russ 155
Jona, Dr Jacob 192-93, 194
Joolen, Stan 'Snowy' 140, 141, 142, 143, 150, 166, 169
Jorgensen, 'Barney' 197

Jory, Percy 76
Junction Oval 9, 10, 34, 75, 234, 255

K

Katamatite 57
Kelly, Bill 224, 229
Kelly, Brian 228, 229
Kelly, Paul 271
Kelynack, Tom 82
Kennedy, John snr 256
Kenny, Sister Elizabeth 220, 275
Kew Asylum for the Insane 47
Killingsworth, Frank 92, 94
King, Jack 205

L

Lahiff, Tommy 197, 202, 205
Laidlaw, Private Wally 68-69
Lake Oval 34, 104, 107, 108, 109, 120, 254, 256
Langford, Jim 165
Languedoc, France 12
Latchford, Albert 94
Launceston 134, 135, 136, 137, 138, 139, 140, 146, 153
Launceston Football Club (NTFA)..... 140, 143, 166, 227, 238
Lawler, Ray 241-42, 263, 281, 332
Lee, Clarrie 141
Lee, Walter 'Dick' 83, 96, 154, 268, 271
Leedham, John 239
Lefroy Football Club (TFL). 135, 143, 153, 154, 161, 162, 165, 166, 167, 223
Lehmann, Rudy 130
Leitch, Allan 142, 143, 164
Lenah Valley 207-09, 211, 213-16, 235, 240, 280
Leonard, Johnny 170
Leopold Football Club (MAFA).. 35, 42, 43, 50, 93, 101, 140
Leslie, Su 325
Lever, Harry 44, 46, 51, 55, 70, 183
Lewis, Norm 146
Lincoln, President Abraham 77
Lindrum, Walter 174
Litchfield-Carron Football Club (NWDFA) 118-19

INDEX

Little Collins Street 26, 27, *27*, 28
Little, William 19
London 12-16, 17, 20, 26, 196, 210, 242, 244
Long, Geoff 237, 238, 239
Longford Football Club (NTFA) . 138, 140, 232
Loring, Harold 224, 226, 228, 233
Lowrie, Bill 73

M

MacDonald, Donald 82
Madden, Bill 73
Main, Jim 268, 272, 328
Marshall, Jack 'Twister' 93, 109, 124, 157, 277, 289
Master Barry 240-41
Mathieson, Jack 196
Matson, Phil 111, 112
Matthews, Herbie *170*, 171, 178, 179, 181, 182
Matthews, Leigh 262, 269, 270
McBrien, 'Likely' 93, 128, 150
McCumisky, Phil 120
McDiarmid, Jack 'Fat' 110, 111, 126
McEacharn, Alex 147
McGregor, Rod 199
McGuire, Eddie 270
McHale, Jock 272
McKenzie, Kenny 48-49
McKenzie, Stan 10
McMurray, Jack jnr 249
McNamara, Dave 48, *48*, 51, 55, 56, 71, 183, 256, 271
McSwain, Charlie 265
Meeske, Billy 93, 124
Melbourne 17, 19, 21, 22, 23, 24-30, 33, 35, 36, 37, 39, 42, 49, 50, 55, 62, 66, 69, 71, 74, 81, 92, 113, 114, 115, 117, 121, 122, 129, 134, 135, 140, 144, 145, 152, 158, 160, 162, 163, 169, 176, 177, 185, 192, 208, 211, 219, 234, 242, 243, 244, 245, 255, 256, 260, 261, 264, 280, 325, 326, 327
Melbourne Cricket Ground 53, 121, 125, 132, 265
Melbourne Football Club (VFA) 34
Melbourne Football Club (VFL) 44, 45, 48, 51, 59, 70, 73, 75, 87, 95, 96, 100, 112, 125, 126, 144, 146, 151, 175, 179, 186, 194, 195, 201, 237, 247
Melbourne Hospital 55, 66, 72
Menzies, Robert 186
Metropolitan Amateur Football Association (MAFA) 39, 42, 50, 150
Metropolitan Junior Football Association (MJFA) 35, 40
Middle Park 35, 36, 93, 174, 196, 254
Middle Park Cricket Club (VJCA) 70
Middle Park junior football clubs 93
Middle Park Wesleys Football Club (PCA) 40-41, 45, 46
Millard, Percy 173
Mills, Bert 193, 197
Mines United Football Club (QFA) 156-57
Minogue, Dan 66, 164
Minyip Football Club (WDFL) 114-18, 119-120, 122, 123, 129, 135, 166, 257, 276, 278
Mohr, Bill 256
Moir, Laurie 237
Moir, Les 143
Monohan, Jack 146, 149
Moore, George 19-20
Moore, Roy 175-76, *176*, 179
Morris, Brian 261
Morrissey, George 43, 53, 55
Moss, Graham 262, 268
Mullally, Dick 179
Mullen, Cec 268
Murtha, Delia (Aggie's mother) 54-55
Murtha, Patrick (Aggie's father) 54-55
Murtoa 114, 116, 257

N

Nash, Alex 199
Nash, Laurie 141, 142, 170, *170*, 172, 173, 176, 178, 181, 186, 188, 189, 190, 230, 247, 249, 255, 267, 268, 269, 271
Nash, Robert 142, 143, 148
Nelson Rovers Football Club (JK Smith Competition) 40
New Guinea 196, 199, 210, 211
Newman, John 'Sam' 261-62
New Norfolk 230, 240
New Norfolk Football Club (TFL) 219, 223, 224, 225, 233
Newton, Bert 261
New Town 221, 249
New Town Football Club (TFL) . 153, 154, 159, 160-68, 223-35, 236, 258, 259, 277, 280
New Zealand 23, 241
Nhill Football Club (WDFL) . 114, 116, 117-18

Nicholls, John 270
Nichols, Rosemary 219-10
Noonan, George 77
North Africa 210
Northcote Football Club (VFA) 146, 148, 149, 189-90
North Hobart Football Club (TFL) .... 135, 138, 140, 152, 153 – 159, 160, 161, 162, 163, 164, 165, 166, 167, 223, 225, 226, 228, 229, 232, 234, 239, 249, 258
North Launceston Football Club (NTFA) 138, 139, 140, 226, 229
North Melbourne Football Club (VFA) 34, 59, 63, 113
North Melbourne Football Club (VFL) 113, 128, 145, 146, 160, 176, 205
North Western District Football Association (NWDFA) 118
Noye, Larry 243, 247, 249, 328

O

Oakleigh Football Club (VFA) 148-49
Oakley, Ross 269, 270
Oborne, Maurie 228
O'Brien, 'Paddy' 111
O'Connell, Jack 110
O'Donohue, John 'Peter' 197, 201, 202
Ogilvie, Albert 156, 167
O'Keefe, Jack 201
O'Meara, Jim 'Brum' 170
Orpwood, Kev 224, 227
Ostberg, Roy 71, 74

P

Palmer, Scott 265
Pannam, Charlie 100, 107, 124, 128
Park, Allan 'Nedda' (son-in-law) ... 211, 224, 225, 226, 229, 233, 240
Park, Cheryl (granddaughter) 213, 221
Park, Roy 52, 58-59
Park, Stephen (grandson) 213, 216, 222
Park, Wayne (grandson) 213, 214
Parker, Harold 73
Parsons, Bobby 224, 225, 226, 228, 233
Patterson, Les 224
Paul, Athol 163, 165
Pavey, Bill 196

Pearson, Charles 'Commotion' 83
Pembroke Football Club 35, 69
Perrett, Ernie 'Codger' ... 116, 120, 135, 136, 140
Perth 89, 110, 125, 175, 239
Peters, Laurie 188, 197, 202, 203, 204, 205
Pettiona, Cecil 128, 166
Pink, Arthur 108
Pitchford, Max 160
Plowman, Hugh 73
Police Football Club (WFL) 131, 132, 150
Poliomyelitis 220-21
Port Melbourne 35, 37, 81, 107, 131, 183, 201, 262
Port Melbourne Cricket Club 73, 75
Port Melbourne Football Club (VFA) 34, 35, 43, 75, 99, 140
Port Phillip Bay 33, 36, 37, 174
Port Phillip Stevedores Association 107
Post and Telegraph Football Club (WFL) ..131, 150, 151
Powell, Len 'Sox' 153, 155
Power, Ted 116, 120, 129
Prahran Football Club (VFA) 146
Pratt, Alfred 'Oxy' 153
Pratt, Bob 170, 171, 175, 178, 179, 181, 186, 190, 270, 271
Press Football Club (WFL) 150
Preston 144-45
Preston Football Club (VFA) 144-49, 151-2, 153, 173, 188, 189, 257
Prider, Harold 267
Puech Bouquet estate 13
Pugsley, Lucinda (Aggie's sister) 57
Pura, Colin 210
Pye, Len 'Apples' 153, 156, 158, *158*, 159, 167

R

Railways Football Club (WFL) 131, 132, 150, 151
Rait, Alan 154, 156, 158, *158*, 159
Ransley, Desmond (son in law) 211, 240
Ransley, Mark (grandson) 213
Ransley, Roy (grandson) 213
Ransley, Teresa (granddaughter) 213, 214
Ransley, Vere (grandson) 213
Red and Checker Cabs Football Club (WFL) .. 150
Reville, Peter 131, 132
Reynolds, Dick 247, 270

INDEX

Richards, Lindsay 166
Richards, Lou 261, 270
Richardson, Trevor 165
Richmond 187, 265
Richmond Football Club (VFA) 34
Richmond Football Club (VFL) 46, 48, 49, 50, 67, 75, 85, 92, 95, 102, 112, 113, 131, 138, 166, 182, 186, 202, 204, 237, 245, 262, 267
Ricketts, Fred 82, 96-97
Robertson, Austin 128, *170*, 171, 175, 181
Robins, Barry (grandson) 213, 214, 222, 230
Robins, Ernest (son in law) 211, 221
Robins, Gail (granddaughter) 213, 214, 221, 240
Rodgers, Stephen 328
Rohan, Jack 164, 170, 171
Rooke, Hedley 163, 165, 166
Ross, Gower 43
Rossi, Keith 210
Rough, Jack 224, 226, 227, 228, 229, 232, 233
Rowing (Ballarat) 21-22
Rowing (England) 15-16
Rowing (Melbourne) 24-26, 28-29
Rudolph, George 131, 166, 249
Rupanyup Football Club (WDFL) 114, 117, 119
Ryan, Joe 241-42
Ryan, Phil 196
Ryan, Stan 155, 156

S

Saker, Alan 201
Sale 77, 198
Sandringham Football Club (VFA) 147-48, 190
Sandy Bay 249
Sandy Bay Football Club (TFL) ... 223, 225, 232, 237, 239, 248
Saturday Industrial League 150
Scanlan, Joe 100, 103-04, 249
Scanlan, 'Paddy' 100, 101, 105, 107, 127
Schmidt, Louis William 'Billy' 49, *49*, 52, 56, 70, 75-76, 77-78, 81, 114, 121, 247, 249
Scott, Doug 225, 232
Scott, Margaret 253
Sealey, Tom 124
Seddon Star Football Club (JK Smith Competition) 40
Seebeck, Lyall 149

Seelenmeyer, Jack 189
Sellars, Ernie 53, 55
Serle, Geoffrey 275, 328
Sharland, Wallace 'Jumbo' 108, 112, 120, 128, 129, 267
Sheahan, Mike 268, 271, 272
Shorten, George 112
Sigley, Ernie 261
Silvagni, Stephen 271
Skilton, Bob 269, 270
Smith, Doug 226, 227
Smith, Frank 155
Smith, George 147, *147*
Smith, Roy 63-64
South Australia 74, 89, 95, 96, 101, 111, 112, 114, 125, 126, 142, 170, 178, 239
South Melbourne 11, 29, 30, 33, 34, 35, 37, 39, 57, 58, 59, 67, 71, 74, 81, 93, 136, 175, 179, 185, 198, 209, 230, 254, 275
South Melbourne Districts Football Club (VJA) 69, 70, 86, 93, 101
South Melbourne Football Club (VFA) ... 34, 35
South Melbourne Football Club (VFL) 35, 41, 51, 52, 61, 68, 69, 71, 75, 77, 78, 80-113, 124-30, 135, 138, 144, 155, 157, 162, 163, 164, 166, 169-84, 186, 187, 192, 194, 197, 199, 205, 220, 243, 245, 254, 255, 256, 267, 268, 276, 277, 278
South Melbourne Open Sea Bathing Club ... 86
South Melbourne Rowing Club ... 29, 40, 47, 50, 57, 100
South Melbourne Wednesday Football Club 42, 43
South Warrnambool Football Club (WDL) 75, 77, 90, 110
Southern Tasmanian Police Team (USFA) .. 208
Spanish Influenza (see also Influenza) 74, 92
Spargo, Frank 147
Spargo, Pierce 147
Sparrow, George 'Sugar' 53, 76
Spinks, Stan 189
Spitalfields 13, 14, 15
Sporting Globe, The 92, 173-74, 326
St Arnaud Football Club (NWDFA) 118
Stamford, Jack 241
Stawell Football Club (WDFL) ... 114, 117, 119
St Kilda 11, 33
St Kilda Football Club (VFA) 34, 35

St Kilda Football Club (VFL) 9, 10, 35, 41, 42-78, 80, 81, 82, 85, 90, 92, 95, 98, 104, 110, 114, 146, 154, 157, 164, 176, 178, 183, 189, 194, 245, 255, 268, 277, 278
St Kilda Wednesday Football Club 42-43
Stoddart, Herb... 44
Stokes, Ray 237, *237*
Strawbridge, Frank 116, 117
Strutt, Horace 230
Stubbs' Baths 37, 65, 125
Sullivan, Jack 228
Sullivan, Peter 263
Sutton, Harry 155, 156
Sutton, Herb.. 128
Sydney 9, 25, 26, 69, 211, 241, 242, 256, 264

T

Tandy, Lily née Ford.................... 196, 243, 254
Tandy, Mark 'Napper' 77, 86, 87, 88, *88*, 89, 90, 92, 94, 95, 96, 97, 101, 102, 104, 105, 106, 107, 110, 111, 112, 113, 127, 173, 179, 196, 224, 243, 245, 249, 254, 267
Tandy, Mark jnr 254
Tandy, Rod 254
Tasmania
   1929 floods.................................... 139-40
   1930 Carnival team................................ 142
   1950 state election............................. 229-30
   1954 Tasmanian team 236-39
   Hare-Clark electoral system.......229-30, 325
   Introduction of Australian
      Rules Football............................... 136
      North – South rivalry............................. 136
Tate, Mayor Levi 59
Taylor, Bert 146, 149
Taylor, Charlie 46
Taylor, George 'Toots'.................................. 123
Taylor, Laurie 197, 202
Taylor, Percy 183
Telephone Exchange Football Club (WFL) 150
Templeton, Kelvin 262
Thiessen, Tony 248
Thomas, Len 128, 171, 179
Thompson family... 219
Thorp, Vic.. 267
Thurgood, Albert 267, 271
Tobruk 210
Todd, Ron..178, 186
Tonks, Bill 224, 226, 227
Townley, Rex 229, 230

Treloar, John 37
Triffett, Gordon 219
Tyson, Des 135, 138, 142
Tyson, Ron 134, 135, 142

U

Umpires 9, 43, 45, 49, 101, 102-03, 109, 112, 126, 127, 131, 132, 150, 155, 167, 177, 197, 249, 260, 261, 269
Unemployment 30, 145, 170
University (VFL)....... 43, 50, 52, 56, 58, 59, 113
'Up there Cazaly'
   Birth of the expression 88-89
   Mike Brady's song............ 251, 254, 262-64, 265, 280
   Summer of the Seventeenth Doll 241-42
   Use during World War II.......................210

V

Vallence, Harry 'Soapy'................................. 186
Veale, Stan 37, 40
Victoria Markets Football Club (WFL)...... 150
Victorian Football Association (VFA)
   Crowds...................................150, 178, 186
   Expansion 145, 192
   Formation 34
   Fracturing 35
   Impact of World War I 59, 62
   Impact of World War II........................197
   Interstate matches 239
   Player payments 178
   Player transfers.................. 51, 146, 178, 197
   Recorder Cup..190
   Rivalry with VFL.............. 35, 113, 177, 186
   Rule changes 34, 74, 177-78, 186
Victorian Football League (VFL)
   Crowds........... 53, 92, 100-01, 104, 150, 198
   Expansion 59, 63, 113, 192
   Finals systems 112
   Formation 35
   Impact of World War I 59
   Impact of World War II........................197
   Interleague matches 129, 154
   Introduction of player numbers................49
   Player payments 47-49, 170
   Player transfers 75, 80-81, 115, 135, 146, 158, 172, 173, 178, 196, 197
   Representative teams...............................129

Rivalry with VFA 35, 113, 177, 186
Rule changes 177
Stewards... 49, 56
Tribunals 56, 102, 103, 104, 109
Umpires 9, 101, 102-03, 132
VFL *Record* 49, *56*, 326

W

Wade, Harry 140
Walker, Bertha.. 198
Walker, Jack.. 73
Walters, Arnie... 146
Warne-Smith, Ivor 247, 268, 271
Warr, Danny 146
Warracknabeal 119, 121, 122
Warracknabeal Football Club (WDFL)......114, 117, 119
Watchem Football Club (NWDFA) 118, 119
Waterside Workers Football Club (WFL) 131, 132, 150, 151, 166, 230
Watson and Sons 26-27, 28, 30
Watson, Colin.............. 75, 77, 90, 110, 247, 271
Watson, Tim... 271
Watts, Albert 126
Weatherboard Hill.. 18
Webb, Athol 237, *237*, 238
Wedd, Bill... 229
Wednesday Football League (WFL) 42-43, 74, 131-32
Wells, Samuel *100*, 104
Welsh, Keith 224-25, 226, 228, 239, 248, 328
Western Australia 30, 55, 89, 99, 110-11, 112, 125, 142, 170, 171, 239
White, Jim 196
Whitecross, Anthony (grandson)...........213, 214
Whitecross, Peter (grandson) 213, 214, 215
Whitecross, Russell (son in law) 211, 215, 221, 222
Whitecross, Susan (granddaughter)......213, 214
Whitten, EJ 'Ted'.................................261, 270
William Leitch Medal (TFL) 156, 234
Williams, Bobby 196, 201, 202, 205
Williamson, David 264
Williamstown.. 107
Williamstown Football Club (VFA)............................34, 35, 178, 186, 201
Willis, Carl 81
Wilmot, Chester.. 210
Wilmot, Reg 63, 267

Wilson, Ernie 111
Wilson, Garry... 262
Wimmera District Football League (WDFL) 114, 117, 119, 129
Windley, Bill.........................34, *34*, 93-94, 124
Witzerman, Roy 224, 226, 228, 233
Wood, Arthur 'Artie'................. 81, 91, 129, 267
Wood, Tom... 116
Woodcock, Bill 42, 74
Woolford family 208, 215, 216
World War I
 Charity fundraising matches 63
 Conscription debate ...59, 63-64, 68, 70, 325
 Enlistments among footballers 10, 54, 58, 59, 61, 62, 67, 69, 71, 73
 Enlistments in South Melbourne........59-64, 69, 71, 325
 Gallipoli 56, 59, 68
 Impact on organised football 56, 58, 61-63, 69
 Industrial disputes.............................. 69-70
 War funds raised 59, 63, 70
 Western Front 54, 56
World War II
 Debate over football continuing............. 187
 Enlistments among footballers 189
 Enlistments in Camberwell 187
 Enlistments in Hawthorn 194
 Impact on organised football ... 186, 193-95, 196, 197-98, 201
 War funds raised 187
Worrall, John 82, 88

Y

Yarraville Football Club (VFA) 87, 151, 194
Yellow Cabs Football Club (WFL) 131, 150
York Park 135, 138, 140, 258

Z

Zahnleiter, Anthony 115, 122
Zschech, Eric................. 116, *116*, 129, 166, 167
Zwar, Henry 145